An Ecological History of Agriculture
10,000 B.C.–A.D. 10,000

An Ecological History
of Agriculture

10,000 B.C.–A.D. 10,000

DANIEL E. VASEY

Iowa State University Press / Ames

DANIEL E. VASEY is professor and chair, Department of Sociology, Divine Word College, Epworth, Iowa.

Manufactured in the United States of America
⊗ This book is printed on acid-free paper.

First edition, 1992

Library of Congress Cataloging-in-Publication Data

Vasey, Daniel E.
   An ecological history of agriculture: 10,000 B.C.–A.D. 10,000 / Daniel E. Vasey.—1st ed.
     p. cm.
   Includes bibliographical references and index.
   ISBN 0-8138-0909-6
   1. Agriculture—History. 2. Agriculture. 3. Agricultural ecology. 4. Agricultural systems.
5. Agriculture—Social aspects. I. Title.
S419.V37 1992
630′.9—dc20   90-48687

Contents

Preface

Agriculture and society have evolved together on a path that can be neatly summarized. First people were few, and farmers nonexistent. Then there were many more people, and most of them were farmers. Now we are billions. Most of us no longer farm, but the few who do support the rest. At our starting point, the first farmers depended upon knowledge of nature accumulated by their ancestors, thousands of generations of collectors of wild foods. That knowledge fed them and formed the base on which agricultural knowledge would be built. Agriculture still builds upon accumulated knowledge, now that of scientists as well as farmers, and present knowledge still feeds the innovators of future technology.

This book is about present agricultural systems, what we know of past ones, and what can be projected about the future. The order is only roughly chronological, because the intention is to present more of a testimony to human skill and adaptiveness than a chronicle. The task of embracing what so many people have done in so many very different places and times is not so formidable as it might seem. Parallel developments abound, making easier the task of generalization. The broad-brush approach may at times leave specialists wanting more details of their area and era, but not all is generalization. Environmental differences and the effects of specific technical innovations are also topics of this book, the many cases of parallel development notwithstanding.

The starting date, 10,000 B.C., falls 1,500 to 2,500 years before the dates of the first positively identified domesticated plants and animals. The date is defensible, however, as well as round. The last glacial definitely ended at about that time, marking the transition from the Pleistocene to the Holocene and the beginning of events that appear to foster the development of full-fledged agriculture. Dates of the first domesticates may yet be pushed back, and, moreover, some period of development must have occurred before the plant or animal reached a state that the archaeologist can identify with domestication. Some scholars argue that some of the origins of agriculture may be way back in the Pleistocene, but the major domesticates of the early Holocene are unlikely to have been cultivated or herded in those same locations under Ice Age conditions.

Another round date is A.D. 10,000. Admittedly chosen for the symmetry it lends to the title, such a seemingly remote year is practically tomorrow in some scales of time and serves to remind us that people, resources, and technology must be matched much longer than just the next few decades or centuries. The near future will witness some continuation of current trends in agriculture, subject no doubt to unforeseen events. Thereafter futurist scholarship (a pair of concepts that come dangerously close to having contradictory meanings) cannot give a clear view through the mists but can offer some probable determinants. Some possible alternative outcomes for the not-so-near-but-not-so-far future will also be described, more for their heuristic value than as actual predictions.

When agriculture is here said to evolve, what is meant foremost is that its history is regular up to a point; parallel circumstances tend to evoke parallels in agriculture, and at least some changes in agriculture recur in widely separated places under similar circumstances. The other meaning of evolution is progress, but here I must express some reservations. Cumulative change is progressive in the long term and when world agriculture is taken as a whole. We cannot say with any certainty that we are better off than our preagricultural ancestors, but we can say that food production enables more food to be produced than was ever collected. Industrially based agriculture, what will from here on for the sake of brevity be called industrial agriculture, uses more inputs to produce still more food. It may or may not be a more complex phenomenon at the farm than preindustrial agriculture—that judgment depends on whether technical or ecological criteria are used—but the structural relations with the whole industrial society are more complex.

Revolution is used here to describe sequences of events that ultimately result in a major transformation of agriculture and society, whether the time span of the transformation is short or long. In many past revolutions, the pace of change is indeed so slow that the actors may not have been aware of it, let alone perceived themselves as revolutionaries. I sympathize with Dovring's (1969) objection to labeling eighteenth-century change in European agriculture a revolution, partly on grounds that the process was too slow. But *revolution* is concise, and clear alternatives are lacking to its use in these situations. And in any period of technical change, the actors cannot know where that change will ultimately take society, even if they are aware that contemporary change is having a powerful impact. The industrial revolution is a perfect example.

A reasonable balance has been sought between preindustrial and industrial agriculture. Chapter 2, about agricultural origins, is the first of six chapters largely devoted to preindustrial agriculture and pastoralism. Chapters 9 and 10 document the rise of industrial agriculture, chapter 11 in large part its spread to the less developed countries, and chapter 12 its projected future development.

Population, environment, and energy are dominant themes of this book, because they are the three principal determinants of agricultural systems, but other variables modify the interaction of each with agriculture. Available technology influences energy needs and the constraints imposed by environment. Population determines how much food must be raised, but demand is also sensitive to economic conditions and cultural preferences in diet. For example, affluence increases the per capita demand on field systems, particularly where crops are used to feed livestock and supply animal products in quantities that are nutritionally superfluous.

Between agriculture and each of these three determinants the relationship is one of mutual action. Chapters 5, 6, and 7 discuss in some detail the shaping of agriculture by the respective environments of tropical, dry or dry summer, and humid temperate climates, but with attention also to the impact of the agricultural systems on their surroundings. Population and agricultural intensity, associated in several parts of the book, are in chapter 8 shown to be mutually dependent. Agricultural systems are both suppliers and consumers of energy. Energy inputs have lately tended to increase much more rapidly than energy output (chapters 9 and 10), and whether future systems will be net suppliers or net consumers is a matter of much import and no certainty (chapter 12).

Many agricultural historians would probably argue that technology is a fourth primary factor shaping agriculture, but technical innovation is here treated more as the substance of change than its cause. Credit must go to the innovators, however many of them are anonymous actors in undocumented history, but this book will give many examples of parallel innovation in widely separated locales. Far from agricultural evolution's ever being retarded by a lack of suitable technology, all humans are inventive and readily come up with needed and feasible innovations. The right time for an innovation is determined by the whole process of social evolution, in which technical innovation plays a central role.

Terms in this book have, as much as possible, been chosen to be global in their applicability. All measures are metric unless otherwise stated. A ton is 1,000 kg unless the short ton, 2,000 pounds, is specified. All temperatures are on the Celsius scale. Southwest Asia and North Africa are used in place of the Eurocentric Near or Middle East, East Asia instead of the Far East. Because the meaning of *corn* varies among English dialects, *Zea mays* is maize. I avoid *arable,* which is cultivated land in one usage, cultivable land in another. However, B.C. and A.D. are used in preference to the culture-free B.P. (before the present), for the reason that B.P. dates change every year. That fact does not bother prehistorians who deal in millennia, presumably because they lack confidence in their readership of the distant future, but is a problem in a book whose time span extends through the present. As for future dates, I do not wish to coin A.P. (after the present).

Reference

Dovring, F. (1969). Eighteenth-century changes in European agriculture: A comment. *Agricultural History,* 43:181–187.

Acknowledgments

The many men and women who till the soil are my subject matter, and among them are more than a few, on three continents and several islands, who have had the patience not only to talk but also to demonstrate. They are the ones who hoe baked soil in the hot tropical sun or climb to timberline meadows in a late spring blizzard to find the lost lamb. I only hope I have done justice to their accomplishments.

To most of the staff at more than a dozen college and university libraries who have been so helpful, I can give only collective thanks. I would, however, express my particular gratitude to Florence Griffin and Sister Fleurette Schmitt for their persistent efforts in obtaining research materials.

William Denevan, Ed Nesman, and Wayne Vasey reviewed early, overly long drafts and did a great deal to give the book needed structure and direction. They pointed out omissions as well as superfluities.

An Ecological History of Agriculture

10,000 B.C.–A.D. 10,000

1

An Ecological Approach

 This chapter introduces concepts that will be used throughout the book: systems concepts in the first part, some prerequisite ecology in the second. The first part is as much defense as explanation. The systems that are of primary interest are agricultural ecosystems contained within the boundaries of human management. Of secondary interest are impinging cultural systems, notably population, economy, technology, and resource exploitation. What is defended is the existence of equilibrium-maintaining, self-regulating mechanisms within many of these systems, and the compatibility of those mechanisms with ongoing change.

Certain schools of thought handle equilibrium and change in contrasting fashion. On one side, classical economists find long-term growth compatible with regulated swings of the economy about equilibrium. Conversely, some biologists in the 1950s and 1960s took from cybernetics a stricter version of equilibrium, called homeostasis, which ecological anthropologists then appropriated and gave the meaning that well-adapted societies are in a stable and general equilibrium with their environments. Only disequilibration causes major change, and only a deus ex machina can upset the perfect machine. A reaction has more recently set in, causing many to junk the whole concept of equilibrium in social systems on grounds that change is the historical norm. I shall plead that the reaction goes too far and that change and equilibrium are compatible and are demonstrable historical conditions.[1]

Systems and Their Dynamics

An adequate history of agriculture should be holistic and informed by ecology – both ecology proper, the study of organisms and their environments, and human ecology, the study of humans and environment. The physical, biological, and cultural environment shapes agricultural systems, and in turn agriculture has an impact on the whole environment. Agriculture itself is cultural behavior, but it also is management of organisms and ecosystems subject to the same biological laws as any others. By managing ecosystems we bend these laws toward our ends but do not change them.

The properties of systems of the most interest here are those that affect stability or give direction to change: openness, boundaries, the nature of equilibrium within the system, endogenous change, and orthogenesis. Openness is easily put aside. All of the systems treated in this book are decidedly open to outside influences.

BOUNDARIES. Natural boundaries, within which elements of the system exchange significantly more energy with one another than with outside elements, are fairly common around ecosystems. For instance, energy moves in and out of a pond ecosystem through predation, water flows, and other means, but apart from the large and essential input of solar energy, the network of transfers within the pond is ordinarily denser than the network extending out from the pond. Even such a general concept as *tropical forest ecosystem* rests on some degree of integration within limits set by temperature, rainfall, and other physical factors.

Human ecologists find boundaries more evasive. Steward (1955) attempts to draw a boundary within cultures by coining *cultural core* to take in functionally related features that are closely tied to subsistence. An appealingly simple concept in principle, cultural core rests on troublesome judgments of what does or does not belong, and few ethnographers try to describe the core of any specific culture. Geertz (1963) uses *cultural ecosystem* to subsume a human community and everything in the environment with which it most directly interacts, but in individual cases, distinguishing organisms and elements that sufficiently interact with members of the human community from those that do not is more or less arbitrary.

Here, because the subject is agriculture, boundaries are not so hard to find. Agricultural activity takes place in a managed ecosystem, and the boundaries of management are usually convenient boundaries of the system itself. Fields, fallows, pastures, stables, livestock, and people in the agricultural food chain are all included. Management tapers off at the margins, for example, where wild foods, green manure, and stable litter are collected from uncultivated, ungrazed land around the periphery, but boundaries are usually far from arbitrary. They are ordinarily more distinct the more intensive the agricultural system.

Agricultural system here refers to agricultural ecosystems under specific forms of management, for example, forest fallow systems. Alternatively, *system* will be dropped altogether, as in *wet rice cultivation,* in order to avoid repetitious language.

EQUILIBRIUM, STABILITY, AND CHANGE.

The concept of equilibrium is the well from which systems theories have been drawn. It was applied to the economy by Adam Smith in the eighteenth century, then by Malthus to population. Today mechanisms that maintain equilibrium are a dominant concern in systems analysis. Unfortunately the widespread demonstration of equilibrium-maintaining mechanisms contributes to the formation of a theoretical encumbrance, an overstress on stability and resistance to change.

The simpler of two common meanings of equilibrium is a balance between opposing forces. Reversible chemical reactions are a familiar example, as when two substances constantly combine to form a third that constantly dissociates into the original two. The equilibrium shifts as the environment changes but would show no net change under constant conditions. The volume of lakes and aquifers is the product of equilibrium between their recharge and discharge. The obvious demographic example is the balance between fertility and mortality, often with immigration and emigration thrown in for good measure, but this example differs in a crucial way from that of the reversible chemical reaction; we have no reason to believe that the population level would be constant under any conditions.

The second meaning is an extension of the first. Forces are so well balanced that the system tends to return to a specific state after a disturbance. The system is thus at least partially self-regulating, though not necessarily to the point of being stable in the absence of outside influences. In fact, disturbances may be of internal or external origin. The business cycle of classical economics is an example; internal and external destabilizing events are as much assumed as are regular swings about the equilibrium growth curve.

An equilibrium state may or may not change significantly in the long term. General systems theorists reserve *steady state* to describe those that do not. Conversely, the business cycle is a a model of equilibrium tendencies against a background of long-term growth.

A conservative form of equilibrium is homeostasis; the system tends toward a narrow range of states or levels so long as it is not stressed beyond certain limits. Homeostasis is well known in living organisms and is commonly built into models of ecosystems (Odum, 1983:47–51). Body temperature is the classic illustration. Ecologists commonly deal with much wider fluctuations—for example, the numbers of a given species—but homeostasis is not wrongly applied if the necessity for maintaining equilibrium and the tendency toward equilibrium can be demonstrated (Ashby, 1956, 1960).

Yet no systems concept has been more troublesome than homeostasis when applied to culture or to ecosystems in which cultural behavior plays a major part. The problem lies in its conservatism. Bender (1978:207) objects, "When organisms are subjected to environmental stress beyond the tolerance of their homeostatic mechanisms, they die; cultural systems do not die, they change." Though she ignores the precedence of homeostasis models of ecosystems undergoing slow change, Bender correctly identifies an implication that many ecological anthropologists draw from biological precedence. Over a few years of ethnographic observation, they find self-regulating mechanisms, quite often sufficient to keep population or the exploitation of some vital resource within sustainable limits, and conclude that change is not likely to occur unless some outside agency disequilibrates the system.

Somehow, in the common vocabulary of ecological anthropology in the 1960s and 1970s, equilibrium was narrowly confined to both steady state and homeostasis, thereby defeating the purpose of coining these terms to isolate specific forms of equilibrium. In rebuttal, an analysis of factors affecting the population of the Tsembaga Maring of Papua New Guinea (Foin and Davis, 1987) finds the model of choice to be one in which regulating mechanisms operate, but the rate of return is so slow in relation to the disturbances that the population most of the time is well above or well below any plausible equilibrium level. They describe the system as one in disequilibrium, on grounds that equilibrium applies only if the population were most of the time kept within a narrow range. If, alternatively, it were simply observed that the population tends toward equilibrium but is well short of being homeostatic, disequilibrium could be reserved for those cases in which exceptional disturbances bring about exceptional change. The latter terminology will be used in this book.

Another troublesome concept from cybernetics is feedback, not the trendy synonym for *reply* or *response,* but any mechanism by which a system responds to changing input. Mechanisms that reduce deviation within the system are negative feedback. Positive feedback, a response of the system that acts to amplify deviation, is an apposite vehicle in which to express changes that spiral over time. It is another concept often used imprecisely, but one that could probably be used in many instances in which *revolution* is now applied with even less precision; I shall continue to use *revolution,* simply because *industrial positive feed-*

back and *agricultural positive feedback* sound awful.

Slow change commonly goes on in spite of negative feedback. In soils the measured equilibrium level of humus and some nutrients tends strongly enough toward a very narrow range of levels that homeostasis is an apt description of the equilibrium state, yet we know that ancient soils tend to be lower in nutrients than more recent soils, and often lower in humus. Population and the economy contrast in that they trend upward while all the time fluctuating within wide ranges.

The systems that interest human ecologists are complex, and so are their equilibrium relations. If it were possible to measure the variation of the principal interacting components of the system, something that is often possible in physical or biological systems, these relations could be precisely defined; that is, negative and positive feedback would be known functions. In the social sciences, including human ecology, we most often face a maze of cause and effect. The complexity leads some social scientists to avoid equilibrium models. Or they reject equilibrium models on the grounds that positive feedback predominates over negative feedback. The line between positive and negative feedback is not really clear in any plausible social cases. For example, the construction of an innovative new factory may be simultaneously a response to the business cycle and something that will generate forces for sustained economic growth.

Though culture and cultural systems are mazes indeed, a frequently useful model is one in which some state tends toward equilibrium in a way that can be accounted for by the action of a limited set of variables or features. To illustrate, take the male:female ratio in a singles bar, an indisputably cultural environment. Negative feedback might be strong if a shortage of patrons of one sex discourages patrons of the other sex from entering or encourages them to leave, a no less meaningful phenomenon if other factors are at work, say, the cost of drinks, a cover charge, or less quantifiable features such as decor, music, behavior of bar staff, all those things that, with the clientele, make up the atmosphere of a bar (Cavan, 1966) or pub (Vasey, n.d.). Equilibrium in our hypothetical bar need not be permanent. Its character may evolve as management and patrons take cues from one another, ending in its expanding into new premises or going out of business. Or external factors — for example, a consultant's report — may force the change.

This book is concerned with greater events than singles bars, but the same principles hold. More or less strongly equilibrated values change in the long term against a background of change in associated features. Distinguishing cause and effect is often difficult but seldom hopeless.

ENDOGENY AND ORTHOGENESIS. Endogeny is change that originates from within. In open systems, exogenous factors, or those operating from outside the system, are inevitably at work, but they may act only to mask endogeny, which should not for that reason be discounted.

Postulated (and testable) mechanisms of social endogeny are nothing new. Marxian dialectics is a model of endogeny, though Marx does not deny the importance of environment.

This book is much concerned with changes in states in equilibrium, particularly with long-term population growth and anthropogenic deterioration of the environment. The latter should be distinguished from environmental deterioration not due to human management or influence, which is typically far slower.

Orthogenesis is another troublesome concept. It is change in separate systems that results in their evolving along essentially the same path. Despite external influences, the initial state of the system predetermines the outcome. The concept has been used in evolutionary biology but never widely favored. In the guise of "unilinear evolutionism" (Steward, 1955), it has often been used to describe, wrongly (Harris, 1968:171–173), nineteenth-century theories of social evolution. Orthogenesis and endogeny should not be equated. Though specific processes of endogeny may tend to produce change in one direction, distinct and separate systems undergoing that change will not necessarily pass through the same stages. Endogeny also goes on in interaction with significant environmental influences that alter outcomes.

MATTER-ENERGY AND MANAGEMENT: BEATING ENTROPY. Social evolution in general is associated with an enormous increase in energy capture (White, 1959), but the association is imperfect. Indeed energy is used so much more efficiently in some modern technologies than in others that we would do well to avoid equating wasteful use of energy with a higher state of the economy or society.

A fundamental principle of cybernetics and general systems theory is that a system exists in spite of a universal tendency toward increasing entropy, that is, toward loss of differentiation and identity.[2] All systems must take in energy in order to maintain themselves against this tendency. Though the proposition is derived from the second law of thermodynamics and can be formally demonstrated to apply to all systems, the use of *entropy* in social analysis often obscures more than it illuminates. We cannot measure entropy in studies of social systems, and even in physical and biological systems we find that information up to a point substitutes for energy. What this means for agricultural ecosystems is that efficient management can to some degree, always limited, replace energy inputs, something evident to the practitioner but occasionally overlooked by the theorist. For example, less irrigation water has to be pumped onto a field if water and plant requirements are carefully matched.

Exchanges of energy are often referred to as exchanges of matter-energy. Without going into the physics, let it suffice that an exchange of matter that is useful to the system is also an exchange of energy. An example would be consumption of one organism by another.

STRATEGY AND NICHE. Subsistence strategies are sets of associated food-getting activities. They fall into two broad classes: food production (agriculture and pastoralism) and food collecting (hunting, gathering, and fishing).

Niche is, strictly speaking, a biological term encompassing the specialized role of an organism or community within its habitat. As an example of social applications, Barth (1956) describes three societies in Swat, Pakistan, that coexist but practice distinctive combinations of agriculture and pastoralism. Bennett (1976:169ff.) objects to the use of *niche* in human ecology on the grounds that it confuses social behavior with what in the natural environment interacts with genetic adaptation, and that it ties a niche to a specific locale. I must differ. Social behavior, not all of it genetically controlled, is so critical to many animal species that they could not occupy their niches without it. Different communities of the same species or subspecies sometimes occupy very different niches. Humans simply diversify more and rely more on culturally transmitted behavior (see also Hardesty, 1975, 1977:115–120).

MODELS OF TECHNICAL CHANGE: KNOWLEDGE TREES AND RESPONSES TO UNINTENDED CONSEQUENCES. Technology is obviously cumulative. The sum total worldwide of know-how and technical artifacts has certainly grown over the centuries and mushroomed in the last few, as much in agriculture as in any field of knowledge, but accumulation is not the whole story of change.

In certain times and places more technology is lost than gained. During the early colonial era many decimated populations lost the knowledge of how to build and maintain complex terrace irrigation systems, raised cultivation beds, and the like.

Despite aggregate accumulation of knowledge, individual modern farmers do not necessarily have more technical knowledge than their predecessors, only different knowledge, and better for modern circumstances. A single farmer in the corn belt possesses different knowledge from that of a swiddener, who slashes and burns the forest and plants by hand, but not more. Each would find it exceedingly difficult to survive in the other's shoes (or bare feet).

Many modern discussions of technical change use an implicit genetic model. Each discovery or invention builds on many generations of predecessors, and, if successful, gives rise to descendants. The model is evident in many histories of science and technology and in conventions for reporting discoveries and inventions. An implicit assumption is that change is fundamentally endogenous. Not to cite scientific precedence is a serious breach of etiquette, but the citation of external conditions such as hunger, eroding topsoil, or government policy initiatives, although common enough, is not obligatory. The genetic model, or knowledge tree, as it is sometimes portrayed, is thus incomplete, because it does not incorporate the influence of external conditions. The model is also incomplete where local knowledge is lost.

The genetic model alone depicts too orderly a process. In reality, change leads to more change not only because the first change is prerequisite but also because of its consequences. Technical change is therefore dialectic as well as cumulative. Either forest clearance by swiddeners or mechanization of cultivation may contribute to soil erosion. New methods may then be needed to manage an altered landscape. The first agriculturalists continued a process of knowledge and technology accumulation begun by food collectors long before but also touched off population growth and processes of environmental modification that would in dialectical fashion compel more change. In this vein it is worth noting that no scientific inquiry is free of potential material consequences. Perhaps the best example whereby seemingly impractical knowledge contributes eventually to high-impact technical change is the line leading from Copernican astronomy to nuclear physics, weapons, and energy.

Agricultural Ecosystems

The remainder of this chapter is intended to serve as an introduction to the ecological factors that shape agriculture. Some readers may want to skip this treatment, which is not meant to be definitive or innovative.

TROPHIC STRUCTURE OF ECOSYSTEMS.

Energy enters ecosystems by means of photosynthesis, and matter-energy passes through ecosystems in food chains, whereby organisms consume other organisms and are in their turn consumed through predation and decomposition. All organisms in the chain, including plants, constantly expend energy through respiration, waste excretion, and other processes.

Ecologists divide ecosystems into trophic levels and classify organisms by placing them within these levels. The first trophic level consists of the photosynthesizing organisms, termed primary producers. The rate at which these organisms produce biomass in a given environment is their net primary productivity, usually expressed as the annual production of dry matter. Herbivores and organisms that feed off the detritus or remains of the primary producers make up the second trophic level. After that, relations among organisms are more complex. Ideally organisms at the third trophic level would consume those at the second trophic level and in turn be consumed by those at the fourth level, and so on. In fact many organisms occupy several trophic levels. Decay organisms and scavengers do not discriminate between carcasses of lower and higher trophic levels, and some carnivores eat herbivores and other carnivores. Because food chains are so interconnected, trophic webs are often a preferred depiction.

Each trophic level invariably contains only a fraction of the biomass and potential energy of the next lower level from which it derives its energy. Although efficiencies vary, on average each level above the first captures roughly a tenth of the next lower level.

Humans as a group derive most of their food from plants but also eat considerable quantities of herbivores, including most of our game and nearly all of our domesticated animals and their products. Dogs and cats are carnivores, but we eat far fewer of them than we eat cattle, pigs, sheep, and goats. Some human communities are primarily at the second trophic level, relying mainly on plant foods. Some are mainly at the third trophic level, either because they hunt for most of their food or because they rely heavily on livestock for meat, milk, and so forth.

We feed from waters at a higher average trophic level than we feed from land—one reason, besides accessibility, that we feed far less from the seas than from a land area one-third as large. We eat few water plants, and most of the fish and other water animals we eat are primarily carnivores, particularly at sea. The primary productivity of the oceans is on average much less than that of most terrestrial ecosystems, one reason being the low concentration of nutrients.

Until very recently the main way that human management extracted more food from environments was to increase the proportion of the biomass that we are able to eat and digest, not to increase the net primary productivity. Irrigation agriculture was long the main exception.

REQUIREMENTS OF THE PRIMARY PRODUCERS. The primary producers, including those wild and domesticated plants from which all our food ultimately derives, need light, oxygen, carbon dioxide, water, favorable temperatures, and nutrient elements. Plants grow in seawater, freshwater, rock surfaces, and, most important here, soils, but plant roots take up nutrients only in the form of salts dissolved in water. Oxygen, carbon, and hydrogen, though essential, are not usually classed as nutrients.

Frequent reference will be made in the text to the limiting factor. Justus von Liebig in the last century stated the law of the minimum: the factor in shortest supply relative to plant requirements determines growth rates and development and is limiting. In a desert, water would ordinarily be limiting, but if irrigation water is supplied, some other factor becomes limiting. Criticisms of Liebig's law are based on the observation that sometimes several factors simultaneously control growth and development, but in preindustrial agriculture one factor is nearly always clearly limiting, and its correction is the immediately practicable way to raise yields. Industrial agriculture provides more circumstances in which all factors are well supplied, and in these cases multiple factors more often determine growth. One summary of experience with high rates of fertilizer application (Sanchez, 1976:315–316) nevertheless finds Liebig's law a good predictor of the economy of fertilizer use.

Heat. Primary producers vary in their temperature requirements. Though a few plants grow well over a wide range of temperature, those that are adapted to cool conditions generally do not thrive in hot weather, or vice versa. The threshold temperature is the minimum temperature at which a particular plant commences growth. The rate of growth in most plants increases rapidly above that temperature, then more slowly until an optimum range is reached. Growth again declines at temperatures above that range, often sharply. At high latitudes some plankton organisms begin growth at temperatures below freezing, some land organisms just above. Many important crops — for example, oats, barley, rye, and peas — commence growth below 5° C. The threshold temperatures of most crops of the temperate zone are below or near 10° but are as high as 18° for some melons. Temperatures of 30° to 35° promote good growth in most plants, but it should be remembered that these are shade temperatures. Temperatures above the optimum are often reached in some crops in full sunlight.

Any single plant variety requires both a minimum amount of accumulated heat above its threshold temperature and an irreducible length of growing season. "Early" crops or varieties of a crop require less accumulated heat to mature than those that are "mid-season," and much less than "late" ones.

Light. Light is much less commonly limiting than might be expected. Photosynthesis increases in response to increasing light but only up to a point at which a given plant is said to be light-saturated. More intense light does not further increase photosynthesis. Even on cloudy days sunlight exceeds the saturation light intensities of most unshaded plants except when the sun is low on the horizon. It is mostly plants with the so-called C_4 photosynthetic pathway (strictly speaking a photorespiratory pathway) that respond to light up to intensities commonly encountered in full sun. Such plants are mainly native to arid or seasonally dry, low-latitude regions. C_4 crops include maize, sorghum, amaranth, and sugarcane. Conversely, plants that are adapted to shady conditions have low saturation light intensities.

Light is limiting in certain situations. Shading of plants by others often limits growth, is an important form of competition among wild plants, and is a phenomenon to be managed in cultivated fields, so that crops shade weeds and not the reverse. In water nearly all photosynthesis goes on in the surface layer, where organisms intercept most of the light—the top meter in fertilized fish ponds, up to 100 m in some relatively unproductive areas of the oceans away from nutrient sources.

Night length controls the flowering of many grasses and legumes. For this reason varieties of maize and soybean that are adapted to one latitude may not be suitable at another.

Large areas lie at high altitudes where sunlight is intense yet low temperatures keep growth slow. Both natural plant communities and agriculture underutilize incoming solar radiation.

Air and Water. Land plants take up oxygen and carbon dioxide directly from the air. Oxygen is often limiting where water excludes access to air. Because root tissues require oxygen for respiration, higher plants that emerge into the air from water or waterlogged soil often have physiological mechanisms that deliver air to the roots. These include a few wild and domesticated plants that supply important human foods—notably rice, taro (*Colocasia esculenta*), and the sago palm (*Metroxylon sagu*)—but most major crop plants do not tolerate prolonged waterlogging.

Oxygen is only slightly soluble in water, less so in warm water than in cold, and nutrient-rich bodies of water are often short of oxygen during warm weather. Oxygen is often limiting in eutrophic bodies of water—that is, those that are highly productive—at times when death and decomposition of organisms use up all the oxygen.

Water is most often and obviously limiting in arid and semiarid lands, but also at times in humid areas. On sandy or gravelly soils even a few days' drought may retard growth and development of plants. Crops today often respond to irrigation on land that was once thought to receive abundant rainfall, because heavy fertilizer applications remove what had been nutrient limitations. Nearly all plants make their best growth when soil is near field capacity, the equivalent of a soil that has been saturated and then allowed to drain for a day or two.

Nutrients. The soil supplies fourteen elements known to be essential to higher terrestrial plants. Those needed in appreciable quantities are the macronutrients nitrogen, phosphorus, potassium, calcium, magnesium, and sulfur. Needed in much smaller quantities are the micronutrients iron, copper, zinc, boron, molybdenum, cobalt, and chlorine.

In freshwater the same macronutrients are required, though requirements in freshwater are probably in different proportions. Micronutrient requirements in freshwater are not yet well known.

All nutrients except nitrogen are mineral elements that originate in the rocks of the earth's crust. Soil gains mineral nutrients from the disintegration and decomposition of parent material. Most of the nutrients in any given soil are in forms unavailable to plants. As they are steadily transformed by further decomposition into available forms, they enter into cycles in which equilibrium levels in the soil are principally maintained through the return of organic matter. Available nutrients are nutrients in soluble forms, most of which continually move by leaching and erosion into freshwater ecosystems and the sea. The oceans are not as a result gaining in productivity except very near the mouths of rivers. The surface layers reached by sunlight steadily lose nutrients to deeper and darker layers, largely through the settling of dead organisms. The world's main fisheries are therefore found either in upwelling zones or where freshwater sources supply nutrients.

Parent material influences the nutrient status of soils. Sources of new parent material include volcanic eruptions, gravitational (colluvial) movements of soil, and movements by wind and water. Alluvial soils and aeolian soils are, respectively, derived from water-borne and wind-borne material. Loess soils are one important type of aeolian soil.

The amount of nutrients held in the soil solution is very small at any one time and would, despite additions from decomposing organic matter, be quickly exhausted by growing plants were it not for a reserve of nutrient ions held on the surfaces of soil particles. Many fine particles carry negative charges on their surfaces and thus attract positively charged ions, or cations. The available forms of these elements are bases, giving an alkaline reaction in the soil. Among the macronutrients, all but nitrogen, phosphorus, and sulfur are normally available only as cations. One form of available nitrogen, the ammonium ion (NH_4^+), is a cation, but the others, as well as the normally available forms of phosphorus and sulfur, are anions carrying a negative charge. Soils made up largely of clay and humus particles have high cation exchange capacities; that is, they can hold a reserve of cation nutrients that are quickly available to plants. Certain clays found in scattered tropical soils have a limited capacity to exchange anions.

Humus is physically and chemically altered organic matter, not a nutrient, but is important for its role as a store of nutrients and for its contribution to soil structure and cation exchange capacity. Plant litter falls on the soil surface, and some of it is dragged below by earthworms, ants, and other animals. Plant roots and soil organisms die beneath the surface. Some of this added organic matter breaks down fairly quickly, but more resistant fractions persist, often in chemically altered form. Several factors determine equilibrium levels of humus. In general, conditions that favor growth also favor the accumulation of humus. Wet conditions favor high equilibrium levels of humus by slowing its mineralization, that is, the release of nutrients through decomposition. The content of humus in a given soil tends strongly toward equilibrium; accelerated decomposition tends to offset unusual additions.

On land, nitrogen is the most commonly limiting nutrient. It circulates among air, soil, water, and living organisms in a complex set of processes known as the nitrogen cycle.

Nitrogen fixation is the process whereby nitrogen, which is unavailable to higher plants, becomes combined nitrogen, either available inorganic compounds or organic matter in living tissues. Lightning fixes a little. Chemical fertilizer nitrogen, fixed in industrial processes, accounts for only a small fraction of total worldwide fixed nitrogen, but on some fields, it supplies well over 90% of the nitrogen taken up by crops. The greatest amount by far of combined nitrogen is contributed by microorganisms: certain cyanobacteria (formerly called blue-green algae), free-living bacteria, and symbiotic bacteria that are mainly active in association with specific higher plants. Of the latter, the most important are the *Rhizobium* species associated with legumes, although some nonleguminous plants harbor other genera of nitrogen-fixing bacteria. The amount of nitrogen fixed by microorganisms varies enormously according to conditions, as can be seen in Table 1.1. In comparison, crops typically remove between 20 and 80 kg/ha/yr of nitrogen under preindustrial management, and up to well over 200 kg/ha/yr under modern, highly intensive cultivation.

Table 1.1. Annual contribution of combined nitrogen in selected environments

| Environment | Contribution (kg/ha) | | Main N-fixing organisms and associated species |
	Average[a]	Maximum	
Seawater	0.5–1	Not established	
Freshwater		>100	Cyanobacteria
Irrigated rice fields	30	100	Cyanobacteria; highest values from *Anabaena azollae*
Permanent grass	8–15		Free-living bacteria in some, *Rhizobium*— legume association in others
Legume crops	80–140	>250	Symbiotic *Rhizobium* bacteria; highest values under forages
Crops other than legumes	5	30	Free-living bacteria; cyano-bacteria under wet conditions

[a]Burris (1977:12).

Soils tend to lose combined nitrogen rapidly to water bodies, and soils and waters lose nitrogen to the atmosphere. Compounds that supply available nitrogen are highly soluble, and under humid conditions most losses of nitrogen are through leaching and erosion. Losses to the atmosphere, or denitrification, occur primarily through the decomposition of organic matter. Losses are normally small but may be quite large when a large amount of organic matter high in nitrogen is available for decomposition.

Only a small fraction of the nitrogen in soils is available at any one time. Most of the rest is stored in humus and fresh organic matter, although some is held in exchangeable form as ammonium cations or in a few soils as nitrate anions. In any given soil the ratio of carbon (in organic matter) to nitrogen is fairly constant. The ratio is commonly around 8:1 to 10:1, though higher and lower ratios occur. Most fresh organic matter has a higher carbon:nitrogen ratio than these typical soil values, and when it is incorporated into the soil, decomposing microorganisms draw down available nitrogen until decomposition of carbon compounds brings the carbon:nitrogen ratio near to the equilibrium ratio of the soil. This also happens in nature when there is a large fall of litter onto the ground or a dying off of much vegetation. When organic matter is added whose carbon:nitrogen ratio is lower than the ratio in the soil (what you expect when adding animal manures, good finished compost, or many kinds of green matter from legumes), rapid decomposition supplies an excess of available nitrogen until the equilibrium ratio is restored.

The tendency is thus strongly toward equilibrium levels of organic matter and total nitrogen in soils, though they may fluctuate seasonally. Management methods, notably irrigation and manuring, raise nitrogen levels by boosting humus content, but after the treatments cease, levels tend to return to equilibrium (but see the section "Cropping Frequencies of Medieval and Modern Systems" in chapter 7 regarding *plaggen* soils).

Available nitrogen levels vary much more. They fall rapidly during heavy rains, though not for long, because mineralization of humus quickly brings levels back toward equilibrium. Flushes of available nitrogen regularly occur in many soils: in tropical soils when rains commence after a dry season, and in soils of temperate regions warming up in spring. In both cases, the rise is brought about by an increase in the activity of microorganisms following a period of relative dormancy.

Phosphorus is, after nitrogen, the nutrient most commonly limiting to plant growth on land. It is nearly always the limiting factor in freshwater and the sea. Although most soils contain far more phosphorus than that required for sustained plant growth, several substances present in soils immobilize available phosphorus; that is, they combine with it in such a way that it is no longer available.

Good agricultural management alone generally maintains available phosphorus close to precultivation equilibrium levels for many years. Even sustained removal by harvesting seeds or tubers will only very slowly lower equilibrium levels if erosion is not serious and crop residues are returned to the soil. Leaching removes very little phosphorus. Applications of chemical phosphorus fertilizers are nevertheless common today, because many soils start out deficient or because modern management has removed other limiting factors. Most of the increment is immobilized, and only a small part, usually about 20%, is available to crops during that season. Crops recover a higher proportion from organic manures. Immobilized phosphorus eventually becomes available, but that may take a great many years for most of what was added in fertilizer. Phosphorus is in a sense put in the bank while other nutrients are quickly spent.

Phosphorus is usually added as phosphate rock, first treated with acids to make the phosphorus more readily available. Bonemeal is a good but scarcer source. Animal manures contain significant amounts, but most are poorer sources of phosphorus than of nitrogen or potassium. Poultry manure is better than other barnyard manures, and bird and bat guano deposits are excellent sources.

The available forms of potassium, the third most commonly limiting nutrient, are highly soluble and quickly leached by heavy rains. Fortunately, colloidal surfaces hold a large reserve of exchangeable cations, and exchangeable potassium so readily enters soil water that it is counted as available. Equilibrium levels of potassium are determined by its abundance in the parent material and by the amount of leaching to which the soil is generally subject. It is fairly easy and inexpensive to raise potassium levels through fertilization, but the effects are short-lived, especially where chemical fertilizers are used, because these are highly soluble and readily leached. Organic manures and composts are generally good sources.

Calcium and magnesium together make up the majority of the cations present in most soils, and calcium is usually the more abundant. High concentrations of either raise soil pH. Calcium, in the form of lime, is commonly added to soils to raise pH, less often for its fertilizer value. Dolomitic lime also supplies magnesium. Most crop plants do best at pH 6.0 to 7.0 (slightly acid to neutral). The minimum pH for most acid-tolerant crops is about 4.8, the maximum for those adapted to alkaline soils about 8.0. Acid soils tend to be found in humid climates, alkaline soils in dry lands.

Sulfur originates from mineral sources but is also, like nitrogen, cycled among soils, living organisms, and water bodies. It is lost to the air as gaseous, acid-forming oxides, from ocean spray and burning vegetation, and as hydrogen sulfide from decaying organic matter. Rainfall washes sulfur oxides back to the soil and surface waters. Sulfur is abundantly supplied in areas subject to sea breezes, and in regions polluted by the burning of fossil fuels it reaches the ground in acid rain. Organic manures and many chemical fertilizer compounds primarily intended to supply other nutrients also contain sulfur, and deficiencies are not widespread, but more are being observed, often attributable to repeated burning of fallow fields and prolonged use of chemical fertilizers that do not supply sulfur.

Micronutrient deficiencies are important in certain environments, most commonly in organic soils and in mature soils on very old parent material. These deficiencies need not be summarized here.

Nutrients must come from somewhere. If cultivators take crops year after year without somehow making up for the removed nutrients, a practice sometimes referred to as mining the soil, available nutrient levels fall to a lowered equilibrium level, but not to nil, because natural additions of available nutrients continue. On a few soils, lowered equilibrium levels continue to support adequate yields by the standards of preindustrial agriculture, but on most the harvests shrink, often to the point that they do not return the effort, sometimes not even the seed. In certain circumstances crop removal stimulates biological nitrogen fixation, but as a rule, compensating additions must come from soil amendments (materials added to soil to increase productivity) imported into the agricultural ecosystem. Tillage, in some historical writings a cause of soil rejuvenation, often improves the availability of nutrients, but does not add them.

Occasional reference will be made to soil orders in the USDA (United States Department of Agriculture) Seventh Approximation. This is done primarily for those readers who are familiar with this internationally used soil classification system. Others may refer to standard soil textbooks.

HUMAN REQUIREMENTS. In this book a daily requirement of 2,000 kcal (large calories) will be assumed per head of population, probably a bit liberal in populations with a large proportion of young children. The Food and Agricultural Organization (FAO) uses a reference standard of 2,000 kcal per diem for adult women and 2,800 for adult men. Some nutritionists lean toward a figure for adult men in the neighborhood of 2,200 to 2,400. Requirements vary, being greater if the person is heavier (why male standards are higher), physically active, fast-growing, pregnant or lactating, or subject to cold or stress.

The present FAO protein standard is 37 to 46 g per day, depending on body weight, climate, and quality of protein, more precisely the balance among the 22 essential amino acids. Most animal proteins are high-quality. Nearly all plant proteins are deficient in one or more essential amino acids, but by matching proteins with different deficiencies the aggregate quality is improved. Especially important in this regard are combinations of cereals and pulses (legume grains and the plants that yield them). Most traditional combinations supply protein whose quality compares well with that of meat. Combinations of maize with beans, many root crops with pulses, or oilseeds with pulses supply protein of enhanced quality, if not as good as that of meat.

The great majority of people get sufficient protein, provided their energy intake is adequate; undernutrition is the cause of most protein deficiencies. Amply fed cereal cultivators have little problem meeting the standard. Roughly 400 g of cereal supplies 1,600 kcal. That much rice provides about 32 g of protein, that much oats or spring wheat about 56 g. Only a little animal protein or complementary plant protein would make protein malnutrition unlikely in most people, with the possible, partial exception of pregnant or nursing mothers. More supplementation is needed where root crops are the principal staples. If enough of the roots are eaten to furnish 1,600 kcal, 24 to 28 g of protein are supplied by potato or taro, 8 to 28 g by sweet potato, and 16 to 20 g by yams, and the proteins generally lack more essential amino acids than those of cereals (Coursey, 1967; Onwueme, 1970:221). Pulses, though useful, do not make up all the deficiencies. Therefore, supplementary sources of quality protein are important. Among the major staples, those that supply the least protein — only 2 to 8 g in a 1,600 kcal portion — are banana, plantain (cooking banana), breadfruit, manioc (cassava, *Manihot esculenta*), and sago, the starch of the sago palm.

Vitamin and mineral nutrition is a complex subject, and no attempt will be made here to outline all the circumstances under which deficiencies occur. Undernutrition causes most severe deficiencies, but the two most serious vitamin B deficiency diseases are aggravated by overreliance on cereal foods processed in certain ways. Beriberi, an often fatal deficiency disease, afflicts people who eat little but polished rice, though processing the rice with lime or lye may improve availability of the needed vitamin, B_1. Vitamin B_2 deficiency results in pellagra, common among people who rely too much on maize. In either case, pulses and animal products are good sources of the lacking vitamin.

Humans have an unusual need for fresh foods or those that retain their value during storage. Besides humans, only guinea pigs and some primates are known to require vitamin C. Scurvy, the C deficiency disease, is, apart from its well-known occurrence among voyagers of the Age of Sail, mainly found among people living on winter stores in the late winter or early spring. Vitamin A deficiencies are surprisingly common, despite that vitamin's being available in some quantity in leafy greens, most yellow or red vegetables, butterfat, and liver.

Iron and calcium are of particular interest, because deficiencies in them are most frequently encountered among women and are aggravated by pregnancy and nursing. Studies of the effects of diet upon fertility often focus on these minerals. Calcium is present in many common foods. Rich sources include fish, shellfish, milk, and cheese, and dark green vegetables, but all except the last are expensive in most places. Most staples supply some iron, and severe deficiency — that is, clinical anemia—is most common in undernourished populations. Among preindustrial agriculturalists, women often evidence slight to moderate iron deficiencies on traditional diets, unless they consume such rich sources as pulses, shellfish, liver, and other organ meats.

Chronic malnutrition cannot be blamed on the agricultural systems themselves, except possibly that seasonal shortages of fresh foods are a frequent product of agricultural adaptations to regions with long winters or long dry seasons. Ecological complementarity of legumes with cereals and other energy staple crops, and the allocation of diverse crops to different microenvironments, tend to make the production of a reasonably balanced diet not only feasible but quite often agronomically advantageous. Fruits and green vegetables do not require a great deal of space. Nutritional studies suggest diverse reasons for chronic malnutrition, but persistent undernutrition is usually an underlying cause. Though much nutritional improvement can be gained in the present world through the improvement of diets and nutritional knowledge, the most important step toward a universally adequate diet is to ensure access to abundant food production.

Notes

1. Another common objection to the use of systems theory in human ecology is that concepts that have precise mathematical definitions in physics, engineering, and biology are used analogically. Doing so may wrongly imply isomorphism among the disparate systems, but I am not convinced that the usefulness of the concepts is necessarily impaired. Many critics, perhaps most notably Berlinski (1976) and Rindos (1984), find that the borrowing adds up to a distortion and simplification of theory grounded in the natural sciences. In fact the critical relationship between equilibrium maintenance and change was foreshadowed more in economics than in physics. The individuals most associated with the founding of cybernetics and general systems theory made their own forays into the psychological and cultural realms (von Bertalanffy, 1967; Wiener, 1950), armed not only with concepts of equilibrium but also with entropy and a host of concepts specific to each theory. Precedence, though, ought not to be the main issue. I would agree with Rindos that homeostasis is often inappropriately applied in human ecological studies but not that equilibrium must therefore be scrapped.

2. An outstanding philosophical difference between cybernetics and general systems theory is that in the latter, living systems and social systems not only resist entropy but also tend to increase negentropy, that is, move toward states of higher differentiation.

References

Ashby, W.R. (1956). *An Introduction to Cybernetics.* Wiley, New York.
_____. (1960). *Design for a Brain.* Wiley, New York.
Barth, F. (1956). Ecologic relationships of ethnic groups in Swat, North Pakistan. *American Anthropologist,* 58:1079–1089.
Bender, B. (1978). Gatherer to hunter: A social perspective. *World Archaeology,* 10:204–222.
Bennett, J.W. (1976). *The Ecological Transition: Cultural Anthropology and Human Adaptation.* Pergamon, New York.
Berlinski, D.J. (1976). *On Systems Analysis: An Essay Concerning the Limitations of Some Mathematical Methods in the Social, Political, and Biological Sciences.* MIT Press, Cambridge.
Bertalanffy, L. von (1967). *Robots, Men, and Minds: Psychology in the Modern World.* Braziller, New York.
Burris, R. (1977). Overview of nitrogen fixation. In *Genetic Engineering for Nitrogen Fixation* (A. Hollaender, ed.), Plenum, New York, pp. 9–18.
Cavan, S. (1966). *Liquor License: An Ethnography of Bar Behavior.* Aldine, Chicago.
Coursey, D. (1967). *Yams.* Longmans, London.
Foin, T.C., and W.G. Davis (1987). Equilibrium and nonequilibrium models in ecological anthropology: An evaluation of "stability" in Maring ecosystems. *American Anthropologist,* 89:9–31.
Geertz, C. (1963). *Agricultural Involution: The Process of Ecological Change in Indonesia.* University of California Press, Berkeley.
Hardesty, D. (1975). The niche concept: Suggestions for its use in studies of human ecology. *Human Ecology,* 3:71–85.
_____. (1977). *Ecological Anthropology.* Wiley, New York.
Harris, M. (1968). *The Rise of Anthropological Theory.* Crowell, New York.
Odum, E.P. (1983). *Basic Ecology.* Saunders, Philadelphia.
Onwueme, I.C. (1970). *The Tropical Tuber Crops.* John Wiley and Sons, Chichester, England.
Rindos, D. (1984). *The Origins of Agriculture: An Evolutionary Perspective.* Academic Press, Orlando, Fla.
Sanchez, P.A. (1976). *Properties and Management of Soils in the Tropics.* Wiley, New York.
Steward, J.H. (1955). *Theory of Culture Change.* University of Illinois Press, Urbana.
Vasey, D.E. (n.d.). *The Pub and English Social Change.* AMS Press, New York. Forthcoming.
White, L. (1959). *The Evolution of Culture.* McGraw-Hill, New York.
Wiener, N. (1950). *The Human Use of Human Beings.* Houghton Mifflin, Boston.

2
The Origins of Agriculture

 To begin with agricultural origins is to introduce several controversies, antiquity for one. The definitive sign of prehistoric agriculture is morphological change indicative of domestication, but its identification is subject to controversy. Unequivocal traces of domestication must have followed a period of evolution of plants and animals under human management. Interested scholars argue whether that period was a few hundred or many thousands of years.

Theories to explain origins are no less controversial. Four prominent types of explanation will be examined: (1) that agriculture was a localized invention that subsequently diffused, (2) that mounting population pressure impelled the turn to agriculture, (3) that environmental changes before and after the end of the last glacial prompted agricultural origins, and (4) that domesticates, human management, and agricultural society coevolved, the development of each furthering the development of the others. Two composite theories are then discussed, and finally my own composite scenario, with all respect due the many specialists on origins, but nevertheless in preference to any of the four explanations taken alone.

The primary task of this chapter is to sift through the many scenarios of the origins of agriculture and present the main explanations. Though I arrive at four, no claim is made that the list is exhaustive, only that these explanations recur in much of the literature. One other should be mentioned, though I would dismiss it as so general that it is hardly an explanation at all, namely, the reasoning that agriculture is a logical outcome of cultural evolution (notably Braidwood, 1960, 1967).

Agriculture transformed the world. Food collecting could not have supported more than a tiny fraction of the world's present population, nor nearly that of two or three thousand years ago. Precolonial California, agricultural only in the extreme southeast, is thought to have been an unusually favorable environment for food collectors, possessing rich resources such as oak groves (for acorns) and salmon runs, and there were settled villages. For all these assets, the population was only between 133,000 and 310,000 (Denevan, 1976:238); the 1980 census showed 24 million in the area. In a few parts of the world, wild food resources of exceptional density permit population densities of several persons per square kilometer. Wild sago palms support sedentary villages of several hundred people in Asmat, West Irian, Indonesia (Rockefeller, n.d.). Harlan and Zohary (1966) report in Southwest Asia dense stands of barley, einkorn wheat, or emmer wheat, the latter sometimes as dense as cultivated wheat fields in the same region.

How Early

Primary dependence upon clearly domesticated plants and animals is demonstrable in widely scattered locations by 8000 B.C. to 4000 B.C. (A summary of both early and somewhat later domesticates is in Harlan, 1975.) How long domestication and agriculture were in an incipient stage is more controversial and has a direct bearing on explanations of agricultural origins.

Direct evidence of domestication, in the form of morphological changes in plants and animals, presently points to dates in the early Holocene, ca. 8500 B.C. to 7000 B.C., in Southwest Asia, Peru, and Mexico. Indirect evidence of cultivation or of domesticated plants dates from ca. 7000 B.C. in the Southeast Asian–Melanesian region. A drainage channel occurs in association with accelerated soil deposition in a Papua New Guinea swamp at about 7000 B.C., where more ambitious drainage and the construction of beds suitable for cultivation are dated to about 4000 B.C. (Golson, 1981). Among plant remains from Spirit Cave, Thailand, ca. 7000 B.C., are what Gorman (1969, 1971) calls probable "cultigens," and Harris (1973) terms semidomesticates, identifications that are disputed (Harlan and de Wet, 1973).

Cases are made for earlier cultivation. Evidence of regular forest burning around 12,000 B.C. in Taiwan (Tsukada, 1966, 1967) is interpreted as a possible consequence of cultivation (Chang, 1976). Sauer (1952) argues that tropical cultivation of vegetatively propagated plants, particularly roots, should have preceded cereal cultivation and could "lie several times seven thousand years in the past" (p. 19), a stance defended by Carter (1975) and Lathrap (1977). Sauer favors Southwest Asia as the earliest site. Lathrap argues from the wide distribution of the bottle gourd (*Lagenaria siceraria*) that its cultivation may have begun as much as 40,000 years ago in its tropical African homeland. But Shaw (1976) notes that after decades of debate, little direct evidence of such early agriculture or domestication as yet exists; as for yam and other vegetatively propagated domesticates in tropical Africa, accepted evidence points to the sixth millennium B.C. at the earliest.

Scholars recognize many degrees of intervention in and control over the life cycles and breeding of plants and animals, and any transition to agriculture would involve a gradual step-up of both. Higgs and Jarman (1969, 1972; also Higgs, 1976; Jarman and Wilkinson, 1972) greatly extend this line of reasoning.

The Higgs-Jarman thesis has several main points, beginning with the now accepted premise that food collectors commonly propagate plants, intervene in ecosystems, and affect the migration and feeding habits of game. Many degrees of dependence fall between full domestication and passive reliance on wild species, and "the origins of agriculture may be as old as the Lower Palaeolithic" (Higgs, 1976:34), that is, older than 100,000 years. Dependence steadily increased over the closing millennia of the Pleistocene; reference is principally to Europe and Southwest Asia.

The Higgs-Jarman thesis differs in at least one major respect from Sauer's early-domestication thesis. Higgs and Jarman seek the early steps toward domestication among Palaeolithic cultures, including many that relied heavily on hunting. Surmising that hunters were unlikely forerunners, Sauer favored instead sedentary collectors exploiting waterside environments.

Much depends on whether or not specialization in particular resources is a valid sign of incipient domestication. Much of the Higgs-Jarman argument is based on evidence of specialization in certain animal species, including reindeer in Europe, where conditions at the time would not have permitted exploitation of plants that were later domesticated. Farther south, grindstones and stone blades that exhibit a polish associated with grass cutting are found in the Nile valley from ca. 13,000 B.C. and in the Maghreb from ca. 14,000 B.C. (Clark, 1976), in either case several millennia before definitely domesticated plants are known to have been present. Moore (1982) suggests the following sequence in Southwest Asia: (1) specialization in certain animal species, including deer, onagers, sheep, and goats, during much of the Upper Palaeolithic (ca. 40,000–10,000 B.C.); (2) selective hunting in "Epipalaeolithic I" (ca. 18,000–10,000 B.C.); and (3) during "Epipalaeolithic II" (ca. 10,000–8500 B.C.) an intensification of the pattern established in the preceding period, along with cereal exploitation. Unger-Hamilton (1989) concludes from analysis of the wear pattern on flint sickle blades that cereals were cultivated, with tillage, from about 10,000 B.C.

Another subject of varying interpretation is sedentism. Agriculture and sedentism are associated, but not in any consistent sequence. A trend is evident in many regions toward sedentism before the appearance of identifiable domesticates. That is not too surprising. Sedentism is known among some contemporary food collectors and in the settlement pattern of littoral hunters of southern Scandinavia in the fourth century B.C. (Rowley-Conwy, 1983). Upper Palaeolithic Siberian mammoth hunters made permanent settlements of some size (Chard, 1974:20–21). However, people who still lived in shifting camps cultivated domesticated plants at Tehuacán, Mexico, though a limited tendency toward sedentism is evident during this "El Riego phase," ca. 7200 B.C. to 5200 B.C. (from uncalibrated C^{14} dates; MacNeish, 1964).

The regions where the earliest domesticates have been identified, Southwest Asia and Peru, offer a striking contrast in the ways that incipient agriculture and settlement developed. In Southwest Asia, sizable permanent settlements (possibly not occupied year-round) preceded definite domestication, though it is uncertain how much these settlements were involved in domestication. The pattern in Peru seems to be more like that at Tehuacán. At Guitarrero Cave, Peru, a horizon dated to 8600–8000 B.C. yielded some large, apparently domesticated beans (*Phaseolus vulgaris*), the remains of a whole pepper (*Capsicum chinense* or *C. baccatum*), and some possible remains of dried tubers, possibly *Oxalis* species now cultivated in the Andes (Kaplan, 1980; Smith, 1980). The cultivators seem to have been nomadic at least part of the year, and they hunted quite a lot.

Domestication

Domestication is the process whereby human management brings about morphological changes in plants or animals. The operational definition frequently used in archaeological investigations is that a plant or animal is said to be domesticated when the remains indicate a form outside the range of variation among wild forms. Cultivars are plants under significant human management, with or without the detectable changes of domesticates.

The identification of a domesticate is subject to the state of knowledge applied, and improvement of that knowledge may push back the dates obtained for earliest domesticates. Some minimal time of transition to a domesticated state must pass, a period that must vary, being shorter the more inbreeding would be obtained. In normally self-fertile plants or those somehow completely isolated from the wild population, the transition might occupy only a few generations (Santley, 1980). In self-sterile plants or in animals that cross repeatedly with wild forms, domestication would be indefinitely prolonged. Although contemporary agriculturalists and pastoralists do not always isolate breeding stock, many do, and isolation could well be an ancient technique. Nearly all cultures recognize sexual reproduction in animals.

Selection is the means by which most of the morphological changes were effected. Both conscious and unconscious selection may be inferred.

The most elementary form of conscious selection is the propagation of those plants that yield the most, the largest, or the best in the breeders' judgment. Some of the effects of domestication on edible parts are fairly consistent and may reasonably be assumed to have been the result of deliberate selection. Edible parts of domesticates tend to be larger than in the wild forms, and those of the main energy staples contain more carbohydrates and less fiber. Domesticates tend to lose defenses against predators — thorns, for example. Toxins and bitter alkaloids necessitating processing for their removal are common enough in wild tubers, pulses, and many seeds other than cereals. Whether or not early cultivators worked out a method of consciously selecting against objectionable substances is problematical, but results were somehow obtained, for example, eliminating toxins from the main varieties of yam and debittering many pulses.

Surveys of plant domestication (Darlington, 1973; Harlan, de Wet, and Stemler, 1976) emphasize unconscious selection. Migration or local isolation of the crop cuts it off from wild forms. Changes due to genetic drift (a form of sampling error, resulting in imperfect replication of a population's genetic code) may be quite rapid if the populations involved are small. Darlington (1973:161–163) lists the following forms of unconscious "operational selection" that likely bring about change: (1) selection for greater vigor and ability to compete with wild forms on plowed, weeded, and fertilized fields; (2) selection for rapid and even germination arising from even sowing; (3) a variety of changes arising from the modes of propagation; and (4) selection for fruits and seeds that remain attached for some time after maturation instead of shattering or dropping. In cereals the last process produces a thicker attachment of seed to seed head, a much used diagnostic trait of domestication. It is not a universal trait in fully domesticated cereals, however (Schwanitz,

1966:32–35), and relevant variation in methods of harvesting is noted in contemporary West African practice (Clark, 1976:83–84).

Many domesticated crops are products of crosses, often between species. Hybridization was probably unintentional and could have happened at any stage in the domestication process, possibly before. Emmer wheat (*Triticum dicoccum*) resulted from a cross of einkorn wheat (*T. monococcum*) and a species of goat grass (*Aegilops*). Subsequent hybridization of emmer and an *Aegilops* species produced bread wheat (*T. vulgare*) (Darlington, 1973:143–144, 162). It is usually conceded that bread wheat arose under cultivation.

Explanations of Domestication and Agricultural Origins

DIFFUSION.   *Diffusion* in this instance refers to the flow of agricultural or protoagricultural practices, ideas, or germ plasm from one place to another, but what is generally meant by a diffusionist theory of origins is one that assigns a primary role to a few areas. In most versions the apparent multiplicity of areas of domestication is reduced to one or two, often one in each of the two hemispheres. Sometimes more are conceded, but many sites of domestication are still assigned a secondary role. Because the early domesticates vary from one region to the next, direct diffusion of the agricultural complex is ruled out, and most proponents settle for the mechanism of stimulus diffusion, that is, the spread of the idea of domestication beyond the main crops or perhaps in conjunction with only one crop.

The greatest difficulty with traditional diffusionist theories, referring to a great deal of thinking before the 1960s and to Carter's (1975) more recent defense, is that they fail to give a plausible mechanism by which the stimulus would take effect. It is assumed that the advantages of cultivation or animal husbandry are apparent; the original invention or inventions are fortuitous. But food production, even in its more developed forms, does not often appeal to food collectors, who resist authorities' efforts to encourage its adoption. Pfeiffer (1976) notes that the Prince of Wales Islanders of the Torres Strait, faced with a failure of their wild yams, obtained domesticated stock from an island to the north, planted for a season, then promptly abandoned the practice the following year. Most interested scholars, for these reasons or others, reject diffusionist theories that are global in scale.

One ingenious hypothesis (Lathrap, 1977) circumvents these flaws, though evidence is thin. Lathrap argues that cultivation of the bottle gourd began in tropical Africa as much as 40,000 years ago, and its cultivation preceded the domestication of other plants in the main areas. A useful industrial product, even to food collectors, it was carried along and propagated in house gardens, which in turn became experimental plots (p. 733) in which weedy species adapted to open, disturbed land thrived. Bottle gourds indeed appear very early in widely scattered locations: Spirit Cave in Thailand; in Tamaulipas (MacNeish, 1958:178–192) and Tehuacán (Flannery, 1973:289), Mexico, in cultural phases dated to 8000–6000 B.C. (uncalibrated C^{14}); and on the central coast of Peru ca. 6000–5000 B.C. (Cohen, 1977). But in none of these early contexts is there positive evidence of domestication or cultivation of the plant. Pickersgill and Heiser (1977:816) alternatively suggest that in the New World, gourds were spread as "camp-following weeds" and probably crossed from Africa before domestication. Whitaker and Carter (1954) conclude from experiments that gourds could float across the South Atlantic and still germinate.

POPULATION. The idea has been around for some time that population pressure provided the impetus for agricultural origins but was usually applied only to particular regions. Smith and Young (1972) apply the explanation in some detail to Southwest Asia. The possibility is raised guardedly by Smith (1976:20) that the explanation might be widely applicable.

By far the most forceful and global application of the population explanation is that of Cohen (1975a, 1975b, 1977). Slow population growth through the late Pleistocene and early Holocene, locally uneven but steady for the world as a whole, forced collectors to turn from megafauna to smaller game and then to a broad spectrum of plants and animals. The change to food production came about because of a world-wide event, as described by the title of Cohen's 1977 book, *The Food Crisis in Prehistory.* Population growth is an underlying cause of the origins of food production, it is argued, and several possible mechanisms are offered by which domestication and agriculture might have arisen.

What most sets Cohen's version off from other demographic explanations is Cohen's insistence that population growth is the independent variable. The mounting pressure and the crisis it generates are separate from the tendency after agriculture develops for growth to accelerate.

The population explanation is roundly criticized by Bronson (1975), who argues that the higher productivity of food production might be attractive even if population pressure were not serious, and that population growth is inherently uneven and too rapid when it does occur to explain the slow rate of technological change that characterizes most of the Pleistocene. The first point is undoubtedly correct under the right circumstances, but that happenstance has little bearing on an explanation of parallel, worldwide developments. The point about uneven population growth is closer to the crux of the dispute. Cohen, particularly in the 1977 book, argues that Pleistocene populations were highly mobile and that this mobility, along with rapid growth in newly inhabited regions, would evenly distribute population pressure and account for the emergence of agriculture in so many places in the space of a few thousand years.

The debate over the population explanation should be rid of one theoretical encumbrance, namely, any need to show that population widely exceeded the carrying capacity of available environments when people first turned to agriculture. Cohen's portrayal of a food crisis is obviously one of great pressure on food resources, but he acknowledges the difficulty of estimating carrying capacity in ethnographic or prehistoric cases. As we shall see in chapter 8, population pressure can stimulate intensification of subsistence activities even if population is well below any absolute limit set by potential food supply and available technology.

ENVIRONMENTAL CHANGE.   If the indisputable dates of first agriculture are not pushed back too much more, their coincidence with the Pleistocene-Holocene transition is hard to explain away. It should be noted, however, that environmental changes were far from uniform over the whole world. Warming, for example, was greater in higher temperate latitudes than in the tropics. Some change was probably experienced virtually everywhere, but not equally dramatic change. Explanations of this type offered thus far are at best too local.

Most authorities now reject the once-popular hypothesis that subtropical regions, sites of much of the demonstrated early domestication, had pluvial (rainier) climates in the late Pleistocene, and that early Holocene desiccation forced the change to agriculture (Childe, 1951; Peake and Fleure, 1927; Pumpelly, 1908; White, 1959:286). This model has some validity at Tehuacán (MacNeish, 1971), but is now rejected in the Southwest Asian region where it was principally applied (Butzer, 1971).

Binford's (1968) domestication scenario makes a less direct connection between origins and changing environment, specifically rising sea levels produced by the melting of the ice sheets in the north. The shrinking land area coincided with increasing sedentism, setting off a process that will be discussed below. An objection to the model as a global explanation is that the loss of the land varied greatly according to whether the coasts were low lying or steep. The loss of area was slight in central Mexico and the central Andean coasts, definite locations of early domestication. In insular Southeast Asia, where the antiquity of food production is still not well known, about half the landmass was submerged.

Origins need not be connected to the same local environmental changes in all regions. A theory might develop the theme that diverse local changes had similar effects on food-collecting populations.

COEVOLUTION. In certain scenarios, domestication is the product of slow and largely involuntary social evolution associated with biologically evolving plants and animals. People are not domesticated in the sense that they change morphologically, but the changes in settlement and society are nonetheless profound.

One early argument of this variety is that the first domesticated crops were weeds that adapted readily to areas around human habitation (Anderson, 1952; Engelbrecht, 1916). Many early domesticated plants are weeds in habit; that is, they compete most effectively in open, disturbed environments and would respond well to fertile soils. Either the plants colonized habitation areas, Engelbrecht's emphasis, or, as in Anderson's "dump heap" scenario, middens became unintended gardens as people discarded propagating parts and organic wastes that would improve the soil. The early stages of the process would depend on neither intentional cultivation nor complete isolation from wild populations of the same plants, but selection would be gradually exercised through a cycle of harvest from the gardens and return of propagating parts. Morphological change, cultivation, and the degree of dependence on the plants would reinforce one another, in positive feedback.

Objections to the scenario are many. Although middens are a recurring feature in the archaeological record and are known from late Pleistocene and early Holocene sites, the migration habits of food collectors vary greatly. The likelihood that the process would result in a sufficient degree of isolation would presumably depend on the plants' tendencies toward cross-fertilization. The theory does not explain animal domestication. Most of all, other means of isolation are at least as credible, including transport by humans to other microenvironments (Flannery, 1965; Lynch, 1973).

Rindos (1980, 1984) expands the coevolution model and in so doing specifically excludes any voluntaristic role for humans until a very late and not clearly specified stage. The coevolution principle is extended to the domestication of animals, but the discussion is almost exclusively about plants.

A brief summary can give themes if not quite do justice to the diverse mechanisms by which Rindos asserts plant domestication could have been fostered. First he draws a parallel from the numerous cases of plants that have coevolved in symbiosis with an animal to the point that the plant now depends upon that animal for reproduction or some other vital part of its life cycle. Then he draws parallels between domesticated plants and the weeds that specialize in cultivated areas. Many weeds are wild plants that have been modified through adaptation to cultivated fields; Harlan (1976) notes that many weeds are descended from cultivated plants, as well as the reverse. Rindos, in a Darwinian variation on the argument of Higgs and Jarman, argues that agriculture is really a late stage in the long evolution of human-plant symbiosis. The alleged novelty of Rindos' model may be contested (Shaffer, 1980), but the exhaustive application of parallels with relations among nonhuman species is unique.

Rindos's 1984 version argues forcefully that increasing human dependency on cultivated plants is partly a response to population growth brought about by the increased supply of food. Rindos is apparently taking pains to correct any impression from his 1980 article that the proposed coevolution process is orthogenetic (Cohen, 1980b). The relationship between humans and domesticates is described as that between predator and prey. Such relationships commonly exist in nature and result in radical increases in the numbers of predator and prey.

The predator-prey analogy falls short of explaining the diverse outcomes of domestication. Although Rindos accomplishes his stated goal of demonstrating that domestication could have been strictly involuntary, that in no way proves that it was. Some involuntary factors could equally have been cultural and uniquely human, and voluntary selection must have been in force at some point that we cannot presume to have been late. Plant and animal domestication commonly result in genetic diversity that far exceeds that within the wild species. Herre (1969) points out that the peculiar variability of domesticated animals is plausibly related to peculiarities of human management, including repeated isolation of small groups from the wild population. The effects of voluntary selection are most evident in characteristics other than the production of edible portions. Woolly sheep were an early and useful achievement, long-haired guinea pigs a later and more esoteric one. In neither case do we know the point at which the variation produced by involuntary selection became something valued and consciously selected.

Devil's claw (*Proboscidea parviflora*) is a fiber plant that the

O'odham (Pima) of Arizona have recently domesticated, probably only since Anglo-American settlers began to encroach on their lands about a hundred years ago. Nabhan and Rea (1987) found that the O'odham distinguish the domesticated variety from wild ones, including those that volunteer in cultivated fields. The folk taxonomy, historical evidence, and present practices of selection all indicate that conscious selection was important early in the domestication process.

Null Cases: Where Food Production Failed to Take Hold

Theories of domestication and the origins of agriculture ought to account for those cases in which conditions were ripe but no such development took place. This idea is not novel. Among recent authors, Harris (1977a) and Rindos (1980, 1984) take some pains to deal with several of these null cases. Australia's particular significance is recognized (Gould, 1973; Harris, 1977a:238–241; Mulvaney, 1975; White, 1971). California is also prominent in many discussions. Cases less often recognized include the Argentine pampas and, until a late date, much of southern Africa. Harris also maintains that plants suitable for domestication are found in the cool maritime coastal areas of North America's northwestern coast and in the American Great Basin. The latter region differs a little in that several centuries before colonial contact, maize-based agriculture was widespread in southwestern Colorado and in Utah as far north as the southern shores of the Great Salt Lake, but then it retreated.

Three of the four explanations offered above for domestication are not readily inverted to explain nondomestication. Nondiffusion would presumably be best applied to Australia, because of its relative precolonial isolation, yet aborigines in the northeast had long contact with agriculturalists in the Torres Strait islands (Harris, 1977b, 1979; Mulvaney, 1975; White, 1971). California and the Great Basin were just beyond the agricultural zone of the southwestern United States. If worldwide population growth was effectively redistributed throughout most of both hemispheres, the problem is to explain why certain regions escaped pressure. The whole point of environmental-change explanations is to yield a general explanation, and it is hard to imagine an environmental change from which Australia, southern Africa, and most of the west coast of North America would somehow be exempt.

Coevolution explanations, alone or in combination with other approaches, offer better possibilities. Explanation is sought in obstacles to coevolution, at the stage of incipient domestication or later.

Formerly offered explanations that particular areas were not amenable to the possible domesticates are not tenable, except perhaps where cold precludes cultivation. Plants suitable for domestication are probably present in most of the areas in question, and conditions suitable for crops of neighboring areas are common. In California's nearly rainless summers, maize cultivation would have required irrigation on most land, but suitable groundwater farming and decrue (cultivation above receding floodwaters) sites may be found. Rivers fed by Sierra and coastal range snows begin to recede only after the weather in many valley locations is warm enough for maize, and I have seen maize grown without irrigation in the Sacramento "inland delta." Decrue farming and irrigation were found in the southwestern United States, the former along the Colorado River in California.

Cohen (1977:205–208) explains nondomestication in California by referring to the richness of wild food resources, including acorns and buckeyes (the nut of *Aesculus californica*). Rich resources support more people than do lean ones, but population pressure is a product not of absolute density but rather of population density relative to resource density. Cohen tries to have it both ways; parallel development occurred among regions with widely varying resource densities because migrations evened out population pressure, but for some unknown reason the adjustment failed where nondomestication must be explained. Why were oaks and buckeyes not domesticated, and why did population growth not lead to maize cultivation in areas suitable for maize but not nut trees? We do know that domestication took place in another region of abundant wild food resources, Southwest Asia.

Rindos (1980, 1984) bases his explanation of nondomestication of California oaks on his hypothesis that a necessary part of the domestication process is the replacement by humans of other animals as agents in propagation and dispersal. He notes that oaks were also not domesticated in Old World regions where many other crops, including olives and tree fruits, were. He maintains that humans could not have replaced squirrels as the main agents of dispersal, because squirrels "not only harvest acorns, but also plant them" (Rindos, 1980:757).

Harris (1977a) also observes that few nut trees were domesticated early, in spite of their importance in some regions that became agricultural, notably the eastern United States. The failure of this "pathway toward agriculture" is attributed to the time needed to reach maturity and the cross-pollination among most of the trees. Neither characteristic is unknown among domesticated plants, but in combination they would be expected at least to slow the domestication process greatly.

Australia forms the least tractable case. Dependence on plants that are probably suitable for domestication was high in certain areas. These plants include a number of grasses, including wild rice (*Oryza* spp.), *Amaranthus* spp., yams (*Dioscorea* spp.), edible aroids, and relatives of sweet potato (Golson, 1971). Three species of the latter are important food sources in central Australia, including *Ipomoea costata, I. muelleri,* and an unnamed species that forms ovoid tubers up to 16 cm long (Yen, 1982). Environments and population densities ranged widely.

Explanation is needed as to why events like those of the Holocene did not occur sooner. Even if cultivation and herding were present in rudimentary form well before the close of the Pleistocene, a reason must be found for the appearance, so close in time, of morphological changes and full-fledged agriculture in far-flung locations not too long after the start of the Holocene. The major domesticates of Southwest Asia and the Mexican highlands would probably not have been in the same habitats under the Ice Age climate but were surviving somewhere, probably at lower elevations and latitudes not too far away. Tropical regions, including Peru and New Guinea, did not have radically lower temperatures during the glacials, and the domesticates of those places probably survived not at all far from their Holocene habitats.

Two Composite Theories: Binford and Harris

Two reviews of domestication and agricultural origins (Binford, 1968; Harris, 1977a) stand out for the concerted effort made to balance the need for a global theory against differences in the course of domestication in various places. Harris's version is the more global, benefiting in no small measure from reports in the late 1960s and the 1970s of work in regions that had previously received little attention.

Binford suggests that specialization in certain food resources, such as migratory fowl and anadromous fish, led to increased sedentism at the end of the Pleistocene. In turn, sedentism stimulated higher rates of population growth in some areas, which became "donor systems" that fed population into receiver areas where domestication subsequently took place. Population pressure was thereby generated in events that were not directly connected but that stemmed from a common cause, a very different circumstance from Cohen's food crisis, which presumes a functional linkage of population pressure in far-flung regions.

Harris's sequence of events is similar in several respects but takes into account the substantial changes in subsistence patterns that had already taken place before the end of the Pleistocene. Diversification of food resources, which some authors call a broad-spectrum revolution, stressed the population-resource equilibrium of food-collecting populations. Suggested sources of stress include extinction of megafauna, sedentism, and anthropogenic modification of the physical environment, by burning, for example. Climatic change is a possible factor, notably desiccation along the Sahara margins, but not worldwide. Like Binford, Harris attributes most subsequent population growth to increased sedentism. He recognizes the principle of coevolution and notes that differences in selection would arise from differing methods of propagation and harvest. Domestication took place in more or less distinctive "alternative pathways to agriculture."

Discussion

A complete theory of the origins of agriculture must do several things: (1) explain parallel developments in widely separated parts of the world, (2) supply a mechanism by which domestication would commence and be followed by increasing reliance on domesticates, and (3) either provide motives for food collectors to turn to agriculture or alternatively demonstrate that motive is not needed.

The first task merits elaboration. Modern humans, *Homo sapiens sapiens,* appeared over much of the Old World 40,000 to 50,000 years ago. Whatever mental and social capabilities are required for agriculture were probably present by that time, if not earlier, long before the definitive manifestation of agriculture in so many places in the early Holocene. Of the four explanations outlined above, all but coevolution can establish a link among remote locations: communication (diffusion), migrations (diffusion or Cohen's population thesis), and change in the world environment. Of Cohen's arguments, worldwide redistribution of population is one of the most contested.

All four explanations are insufficient without at least a small dose of another, which is not to say that no explanation can be dominant. Indeed Cohen (1977) recognizes as much. He notes that domesticates spread, some conditions around food collectors' camps were conducive to plant domestication, and the early Holocene witnessed growing mutual dependence of humans and domesticates, but he insists that these putative causes of agriculture are insufficient without the population-induced food crisis.

Diffusion, for reasons already discussed, most obviously does not stand on its own, but it occurred. No matter how dispersed the domestication process — Harlan (1971) argues that domestication took place not in centers but in "non-centers" — diffusion must be invoked to explain the spread of crops and livestock far from their places of origin. Lathrap's theory is mixed, as it makes the diffusion of gourd cultivation an initial cause, the precipitating agent of coevolution in experimental plots. His enthusiastic endorsement (1985) of Rindos's 1984 book is therefore consistent.

Coevolution is indispensable. Even if conscious selection were early, unconscious selection must have been highly significant. Even preindustrial cultivators who consciously selected seeds or made far-reaching management decisions were presumably not prophets capable of seeing where their efforts would lead plants, animals, and society.

Coevolution could also stand alone, were it not for the need to explain parallel development. The analogy with biological evolution is weak at this point. Separate species evolve in sometimes striking parallels but not on a common schedule. Rindos (1984:33–34) addresses the point only by accusing Cohen of making events more synchronous than they were. Rindos notes that the spread among dates of known agriculture in major regions is as much as 8,000 years, and wonders how much of a spread would lead to rejection of the hypothesis. The range among known dates in Peru, Mexico, Southwest Asia, and possibly Papua New Guinea is remarkably slight, however, and even a spread of a few thousand years is remarkable in comparison with the prior passage of time since modern humans appeared. If no connection exists, the parallels must be either coincidence or else orthogenesis, the very interpretation that Rindos works so hard to exclude. We are left with population and environmental change to explain parallel development until such time that alternative, credible hypotheses are advanced.

Cohen's scenario is based on the shaky premise that population pressure is the independent variable. His assumption that Pleistocene population is independent of food supply does not follow from any valid general property of population (chapter 8), and Cohen himself (1980a) acknowledges that population growth accelerated in the early Holocene following the development of agriculture.

The end of the Ice Age would almost certainly result in a large worldwide increase in available wild foods, raising the question of why population pressure was not thus relieved. Net primary productivity would substantially increase unless the rise in mean temperatures was widely offset by desiccation, a now rejected hypothesis. Many widespread Holocene environments, including temperate hardwood forests, steppes, and Mediterranean scrublands, tend to produce a high proportion of biomass that is edible to humans. Arguments that European mesolithic cultures of this time faced a decreasing subsistence base as Pleistocene game were eliminated from the region (Dolukhanov, 1973; Price, 1973; Waterbolk, 1968) are difficult to sustain. Hunters would have lost a very convenient source of meat, in the form of megafauna and gregarious herd animals of the Pleistocene tundra, but abundant compensating resources should have been available (Clark, 1968).

The more credible interpretation is that population growth was responsive to changes in the resource base and settlement, as for example in the scenarios of Binford and Harris. Accelerated growth of the early Holocene may actually have begun earlier. Cohen (1977:126–130) grants that mesolithic European populations increased markedly, and sites in the New World are far more numerous toward the end of the Pleistocene, whether because of first settlement or belated growth is not yet clear.

The first steps toward domestication should be separated from increased reliance on agriculture.[1] Cohen's long-building population pressure is a more believable explanation of the broad-spectrum revolution than of subsequent events. Population pressure would have stimulated a shift to broad-spectrum collecting and even incipient cultivation or herding at a much lower population density than that which would impel reliance on agriculture. By the time agriculture is indisputably present, the early Holocene, it could not be independent of the changes of the late Pleistocene or of early post-Pleistocene adaptations.

In this scenario, change accelerated, but no prior steady state existed. Binford and Harris invoke disequilibration, assuming exogenous cause, a premise stated more clearly by Clark (1976:96): "The change from gathering to cultivation was unlikely to have taken place where the human population was in a state of equilibrium with its environment." I would scrap the notion that food-collecting populations are homeostatic or in a steady state, but without junking negative feedback altogether.

The point made in the previous chapter was that more or less rapid change exists in the face of mechanisms that produce tendencies toward equilibrium in various quantifiable states. If change is compatible with mechanisms that tend to maintain stability, then relative stability does not preclude long-term change, nor does accelerated change mean that equilibrium-maintaining mechanisms must have broken down.

To continue the scenario, after long-building population pressure brought about the broad-spectrum revolution, changed mechanisms of fertility or mortality regulation went into motion, resulting in growth rates that more than offset any relief of pressure brought about by the end of the Ice Age. Coevolution of humans and domesticates entered the picture at some point. The environmental changes of the early Holocene at the very least facilitated the dispersal of domesticates and the spread of agriculture. My own preference is also to reject coincidence and assume that the diverse environmental changes of the Pleistocene-Holocene transition somehow precipitated significant events and therefore explain synchronous events.

The absence of agriculture from Australia should challenge all theorists. Diffusion did not take place, despite opportunities. Evidence for early *Homo sapiens sapiens,* say, by 35,000 years ago, is stronger than in the Americas, raising the question of how Australia escaped rising population pressure. What environmental change of the Pleistocene-Holocene transition would have skipped a continent? Rindos takes on nondomestication by choosing California, the more tractable case, instead of Australia, where aborigines had domesticated dogs and developed varying degrees of dependence on plants that are suitable for domestication.

Note

1. William Denevan first pointed out to me the importance of this distinction but should not be held responsible for my use of it.

References

Anderson, E. (1952). *Plants, Life, and Man.* Little, Brown, Boston.

Binford, L.R. (1968). Post-Pleistocene adaptations. In *New Perspectives in Archaeology* (S.R. Binford and L.R. Binford, eds.), Aldine, Chicago, pp. 313–341.

Braidwood, R.J. (1960). The agricultural revolution. *Scientific American,* 203(9):130–149.

_____. (1967). *Prehistoric Men.* 7th ed. Scott, Foresman, Glenview, Ill.

Bronson, B. (1975). The earliest farming: Demography as cause and consequence. In *Population, Ecology, and Social Evolution* (S. Polgar, ed.), Mouton, The Hague, pp. 53–78.

Butzer, K.W. (1971). *Environment and Archaeology,* 2d ed. Aldine, Chicago.

Carter, G.F. (1975). *Man and the Land.* 3d ed. Holt, Rinehart and Winston, New York.

Chang Kwang-chih (1976). *Early Chinese Civilization.* Harvard University Press, Cambridge.

Chard, C.S. (1974). *Northeast Asia in Prehistory.* University of Wisconsin Press, Madison.

Childe, V.G. (1951). *Man Makes Himself.* Mentor, New York.

Clark, J.D. (1976). Prehistoric populations and pressures favoring plant domestication in Africa. In *Origins of African Plant Domestication* (J.R. Harlan, J.M.J. de Wet, and A.B.L. Stemler, eds.), Mouton, The Hague, pp. 67–106.

Clark, J.G.D. (1968). The economic impact of the change from late glacial to post glacial conditions in northern Europe. In *Eighth Congress of Anthropological and Ethnological Sciences, Proceedings,* Science Council of Japan, Tokyo, pp. 241–244.

Cohen, M.N. (1975a). Archaeological evidence of population pressure in preagricultural societies. *American Antiquity,* 40:471–474.

_____. (1975b). Population growth and the origins of agriculture: An archaeological example from the coast of Peru. In *Population, Ecology, and Social Evolution* (S. Polgar, ed.), Mouton, The Hague, pp. 79–122.

_____. (1977). *The Food Crisis in Prehistory.* Yale University Press, New Haven, Conn.

_____. (1980a). Speculations on the evolution of density measurement and population regulation in *Homo sapiens.* In *Biosocial Mechanisms of Population Regulation* (M.N. Cohen, R.S. Malpass, and H.G. Klein, eds.), Yale University Press, New Haven, Conn., pp. 275–304.

_____. (1980b). [Comment on D. Rindos, Symbiosis, instability, and the origins and spread of agriculture: A new model]. *Current Anthropology,* 21:766–767.

Darlington, C.D. (1973). *Chromosome Botany and the Origins of Cultivated Plants.* 3d ed. Allen and Unwin, London.

Denevan, W.M. (1976). Introduction [to D.H. Ubelaker, The sources and methodology for Mooney's estimates of North American Indian populations]. In *The Native Populations of the Americas* (W.M. Denevan, ed.), University of Wisconsin Press, Madison, pp. 235–244.

Dolukhanov, P.M. (1973). The neolithization of Europe: A chronological and ecological approach. In *The Explanation of Culture Change: Models in Prehistory* (C. Renfrew, ed.), University of Pittsburgh Press, Pittsburgh, pp. 329–342.

Engelbrecht, T. (1916). Über die Entstehung einiger feldmassig angebauter Kulturpflanzen. *Geographische Zeitschrift,* 22:328–334.

Flannery, K.V. (1965). The ecology of early food production in Mesopotamia. *Science,* 147:1247–1256.

_____. (1973). The origins of agriculture. *Annual Review of Anthropology,* 2:271–310.

Golson, J. (1971). Australian aboriginal food plants. In *Aboriginal Man and Environment in Australia* (D.J. Mulvaney and J. Golson, eds.), Australian National University Press, Canberra, pp. 196–238.

_____. (1981). New Guinea agricultural history: A case study. In *A Time to Plant and a Time to Uproot: A History of Agriculture in Papua New Guinea,* Institute of Papua New Guinea Studies, Port Moresby, pp. 55–64.

Gorman, C.F. (1969). Hoabinhian: A pebble-tool complex with early plant associations in Southeast Asia. *Science,* 163:671–673.

————. (1971). The Hoabinhian and after: Subsistence patterns in Southeast Asia during the late Pleistocene and early Recent periods. *World Archaeology,* 2:300–320.

Gould, R.A. (1973). Australian archaeology in ecological and ethnographic perspective. *Warner Module in Anthropology,* no. 7, pp. 1–33. Andover, Mass.

Harlan, J.R. (1971). Agricultural origins: Centers and non-centers. *Science,* 174:468–474.

————. (1975). *Crops and Man.* Agronomic Society of America, Madison, Wis.

————. (1976). Plant and animal distribution in relation to domestication. *Philosophical Transactions of the Royal Society of London,* 275:13–25.

Harlan, J.R., and J.M.J. de Wet (1973). On the quality of evidence for origin and dispersal of cultivated plants. *Current Anthropology,* 14:51–61.

Harlan, J.R., and D. Zohary (1966). Distribution of wild wheats and barley. *Science,* 153:1074–1079.

Harlan, J.R., J.M.J. de Wet, and A.B.L. Stemler (1976). Plant domestication and indigeneous African agriculture. In *Origins of African Plant Domestication* (J.R. Harlan, J.M.J. de Wet, and A.B.L. Stemler, eds.), Mouton, The Hague, pp. 3–22.

Harris, D.R. (1973). The prehistory of tropical agriculture: An ethno-ecological model. In *The Explanation of Culture Change: Models in Prehistory* (C. Renfrew, ed.), University of Pittsburgh Press, Pittsburgh, pp. 391–417.

————. (1977a). Alternative pathways toward agriculture. In *Origins of Agriculture* (C.A. Reed, ed.), Mouton, The Hague, pp. 179–243.

————. (1977b). Subsistence strategies across Torres Strait. In *Sunda and Sahul: Prehistoric Studies in Southeast Asia, Melanesia, and Australia* (J. Allen, J. Golson, and R. Jones, eds.), Academic Press, London, pp. 421–463.

————. (1979). Foragers and farmers in the Western Torres Strait Islands: An historical analysis of economic, demographic, and spatial differentiation. In *Social and Ecological Systems* (P.C. Burnham and R.F. Ellen, eds.), Academic Press, London, pp. 75–109.

Herre, W. (1969). The science and history of domesticated animals. In *Science in Archaeology* (D. Brothwell and E.S. Higgs, eds.), Thames and Hudson, London, pp. 257–272.

Higgs, E.S. (1976). Archaeology and domestication. In *Origins of African Plant Domestication* (J.R. Harlan, J.M.J. de Wet, and A.B.L. Stemler, eds.), Mouton, The Hague, pp. 29–39.

Higgs, E.S., and M.R. Jarman (1969). The origins of agriculture: A reconsideration. *Antiquity,* 43:31–43.

————. (1972). The origins of animal and plant husbandry. In *Papers in Economic Prehistory* (E.S. Higgs, ed.), Cambridge University Press, Cambridge, pp. 3–14.

Jarman, M.R., and P.F. Wilkinson (1972). Criteria of animal domestication. In *Papers in Economic Prehistory* (E.S. Higgs, ed.), Cambridge University Press, Cambridge, pp. 15–26.

Kaplan, L. (1980). Variation in the cultivated beans. In *Guitarrero Cave: Early*

Man in the Andes (T.F. Lynch, ed.), Academic Press, New York, pp. 145–148.

Lathrap, D.W. (1977). Our father the cayman, our mother the gourd: Spinden revisited. In *Origins of Agriculture* (C.A. Reed, ed.), Mouton, The Hague, pp. 713–751.

———. (1985). Review of D. Rindos, *The Origins of Agriculture: An Evolutionary Perspective. Economic Geography,* 60:339–341.

Lynch, T.F. (1973). Harvest timing, transhumance, and the process of domestication. *American Anthropologist,* 75:1254–1259.

MacNeish, R.S. (1958). *Preliminary Archaeological Investigations in the Sierra de Tamaulipas, Mexico.* Transactions of the American Philosophical Society, n.s. 48, pt. 5. Philadelphia.

———. (1964). Ancient Mesoamerican civilization. *Science,* 143:531–537.

———. (1971). Speculation about how and why food production and village life developed in the Tehuacan valley, Mexico. *Archaeology,* 24:307–314.

Moore, A.M.T. (1982). Agricultural origins in the Near East: A model for the 1980's. *World Archaeology,* 14:224–236.

Mulvaney, D.J. (1975). *The Prehistory of Australia.* Penguin, Harmondsworth, England.

Nabhan, G.P., and A. Rea (1987). Plant domestication and folk-biological change: The Upper Piman/devil's claw example. *American Anthropologist,* 89:57–73.

Peake, H.J., and R. Fleure (1927). *Peasants and Potters: The Corridors of Time.* Vol. 3. Oxford University Press, Oxford.

Pfeiffer, J.E. (1976). A note on the problem of basic causes. In *Origins of African Plant Domestication* (J.R. Harlan, J.M.J. de Wet, and A.B.L. Stemler, eds.), Mouton, The Hague, pp. 23–28.

Pickersgill, B., and C.B. Heiser (1977). Origins and distributions of plants in the New World tropics. In *Origins of Agriculture* (C.A. Reed, ed.), Mouton, The Hague, pp. 803–835.

Price, T.D. (1973). A proposed model for the procurement systems in the Mesolithic of northern Europe. In *The Mesolithic in Europe* (S.K. Kozlowski, ed.), Warsaw University Press, Warsaw, pp. 455–476.

Pumpelly, R. (1908). *Explorations in Turkestan: Expeditions of 1904, Prehistoric Civilization of Anau.* Carnegie Institution Publication no. 73. Washington, D.C.

Rindos, D. (1980). Symbiosis, instability, and the origins and spread of agriculture: A new model. *Current Anthropology,* 21:751–772.

———. (1984). *The Origins of Agriculture: An Evolutionary Perspective.* Academic Press, Orlando, Fla.

Rockefeller, M.C. (n.d.). *The Asmat of New Guinea,* ed. A. Gerbrands. Museum of Primitive Art, New York.

Rowley-Conwy, P. (1983). Sedentary hunters: The Ertebolle example. In *Hunter-Gatherer Economy in Prehistory* (G. Bailey, ed.), Cambridge University Press, Cambridge, pp. 111–126.

Santley, R.S. (1980). [Comment on D. Rindos, Symbiosis, instability, and the origins and spread of agriculture: A new model]. *Current Anthropology,* 21:767-768.

Sauer, C.O. (1952). *Agricultural Origins and Dispersals.* American Geographical Society, New York.

Schwanitz, F. (1966). *The Origin of Cultivated Plants.* Harvard University Press, Cambridge.

Shaffer, J.G. (1980). [Comment on D. Rindos, Symbiosis, instability, and the origins and spread of agriculture: A new model]. *Current Anthropology,* 21:768.

Shaw, T. (1976). Early crops in Africa: A review of the evidence. In *Origins of African Plant Domestication* (J.R. Harlan, J.M.J. de Wet, and A.B.L. Stemler, eds.), Mouton, The Hague, pp. 107-154.

Smith, C.E., Jr. (1980). Plant remains from Guitarrero Cave. In *Guitarrero Cave: Early Man in the Andes* (T.F. Lynch, ed.), Academic Press, New York, pp. 87-119.

Smith, P.E.L. (1976). *Food Production and Its Consequences.* Cummings, Menlo Park, Calif.

Smith, P.E.L., and T.C. Young (1972). Greater Mesopotamia: A trial model. In *Population Growth: Anthropological Implications* (B. Spooner, ed.), MIT Press, Cambridge, pp. 1-59.

Tsukada, M. (1966). Late Pleistocene vegetation and climate in Taiwan (Formosa). *Proceedings of the National Academy of Sciences,* 55:543-548.

_____. (1967). Vegetation in subtropical Formosa during the Pleistocene glaciation and the Holocene. *Palaeogeography, Palaeoclimatology, Palaeoecology,* 3:49-64.

Unger-Hamilton, R. (1989). The Epi-Palaeolithic southern Levant and the origins of cultivation. *Current Anthropology,* 30:90-103.

Waterbolk, H.T. (1968). Food production in prehistoric Europe. *Science,* 162:1093-1102.

Whitaker, T.W., and G.F. Carter (1954). Oceanic drift of gourds: Experimental observations. *American Journal of Botany,* 41:697-700.

White, J.P. (1971). New Guinea and Australian prehistory: The "Neolithic problem." In *Aboriginal Man and Environment in Australia* (D.J. Mulvaney and J. Golson, eds.), Australian National University Press, Canberra, pp. 182-195.

White, L. (1959). *The Evolution of Culture.* McGraw-Hill, New York.

Yen, D.E. (1982). Sweet potato in historical perspective. In *Sweet Potato: Proceedings of the First International Symposium* (R.L. Villareal and T.D. Griggs, eds.), Hong Wen, Taiwan, pp. 17-30.

3

An Overview of Preindustrial Agriculture

 This chapter introduces the diversity of preindustrial agricultural systems and the major factors that mold these systems. The approach is typological. The sources are ethnographic, historical, and archaeological, but ethnographic data generally provide the most complete picture of agricultural systems, and coverage is necessarily less complete of past possibilities than of present practices. Not all recent systems that rely on preindustrial technology were present in the more distant past, and some ancient systems may have become extinct. Of particular interest are agricultural systems at the beginnings of food production, when population was thin, most cultivars less modified than later, and landscapes less altered by human activity. Many archaeologists are interested in such reconstructions, a few of which are given in chapters 6 and 7.

Agriculture is here the cultivation of crops with or without animal husbandry. Although pastoralism, a primary reliance on animals, is agriculture in the broadest sense, it will be separated from the rest and treated in chapter 4.

Some anthropologists and historians distinguish agriculture, in its original meaning of cultivation with plows, from horticulture, in which only hand tools are used. I would instead follow the practice of the agricultural sciences and make agriculture inclusive, with horticulture a specialized branch taking in such pursuits as greenhouse management and ornamental gardening. Plows are but one of many variables separating more and less intensive systems, not a critical, diagnostic trait that divides agriculture in two. Plowing is important, though, because of its significance for land preparation, and because it nearly always demands the use of draft animals. The degree to which the husbandry of grazing animals is integrated with cultivation shapes agricultural systems whether the animals are kept for draft or for other purposes.

Intensity

Intensive and *extensive* designate, respectively, the greater and lesser use of inputs intended to increase production. The most extensive agricultural systems are those few in fortunate situations where little is done except to plant and to harvest. The most intensive agriculture is probably that found in greenhouses, where much energy and equipment are invested, and crops receive irrigation, hand care, and heavy applications of fertilizer. In this and many other situations, intensification stimulates further intensification, because of the need to maximize the return on the first set of inputs, and because the removal of one limiting factor generally makes some other factor limiting and subject to alleviation. Irrigated wheat fields also illustrate the principle. Under modern management they tend to receive more fertilizer than dry (nonirrigated) wheat fields, both because the cost of water and irrigation equipment must be recouped and because moisture no longer limits crop growth.

Intensification is often broken down into the kinds of input. The terms *labor-intensive, capital-intensive,* and *energy-intensive* are common in the literature and will be used throughout this book. *Labor* and *energy* are fairly synonymous in a preindustrial system lacking draft animals. Other energy enters the system, notably solar energy for photosynthesis, and energy is expended when brush is burnt or livestock is moved about, but human labor is the main source that is fully under human control. If draft animals are used, their energy replaces human labor, raising the total energy expenditure; unlike their masters, they are kept and fed only if they till the fields. In industrial agriculture, *capital* and *energy* become partially synonymous, because fossil fuel energy is spent on the main inputs that capital buys—for example, in digging ditches and producing chemical fertilizers.

Not all innovations that improve yields constitute intensification, only those that require heightened labor, capital, or energy inputs. An improved plow design does not make a system more intensive unless that plow is used more than the old one or demands more horses or horsepower to pull it. A new and higher-yielding seed might constitute intensification, but only if it costs more than the old seed or requires more fertilizer or care. The concept of skill-intensive agriculture appears in the literature, but in practice, skill is better treated as beneficial management.

No law ordains that one must always put more in to get more out. Cultivators seek to maximize yields at some acceptable level of inputs and in many instances succeed in reducing inputs while simultaneously raising yields. The ancient Egyptians readily diverted the Nile to fertilize their fields, irrigate, and, to a point, control weeds. The construction of rice paddies can result in a net increase in productivity per unit of human labor or animal energy. During the European agricultural revolution of the sixteenth, seventeenth, and eighteenth centuries, production per unit of land and per worker increased as the management of biological factors improved. Even in modern agriculture, in which yield gains are largely won with the help of massive inputs of fossil-fuel energy, some innovations lead to simultaneous increases in yields and savings in all significant inputs.

Cropping Systems

POPULATION PRESSURE AND CROPPING FRE-QUENCY. *Frequency of cropping* is sometimes used synonymously with *intensity,* particularly with respect to preindustrial systems. Albeit a bit imprecise, the usage is correct in the sense that if cropping is more frequent, and fallowing therefore less so, a given area of land receives more work over a period of years and, it is hoped, produces more. Tillage, weeding, the use of soil amendments, and other inputs tend to be used more on frequently cropped land than on land that lies fallow for long periods, but there are exceptions, and we should not presuppose the association.

Boserup's (1965) influential model is a series of stages that evolve under increasing population pressure, each a specific combination of cropping length and fallow length. Under the least population pressure, cropping for a year or two alternates with fallows of 20 to 25 years. This is termed forest fallow cultivation, because tall secondary forest develops by the end of the fallow. As population pressure rises, cultivators must sooner return to the same plot, or cultivate longer, leading in turn to bush fallow cultivation, in which fallows of 6 to 10 years allow only short, mostly woody vegetation to regenerate; short fallow cultivation, in which wild grasses dominate fallows; annual cropping, with only seasonal fallows; and multicropping, a close sequence of crops.

Much of the literature describes forest and bush fallow systems as slash-and-burn or swidden cultivation, and the fields being cropped as swiddens. The term *permanent cultivation* usually lumps annual cropping and multicropping.

Boserup's model is apparently based upon experience in the tropics, and she acknowledges that it must be modified to fit other environments. Grasses can dominate long fallows, either because environmental conditions limit forest growth or because human interference thoroughly suppresses forest growth. Prolonged cultivation, say, for four or more years, along with thorough weeding of woody regrowth during cropping can long delay secondary forest development. So can frequent burning. Widespread maintenance of *leys* — that is, pastures of many years' duration that alternate with cultivation — was one significant development of late preindustrial agriculture in Europe. Fallows of a few months to a year or two are managed in widely varying fashion. Some are left alone, in which case grass and a few broadleaves indeed dominate, but plowing is sometimes done at regular intervals. As we shall see, the latter practice is common in many dry lands and was also the rule in much of medieval Europe. *Bare fallow* is a common description, but sometimes grass quickly grows back; *plowed fallow* is more generally appropriate.

An objection to the Boserup model is that agriculture at low population densities may incorporate short fallows or none (Bronson, 1972; Sherratt, 1980). Environment dictates many examples, such as gardens made in compost pits on some infertile coral islands and agriculture in desert oases, and in these cases population pressure may still be high on the limited area of cultivable land. Some prehistorians assert that the first agriculture in many regions should have consisted of permanent cultivation of exceedingly fertile or better-watered patches, and that long fallow systems are associated with less fertile soils and must have developed later as population spread (Allan, 1972; Sherratt, 1980). Some archaeological evidence supports the argument in humid temperate and dry lands (chapters 7 and 8), but the assertion that long fallow systems are not found on inherently productive soils is wrong. Examples to the contrary include the Gazelle Peninsula of Papua New Guinea (Bourke, 1976) and parts of northern Haiti (Wood, 1963). In both places, fallows were subsequently eliminated, mostly without benefit of soil amendments. Soil fertility seems to have declined, but cultivators responded by emphasizing less demanding crops.

One community, even a single holding, may contain systems with different cropping frequencies. Lambert (1985) reports the practice in Pahang, Malaysia, of starting rice seedlings on swiddens for transplanting to permanently cultivated, rain-fed basins. The pasturing of livestock, in general a less labor-intensive activity than cropping, is to varying degrees integrated with cropping. Grazing animals may be kept on grass fallows as well as on pasture. Some of the most common combinations are those in which short fallowed or permanently cultivated gardens or orchards predominate near human dwellings and stables or pens, longer fallows away from the settlements. Ashes, food scraps, crop byproducts, litter, human and animal excrement, and other organic wastes end up mainly on the so called *infields,* either intentionally or because they are hard by home and corral. The resulting productivity gains and the relative accessibility of bulky, daily harvested foods in the infields are sufficient motives to cultivate these areas more frequently than the *outfields.*

Most forest fallow cultivators have few livestock, and the amount of fertility that settlement wastes provide is not large. Infields, though frequently encountered, are small. Some Southeast Asian forest fallow cultivators efficiently utilize settlement wastes on infield gardens, but most swiddeners use them more haphazardly. Many do not deliberately use manures at all, and most avoid applying human feces.

One way to increase the flow of nutrients from outfields to infields is to let livestock do the work. Where fallows are grazed and the animals folded, stabled, or tethered at night in the inner area, most of the movement has been accomplished, all of it if they are folded or tethered on a site destined for planting. The nutrients are in the handy and fairly available form of animal manure. Where the literature refers to infield-outfield systems, they generally take this form. Examples were once to be found in parts of Europe and are still widely distributed across the grasslands of Africa lying between the equatorial forests and the Sahara. Particularly if livestock are numerous, infield crop production may exceed that from the outfields.

Uncultivated land as well as fallows may furnish nutrients. Manure from livestock fed on outlying pastures may go to build or maintain the fertility of cropland, and animals that feed on pastures by day may be managed so that they leave their excreta in folds or pens at night. The ground is cultivated after the fold is moved. The East Asian landscape bears the mark of centuries of stripping vegetation from hillsides for green manure and composts to enrich valley farms. Long grazing or stripping tends to lower equilibrium levels to the point that the vegetation on the uncultivated land is thin.

TECHNOLOGY AND CROPPING SYSTEMS. Specific tools and techniques are strongly associated with particular cropping systems. The fallow vegetation at the time of clearing determines the tools used for tillage and cultivation.

Axes, machetes, and other chopping tools are the requisites for preparing forests. Cultivators slash undergrowth before attacking the trees. Steel axes can fell quite large trees, but the going is too slow with stone (Iversen, 1956). According to the few extant accounts, cultivators who lack steel tools use stone axes to clear undergrowth and small trees, lop branches, and girdle (ringbark) larger trees. Burning around the base is also used to kill large trees. It is sometimes possible on hillsides to use falling trees to help fell other trees, a difficult skill of great value.

Burning follows clearing, after the slash is allowed to dry. The timing of the slash and the burn can be critical, and seasonal changes in weather are never entirely predictable. Some cultivators stack unburnt slash for a second burn. Others do not.

Subsequent work is fairly light. Forest soils are typically loose, and simple preparation does not compact them. Little tillage is needed, though "stump-jumper" plows were used on newly cleared forests in colonial North America and Australia and in a few historical forest fallow systems of Europe. Many cultivators simply broadcast seed directly after the burn or when the rains begin. Some use hoes and digging sticks to plant root crops and other vegetatively propagated plants or to build low mounds. The predominant native plants of the forest floor do not readily adapt to the sunlit, disturbed conditions of the swidden, and many are destroyed by clearing and burning. Coppice may grow from stumps but is easily controlled and does not shade out the crops. One to three hand weedings thus suffice during the first season. In the following seasons, weeds adapted to open habitats invade and demand more weeding.

Once shorter, open growth dominates the preceding fallow, hoeing becomes the rule. There is still a slash and a burn, but the soil is not so loose, because less litter lies near the surface. Weed species adapted to open environments are already present. Hoes are also used for weeding, which must be done often in the first season and thereafter.

Plows most often make their appearance with grass fallows. The fallow species become the main weed species of the cropping period, and plowing, besides breaking ground, is also an important part of weed control. Draft animals pull most plows. Exceptions, like the *taclla* (foot-plow) of the Andes, are rare.

Permanent cultivation tends to reduce again the demands of land preparation, because weeds are not given free rein at any time. The other function of tillage, preventing soil compaction, becomes important on fine-textured soils. Plowing is common among permanent cultivators, but if they must till by hand, it is easier to dig a previous garden than to break sod.

Hoes and plows are not absolute necessities at any stage. Throughout much of the Pacific, soil preparation is done with digging sticks, regardless of fallow vegetation or frequency of cultivation. In the populous highlands of Papua New Guinea and West Irian, grass fallow systems supply most of the food, and digging sticks were the only tool used to break ground (Steensberg, 1980) until steel spades lately came into general use. Digging sticks are also used to build large mounds for the principal crop, the sweet potato.

Boserup (1965) exposes a frequent overemphasis on technical innovation. Long fallow cultivators are not primitives in waiting for more-intensive methods, a colonial-era characterization that reveals a lack of appreciation for the less concrete side of technology. Forest and bush fallow systems require a great deal of know-how in order to time operations, exploit the diverse microenvironments of the swidden, schedule plantings to assure a steady food supply, and more. Given what they already know, it seems unlikely that fallow cultivators of any sort would fail for long to invent or borrow the tools of tillage. The tools of hand cultivation are conceptually simple and nearly global in their distribution. The plow is nearly as ubiquitous wherever animals suitable for draft are available, and their husbandry can be readily integrated with cultivation.

IRRIGATION, DRAINAGE, AND CROPPING SYSTEMS. In keeping with the principle that intensification stimulates more intensification, irrigated or drained fields are generally cropped at least once a year. Nutrients gained or made more available through irrigation or drainage often help make this possible. Irrigation water may contain little more nutrients than rainfall holds, or it may supply an appreciable part of crop requirements. Drainage and aeration accelerate the mineralization of humus, which tends to be at high equilibrium levels in wetland soils. Exceptions to the rule are common enough but only partial; irrigated or drained fields are sometimes fallowed, but the cropping:fallow ratio is nearly always high.

Pest and Disease Control

Preindustrial cultivators control pests and diseases primarily by managing agricultural ecosystems, for example, by plowing, intercropping, and rotating crops. Diagnosis with the naked eye is more or less effective, depending on the pest or disease. Hand control is used, as well as some naturally occurring insecticides.

Diversifying crops reduces transmission and cuts losses in the event of a serious blight, yet heavy dependence on a single crop is common. Causes for that dependence vary. Sometimes population pressure and the special suitability of one staple to an environment combine to make one crop dominant. This has happened in the highlands of West Irian and Papua New Guinea, and indeed without pests and diseases exacting much penalty; failures of sweet potato are reported but result from frost. Crop diversity tends to be greatest in forest fallow systems and least under annual cropping, but exceptions to both generalizations are numerous. The continuation of long fallow cultivation is not certain protection against disastrous crop failures; the current blight (*Phytophthora colocasiae*) sweeping Pacific taro fields moves readily among widely separated swiddens and causes total losses.

Pest and disease problems mounted during the last century or so, sometimes posing difficulties for preindustrial cultivators whose ancestors had managed quite well. Pests and diseases moved from their endemic regions with unprecedented speed once the steamship was in general use.

Crops and Livestock

The large numbers of cultivars and domesticated animals make some sort of classification handy. Vavilov (1949–50) lists 738 cultivars, mostly food plants, but omits a few fruits and nuts, many of the forage and fodder cultivars, and some occasionally cultivated succulent vegetables. I count 25 domesticated animals used for food, fiber, or traction.[1]

CROPS.   A classification based on crop ecology resembles one based on the crops' roles in human or animal nutrition. The following classification uses both criteria and is in line with much of the literature.

Energy staples are productive crops that accumulate a lot of starch or sugar in the edible portion. Starchy staples are more prevalent than sugar crops.

In these and all other crops, nearly all nitrogen is in the form of protein or related compounds, and the amount of nitrogen removed is proportional to the yield and protein content of the harvested portion. High yields of cereals, which contain about 6% to 18% protein on a dry-weight basis, require high levels of available nitrogen during crop growth and development. At maturity the grains contain most of the protein, whereas the straw has a low protein content. Nonlegume forage and fodder crops, mostly grasses like the cereals, contain much nitrogen in the harvested portion and supply the bulk nutrients to livestock that cereals so often supply to humans. Comparable harvests of low-protein staples, such as manioc (*Manihot esculenta*), banana, and sago, remove less nitrogen. Acceptable yields are often obtained on soils low in available nitrogen, but high yields still require a high uptake, because so much nitrogen is locked up in the foliage. After harvest, however, most of the nitrogen remains in crop residues and may be returned to the soil.

Sugar crops, that is, sugarcane, sweet sorghum, and sugar beets, are a special case. These crops remove much nitrogen from the soil, because so much of the plant is taken away for processing, but most of the nitrogen remains in the residues after the sweet juices are pressed out. The residue may be returned, but other uses compete: fuel and, in the case of cane and sorghum tops, fodder. Preindustrial cultivators often do not process sugar crops, but chew cane and sorghum stalks.

Legumes complement the energy staples ecologically, because of their association with nitrogen-fixing bacteria, and nutritionally. All parts of legume crops tend to be high in protein. Even the straw that remains behind after harvest is a useful stock feed, though inadequate alone. The nitrogen contribution to the soil from fodder and forage legumes is generally much greater than that from pulses, making more available to an interplanted or following crop, in spite of the high crop removal in fodder crops. Among common pulses, the soybean most closely approaches the forage and fodder legumes in nitrogen contribution.

Oilseeds also yield less than the cereals but, like the cereals, draw all their nitrogen from the soil. Most oilseeds contain a high proportion of protein, though of low quality, but are valued for their oil. Much of the remainder of the edible kernel is fed to livestock as press cake, even in preindustrial systems. Two major edible oil crops, soybeans and peanuts, are legumes and not included in this class. A few oilseed crops, such as sunflower and rape, yield useful forage or fodder if harvested before the seeds mature.

Tree fruits and nuts can be nutritionally valuable, and some give yields that under preindustrial management compare well with annual energy staples or oilseeds. It is therefore remarkable that their contribution to world food supply is rather small. Advocates of permaculture (Mollison, 1979), which emphasizes tree crops and other perennials, point out that good yields can be maintained with low inputs of labor or mechanical or animal energy. Root systems generally go deeper for nutrients than those of annuals, and nutrients recycle more effectively. The Mediterranean basin provides the best example of a major region in which perennials—in this case, vines, olive trees, and stone fruits—contribute significantly to the total energy supply. Banana, mango, and coconut are even more prominent on some Pacific islands, but in most agricultural communities, perennials have a small role and are frequently not grown at all.

Explanations for why something is not done are inherently speculative, but the delay from planting to harvest is a likely reason these crops are not exploited more. A few tropicals, such as papaya (*Carica papaya*) and banana, yield in about a year, but most tree crops take several years before bearing fruit and often several more before full production. Deferred returns on effort and land are not the only disadvantage of the delay. Feuding, vandalism, warfare, lack of assured tenure, and sharecropping arrangements that are subject to unilateral revision by the landowner combine to undermine cultivators' confidence in the security of their invested labor.

The final class includes annual fruits, such as melons and tomatoes, and green vegetables. In spite of their nutritional value, these are rarely field crops, except where grown to supply an urban populace.

The production of major crops (excluding forage crops) is shown in Table 3.1. Yields are expressed in dry weight of the edible portion.

Table 3.1. World production of major crops, 1978, in thousands of metric tons

Crop	Yield	Crop	Yield
Wheat	425,478	All pulses	51,873
Maize	394,231	Manioc	117,201 (44,500)[a]
Paddy rice	379,814	Oats	42,909
Barley	172,175	Sweet potato	113,954 (38,700)[a]
Potato	284,470 (71,100)[a]	Millet	32,962
Sorghum	67,268	Rye	23,705

Source: FAO (1980).
[a]Dry weight in parentheses.

LIVESTOCK. Land animals raised for food are usefully divided into two classes: (1) the grazers and browsers, which can feed entirely upon bulk foliar growth, so long as it contains a sufficient proportion of protein and digestible carbohydrates; and (2) those that require more-concentrated feed, much of which can sustain humans, such as cereal grains, tubers, oilseeds, or press cakes. Livestock in the first class include cattle and other bovines, sheep, goats, camels and the

South American cameloids, reindeer, and horses. In preindustrial systems they rarely receive much cereal or other feed suitable for humans, except for culls, something defined partly by taste and aesthetics. Small animals that graze effectively, such as geese, rabbits, and guinea pigs, are more likely to receive grain. Animals in the second class often consume food that, though digestible by humans, is disdained. Pigs and most poultry take worms, grubs, and insects in quantity, and pigs also perform a useful sanitary function by eating the feces of humans and livestock. Pigs can feed themselves quite well if a forest is at hand with nut trees and a good worm or grub population.

Livestock vary in their conversion efficiency, the rate at which what they eat ends up available for human consumption. The milk from good dairy cattle under optimum management retains about 33% of the digestible energy content of a fairly concentrated diet, and a substantially lower percentage is retained from rough feeds with a high proportion of fiber. Eggs retain at best about 16% of the original energy fed to the whole population of chickens, and beef generally less than 10% of what the breeding and producing herd is fed (figures from Brody, 1979:51–52, 56). The maximum efficiency of swine production is usually estimated at about 25%. That calculated for the individual animal, not taking into account what the breeding stock is fed, declines from 80% in young pigs to 27% in those grown to 60 to 100 kgs (Cullison and Lowrey, 1987:550). The efficiency with which fed protein is retained in the usable portion is generally higher than that for energy unless protein is fed to excess and metabolized.

Conversion efficiency varies with body size, the rate of growth and maturation, and the rate of reproduction. Large body size improves efficiency, because less heat is lost in proportion to body mass, and metabolic requirements are thereby less. Fast-growing animals put more of their food into growth and less into metabolism. High reproductive rates improve efficiency by reducing the number of breeding stock that must be fed.

Grazing and browsing livestock, when raised for meat, have low conversion efficiencies relative to those of pigs and poultry. Cattle, camels, reindeer, sheep, and goats are large animals but grow comparatively slowly and bear but one or two young at a time. Thus the livestock that compete least with us for crops and cultivable land are also the least efficient converters. Dairy production, in order to achieve its highest efficiency, requires either very good pasture or the inclusion of some grain in the diet.

Management affects conversion efficiency. Preindustrial farmers and herders ordinarily obtain much lower efficiencies than those obtained under industrial agricultural management, in part because they select animals for hardiness or other qualities besides yield, and the animals often fend for themselves or are fed culls and rough feedstuffs. The best conversion efficiencies are obtained by feeding the best breeds of stock a good-quality diet or giving them access to good pasture. The poorest efficiencies are obtained under hardship conditions. Underfed animals must use a higher proportion of their diet to meet metabolic needs, leaving less for growth or milk and egg production. Other hardships, such as exposure to cold or the need to graze a large area, increase metabolic needs.

THE EFFICIENCY OF CANNIBALISM. Human flesh is presumably as nutritious as any other. After many years during which anthropologists paid attention mostly to ritual and other nongustatory functions of cannibalism, some parted company, arguing that the contribution to food supply is important and even constitutes a sufficient explanation of the practice, particularly where protein or a specific amino acid is deficient in the rest of the diet (Dornstreich and Morren, 1974; Harner, 1977; Harris, 1985; Vayda, 1970; Walens and Wagner, 1971). The argument has its critics (Garn and Block, 1970). It is therefore worth inquiring how humans measure up to other livestock raised for meat.

Humans are such inefficient converters of food into flesh that gustatory cannibalism must be viewed as nutritional imperialism of benefit to the consumers but a draft on the greater ecosystem of both eaters and eaten. The obvious fact that humans are raised on human food, making them a sort of especially demanding pig, underlines their poor performance. We are inefficient converters because of our slow rates of reproduction and growth. Pigs are born in large litters and develop in about six months to a subadult stage roughly equivalent to that of a human in its early teens.

To get a rough idea of the actual conversion efficiencies of humans, assume that a 15-year-old male grows to 60 kg on a daily food intake that averages 25 g of protein and 1,400 kcal. Then, assuming (after Dornstreich and Morren, 1974) a 60% dressed-out proportion, the slaughtered carcass would supply about 6,500 g of protein and 120,000 kcal. The energy retained in the edible portion would be about 2% of lifetime intake, protein about 5%. Even these rates might well be halved if account is taken of breeding adults and of older persons who have for years used all their food for maintenance. Such conversion efficiencies are clearly much poorer than those of common livestock.

Arguments for and against the economic or adaptive value of cannibalism should specify the community that supposedly benefits. If both eaters and eaten are considered, humans are an awful substitute for pigs or fowl. Eating no livestock would be preferable to cannibalism. If the analysis takes into account only the eaters, cannibalism is as adaptive and functional as any other food-getting activity, so long as the costs of the hunt are not excessive. Conversion efficiencies are irrelevant if someone else bears the costs. Other sources of protein need not be proved inadequate, any more than this must be done to demonstrate the rationality of fishing or of normal hunting. The argument that the protein contribution from cannibalism is small and that ritual or social functions must therefore supply its rationale (Garn and Block, 1970) is never raised to plead that hunting ritual or coming-of-age hunts themselves explain hunting. Explanations of cannibalism should not be burdened with a need to exclude other explanations. Cannibalism may or may not be especially prevalent in communities where protein is in short supply, but its presence elsewhere does not negate a nutritional function. Meat is meat.

Eaters and eaten are sometimes from the same community, with the cause of death other than slaughter for the table. Ecological efficiency is then irrelevant. The practice is horribly maladaptive in one celebrated case. The Fore of Papua New Guinea have suffered many deaths from the incurable disease *kuru,* which is transmitted by contact with the tissues of the dead on their way to the table (Gajdusek and Farquhar, 1981; Gajdusek and Gibbs, 1969).

Agricultural Systems and Settlement Patterns

Because cropping frequency and some other measures of agricultural intensity correlate positively with population pressure, a relationship might also be expected with size or permanence of settlement. The inference is in fact controversial and worth some elaboration.

RURAL SETTLEMENT PATTERNS. The most dispersed settlement pattern, an array of individual family homesteads, is found in most parts of the world (Allan, 1972:220–221), as is its counterpart, the nucleated farming village. The dispersed pattern is not associated with any particular cropping frequency, but generalizations can be made about cropping frequency and associated farming villages.

Long fallow cultivation is often called shifting cultivation, after the frequent moves of both cultivation and settlements. Some villages are permanent, not shifting, but the most common practice is to move with each clearing of new fields. Villages are typically small, but some hold several thousand inhabitants (Allan, 1972:220; Carneiro, 1961; Nye and Greenland, 1960:5-6). Cultivators from large villages must make long walks to fields, and Allan (p. 220) notes that "most" Tswane, Serowe, and Kgwaketse spend part of the year away from the villages. Carneiro (1961) associates permanence and size; the logistics of frequently moving a large village are certainly forbidding.

Short fallow and permanent cultivation systems are usually associated with permanent settlements. Even small villages also tend to be fairly permanent. Large settlements exist in a variety of forms that is beyond the scope of this treatment; Smith (1972:416) generalizes that increased population pressure leads to a greater variety of settlement types.

SOCIOPOLITICAL TYPES AND ASSOCIATED AGRICULTURAL SYSTEMS.

Shifting cultivation and settlement are often, but by no means always, associated with what social anthropologists term segmentary lineages. The members of the lineage, which comprises most of the resident community, have known kinship ties to one another, through either patrilineal (father-child) or matrilineal (mother-child) descent from a common ancestor. Lineages must sooner or later segment, because of limits to genealogical knowledge, although personal or group disputes are often the immediate cause. Authority tends to be informal and impermanent.

Societies tend to acquire more complex and formal social and political organization along with larger settlements. More and more of the adults take no part in food production. In a cross-cultural study, Harner (1970) links the evolution of formal, centralized authority and the formation of social classes with population pressure on the food production system, though his measure of pressure on agricultural communities — that is, the percentage of the diet got by hunting and gathering — is indirect.

Short fallow and permanent cultivation systems support all past and present urban civilizations. Labor intensity marked agriculture of the early and classical civilizations of both hemispheres. What was for many years thought the exception, the lowland Classic Maya, has now been found to follow the rule. The long fallow agriculture of contemporary Maya had been thought to be representative of earlier systems, by some writers out of a belief that the region's soils cannot support more frequent cropping. Revision came when research (summarized in Harrisson and Turner, 1978; Wilken, 1971) revealed remnants of island beds, terraces, tree shelter belts, permaculture of breadnut (*Brosimum alicastrum*), and other evidence of high cropping frequencies and appreciable labor investments.

Increases in regional populations leading up to the development of early civilizations and the dynastic Egyptian state are documented in several sources for the Old World (Harris, 1977:155–156) and are evident in the so-called Formative stages of the New World. There must therefore have been a concomitant intensification of agriculture as a whole.

One hoary theory that links intensification and state formation is that intensive agriculture alone permits elites and other nonproducers of food to live on farmers' surpluses. The notion is flawed, because a capacity to produce surpluses is not unique to intensive agriculturalists. The nonagricultural population in the early civilizations was small, generally 10% to 20% of the total, and would not have demanded a great surplus.

A more plausible connection is that intensification and attendant population growth favor occupational specialization, a prerequisite of state formation. Over several generations, farmers witness the closing of the landscape, the interposing of other communities between themselves and distant resources, and, where a high proportion of land can be cultivated, declining availability of resources from uncultivated land. The demand on the farm for labor might also increase, but that appears to be a variable condition; a feature of many early states and civilizations is the coexistence of systems that are both labor-intensive and labor-inefficient with other systems that are neither.

Numerous theories of the origins of the state and civilization already emphasize the significance of pressure upon resources, agricultural or otherwise. Widening differentials of access to resources are a central theme in Fried's (1967) influential treatment and in Marx and Engels. Another theory links state formation to circumscription by geographical or political barriers and resultant pressure on the system of production (Carneiro, 1970). The thesis that the emerging lower Mesopotamian states controlled trade in distant resources—that is, wood for construction, precious stones, metals, "and perhaps even flint and construction stone as well"—is offered by Adams (1981:80). I would add that intensification and the growth of trade should reinforce one another, especially if the trade is at a distance.

Peasant farmers made up most of the population of the early states and civilizations. I suggest that more attention be paid to reconstructing their circumstances and their response as cultivators.

The appearance of cities could be a normal outgrowth of state formation, but some tie with population growth is also plausible. Some minimal population density is obviously conducive, though a few trade cities sprung up in the thinly populated margins of the Sahara. Some geographers go further and support the central place theorem, which associates density with nucleation of settlement.

DISTRIBUTIONS OF AGRICULTURAL SYSTEMS AROUND SETTLEMENTS. Nonagricultural populations, particularly those of cities, generate demand for food and fiber, increasing the pressures for intensification. Thus intensification is sometimes associated with declining population in agricultural settlements as excess population moves to urban centers. The phenomenon is best witnessed where industry makes the mechanization of agriculture possible but is also known in preindustrial contexts. Industrial development may also create demand for agricultural products, even if the industry is of the cottage variety. Raw material for textile manufacture is the outstanding example. Boserup's (1965) model is criticized (Dovring, 1966) or amended (Brookfield, 1972) partly on the grounds that growing commerce is often the primary cause of intensification, but in a preindustrial population with little luxury consumption of agricultural products, population growth, either near at hand or in distant markets, is the cause of commerce.

Cities and nonagricultural towns might be expected to generate the greatest pressure for intensification in their immediate environs, because of their demand for such bulky goods as fresh vegetables and milk and because of heightened competition for land. Von Thünen's *Der isolierte Staat in Beziehung auf Landwirtschaft und Nationalokonomie* (1826), a classic of geography, sets out a model of concentric rings around a city. Intensity decreases from the inner rings to the outer. The model is an ideal, based on assumptions of isolation from other urban centers, settlement in the hinterlands, uniform topography and other environmental factors, cultural homogeneity, a lack of disturbance from the transportation network, and market participation and optimal decision making on the part of the cultivators. Such conditions cannot be met in the real world, but the model has been found to underlie the spatial patterning of agricultural intensity in a number of preindustrial and industrial settings (Dickinson, 1967; Griffin, 1973; Horvath, 1969; Jonasson, 1925–26).

The infield-outfield strategy adapts well to settlements of many sizes. The benefit from wastes drawn from a large catchment area are greater the larger the settlement. The logistics and the sanitary hazard of using wastes in agriculture in or near a city are discussed in Vasey (1980), along with some history (see also Fahm, 1980). Briefly, two designs evolve. In one, the cities remain densely settled, and trash, ashes, food scraps, horse and human excrement, and other wastes are carted to suburban gardens, creating a belt of very productive soils, exploited for dairying in Europe and for vegetables in East Asia. The other solution is to disperse all or a part of urban settlement and incorporate intensively worked small gardens. The lowland Classic Maya cities, above all Tikal (Haviland, 1969; Sanders, 1973), are exemplary.

Note

1. I offer the alpaca, the ass, the Bactrian camel, the dromedary, cattle, chickens and closely related fowl, dogs, donkeys, the common breeds of ducks, the Muscovy duck (*Cairina moschata*, actually from South America), the common breeds of geese, the Egyptian goose (*Chenalopex aegyptiacus*), goats, guinea fowl, guinea pigs, horses, the llama, the pig, pigeons, quail, rabbits, reindeer, sheep, turkeys, yaks, and water buffalo. This list splits the subspecies of *Lama* — llamas (*L. glama glama*) and alpacas (*L. glama pacos*) — but lumps as cattle what some authorities divide into European cattle (*Bos taurus*) and the zebu (*B. indicus*) (Laben, 1974:132), possibly drawing the wrath of taxonomists. It omits a number of animals: some pets that are not commonly used for food, for example, cats, at the risk of ethnocentrism; laboratory animals; mules and other infertile hybrids; and such animals as the capybara, the cassowary, elephants, the guanaco, and the vicuña, which have been kept and sometimes bred in captivity without becoming fully domesticated. Also ignored are eland, the musk ox, and other species that are under serious investigation, including breeding, for food and fiber. The count is thus rough; some might delete quail, and others would add the chukar partridge.

References

Adams, R.M. (1981). *Heartland of Cities: Surveys of Ancient Settlement and Land Use on the Central Floodplains of the Euphrates.* University of Chicago Press, Chicago.

Allan, W. (1972). Ecology, techniques, and settlement patterns. In *Man, Settlement, and Urbanism* (P.J. Ucko, R. Tringham, and G.W. Dimbleby, eds.), Schenkman, Cambridge, Mass., pp. 211–226.

Boserup, E. (1965). *The Conditions of Agricultural Growth.* Aldine, Chicago.

Bourke, R.M. (1976). Food crop farming systems used on the Gazelle Peninsula of New Britain. In *1975 Papua New Guinea Food Crops Conference Proceedings,* Department of Primary Industries, Port Moresby, Papua New Guinea, pp. 82–110.

Brody, S. (1979). *Bioenergetics and Growth.* Hafner, New York.

Bronson, B. (1972). Farm labor and the evolution of food production. In *Popu-*

lation Growth: Anthropological Implications (B. Spooner, ed.), MIT Press, Cambridge, pp. 190–218.

Brookfield, H.C. (1972). Intensification and disintensification in Pacific agriculture: A theoretical approach. *Pacific Viewpoint,* 15:30–48.

Carneiro, R. (1961). Slash-and-burn cultivation among the Kuikuru and its implications for cultural development in the Amazon basin. In *The Evolution of Horticultural Systems in South America, Antropología,* supplement no. 2, Caracas, pp. 47–67.

_____. (1970). A theory of the origin of the state. *Science,* 169:733–738.

Cullison, A.E., and R.S. Lowrey (1987). *Feeds and Feeding.* 4th ed. Prentice-Hall, Englewood Cliffs, N.J.

Dickinson, J.C., III (1967). Variations on the von Thünen theme in a semi-traditional society. *Annals of the Association of American Geographers,* 57:172.

Dornstreich, M.D., and G.E.B. Morren (1974). Does New Guinea cannibalism have nutritional value? *Human Ecology,* 2:1–12.

Dovring, F. (1966). Review of *The Conditions of Agricultural Growth,* by Ester Boserup. *Journal of Economic History,* 26:380–381.

Fahm, L.A. (1980). *The Waste of Nations: The Economic Utilization of Human Waste in Agriculture.* Allanheld-Osmun, Montclair, N.J.

FAO (1980). *The State of Food and Agriculture 1979.* Food and Agricultural Organization, Rome.

Fried, M. (1967). *The Evolution of Political Society.* Random House, New York.

Gajdusek, D.C., and J. Farquhar (1981). *Kuru: Early Letters and Field-Notes from the Collection of D. Carleton Gajdusek.* Raven, New York.

Gajdusek, D.C., and C.J. Gibbs, Jr. (1969). Attempts to demonstrate a transmissible agent in kuru, amyotrophic lateral sclerosis and other subacute and chronic nervous system degeneration of man. *Nature,* 204(4955):257–259.

Garn, S.M., and W.D. Block (1970). The limited nutritional value of cannibalism. *American Anthropologist,* 72:106.

Griffin, E. (1973). Testing the von Thünen theory in Uruguay. *Geographical Review,* 63:500–516.

Harner, M.J. (1970). Population pressure and social evolution. *Southwestern Journal of Anthropology,* 26:67–86.

_____. (1977). The ecological basis for Aztec sacrifice. *American Ethnologist,* 4:117–135.

Harris, M. (1977). *Cannibals and Kings: The Origins of Culture.* Random House, New York.

_____. (1985). *Good to Eat: Riddles of Food and Culture.* Simon and Schuster, New York.

Harrisson, P.D., and B.L. Turner II, eds. (1978). *Pre-Hispanic Maya Agriculture.* University of New Mexico Press, Albuquerque.

Haviland, W.A. (1969). A new population estimate for Tikal, Guatemala. *American Antiquity,* 34:429–433.

Horvath, R.J. (1969). Von Thünen's isolated state and the area around Addis

Ababa, Ethiopia. *Annals of the Association of American Geographers,* 59:308–323.

Iversen, J. (1956). Forest clearance in the Stone Age. *Scientific American,* 194(3):36–41.

Jonasson, O. (1925–26). Agricultural regions of Europe. *Economic Geography,* 1:277–314, 2:19–48.

Laben, R.C. (1974). Dairy cattle and other dairy animals. In *Animal Agriculture: The Biology of Domestic Animals and Their Use by Man* (H.H. Cole and M. Ronning, eds.), W.H. Freeman, San Francisco, pp. 131–146.

Lambert, D.H. (1985). *Swamp Farming: The Indigenous Pahang Malay Agricultural System.* Westview, Boulder, Colo.

Mollison, B. (1979). *Permaculture Two: Practical Design for Town and Country in Permanent Agriculture.* International Tree Crops, Winters, Calif.

Nye, P.H., and D.J. Greenland (1960). *The Soil under Shifting Cultivation.* Commonwealth Bureau of Soils Technology, Harpenden, England.

Sanders, W.T. (1973). The cultural ecology of the lowland Maya: A reevaluation. In *The Classic Maya Collapse* (T.P. Culbert, ed.), University of New Mexico Press, Albuquerque, pp. 325–365.

Sherratt, A. (1980). Water, soil, and seasonality in early cereal cultivation. *World Archaeology,* 11:313–330.

Smith, P.E.L. (1972). Land-use, settlement patterns, and subsistence agriculture: A demographic perspective. In *Man, Settlement, and Urbanism* (P.J. Ucko, R. Tringham, and G.W. Dimbleby, eds.), Schenkman, Cambridge, Mass., pp. 409–425.

Steensberg, A. (1980). *New Guinea Gardens: A Study of Husbandry with Parallels in Prehistoric Europe.* Academic Press, New York.

Thünen, J.H. von (1826). *Das isolierte Staat in Beziehung auf Landwirtschaft und Nationalokonomie.* Perthes, Hamburg.

Vasey, D.E. (1980). City wastes that grow city food: Ecological and social strategies. In *Urbanisation and Its Problems in Papua New Guinea* (R. Jackson, J. Odongo, and P. Batho, eds.), University of Papua New Guinea, Port Moresby, pp. 165–173.

Vavilov, N.I. (1949–50). *The Origin, Variation, Immunity, and Breeding of Cultivated Plants,* trans. K. Starr Chester. Chronica Botanica, vol. 13, Waltham, Mass.

Vayda, A.P. (1970). On the nutritional value of cannibalism. *American Anthropologist,* 72:1462–1463.

Walens, S., and R. Wagner (1971). Pigs, protein, and people-eaters. *American Anthropologist,* 73:269–270.

Wilken, G. (1971). Food-producing systems available to the ancient Maya. *American Antiquity,* 36:432–448.

Wood, H.A. (1963). *Northern Haiti: Land, Land Use, and Settlement: A Geographical Investigation of the Departement du Nord.* University of Toronto Press, Toronto.

4

Pastoralism

 Pastoralism, the reliance on domesticated animals for most of one's livelihood, has its own chapter because of its distinctiveness from agriculture proper in environmental impact, the demands of management, and commonly associated sociopolitical forms. Although their contribution to world food supply has always been much smaller than that of agriculturalists, the place in history of such pastoralists as the Mongols, the Scythians, and the Ngoni (Zulu) alone warrants special treatment.

Preindustrial pastoralism in the ethnographic present is concentrated in the wet-dry tropics, dry lands, dry summer lands, and some cold highland and high-latitude regions. Historic or known prehistoric distributions are little different, except for past extensions into humid temperate climates, northwestern Europe in particular. Describing pastoralists in one chapter, instead of in scattered parts of chapters 5 through 7, facilitates comparison. Similarities are striking, but the effects of widely varying environments should not be overlooked. For example, although reindeer herders of the Arctic face many of the same challenges as East African cattle pastoralists and have developed similar solutions, the former add to their food supply by hunting and fishing, the latter by cultivating crops.

Pastures and Pastoralism

DISTRIBUTION OF GRASSLANDS AND PASTORALISM. Most pastoralism is on grassland or open woodland with grass ground cover. A few exceptions are worth noting. Mixed forest and steppe is important in parts of Siberia in season, usually the winter. Goats, which are occasionally the main live-stock, particularly around the Mediterranean, can browse dense scrub and wooded steppes, where they easily reach most of the foliage and young branches. Pigs and poultry, animals that get little of their food from graze or browse, are usually absent and always few in number.

Grasses dominate climax vegetation mostly where low growing-season temperatures or low moisture limits tree growth. A few grasslands develop on land with a high water table but are not much exploited by pastoralists, except in the minor instance of water-buffalo herding in the Tigris-Euphrates marshes. Of the more usual livestock, cattle best tolerate wet conditions but are not normally kept successfully on wetlands for extended periods.

Pastoralists call drought-induced grasslands and thinly grassed deserts home over vast tracts of East Africa, the Sahel and Sudan belts below the Sahara, the Mediterranean, Southwest Asia, Central Asia, Tibet, southern Siberia, and Mongolia. Those who figure the most prominently in written history and in contemporary geographic and ethnographic accounts inhabit these regions.

Others exploit cold-induced grasslands across a broad belt south of the Arctic Ocean and north of the boreal forests of North America and Eurasia. They also dominate Iceland, historically the margins of Greenland, and a number of smaller islands of northern waters.

Pastoralism is historically an Old World phenomenon. It was absent from the precolonial Americas, except that some peoples of the Andes may have made their living from llamas and other cameloids, used as much to carry loads as for anything else. The Vikings carried the Scandinavian version of cattle and sheep pastoralism across the Atlantic to the Faeroes, Iceland, Greenland, and briefly to Newfoundland (Ingstad, 1969), during a forerunning phase of European expansion. In the form of ranching, pastoralism has spread with European settlement to arid and semiarid regions of Australia and North and South America.

People and livestock have contributed to the scarcity of trees on many of today's pasturelands. Treeless grasslands are most often a climax form in the form of Arctic, subarctic and mountain tundra and meadow. Dwarf trees are common in slightly more favorable areas but do not readily withstand the depredations of livestock. Most drought-induced grasslands once carried more trees, often deeply rooted species that reach pockets of soil moisture. Fires, which human activity inevitably increases, suppress the more slowly recovering woody vegetation and thus favor grasses and associated legumes and broadleaves. Frequent cultivation has the same effect. Where stocking densities are high, grazing and browsing livestock damage bark, compact soils, and destroy tree seedlings. Goats may girdle (ringbark) trees. Conditions that are marginal to tree growth exacerbate these factors by delaying recovery.

Woody growth may return on overgrazed pastures, but too often its forms are detrimental to pastoralism. A common outcome is a stand dominated by a narrow range of scrub species that are unappealing or inedible to most livestock, often thorny scrub in dry lands.

THE CYCLE OF SEASONS. A significant feature of grasslands is the alternation of rich and lean seasons. The difference in the area of land required to support a given animal is typically many-fold. The lean season in drought-induced grasslands extends roughly from the time during the dry season that soil moisture approaches the wilting point until shortly after regular rains begin, when new growth appears. In temperate climates, winters are lean, spring and summer rich. Growth slows where summers are hot and dry but briefly peaks again in autumn, where rainfall permits. Desert rains are sporadic; though monthly mean precipitation totals taken from many years of observation commonly show a definite seasonal peak, the onset of the rains is typically unreliable, and their amount highly variable. Flushes of rapid growth follow desert rains and furnish rich pasture. In high latitudes, summer is the season of bounteous pasture, and winter is the lean season. Low growing-season temperatures limit evaporation, and growth goes on all summer.

The poverty of lean-season pasture and browse arises from plant maturation and the slowing or cessation of growth. Grasses and legumes include annual and perennial species. Annuals at first produce lush, nutritious growth, but as they produce seed near the end of their growth period, their straw loses protein and carbohydrates to seed production. The nutritive value of grasses is then very low, of legumes a bit better. Livestock eat little of the seed, because seed heads and pods of wild species tend to shatter quickly on maturation, and many native pulses contain toxic and bitter compounds. Perennials do not as a rule produce quite as nutritious new growth as annuals, but their quality holds up better. Their root systems are typically deeper and take up effective moisture longer than those of most annuals. Species vary, but in general, low or nil seed production in perennials allows mature foliage to retain more feed value than it does in annuals.

Some preindustrial agriculturalists convert forests of humid and subhumid lands into grasslands, usually creating meadows interspersed with croplands and remaining forests. Fire and an ax may be the only tools. The pasture suffices for their livestock. It is not ordinarily extensive enough to support communities of specialized pastoralists, but there are at least two significant historic exceptions. In northern Europe, shepherds' holdings have often followed wood cutting or replaced cultivation on hill farms. In nineteenth-century New Zealand, graziers built a large sheep and dairy industry after a series of great forest fires. Pastures carved from forests typically hold their quality better through the lean season than do those in the more usual pastoral lands. A drawback is that scrub readily invades, and industrial technology, in the form of mechanical suppression and herbicides, is today applied to prevent this from happening.

Within the main pastoral regions, crop plants and edible wild plants experience the same seasons as pasture species do, but the rich and lean seasons are later for human consumers than for grazing species. Humans cannot utilize much of the new growth, but they can effectively harvest and eat the seeds, tubers, and other plant portions produced by maturing plants.

Because of these differing peaks, dairying is a better complement to cultivation or gathering than meat production is, perhaps partly accounting for its greater importance among pastoralists. Dairy production peaks during the period of new growth, when milch animals are well fed. If herds were culled for meat at this time, poor use of the best pasture would result, along with excessive slaughter of young animals. Some African pastoralists consume in small quantities the blood of their cattle, like milk a sustained-yield product and one that might be in best supply when pasture quality peaks, though available data on seasonal production of blood are not adequate to test this assumption.

Livestock store food from good years to bad, and in hard times meat often becomes the main food for humans. Pastoralists increase their stock in good years but are forced to slaughter to feed the community when drought or other hardship conditions are severe. In these circumstances milk production will usually fall off, because the cows are underfed.

Pastoralism and Agriculture

If we were to call only those people who live off their animals and cultivate no crops pastoralists, they would be few, and in many more instances it is hard to establish clear criteria to distinguish pastoralism from agriculture. Nomadic pastoralists are the easiest to identify, possibly one reason anthropologists tend to ignore sedentary forms. Although a few nomads obtain more food by cultivating than they get from their herds, to class nomads as pastoralists is usually acceptable, as long as the animals' need for pasture determines the movements of the group. Some settled peoples rely almost entirely on domesticated animals, and we should call them sedentary pastoralists, whereas others mix cultivation and animal husbandry in diverse ways. I suggest a continuum between sedentary pastoralism and mixed farming.

The usefulness of pastoralists' territories for crop production varies but is most often limited. Agriculture is not practicable on the tundra on any significant scale. The driest grazing territories permit cropping only around the few water sources, which in most places are already well developed within the limitations of preindustrial technology. Rugged terrain usually offers only small areas of cultivable land, which may or may not be cultivated. Nevertheless, some nomads graze their livestock over extensive areas of land that could be in crops, particularly in parts of East Africa. Irrigation works could greatly extend cultivation in most semiarid regions.

Most pastoralists, and nearly all in Africa and Southwest Asia, rely to an appreciable degree on crops obtained through their own efforts or by exchange with agriculturalists, leading some observers (Johnson, 1969:11; Kottak, 1987:122; Lees and Bates, 1974) to conclude that pastoralism is not viable by itself. Spooner (1973) reaches a similar conclusion, noting the importance of hunting, gathering, and fishing to northern reindeer herders. This line of reasoning is misleading. One could equally argue that a partial reliance on animals by mixed farmers shows that vegetarians could not survive, or that agriculture alone is not viable where it is presently supplemented by hunting, gathering, and fishing. That many pastoralists lack sufficient animals to provide their whole subsistence does not necessarily mean their territories cannot support a purely pastoral strategy, though possibly the pastoralists would have to be fewer where their stocking rates are already at or near their sustainable limit.

Several accounts describe pastoralists who subsist from little else but their herds. These include the Altai and many Mongols of Outer Mongolia (Krader, 1959) and in southern Siberia the Buryats and Kalmyks and some other of the more nomadic Mongols (Vainshtein, 1980). Though some Central Asian Kazakhs cultivate (Krader, 1959), within the center of their territory only a few families do so or regularly eat agricultural foodstuffs (Bacon, 1954).

The inland Same (Lapps) turned from slight dependence on reindeer pastoralism to primary dependence after colonial expansion and pressure on land brought about depletion of game and intense competition for fishing rights (Gjessing, 1954:14–22; Ingold, 1976:2; Paine, 1957,

1972). An early observer, seeing the sparse pasture and modest milk production of reindeer, might well have wrongly predicted that pastoralism would not be viable. The Nentsy of northwest Siberia gained about 85% of their diet from domestic reindeer in the early historic period (Prokof'yeva, 1956:556), also following some decline in the relative importance of hunting.

Among sedentary pastoralists, many remote Icelandic farms were once nearly self-sufficient, particularly at times when foreign merchants imposed unfavorable trade terms. Fish, birds, and birds' eggs were important, but many farms lacked rights to these resources.

Sub-Saharan African pastoralists derive a particularly large part of their food supply from cultivation. The risks or costs of pastoralism may discourage greater reliance on the animals, probably the costs more than the risks. Though northern pastoralists incur the costs of winter, in the form of difficult measures, variously haymaking, cutting branches for fodder, moving stock over wind-blown slopes in stormy weather, and spading or plowing snow from pastures (Vainshtein, 1980:63), their rewards seem to be comparatively good. East African animals furnish very low yields of milk. Table 4.1 gives comparative data for milch animals in various regions.

Two explanations are likely for the prevalence of low milk yields in East Africa. One is that high milk production was never bred into cattle races, possibly because of a limited gene pool and the need to maintain disease resistance. The other is the poor nutritional quality of the dominant grasses. Under improved feeding schedules on government farms in Uganda, yields from local races increased, but only to between 430 and 530 l/yr ("200–250 gallons per lactation"; Mahadevan and Parsons, 1970:336).

The risks in Africa are not demonstrably worse than elsewhere. Tropical African herds once suffered terrible losses from rinderpest and sleeping sickness, sufficient in many areas to wipe out pastoralism, but these diseases do not cause recurrent losses of great magnitude in the ethnographic present. Otherwise, occasional losses are probably no worse than in northern pastoral zones. The Dodoth of northern Uganda lose up to 10% to 15% of their cattle in a drought year (Deshler, 1965:160), but losses in Siberia and Central Asia over a severe winter can be as high as 25% (Krader, 1955:320; Vainshtein, 1980:80).

Even in Africa, purer forms may be found. The Samburu of Kenya herd their animals and practice no cultivation. They make relishes of wild vegetables and "supplement their diet with small supplies of grain bought from the handful of shop owners in the district" (Spencer, 1965:3). Pastoralism in the extreme south was once unsupported by

Table 4.1. Milk yields of pastoralists' livestock, in liters

Pastoralists (Source)	Cows	Ewes	Goats	Mares	Reindeer	Camels
Tuva (Vainshtein, 1980)	500	≤65	≤115	300	25–65	
Chukchi (Bogoras, 1904–9)	560				"Small"	
Dodoth, northeastern Uganda (Netting, 1977; Deshler, 1965)	140–180					
Nuer, Sudan (Evans-Pritchard, 1940)	350–460[a]					
Karimojong, northern Uganda (Dyson-Hudson and Dyson-Hudson, 1970)	250					
Northern Kenya (Spencer, 1973)	150–200					700
Northern Arabian Bedouin (Sweet, 1965)						200–1,300
Northern Arabian Bedouin (Dahl and Hjort, 1976)						700
Somalia (Dahl and Hjort, 1976)						1,100
Eritrea (Mason and Maule, 1960)						900–1,100
Afar (Dahl and Hjort, 1976)						80–160

Note: Yields are the amount available for human consumption per annum from females of milking age, with nonproducing periods included.
[a] No seasonal variation is given. The value is probably projected from wet-season yields only.

cultivation (Smith, 1983). The cereals grown farther north face unfavorable conditions, particularly in the winter rainfall zone of the southwest.

The Antiquity of Pastoralism

Past scholarly opinion largely held that pastoralism evolved from hunting. This was the view of Morgan ([1877] 1963), and Engels ([1884] 1942), who thought pastoralism more primitive than agriculture and therefore probably earlier.

Most interested scholars (Adams, 1974; Bobeck, 1962; Lees and Bates, 1974; Sauer, 1962; Smith and Young, 1972; Vainshtein, 1980) now argue that pastoralism as we know it grew out of agriculture and first developed on the margins of agricultural regions, but the issue is far from settled. The gist of their argument is that Old World agriculture as a whole preceded anything resembling contemporary pastoralism. Pastoralism apparently antedated agriculture in some other regions, albeit at comparatively late dates in most, leaving an unresolved choice as to whether these particular pastoral adaptations were local developments or products of migration or diffusion from the regions of early agriculture.

Early pastoralists might have left few traces recognizable from ethnographic descriptions of pastoralism. Higgs and Jarman apply their thesis of early and prolonged domestication to both plants and animals (chapter 2), and animals would necessarily have been the main domesticates in high latitudes during the last glacial.

Southwest Asia is of special interest because cattle, sheep, and goats, as well as many food plants, were domesticated there, and mixed farming was a common early form of agriculture. At some early sites, animal bones have been found with no plant remains, but this evidence of pastoralism is unreliable because bones are better preserved than plants. Thus far no remains of domesticated animals have been found in the early phases anywhere that cultivation would not have been practicable, say, in high mountain pastures and nonirrigable desert.

Lees and Bates (1974) infer that nomadic pastoralism developed late in Southwest Asia, a result of the spread of canal irrigation. They reason that irrigation agriculture pushed permanent settlement into drier areas, reducing the mobility of cultivators and their opportunities to keep large numbers of livestock. Another argument, that nomadic pastoralism depends upon grain subsidies from outside sources, is based on too rigid an application of ethnographic models from the same region. Pastoralists, if early on the scene and not forced into a corner by the expansion of irrigation, might have been under less population pressure than later ones and better able to subsist from their herds.

Nomadic pastoralism began later than cultivation in the central Zagros Mountains of Iran, concludes Gilbert (1983), with reservations concerning the quality of evidence, and he suggests other plausible pastoral strategies that could have been earlier, including herder-gatherers, and pastoralism on grasslands surrounding the highly localized sites of early agriculture. Some evidence points toward graziers' exploitation of multiple altitudinal zones.

In Africa, domesticated animals spread from north to south, appearing in some places before domesticated plants and in others at about the same time. Clark (1976:71–74) associates early herding near the Mediterranean with food collecting. Herding in the Maghreb may date from the sixth millennium B.C. (Bender, 1975) and is not known to have been associated with definitely domesticated plants. Earliest remains of domesticates in the Sahara reveal only animal remains, mainly those of cattle (Clark, 1976:75–76; Mori, 1965; Munson, 1976). In the Nile valley, established sedentary food-collecting populations apparently adopted intact the Southwest Asian complex of domesticated plants and animals. The record farther south is as yet unclear. Linguistic evidence suggests that the major pastoral populations of East Africa intruded at a late date into older agricultural populations (Schneider, 1979:30–36), but Robertshaw and Collett (1983) conclude from the archaeological record that a pastoral strategy incorporating some cultivation was established in the Rift Valley before A.D. 200–300, about the time agriculturalists arrived from the north. Near the southern Cape, pastoralism developed in the absence of cultivation in the early Christian era. An intriguing feature was the presence of sheep, which are almost entirely missing from tropical Africa (Smith, 1983).

Mori (1965) suggests that African cattle were domesticated from the wild *Bos* of northern Africa independently of domestication in Southwest Asia. If that is correct, and cultivation was unknown to the early herders of the Sahara and the Mediterranean littoral, pastoralism in at least these places evolved from cattle hunting.

Camel pastoralism is a late development in the regions where it was later prominent, first appearing in deserts along interurban routes, suggesting a commercial function from the start. Sherratt (1983) suggests, on admittedly partial evidence, that camels were carrying cargo on major trade routes in the fourth millennium B.C., by which time oasis agriculture was firmly established.

Fleming (1972) argues that northwest European pastoralism, entailing movement in the manner of some later Celtic and Germanic communities, dates back to only the first millennium B.C. At that time, cultivation and other activities of the agricultural population had already created extensive grasslands.

Reindeer pastoralism arose far north of agriculture or cattle and sheep pastoralism, thus either by distant stimulus or independently out of reindeer hunting. In the east the Reindeer Chukchi and Koryak are about 5,000 km from the steppes of Manchuria and Mongolia-Buryatia, the Samoyed slightly less from the Central Asian steppes. Collectors of the boreal forest occupy the intervening territory. Their use of reindeer is slight or absent, except for the Yakut, who are substantial reindeer, horse, and cattle pastoralists (Iokhel'son, 1933; Tokarev and Gurvich, 1956). Distances in the west from the Same cattle and sheep pastoralists to the Scandinavian are less, although mountains intervene.

The late date at which the Same and Nentsy became primarily reliant upon reindeer pastoralism (above) might be representative. In the early historic record many were still basically hunters and fishers who kept a few reindeer, principally for pulling loads. Even among the Chukchi—who are, with the Same, often taken to be the best examples of reindeer pastoralists—some groups mainly rely upon coastal fishing and sea-mammal hunting; how long the inland people have depended on reindeer is not known.

Domesticated reindeer were early in southern Siberia, perhaps as early as 1000 B.C. (Vainshtein, 1980:120), though the evidence—bridles and rock drawings of people riding reindeer—points only to their use for draft. A plausible hypothesis is that reindeer were first domesticated on the margins of cattle and sheep pastoralism and that herding and breeding spread north from there. The fact would remain that northern peoples adapted reindeer herding and breeding to a hunting and fishing strategy and reinvented the classic pastoral strategy when the need subsequently arose.

In short, the chronological and evolutionary relationships among pastoralism, agriculture, and collecting are anything but clear. Pastoralists' animals appeared earliest near crop domestication, except for the camel and the horse, which were later, and the reindeer, which was domesticated some distance from effective agriculture. The most familiar pastoralists of the historical and ethnographic literature are either intertwined with agriculturalists within their own regions or, like the Mongols of the Gobi, have a long history of interaction with settled but distant cultivators. An uncertain number of pastoral strategies evolved from hunting, and we do not know the role of distant agriculturalists in furnishing domesticated animals or requisite knowledge.

Classes of Pastoralism

Confusion surrounds the classification of pastoral strategies, largely because distinguishing criteria are used inconsistently. The two most often applied criteria are the pattern of herd movements and the permanence or lack of permanence of human settlement, obviously connected phenomena, but by no means synonymous. Another criterion, the degree of participation in agriculture, is strongly associated with permanence of settlement, though Johnson (1969:17) notes exceptions.

VERTICAL AND HORIZONTAL HERD MOVE- MENTS. The majority of pastoralists outside the tropics exploit territories whose climates and seasons of best pasture vary with elevation. The most common strategy is to go up for the summer and down for the winter. With few exceptions, mountains receive more rain than the land below, and their cooler temperatures slow evaporation, so that summer pastures remain green and growing when the grass at lower elevations has slowed its growth or withered. In winter some mountains are deep in snow, while the nearby plains are green under mild, wet conditions. In tropical East Africa, there is no winter, but pastoralists often find the best dry-season pasture in the mountains.

A few pastoralists of the Eurasian steppes reverse the pattern. In winter the eastern Kazakhs, Darkhats, Altai-Kizhi, and most Kirghiz and Tuvinians move their herds onto open mountain slopes where wind blows away the snow (Vainshtein, 1980:83ff.). Some pastoralists of Iranian Baluchistan descend in late summer or early autumn to harvest dates; high and low pastures alike are dry at this time (Salzman, 1972).

Herds also move among pastures whose elevation varies little. Johnson (1969) begins his classification with the division of vertical and horizontal nomadism. Vainshtein (1980:91–92) makes a similarly broad distinction between vertical and meridional migration.

Most detailed descriptions of nomads' horizontal paths show meaningful patterns rather than aimless wanderings. One type of movement, to the vicinity of water holes or wells at the driest time of year and away into the desert with the arrival of seasonal rains, is a common feature in arid lands, particularly among camel pastoralists, who make use of that animal's speed to move away from overgrazed pastures near permanent water. The Kababish of the Sudan move their camels to the south to meet the rains of the northward-moving intertropical convergence. Their other livestock, sheep and goats, remain near wells until the rains approach (Johnson, 1969:82–89). In Central Asia, large aggregates of livestock and people move among winter pastures, then disperse in summer onto fresh pastures. Conservation is one motive. Some pastures are allowed to grow long by winter, whereas others are grazed at the peak of their nutritional value (Krader, 1959). Reindeer pastoralists move their herds frequently, to avoid insect pests, to exploit wild food resources, and to preserve the highly fragile and slowly growing pastures (Leeds, 1965:99–100). A common movement is onto the treeless tundra near the Arctic Ocean in summer and back to the partly treed forest-tundra for the winter. An exception to the rule of patterned, purposeful migration: Salzman (1972) insists that ad hoc decisions are the rule in Iranian Baluchistan.

PERMANENCE OF SETTLEMENT. Several common classifications divide pastoralism into sedentary, seminomadic, and nomadic forms. I concur but wish to find a way through variable meanings of *seminomadic* and a plethora of subtypes peculiar to specific regions.

Sedentism is obvious enough — a permanent settlement is occupied year-round — but there are borderline cases. A few Tibetan pastoralists move only once every three years. They share most of the culture of the nomads but live in "half-cave, half-sod" houses instead of the nomads' tents (Ekvall, 1968:33). Some other communities stay in place, while only the herders move with the animals. They are sedentary inasmuch as the community has a fixed focus of social and economic activity. For European strategies of this sort, French geographers coined *transhumance,* also applied by Braudel (1966:86, 101) to shepherds whose moves from their home village are short and seasonal. The term has in English unfortunately come to be applied to all sorts of movements, with or without permanent settlements.

Many northern European herders go to mountain pastures in summer, but the distances are usually short and contacts with the household below frequent. By Icelandic tradition (field notes, 1969, 1970), one member of each household, often the oldest unmarried daughter, herds the sheep on mountain pastures for the summer. Mountain huts are common but seldom equipped for full housekeeping.

Shepherds of southern Europe sometimes move their flocks hundreds of kilometers, losing contact with their home villages for months, but nevertheless are no more nomadic than fishermen who go to sea for much of the year. Social and economic ties center on the village. Away from home the shepherds are outsiders, and relations with local people are traditionally uneasy, even hostile.

In some places, sedentary pastoralists and settled agriculturalists share a common community and culture, but in others they are more separate. In northern Europe the resemblances stand out; homesteads are similar, and social networks intertwine. Social separation is traditionally far greater in Mediterranean Europe, despite economic interdependence. Colonial European settlement of favorable regions in the Americas gave rise to a distinctive pastoral pattern that Strickton (1965) calls the Euro-American ranching complex, and much the same can probably be said of Australia.

At least two different seminomadic strategies are in the literature. In one, part of the community remains behind in a permanent settlement, while the herders migrate. In the other, the entire community spends part of the year in a permanent settlement and part in encampments or temporary shelters following the herds.

The first strategy is simply transhumance in a non-European context. Many descriptions highlight mobile male herders more than in European accounts, but the difference may be in the eye of the ethnographer. Social life goes on in the settlements, whether or not it is recorded. The Karimojong of northern Uganda are one of several East African peoples counted as virtual nomads, and by most accounts the whole herd and all able-bodied men and older boys make a decisive move away from the permanent settlements and live in temporary shelters during the rainy season, something unusual in European transhumance. But Dyson-Hudson (1972) objects that the rule is often breached — for example, by keeping part of a herd and some adult male herders at the settlement year-round. One herd stayed for fifteen consecutive months. Judging from this account, "transhumance" is an apt label for Karimojong pastoralism.

The second strategy is more legitimately set apart as seminomadic. In its most common expression the community has one permanent settlement but moves en masse among encampments for part the year. In the main variants, everyone moves, but they build huts rather than carry tents. These include Siberian peoples (Tokarev and Gurvich, 1956; Vainshtein, 1980:97–98) who maintain permanent settlements in both summer and winter pasturelands and some in Bosnia-Herzegovina, Yugoslavia, who maintain permanent settlements on summer, winter, and spring-autumn pastures (Matley, 1968). One settlement is by far the best furnished in both Yakutia, Siberia (Tokarev and Gurvich, 1956), and Bosnia-Herzegovina.

Nomads by definition do not maintain permanent settlements. As for borderline cases, many nomads often camp repeatedly in the same spots, not permanent settlements but places that may acquire special significance as political or religious centers.

Portable dwellings are the mark of the nomad. In North Africa and Southwest Asia, people who live in tents all year are separate in both popular thinking and the scholarly literature. Wheeled dwellings and yurts are equally important on the Eurasian steppes. Of the inhabitants of the Eurasian tundra and northern forests those who rely on the highly migratory reindeer are the most likely to live year-round in tents.

The division of pastoralism into sedentary, seminomadic, and nomadic forms offers the best way out of the maze of regional classifications. Transhumance pastoralism is a variant of sedentary pastoralism whereby only the specialist herders and animals go on seasonal migrations. Seminomads maintain a permanent settlement but abandon it for part of the year. Nomads are nomads.

Land and Herd Management

Pastoralism is an extensive form of land use. Yields of food energy or protein from a given area are less than from crops, and inputs of labor, energy, and capital are less.

The trophic level interposed between primary producers and humans lowers productivity. Although the conversion efficiency of domestic livestock under intensive management is considerably better than the typical 10:1 ratio of energy transfer from one trophic level of a natural ecosystem to the next, preindustrial pastoralists' animals are not so efficient. Their milk production under the best conditions is poor by industrial standards, growth of young animals is slow, and butchering often takes place at an advanced age. The lands themselves are often marginal and provide low concentrations of available feed. The population densities of pastoralists are thus low in comparison with those of most agriculturalists.

Pastoralists have few incentives to make yield-raising inputs. Under preindustrial conditions, pasture rewards an input like tilling or planting much less than would crops for direct human consumption. Hay cutting is exceptional. Nomads and seminomads make the fewest inputs into land. Their animals are their wealth. The land is not, hence it receives little investment. Individual rights apply rarely to whole grazing territories, more often to critical resources, notably water holes or portions of pasture that remain green in the dry season. Even these rights are by no means universal among nomads and seminomads.

Some observers declare not only that nomads do little to improve pasture but also that their attitude is thoroughly exploitative. They are little concerned with exhaustion and degradation of pastures but believe they can always expand onto someone else's territory (Spooner, 1973:16). The judgment may be premature. Some nomads and seminomads operate in tightly bounded tracks and seasonally graze their stock on the fields of agriculturalists, thus operating under constraint. Even in the tundra, both well-conserved and degraded pastures are reported. A good cross-cultural study has yet to be done, and generalizations based on experience in single regions may be ill advised.

Historic Scandinavian sedentary pastoralists built walls around fields, drained marshy grasslands, and sometimes spread manure from the winter stables, but these practices were nearly always confined to the *tún,* or home field, used to grow hay and occasionally to feed particularly valuable stock, such as pregnant or lactating cows. By modern standards these pastoralists cut hay in small amounts. Women in charge of feeding cattle were admired if they could feed just enough to get the animals through the winter, and survivors frequently had to be carried to spring pasture.

A few seminomads living where winter restricts movement make hay. Ekvall (1968:34–35) describes Tibetan practice. Not all households do so, and the amount made is small, just enough to reduce winter mortality of stock but not enough to keep milk production and growth up to summer standards. Because hayfields are unfenced and must be protected from stock, summer grazing is at a distance, and hayfield grass is not cut until it goes to seed, when the nutritional value of the hay should be well past its peak.

Preindustrial pastoralists of the tropics do not make wet-season hay for dry-season feeding. One likely obstacle is that conditions are too wet to dry grass at the time it is most palatable and nutritious, shortly after the rains begin, and the senescent growth of the late rainy season is poor feed that does not adequately reward the effort of cutting it.

A land management technique used by most pastoralists in drier lands is burning. This is done to encourage green growth when the rains arrive and sometimes to suppress insects.

In the absence of land improvements the required skills are those of managing the animals. Breeding is a recognized art. Though some reindeer pastoralists allow crossbreeding with wild males, most of them nonetheless practice selection. Nomadism places special demands upon the herders. Long-distance moves of large herds, often over difficult terrain and sometimes in severe weather, require stamina, intimate knowledge of the territory, insight into the animals' behavior, and timing of moves in anticipation of weather. Vital knowledge can help prevent disease in the herd. Nowhere is this better illustrated than in the tsetse fly zones of sub-Saharan Africa. The wise herder knows and avoids infested bush but, when necessity demands it, can drive the herds at night and take other measures that get most through without tsetse bites and certain death from sleeping sickness (trypanosomiasis) (Kjekshus, 1977:54–55).

The Technology of Pastoralists

The people of neighboring, literate, urban civilizations commonly portray pastoralists as barbarians, a judgment that is wrong in the technical domain at the least. Nomadic pastoralists for obvious reasons do not construct great edifices. Nor do the thin populations of sedentary pastoralists; Iceland lacked a single sizable bridge until the late nineteenth century. Yet pastoralists' knowledge of basic tools, techniques, and materials is generally much the same as that of their nearest agricultural or urban neighbors, or was at least until the arrival of the industrial age. Many pastoralists maintain centers of cottage industry, where crafts reach a high level and artisans work glass, metal, and leather.

Metalworking displays well the accomplishments of pastoralists, because many know the craft, one that is rightly or wrongly thought a hallmark of technological sophistication. The Scythians made gold and bronze castings that are today renowned for their artistic conception and skilled casting, and they worked iron and silver as well. The Sarmatians, who displaced the Scythians in the western Eurasian steppes, seem to have led in the development of whole-body plate armour. This, and their crossbows, intimidated the "civilized" Roman legions sent to fight them. Ironworking extended early across the steppes to Tibet, Mongolia, and southern Siberia. When the Russians reached east-central Siberia, the Yakut knew smelting and iron-smithing (Tokarev and Gurvich, 1956:257). Although present-day pastoralists of Southwest Asia and North Africa commonly trade for metal goods, many used to do their own smelting and smithing. East African pastoralists also know ironworking, though it is a fading art in the colonial and postcolonial eras. If nomads have enough horses, camels, yaks, or reindeer, they carry impressive loads. Excavations of royal Scythian burials corroborate Herodotus's vivid account of their wealth.

War and Conquest

War absorbs much of the pastoralists' technical skill, which goes into making iron weapons and armor, crossbows, siege machines, and more. The Mongols acquired rocketry from the Chinese but took its use further, employing mass incendiary bombardments in sieges (von Braun and Ordway, 1969:26–27).

Pastoralists conquered agricultural and urban populations much larger than themselves. The Great Wall failed to keep Huns and Mongols out of China. The Turkic-speaking hordes of Central Asia and the Cimmerians, Scythians, and Sarmatians of the western Eurasian steppes dominated agriculturalists in their midsts and were the bane of urban civilizations beyond their borders. Imperial Rome just held off the pastoral Huns before falling to Germanic tribes that included major pastoralist contingents. The Bedouin figured large in the spread of Islam by the sword. Pastoralists in Africa never mounted armies on quite the same scale, but the Maasai and Tuareg and many Bedouin have a similar reputation for successful warfare. Schneider (1979:45) maintains that organized warfare in East Africa was with few exceptions waged by the Maasai, Nandi, and "others of the southerly Eastern Nilotes," predominantly pastoralists. Nor is it the nomads alone who excel at war and raiding. The vanguard of the Viking expansion to the west was made up of sedentary pastoralists from the outer coasts.

Pastoralists founded conquest states and ruling dynasties: the Mongols and Manchu in China; and Ankole, Rwanda, and Burundi in Africa. The Bedouin played a major role in the formation of ruling elites and states in Arabia (Rosenfeld, 1965). Ironically, numerically inferior pastoralists are liable to assimilation by the settled peoples, just what happened to the Mongol court of Kublai Khan in China.

Several factors contribute to the might of pastoralist armies. Mobility is foremost. Horse nomads of the Eurasian steppes and the camel nomads of the great deserts move their armies with great speed, and the rest of the human community can shift, taking animals, to provide logistical support or avoid attack at the rear. Spending a lifetime on horseback or camelback is excellent military training for both warrior and mount. Even the Vikings, though they went abroad on their longboats, made the most of their wealth in domesticated animals, moving ponies and lactating cows to new colonies in the outer islands, thus quickly establishing both a food supply and mounts. Ekvall (1961) lists some additional advantages of Tibetan nomads at war: the ability to mobilize a force quickly, rapid communication, early training, knowledge of a wide territory, and esprit de corps. These can fairly be generalized, but in viewing pastoralists primarily through the looking glass of ethnographic description, we see only a shadow, because we cannot witness the mobilization, organization, and sustained movement of the great hordes of the past.

The Culture of Pastoralists: How Different?

This chapter began with the recognition that pastoralism is distinct from agriculture, and it fittingly ends with a note on the distinctiveness of pastoralists' culture. The uniqueness is clear in some respects, controversial in others.

Life with the herds leaves its mark. Social life must be fit to the demands of herd management, and the animals dominate folklore. Nomadic pastoralism generates settlement patterns unlike those of either settled agriculturalists or nomadic food collectors.

The more-controversial contrasts deal with social norms, personality, and social and political organization. In any given locality the differences between pastoralists and their agricultural neighbors may be both diverse and striking, whereas in others the similarities are more compelling. Modern anthropologists have made only a few attempts to draw global generalizations about pastoralist society. Salzman (1967) deals mainly with political organization and the exercise of legal authority. Spooner's (1973) treatment is broader—taking in such larger social issues as kinship, the stability of local groups, a few personality characteristics, and religious ideas—but is not comprehensive.

Pastoral communities and polities vary greatly in size, the degree to which power and authority are centralized, and the development of social classes. Polities include small, independent bands and have included states. Influence from agricultural societies and urban civilizations accounts for some of the variation, notably in the case of pastoralists who adopt a major world religion and its supporting institutions, yet pastoral states and empires retained their own character over several millennia in the Eurasian steppes.

Ethnographic descriptions of pastoralists' behavior and personality are also varied, but reasonable arguments are made that some behavioral characteristics are adaptive in the pastoral context. Edgerton's (1971) analysis of data from the Culture and Ecology in East Africa Project is of particular interest, because pastoralists and agriculturalists of close ethnic relationship are paired, and fairly consistent contrasts in behavioral norms and some aspects of personality do emerge. Edgerton's

(1971) study, Leeds's (1965) analysis of the Reindeer Chukchi, and Spooner's (1973) work also link the demands of herding to specific behavioral norms.

Attention might be given warfare and, more realistically if the data are ethnographic, the nature of wealth. Nowhere does wealth beget wealth more than in a pastoral economy, where it consists of animals that reproduce themselves. Growth, if unchecked, would be exponential. Poverty begets poverty. Dahl and Hjort (1976:75) note the often narrow margin between calves' milk requirements and cows' production and conclude that impoverished herders consume the milk of their cows to the detriment of the calves, increasing mortality and making it hard to maintain herd size. The same principle can fairly be extended to milch animals in general. Excessive and early breeding puts females at risk, excepting camels because of their late fertility and seasonal breeding.

But the growth of herds is restrained, among sedentary pastoralists by land resources and more ubiquitously by theft, predation, and escape. Horses and reindeer especially tend to go wild. Wealthy herders have an obligation to provide for poor relatives, and food exchanges presumably relieve pressure on the latter's herds. Poor Chukchi herders "accidentally" drive their reindeer through large herds, which inevitably lose some of their number (Leeds, 1965:100–110).

Pastoralist culture, however distinct, is threatened. Political autonomy was lost some years ago. Sedentary pastoralism has already largely merged into modern industrial farming and ranching, whether in Scandinavia or Soviet Central Asia. As for nomads, modern nations seek to settle them (chapter 11).

References

Adams, R.M. (1974). The Mesopotamian social landscape: A view from the frontier. In *Reconstructing Complex Societies* (B. Moore, ed.), Supplement to the Bulletin of the American School of Oriental Research, no. 20, pp. 1–13.

Bacon, E.E. (1954). Types of pastoral nomadism in Central and Southwest Asia. *Southwestern Journal of Anthropology,* 10:44–68.

Bender, B. (1975). *Farming in Prehistory.* St. Martin's, New York.

Bobeck, H. (1962). The main stages in socio-economic evolution from a geographical point of view. In *Readings in Cultural Geography* (P.L. Wagner and M.W. Mikesell, eds.), University of Chicago Press, Chicago, pp. 218–247.

Bogoras, W. (1904–9). *The Chukchee: The Jesup North Pacific Expedition.*

82

CHAPTER 4

Memoirs of the American Museum of Natural History, vol. 7. New York.

Braudel, F. (1966). *The Mediterranean and the Mediterranean World in the Age of Philip II.* Vol. 1, trans. Sian Reynolds. Harper and Row, New York.

Braun, W. von, and F. Ordway (1969). *History of Rocketry and Space Travel.* Crowell, New York.

Clark, J.D. (1976). Prehistoric populations and pressures favoring plant domestication in Africa. In *Origins of African Plant Domestication* (J.R. Harlan, J.M.J. de Wet, and A.B.L. Stemler, eds.), Mouton, The Hague, pp. 67–106.

Dahl, G., and A. Hjort (1976). *Having Herds: Pastoral Herd Growth and Household Economy.* Stockholm Studies in Social Anthropology, no. 2. Department of Social Anthropology, University of Stockholm, Stockholm.

Deshler, W.W. (1965). Native cattle keeping in eastern Africa. In *Man, Culture, and Animals* (A. Leeds and A.P. Vayda, eds.), American Association for the Advancement of Science, Washington, D.C., pp. 153–168.

Dyson-Hudson, R. (1972). Pastoralism: Self-image and behavioral reality. In *Perspectives in Nomadism* (W. Irons and N. Dyson-Hudson, eds.), E.J. Brill, Leeds, England, pp. 30–47.

Dyson-Hudson, R., and N. Dyson-Hudson (1970). The food production system of a semi-nomadic society: The Karimojong, Uganda. In *African Food Production Systems* (P.F.M. McLoughlin, ed.), Johns Hopkins University Press, Baltimore, pp. 91–123.

Edgerton, R.B. (1971). *The Individual in Cultural Adaptation.* University of California Press, Berkeley.

Ekvall, R. (1961). The nomadic pattern of living among Tibetans as preparation for war. *American Anthropologist, 63:*1250–1263.

———. (1968). *Fields on the Hoof: Nexus of Tibetan Pastoralism.* Holt, Rinehart and Winston, New York.

Engels, F. ([1884] 1942). *The Origin of the Family, Private Property, and the State: In the Light of the Researches of Lewis H. Morgan.* Reprint. International Publishers, New York.

Evans-Pritchard, E.E. (1940). *The Nuer: A Description of the Modes of Livelihood of a Nilotic People.* Clarendon, Oxford, England.

Fleming, A. (1972). The genesis of pastoralism in European prehistory. *World Archaeology, 4:*179–191.

Gilbert, A.S. (1983). On the origins of specialized nomadic pastoralism in western Iran. *World Archaeology, 13:*301–326.

Gjessing, G. (1954). *Changing Lapps: A Study in Culture Relations in Northernmost Norway.* London School of Economics, Monographs in Anthropology, no. 13, London.

Ingold, T. (1976). *The Skolt Lapps Today.* Cambridge University Press, Cambridge.

Ingstad, H. (1969). *Westward to Vineland,* trans. E.J. Friis. Harper and Row, New York.

Iokhel'son, V.I. (1933). *Peoples of Asiatic Russia.* American Museum of Natural History, New York.

Johnson, D.L. (1969). *The Nature of Nomadism*. University of Chicago, Department of Geography, Research Paper 118. Chicago.

Kjekshus, H. (1977). *Ecology Control and Economic Development in East African History: The Case of Tanganyika 1850–1950*. University of California Press, Berkeley.

Kottak, C.P. (1987). *Cultural Anthropology*. 4th ed. Random House, New York.

Krader, L. (1955). Typology of Central Asian pastoralism. *Southwestern Journal of Anthropology*, 13:301–326.

———. (1959). The ecology of nomadic pastoralism. *International Social Science Journal*, 11:499–510.

Leeds, A. (1965). Reindeer herding and Chukchi social institutions. In *Man, Culture, and Animals* (A. Leeds and A.P. Vayda, eds.), American Association for the Advancement of Science, Washington, D.C., pp. 87–128.

Lees, S.H., and D.G. Bates (1974). The origins of specialized nomadic pastoralism: A systemic model. *American Anthropology*, 39:181–186.

Mahadevan, P., and D.J. Parsons (1970). Livestock. In *Agriculture in Uganda* (J.D. Jameson, ed.), Oxford University Press, London, pp. 333–344.

Mason, I.L., and J.P. Maule (1960). *The Indigenous Livestock of Eastern and Southern Africa*. Commonwealth Agricultural Bureaux, Farnham Royal, England.

Matley, I.M. (1968). Transhumance in Bosnia and Herzegovina. *Geographical Review*, 58:231–261.

Morgan, L.H. ([1877] 1963). *Ancient Society*. Reprint, ed. Leacock. Meridian, New York.

Mori, F. (1965). *Tadrant Acacus: Arts Rupestre e Culture del Sahara Preistorica*. Einaudi, Turin, Italy.

Munson, P.J. (1976). Archaeological data on the origins of cultivation in the southwestern Sahara and their implications for West Africa. In *Origins of African Plant Domestication* (J.R. Harlan, J.M.J. de Wet, and A.B.L. Stemler, eds.), Mouton, The Hague, pp. 187–210.

Netting, R.M. (1977). *Cultural Ecology*. Cummings, Menlo Park, Calif.

Paine, R. (1957). *Coast Lapp Society*. Tromsö Museum, Tromsö, Norway.

———. (1972). The herd management of Lapp reindeer pastoralists. In *Perspectives in Nomadism* (W. Irons and N. Dyson-Hudson, eds.), E.J. Brill, Leeds, England, pp. 76–87.

Prokof'yeva, E.D. (1956). The Nentsy. In *The Peoples of Siberia* (M.G. Levin and L.P. Potapov, eds.), University of Chicago Press, Chicago, pp. 547–570.

Robertshaw, P.T., and D.P. Collett (1983). The identification of pastoral peoples in the archaeological record: An example from East Africa. *World Archaeology*, 15:67–78.

Rosenfeld, H. (1965). The social composition of the military in the process of state formation in the Arabian Desert. *Journal of the Royal Anthropological Institute*, 95:75–86, 174–194.

Salzman, P.C. (1967). Political organization among nomadic peoples. *Proceedings of the American Philosophical Society*, 111:115–131.

_____. (1972). Multi-resource nomadism in Iranian Baluchistan. In *Perspectives in Nomadism* (W. Irons and N. Dyson-Hudson, eds.), E.J. Brill, Leeds, England, pp. 60–68.

Sauer, C.O. (1962). The agency of man on the earth. In *Readings in Cultural Geography* (P.L. Wagner and M.W. Mikesell, eds.), University of Chicago Press, Chicago, pp. 539–557.

Schneider, H.K. (1979). *Livestock and Equality in East Africa: The Economic Basis for Social Structure.* Indiana University Press, Bloomington.

Sherratt, A. (1983). The secondary exploitation of animals in the Old World. *World Archaeology,* 15:90–104.

Smith, A.B. (1983). Prehistoric pastoralism in the southwestern Cape, South Africa. *World Archaeology,* 15:79–89.

Smith, P.E.L., and T.C. Young (1972). Greater Mesopotamia: A trial model. In *Population Growth: Anthropological Implications* (B. Spooner, ed.), MIT Press, Cambridge, pp. 1–59.

Spencer, P. (1965). *The Samburu: A Study of Gerontocracy in a Nomadic Tribe.* Routledge and Kegan Paul, London.

_____. (1973). *Nomads in Alliance: Symbiosis and Growth among the Rendille and Samburu of Kenya.* Oxford University Press, London.

Spooner, B. (1973). *The Cultural Ecology of Pastoral Nomads.* Addison-Wesley Module in Anthropology 45. Reading, Mass.

Strickton, A. (1965). The Euro-American ranching complex. In *Man, Culture, and Animals* (A. Leeds and A.P. Vayda, eds.), American Association for the Advancement of Science, Washington, D.C., pp. 229–258.

Sweet, L.E. (1965). Camel pastoralism in North Africa and the minimal camping unit. In *Man, Culture, and Animals* (A. Leeds and A.P. Vayda, eds.), American Association for the Advancement of Science, Washington, D.C., pp. 129–152.

Tokarev, S.A., and I.S. Gurvich (1956). The Yakuts. In *The Peoples of Siberia* (M.G. Levin and L.P. Potapov, eds.), University of Chicago Press, Chicago, pp. 243–304.

Vainshtein, S. (1980). *Nomads of South Siberia.* Cambridge University Press, Cambridge.

5

The Tropics

Coverage of preindustrial agriculture and environment quite properly begins with the tropics, latitudes of special interest for several reasons. With the exception of East Asia, nearly all the less developed countries are in the tropics and subtropics. Underdevelopment often extends to agriculture, yet the potential productivity is greater than in higher latitudes. Population densities were once comparable to those of temperate lands, before the colonial era brought drastic depopulation in its wake. Presently rapid population growth makes higher agricultural yields imperative.

This chapter includes less coverage of the prehistoric or historic evolution of agriculture than the next two chapters, because appropriate historical records lack depth, and knowledge of tropical prehistory, though rapidly improving, is still limited. The approach is therefore primarily typological, with the typology based mainly on contemporary or recent historical descriptions.

Ethnographic Sources

Available ethnographic sources should not be used alone to portray traditional tropical agriculture as if it were unchanged since the precolonial era. Those few countries that escaped conquest were visited by threats of force, disruption and redirection of trade, and diseases against which they had acquired no immunities. The combined impact was appreciable everywhere. At the extreme, populations of the Amazonian lowlands suffered such early and drastic losses (Denevan, 1976) that ethnographically documented societies can only be a pale shadow of those past. Evidence of relict agricultural systems abounds in South America, Africa, and the Pacific, underlining the importance of continuing archaeological investigation.

Ethnographic description of agriculture best covers Africa, which consequently has a strong influence on much of the literature on the tropics in general. Not only do anthropologists and geographers supply numerous postcolonial accounts, but agricultural authorities provide detailed descriptions. There are excellent regional surveys and summaries (Allan, 1965; Dumont, 1957; Miracle, 1967; Ruthenberg, 1971). Colonialism had an impact on Africa too, and certain scholarship aims to reconstruct precolonial ecosystems and modes of production (Kjekshus, 1977).

Climates

The climates in question are always warm, and wet for enough of the year to support staple crops without the aid of unusual moisture-conserving measures. The climates are roughly the tropical (A) climates of the Köppen classification. Many of the generalizations made here also apply to subtropical lands within the humid temperate (Ca) zone.

Rainfall distribution, as much as annual accumulation, determines the moisture regime and vegetation. When the rains arrive, the soil quickly approaches the optimum (field capacity), and moisture continues to be ample for some months. Dry spells within the rainy seasons may affect crops, but the relative lengths of wet and dry seasons most significantly influence the choice of crops and the system of cultivation. The Köppen classification accordingly divides tropical climates by length of dry season.

Köppen's tropical rain forest (Af) climates straddle the equator, where the intertropical convergence produces a well-distributed rainfall, including two peaks per year in most places. Other areas are a bit farther poleward, found where trade winds encounter mountains, as in the Hawaiian Islands.

Over the western and central parts of the great tropical land masses and in the absence of mountain influences, the annual dry season gradually lengthens with increasing latitude. The Af zone gives way to a narrow belt of monsoon (Am) climates, followed by a broad zone of the wet-dry tropics (Aw), and finally the steppes and deserts discussed in chapter 6.

In the eastern parts, Af and Am climates give way poleward to humid temperate climates. Here are subtropical forests, which in their structure and ecology strongly resemble tropical forests, though many species differ.

Large upland and mountain areas lie within the tropics, and their climates are both distinctive and diverse. Temperature decreases with altitude, but because mean temperatures vary little from month to month, these climates are not to be equated with temperate climates that may share the same mean annual temperature. Rainfall increases up to a point, so that montane rain forests often rise above lowlands with Am or Aw climates, but drier regimes are found, often upslope of montane forests at very high altitudes, as well as in the rain shadow of high ranges. Many valleys and plateaus are important agricultural lands and support dense populations, usually up to the elevation at which frost is frequent, though Andean farmers have found ways to cope with almost nightly light frosts. This chapter will not treat highland agricultural systems in as comprehensive a fashion as those of the lowlands, because there is a dearth of good description and analysis and because the environmental diversity confounds generalization.

The Humid Tropics

Following an established convention, the Af and Am climates will be lumped as the humid tropics. The Köppen scheme divides them, stipulating that Am climates have a dry season (6 cm or less of rain per month for one to three consecutive months). Significant differences between the two zones may be found in natural vegetation and in agricultural possibilities (Chang, 1968), which will be noted when especially pertinent. The natural vegetation on nearly all well-drained land is forest, differing only in height and somewhat in structure.

FOREST ECOLOGY. Forest growth is luxuriant because potential photosynthesis is high year-round, moisture is adequate most of the time, and sufficient nutrients recycle through the ecosystem. The lush appearance of the forests led early colonial observers to overestimate their immediate promise and in many instances to denigrate the efforts of indigenous cultivators. Favorable temperature, sunlight, and rainfall were easy to witness, but not the miserly recycling of nutrients, and Europeans often formed the impression that the soils were highly fertile. The soils in fact range from severely leached sands to moderately fertile soils, but the average nutrient status is moderate at best, certainly much less than the lush growth signals. Net primary productivity varies a little with soil, but growth is rapid even on soils that are low in several essential nutrients, and agricultural performance on these may be extremely disappointing. Efforts to transplant European agricultural systems were mostly failures before industrial technology and ecological studies were brought to bear, although European settlers (as managers, rarely as cultivators) were more successful at establishing tree plantations.

Adequate sunlight coincides year-round with warm temperatures, but high humidity and cloud cover reduce received sunlight below that which falls on drier parts of the tropics and subtropics. Day length varies little, making daylight hours less at all times of year than during the growing season of higher latitudes. Potential photosynthesis is also restricted by high temperatures, particularly at night, leading to high respiration rates (Chang, 1968), though with less effect on maize and other crops with a C_4 photosynthetic pathway. In spite of these limitations, tropical forests achieve some of the highest net primary productivity rates of any ecosystem, partly because the multilayered vegetation intercepts so much of the sunlight.

Classification of tropical forests roughly parallels the Köppen scheme. The evergreen forest typical of the Af zone contains few deciduous trees. In the Am zone, deciduous species are more frequent, and the canopy becomes noticeably thinner during the dry season. Regional variation is substantial. For example, deciduous species are nearly absent from Australia's tropical eucalyptus forests, whereas in some forests along the windward shores of Southeast Asia the upper canopy loses nearly all its leaves during the dry season, with only lower layers staying green (Walter, 1971).

An outstanding feature of soil-plant relations in tropical forests, and the one most pertinent to their agricultural exploitation, is that so much of the recycling nutrients are at any one time tied up in the mass of trees and other higher plants—the phytomass—and in partly decayed vegetation that is not yet incorporated into the soil. The phenomenon partly explains the development of tall forest on sands of very low nutrient status (Stark, 1971). In one study, the phytomass on a tropical forest soil with higher phosphorus and bases than most was found to contain 11 times as much phosphorus in mobile forms as the top 30 cm of soil, 3 times as much potassium, about as much calcium and magnesium, and about 40% as much nitrogen (Greenland and Kowal, 1960). Golley (1975:114) reports similar distributions of mobile phosphorus and potassium in a Panamanian forest, but the phytomass contained only about half as much calcium and magnesium as the soil. Laudelout (1961) and Moss and Morgan (1970) report in several African locations about equal amounts of nutrients in the soil and phytomass, except that more than 90% of the phosphorus was in the soil, a variation that may be due to a different method of extracting phosphorus.

Tropical forests do not generally respond to experimental additions of fertilizer nitrogen (Longman and Jenik, 1974:39), but crops on cleared sites do. Either much of the nitrogen is fixed by microorganisms in symbiotic association with forest species, or the cover is essential to fixation by free-living microorganisms.

Nutrients recycle more rapidly and efficiently than in other ecosystems. Litter accumulates at rates of 5.5 to 15.3 t/ha/yr in tropical forests and 1.0 to 1.8 t/ha/yr in temperate forests (Sanchez, 1976:356). Organic matter decomposes faster in the tropics, however, and equilibrium humus levels are not far out of line with those of the same soil orders under temperate forests. A dense mass of feeder roots near the surface intercepts most nutrients released by decomposition before they are leached away. Stark (1971) suggests that mycorrhizae in some sandy Amazonian soils directly transfer from litter to plant roots a high proportion of nutrients, which are therefore at no time mobile in the soil.

OTHER ECOSYSTEMS. Most grasslands in the humid zone, if on well-drained soils, are a product of human intervention. When grassland replaces forest, fewer nutrients accumulate in the phytomass. Neither in this zone nor in the wet-dry tropics is the net primary productivity of grasslands much less than that of forests receiving similar rainfall (Murphy, 1975; Rodin, Bazilevich, and Rozov, 1975:16), but forests accumulate far more phytomass, enough to offset the smaller proportion of each nutrient contained in wood as compared with grass or foliage.

Forests cover most wetlands. Primary productivity is high from them or the few grasslands. Soils tend to have a high content of nutrients, mainly in organic forms.

The Wet-Dry Tropics

Annual rainfall in the wet-dry (Aw) climates exceeds that of the steppes (BSh) and may be fairly heavy, but the dry season (6 cm or less of rain per month) is four months or longer. In Trewartha's (1957) modification of the Köppen classification, wherever mean temperatures are those typical near sea level, the wet-dry climates supersede steppe as annual rainfall rises above about 500 mm. The boundary is supposed to represent the limits of rain-fed agriculture without resort to the moisture-conserving measures of agriculture in semiarid lands, but early-ripening cereals can often be grown without such measures somewhat inside the steppe zone if the rains mostly fall in one short season.

A weakness of purely climatic classifications, one that is most apparent in transitional zones, is that soils vary in their ability to hold water and sometimes in the amount of runoff. Vertisols—that is, soils made up largely of clays that swell markedly when wet and crack when dry—shed rain when dry and retain only a modest amount of moisture. They are frequently encountered in the Aw zone and pose a challenge to management.

Vegetation of the wet-dry zone includes forests and woodlands, savannas, and grasslands. *Savanna* is here a form unique to the tropics (Walter, 1971), that is, a predominantly grass-covered landscape studded with trees at wide intervals. What some call savanna, grassland interspersed with woodland patches or gallery forest, is here just called grassland.

Forests near the humid zone are fairly tall, up to 50 m, but more open than those across the boundary. Trees lose leaves throughout the dry season but retain some by the end.

In drier locations, woodland growth is shorter and more deciduous. Growth also tends to be more open, though low, dense scrub is also common. Particularly in Africa, the latter often carries thorns that protect the plants from indigenous browsing animals.

Most of the grasslands and savannas are anthropogenic, a consequence of clearing, grazing, and fire. Just how much is natural, either a climax or a product of such nonhuman causes as lightning-set fires, is controversial, but pioneer agriculturalists in the Aw zone probably found greater expanses of forest and woodland than are now present, especially in the more humid areas. Grass more readily replaces trees the longer the dry season. The fire hazard mounts, especially from activities related to agriculture and settlement.

Annual rainfall and dry-season length markedly affect soils. Drier conditions reduce net primary productivity and additions of organic matter; because decomposing bacteria are active when soil moisture falls below the wilting point, decomposition continues for some time after growth has ceased. Consequently, soil humus and nitrogen tend to decline. A benefit from reduced rainfall is that leaching removes fewer nutrients. Bases tend to be higher, often accumulating in the lower rooting zones. Nitrogen is the nutrient most likely to be limiting.

Humus levels are on average higher under forest or woodland than under savannas produced by human intervention under comparable conditions (Moss and Morgan, 1970; Walter, 1971:240). If parent material is favorable, highly productive soils are found under forest cover near the border with the humid tropics, where leaching is less than in the wetter regions, and organic matter accumulates nearly as rapidly.

Subterranean water can greatly benefit soil nutrient status where capillary action or gravitational seepage brings it to the surface. During the dry season, water and dissolved nutrients move upward rather than away from the rooting zone. Groundwater extends the growing season, and organic matter accumulates longer. Seepage zones are often very important for indigenous agriculture, unless excess seepage leaches nutrients.

The alternation of wet and dry seasons brings seasonal floods and drought to low-lying land, including the vast llanos of the Orinoco basin and northeastern Bolivia. Because organic matter decomposes rapidly when the land is not inundated, equilibrium humus levels are low. Floodplains are more promising where the floods leave behind good alluvial soil borne from better soils upstream.

Crops

Annuals must mature before low soil moisture limits growth and development, but the onset of the dry season may be essential to trigger formation of the edible portion, as in most yams. Dry weather aids ripening of cereals and drying of grain for storage.

Some perennials do not tolerate drought well and are best adapted to the humid zone. Others need some length of dry season to initiate fruiting or to provide some protection from disease.

Chang (1968) notes that several important crops of the Am zone have a minor role in the Af zone. He finds in the wetter zone that coffee, cacao, cotton, and tobacco, albeit not food crops, are particularly susceptible to disease, and mangosteen and durian blossom and set fruit irregularly. He stresses the difficulties of cereal cultivation. Rice is the dominant crop of the Am zone but occupies a lesser role in the Af lands. Ripening and drying the grain is a problem in the latter, but a surmountable one, as many Southeast Asian cultivators demonstrate.

Palms are characteristic of both Af and Am zones. They include several crop species, some of them true domesticates, others not. The coconut is the most familiar food palm; because the nuts float on the sea and often survive the voyage, its range is pantropical along the coasts. Not only are the nuts eaten, but the sweet juice collected from the flowers is also boiled down to make palm sugar or fermented into palm wine. The next most important palm is the sago palm (*Metroxylon sagu*), cut down at six to eight years of age for the pith, from which starch is washed and collected. Sago is planted and the stands managed in many parts of its range, from coastal Southeast Asia to Papua New Guinea, and as a wild food resource is also the main staple of other communities in the region. Sago palm sap is in a few places processed into sugar and fermented drinks. Another species exploited for its starchy pith is the Mauritius palm of the Orinoco delta, Venezuela (Kirchhoff, 1948). The oil palm (*Elaeis guineensis*), valued for nuts that are rich in edible oils, is an old cultivar in West Africa and a recent subject of scientific breeding and commercial development. Other nuts and fruits are important in many localities, as well as the buds of the cabbage palm (*Sabal palmetto*). Add to these diverse products the fiber and useful timber from these and other species, and the importance of palms is apparent.

Numerous crops that are widely grown in the wet-dry tropics are largely or wholly missing from the humid zone. These include peanut, sorghums, millets, and assorted minor pulses and cereals.

In the driest Aw lands the main staples are usually cereals that are both early and resistant to short dry spells. These species or varieties are usually missing or less important in areas with longer or more dependable rainy seasons, not because they cannot be grown but because low yields or other characteristics make them less valuable than later sorts. Africa has the greatest variety of such crops: bulrush millet, some sorghums, and teff (*Eragrostis abyssinica*). Maize in tropical America was domesticated in a highland steppe region and was in precolonial times bred for these conditions more than would be guessed from the requirements of most modern commercial varieties. Manioc fills the same role in South America; the crop takes a year or more to produce mature tubers but withstands drought by slowing or ceasing growth and maturation until soil moisture is again adequate. Manioc, like maize, is also widely grown in the humid zone.

Fallow Systems of the Humid Zone

WOODY FALLOW SYSTEMS. An outstanding feature of the humid tropics is the continued prevalence of swidden systems. Rather than distinguish between bush and forest fallows, all will here be lumped as woody fallows. These systems seem to have long predominated in some areas, in others to have coexisted with permanent cultivation of sizable fields. Colonial-era depopulation encouraged their spread in many areas where permanent cultivation had formerly been the rule (Brookfield, 1972; Denevan, 1970; Kjekshus, 1977).

Active cultivation, which takes in weeding and light tillage, usually lasts but a few years. One season is the rule in reports of Asian upland rice swiddeners. Elsewhere 2 years is most common, and more than 3 years uncommon, but variations can be found most places, even where a single crop dominates. Native South American cultivators of the Amazon abandon their fields after an average of just over 3 years, but the range is commonly from 1 to 6 years, occasionally to as much as 15 (Beckerman, 1987:70–72). Cultivation also goes on for 3 or more years among some mountain peoples of northern Thailand, and maize and opium are main crops in addition to rice (Kunstadter, 1987:130–133). The Hmung Njua cultivate opium poppies for 10 years (Geddes, 1976).

Secondary forest grows rapidly once it starts and is not replaced by primary forest for 25 or more years. Repeated fallows of about 4 to 8 years can result in a predominance of shrubby or medium-height growth structurally distinct from secondary forest.

Slashing without burning is a rare exception to the rule of slash-and-burn clearance. Usually, low secondary growth is cut and the litter allowed to settle before planting. The practice is reported in several places in Colombia's western coastal belt (Beckerman, 1987:77; Snedaker and Gamble, 1969; West, 1957) and in Manus (Rooney, n.d.) and the southern Finschhafen Peninsula (author's observations at Lae, several pers. coms.) of Papua New Guinea. An intriguing variant is found on the Great Papuan Plateau, Papua New Guinea (Schiefflin, 1975). Undergrowth is cleared on slopes from primary or well-developed secondary forest. Banana, breadfruit, and *Pandanus,* all tall standing crops, are planted through the litter. After five days the forest trees are felled on top of the crop, which sustains little damage and later emerges from the slash. Sugarcane and *pitpit (Saccharum edule)* are cultivated on separate ridgetop fields, from which the slash is removed without burning. The Uarina of Peru's Amazonian lowlands also fell trees after clearing undergrowth and planting banana (Beckerman, 1987:77).

The reported locations of such "slash-and-mulch" cultivation (Beckerman, 1987:77) are among the world's rainiest, with the probable exception of the Uarina territory. Examination of weather records at Lae, Erave, and Lorengau, Papua New Guinea — stations near reported locations — indicate that dry spells occur in most years but are far from dependable. The practice may be in part an adaptation to a lack of reliable conditions for burning, but some of its practitioners burn other fields, and peoples around the Uarina make burning the rule.

Slashing and burning effectively clears growth and has other advantages. The ashes retain most nutrients, and their alkalinity often makes more soil nitrogen available (Webster and Wilson, 1966:173). Burning loses nitrogen and sulfur to the air, but not all the slash is burnt; Seubert reports that unburnt slash from a 17-year-old fallow added 7 kg of nitrogen per hectare (Sanchez, 1976:364). The completeness of the burn varies with such practices as stacking and reburning.

Swiddens disturb the forest ecosystem, a disturbance that considerably reduces the work of controlling weeds. If the forest had shaded the ground well, weeding is light and infrequent the first season after clearance. Weeds adapted to open ground gradually invade, making the work greater from the second season on. Coppices begin to emerge from stumps shortly after clearance. Some cultivators rigorously suppress their growth in the early stages of cultivation, others do not, but most allow enough regrowth later on to give trees a head start on the fallow. Some Sierra Leone cultivators cut trees at different heights to encourage early regrowth of particularly valued species (Hoskins, 1984:47).

Several other commonly encountered practices favor woody vegetation in the fallows. Clarke (1976:249) lists short cultivation periods, tree planting, and fire prevention. Beckerman (1987) adds small clearings, which the surrounding uncut forest readily invades.

Scattered reports of tree planting come from Southeast Nigeria (Nye and Greenland, 1960:31; Vine, 1968); Pahang, Malaysia (Lambert, 1985); Java (Soemarwoto et al., 1985a); and the central highlands of Papua New Guinea (Clarke, 1976; Newton, 1960). The word *fallow* is used guardedly; the timber is used for fences, construction, or fuel. Species include *Casuarina* in highland Papua New Guinea, *Acioa barteri* in Southeast Nigeria, and a diverse mixture of trees and bamboo in Java. *Casuarina,* perhaps significantly, is a nonlegume associated with fairly active nitrogen-fixing bacteria. Although all woody fallows have their uses – Hoskins (1984) describes the folly of overlooking the value of natural fallows – planted fallows are utilized more intensively because the proportion of useful species is greater. The Javanese-planted fallow, or *talun,* produces large timbers and bamboo for sale and small branches for fuel wood; only leaves and debris remain to be burnt when the *talun* is cleared (Soemarwoto et al., 1985:49).

The longer that cultivation continues, the harder it is to reestablish woody growth. Herbaceous weeds and fast-growing softwoods predominate after short periods of cultivation, and growth has reached 7 to 12 m in 2 to 3 years (Richards, 1952:383). The length of cultivation that disturbs this succession varies with the cultivation methods used. Among the Hmung Njua, 50 years of fallow are needed after 10 years of opium cultivation to restore what they consider a satisfactory forest regrowth, and 10 fallow years are needed after 1 year of upland rice cultivation (Geddes, 1976). Cultivation may last only one season in most Southeast Asian upland rice fields, because invading grasses take over fields cultivated longer and crowd out woody regrowth. In contrast, secondary forest develops rapidly after 3 or more years of manioc cultivation in Amazonian swiddens. Light weedings and small fields allow rapid woody regrowth, and harvests may go on for some years after cultivation ceases, from crops—notably banana and manioc (*Manihot esculenta*)—that survive among woody regrowth (Beckerman, 1987).

Assurance of woody regrowth is a more ubiquitous function of short cultivation periods than is declining fertility. A sharp decline in available soil nutrients usually follows the first season, because leaching has by then removed from the root zone most of what ashes added. Declining yields are also commonly reported, though it is sometimes uncertain whether lower nutrient levels or invading weeds are the greater cause. Further declines in nutrients and yields are reported in a few instances in a third year but not in all. Certainly decreases are less in later years than in the second year. Yet short cultivation periods predominate on better and poorer soils. In some areas where woody fallows were once the rule, cultivation is now permanent despite an absence of soil amendments, evidence that long cultivation periods could have been maintained but for their effect on fallow vegetation.

GRASS FALLOW SYSTEMS. Grasses dominate fallows in the event that woody vegetation is not reestablished. Grass fallow systems occur in the humid tropics, but all indications are that they are less advantageous than woody fallows and are often unstable or even destructive of fertility. As a result, their extent is less than that of woody fallows or permanent cultivation, in marked contrast to their stability in other climates.

Examples abound whereby grass succession in fallows prompts abandonment of cultivation. Gourou (1947) attributes vast deforested and uncultivated stretches to past overcultivation, and their extent has clearly increased since then. On the Sepik plains of Papua New Guinea, Lea (1965:200) found nutrient status and yields declining in spite of 10-year grass fallows, and a frontier of abandonment was moving across a once-forested landscape.

Alternations are reported of long cultivation periods and prolonged grass fallows, though much less frequently than in the wet-dry tropics and under circumstances that point to the system's disadvantages. Stable and productive systems of this sort are found on some good alluvial or volcanic lowland soils in Papua New Guinea, but the crop mix favors those crops that produce acceptable yields where the soil nutrient status is fairly low (Vasey, 1981).

Grass fallows do not appear to be as effective in the humid tropics as woody fallows in performing the functions listed by Vine (1968): (1) rebuilding a reserve of mineral nutrients, (2) suppressing weeds, and (3) restoring equilibrium humus and nitrogen levels. Some observers (Webster and Wilson, 1966:171) would add improvement of soil structure − forest soils tend to be well aerated − but others disagree. Because more nutrients eventually accumulate in the phytomass of secondary forest than in a grass fallow of equal age, the ashes and unburnt litter of the forest supply more to a crop. Phosphorus is especially critical in this regard; Nye and Greenland (1960:24–25) estimate that residues from a 10-year-old woody fallow typically supply three to six times as much available phosphorus as those from a grass fallow. Weeds adapted to open habitats thrive in grassland, and the grasses themselves become troublesome weeds in the newly cleared fields. Finally, the typical volunteer grasses of humid tropical fallows afford poor grazing, and the few mixed farming systems that exist are not equal to those of temperate lands in their integration of cropping and animal husbandry.

Some differences are worth noting among dominant fallow grasses. Elephant grass (*Pennisetum purpureum*) is recognized in Africa as especially desirable and effective, and in Zaire the Zande prefer *Pennisetum pedicelatum* to *Imperata cylindrica* (de Schlippe, 1956), but no one reportedly exercises such preferences by planting grasses, at least not under preindustrial circumstances.

Grass fallow systems in some humid tropical highlands are both far more common and more stable than in the lowlands. Examples may be found along the eastern slope of the Andes, in some parts of equatorial East Africa, and in the central highlands of West Irian and Papua New Guinea. One explanation that can be ruled out is a difference in the dominant grass species. Up to elevations of 1,500 m, they are often the same as in the lowlands, for example, *Imperata cylindrica* var. *major* in Southeast Asia and Papua New Guinea.

In the central highlands of Papua New Guinea a shift from a varied crop mix to one dominated by sweet potato generally accompanies the replacement of secondary forest fallows by grass fallows (Vasey, 1981), a change that seems to help assure sustained and stable production. Sweet potato has an unusual capacity for growth and development on soils that are low in available phosphorus as measured by standard procedures

(Nishimoto, Fox, and Parvin, 1977) and rarely responds to added fertilizer phosphorus (van der Zaag, 1979). Many of these soils are low in available phosphorus.

Mounds and ridges commonly dot cleared grassland. Low ridges are the rule on plowed lands, broad high furrows in tropical India. Cultivators of Melanesia and sub-Saharan Africa build mounds by hand. The largest are planted with root crops and presumably provide a large volume of loose, well-aerated soil for their development. Sweet potato mounds are as high as 1 m in the highlands of Papua New Guinea (Waddell, 1972). Yams are grown on large mounds in several parts of Melanesia. The ceremonial yams (*Dioscorea alata*) of the Maprik area (Lea, 1966) and Trobriand Islands (Malinowski, 1935, 1965), Papua New Guinea, have gained some fame. A hole up to 1.5 m deep is filled with topsoil and surmounted by the usual mound. The tubers grow as long as 3 m.

Mounds and ridges are built in varied circumstances, pointing to multiple functions. Aeration is a likely function anywhere, and drainage a likely function where the water table is high. Waddell (1972) demonstrates at high elevations in Papua New Guinea that air drains from the top of the mound, providing some frost protection. Mounds and ridges can help control erosion, but variations in their design and in soil affect their usefulness. To give an example of local variation, the author has seen sweet potato mounds on steep slopes in the highlands of Papua New Guinea staggered on contours side by side with others having straight downhill ditches made to order for gully erosion. Tied ridges, those connected by cross ridges, appear to be an especially effective erosion control, are indigenous at widely scattered locations, and are advocated by some agricultural extension services (Wrigley, 1969:121–122).

Fallow Systems of the Wet-Dry Zone

The wet-dry zone occupies about half the tropics, the more densely populated half outside Southeast Asia. Fallow systems here are highly varied. Some resemble those of the humid zone, allowing for differences imposed by the long dry season, but others integrate cropping and animal husbandry or combine cultivation periods and fallows in ways absent from the humid zone. Grass fallow systems are far more prevalent in the wet-dry zone.

Several differences from the humid tropics appear to reduce the advantages of woody fallows over grass fallows. The difference in biomass between secondary forest and grassland savanna decreases as the dry season lengthens. Moreover, reserves of mineral nutrients contained in the biomass are less likely to be of critical importance where soils are not as leached. The more-open forest and woodland of the wet-dry zone allow an understory of grasses and other weeds to develop and, after clearing, present cultivators with weed control problems similar to those encountered in grassland or savanna, though not necessarily as severe. Finally, the grasses of the zone provide fair-quality grazing.

WOODY FALLOW SYSTEMS. As long as secondary forest remains, woody fallow systems are much like those of the humid zone. Most cultivation periods are in the range of one to three years, and similar practices assure woody regrowth. Protection from fire becomes more difficult, however. Cereals play a larger role in the crop mix where they are available, though sweet potato, yam, and manioc are important in places. The long dry season limits the number of crops of all sorts taken in a year.

In the middle of the Aw zone, where the dry season lasts four to six months, reported fallow vegetation and cultural practices show much variation. Three years of cultivation alternate with several years of thorn forest or thicket in several African cases, and cereals dominate the crop mix (Allan, 1965:144, 200–210). In the vicinity of Port Moresby, Papua New Guinea, two years of cultivation of banana and root crops are followed by regrowth of secondary eucalypt-dominant forest, which grows tall in spite of an annual rainfall of only 1,000 to 1,200 mm (Vasey, 1982). In still drier parts of the zone, woody vegetation is so fragile that its regrowth is hard to ensure.

A distinctive variant is the *chitemene* system, reported at many locations around the Congo-Zambesi watershed, taking in much of Zambia and adjacent parts of Zaire (Allan, 1965:18–20, 69, 140–143; Miracle, 1967:124; Peters, 1950; Richards, 1939). Woodland is slashed in the usual manner, but the litter is then gathered into a smaller area before being burnt, thus concentrating nutrients. The exact spatial arrangement varies, but the ratio of cleared area to burnt area is consistently high, about 14:1 among the Lala (Peters, 1950). Several observers report that *chitemene* is practiced on soils of low nutrient status, and the woodland is a low growth that would presumably hold fewer nutrients than a taller one. Soil heating could be another function. Relevant data are lacking from the reports, but significant heating can occur under reburn stacks during normal swidden operations (Sanchez, 1976:359–360).

Most production comes from the burnt areas. Some cultivators take one or two crops of sorghum from the larger unburnt area, and a variety of crops from the burnt areas in a complex succession lasting three to five years, a contrast that points to an important nutrient-enrichment function of *chitemene,* although we do not have available analyses to show that the extra ashes remove limitations.

Fallows last 18 to 40 years. Regrowth is slow regardless but is affected by clearing methods. In the Bangwela area of Zambia, fallows are 20 years if the trees are only lopped, 34 to 40 years if the trees are felled.

GRASS FALLOW SYSTEMS. Grass fallow systems predominate over woody fallow systems in most of the wet-dry zone. The main exceptions are the Yucatán Peninsula and parts of northern Colombia. Grass succeeds woody regrowth most readily in the driest locations.

Grass fallow systems exist in many forms, and fallow takes up as much of some cycles as in woody fallow systems. In three reported African cycles the ratios of fallow years to years of cultivation are slightly less to substantially greater than those of woody fallow systems practiced by the same cultivators. The ratios in the Kilombero valley, Tanzania, are about 4:1 in a complex grass fallow system and range from 5:1 to 12.5:1 in woody fallow systems (calculated from Baum, 1968). The ratios for grass fallow systems are about twice as high as those of woody fallow systems at Kuba, Zaire (Miracle, 1967:109) and apparently much greater at a location in the northern savannas of Ghana (Allan, 1965:233–234).

Methods of bringing grass fallows under cultivation are rather like those of the humid zone. Animals are more likely to be used for draft, however. Plows drawn by oxen or water buffalo are common in the zone in tropical India and Southeast Asia and among nonindigenes of tropical Latin America. They are an innovation in sub-Saharan Africa but are not prevalent thus far. Suitable livestock were absent from the precolonial Americas.

One unique local method is the Sudanese *hariq* method of clearing grass, used along the border of the Aw zone and the steppes (Tothill, 1948). A properly timed burn saves tillage and weeding in the early stages of cultivation. The grass is cut in the dry season but is not burnt until a short time after the rains begin, when the new grass has just emerged through the soil and litter. At this time the grass plants have used up their carbohydrate reserves, and they are slow to recover. Cereals are undersown without tillage shortly after.

A much more labor-intensive method of land preparation is denshiring (an old English term): the cutting, drying, stacking, and burning of sod, reported in the Sudan and northern Zambia (Bartlett, 1962) and among the Ngoni-Chewa of southern Zambia (Allan, 1965:99). Ashes and soil are spread before planting.

Mounds and ridges are more general in this zone than in the humid tropics, mainly because grass fallow systems are so much more common. Mounds and ridges are the rule in sub-Saharan Africa and for yam cultivation in wet-dry areas of Melanesia. Their functions appear to be much the same as in the humid zone.

Cropping periods average a little longer in grass fallow systems than in woody fallow systems (Sanchez, 1976:348). My examination of 63 published descriptions in Aw climates, mostly in Africa, shows a range from as little as a single season up to as much as 20 years. In the last case, in the Tewa District, Uganda (Allan, 1965:31–32), the fallow lasts only 3 years, demonstrating that grass fallow systems at the highest cropping frequencies grade into permanent cultivation. Most cultivation periods in the African cases are from 2 to 5 years.

Lengthy cultivation periods do not prevent the reestablishment of grass fallows, and in many situations other penalties of extended cultivation are also less than in woody fallow systems. Available nutrients and yields decline less sharply than in swiddens (Nye and Greenland, 1960; Nye and Stephens, 1962), one reason being that first-year crops following grass do not receive so large a dose of nutrients from the ashes of the fallow, and first-year yields are generally less (various cases in Allan, 1965; Sanchez, 1976: Figs. 10.13 and 10.15). Some cultivators of grasslands in the Aw zone have the unenviable opportunity to extend cultivation until equilibrium nutrient levels are low but crops of a sort can still be taken. Cultivation for 10 to 12 years on poor hill soils around Port Moresby, Papua New Guinea, results in nitrogen deficiencies, and the crop mix consists mainly of peanut, widely spaced manioc, and a few stunted banana plants (Vasey, 1982, 1985).

Grass fallows last anywhere from months to several decades. Alternations are often complex. To use the Kilombero valley of Tanzania as an example, 3 years' cultivation and 3 years' fallow alternate through three cycles, followed by a 30-year fallow (Baum, 1968). Long cycles may be especially subject to the influence of land tenure, warfare, internal politics, and other nonagronomic factors.

The functions of grass fallows need to be clarified in those instances in which the fallow goes on longer than the accumulation of potentially useful biomass. Most grasslands accumulate almost as much standing biomass in one year as they ever will, particularly in the moister parts of the Aw zone. Very rarely does the standing biomass exceed three times the net annual primary production. Thickening stems on woody perennials may accumulate a small reserve of nutrients for some years, but not if fire sweeps the fields every dry season, which it quite often does.

Organic matter accumulation in the root zone may be a continuing benefit of grass fallows, but at least two factors appear to limit it. Burning reduces litter, and the seasonal dieback of the root system found in temperate grasslands is absent in the tropics.

Species succession during prolonged grass fallows might be a factor in their favor. Particularly troublesome species are common in the early stages. Most descriptions of grass species succession are at best sketchy, but according to some accounts of old fallows the dominant species are those of uncultivated grasslands and savannas, not the prevailing weeds of cultivation.

Soil amendments are much more frequently used in grass fallow systems than in woody fallow systems and more in the wet-dry tropics than in the humid zone, but on the whole their application is exceptional where chemical fertilizers are not in use. Because cultivation periods are longer in grass fallow systems, amendments are more likely to be needed. Animal manures and green matter from young growth in grasslands supply nitrogen fairly quickly, an advantage in most of these soils. The collection area is usually small. In most published accounts from the wet-dry zone of Africa, crop residues and weeds from the immediate environs of the mound are the usual amendments.

Permanent Cultivation

Many permanent cultivation systems are common to both the humid and the wet-dry tropics. Soils of both zones include a few that readily support acceptable yields from permanent cultivation, even where soil amendments are few or nil. Amendments can make a satisfactory return possible on most soils whose physical properties permit cultivation. Animal manures are far more often available in quantity in the wet-dry zone, where permanent cultivation is sometimes integrated with grazing or stall feeding of livestock. Perennial cultivation is found throughout the tropics, with or without an understory of annual crops. Particularly important are the plantation tree crops, though the species often vary between the zones. Colonial and postcolonial plantations used few industrial inputs until the past few decades. Wetland or inundated field systems, of which wet rice is the most familiar, are found in both zones; in the wet-dry zone the flooding is seasonal unless fields are irrigated.

Decrue cultivation is to be found in floodplains of the Aw zone.

Decrue refers to the practice of planting just above receding floodwaters to take advantage of residual soil moisture and the slowly receding water table. Planting is occasionally done in the same situation on floodplains of the humid zone, as on the Amazonian *varzea,* but not to conserve moisture.

Most of the techniques used to sustain permanent cultivation are also found in association with nearly permanent cultivation, in which long cultivation periods alternate with fallows of only a year or two. Reasons for short breaks in cultivation may have little to do with the maintenance of soil nutrient status — for instance, the control of a particular weed or just local politics. No further attempt will be made here to distinguish between permanent and nearly permanent cultivation.

SOIL AMENDMENTS AND PERMANENT CULTIVATION. The main soil amendments available to the preindustrial cultivator are animal manures and green manures. The latter is any vegetation incorporated into the soil, including not only cover crops grown to be plowed under, the North American meaning, but also that brought in from elsewhere. The term *compost-dependent,* often applied to systems in which applications of organic matter make permanent cultivation possible, is used here despite the reservation that few cultivators first allow the added organic matter to decompose in compost heaps. Preindustrial cultivators use few inorganic amendments other than ashes.

The usual green manures are crop residues, weeds from near the crops, kitchen scraps, and grass and leaves from the immediate environs. As in fallow systems in which green manures are applied, the labor required to collect and move bulky material appears to discourage collecting foliage too far afield. Labor savings might be gained by using dry matter, although the carbon:nitrogen ratio is high if senescent vegetation is used.

The high average carbon:nitrogen ratio of forest foliage probably limits its direct application to soils, except for carefully selected foliage. Many Pacific islanders place the leaves from selected species under and around planting parts of taro.

The amount of organic matter needed to maintain or improve yields obviously varies with the nutrient status and other properties of the soil. Almost any soil with satisfactory physical characteristics can be permanently cultivated if the holders are prepared to range far enough afield in search of organic matter. A remarkable account relates such an accomplishment on sandy, thin soils on Ukara Island in Lake Victoria by a refugee population working long and hard hours to gather organic matter from land and lake (Ludwig, 1968). Market gardeners in Singapore maintain high yields on thin hill soils (Fong, Lian, and Wikkramatileke, 1966) by using organic manures, either those originating on the holding or purchased prawn dust, a rich source of nitrogen. Compost-dependent gardens are often one source of subsistence on those Pacific atolls whose surface soils are only partly formed from the parent coral.

Home (dooryard) gardens are often cultivated for the duration of household occupation and receive regular additions of organic matter, intended or not. Kitchen scraps, hearth ashes, and manure from any domesticated animals kept near the house are used most effectively if they are purposefully applied but are still of value where methods are more casual and the materials more or less happen to end up in the rooting zones of the crops. The same may be said of human excrement; deliberate use on crops is a scattered phenomenon throughout much of the tropics but is exceptional. Latrines were uncommon until recently and are still absent from many households, however, and we may assume that much excrement ends up near the household, particularly by night. Clarke (1971:72) notes that the Maring of highland Papua New Guinea, a region where most peoples will not knowingly apply human excrement to crops, cultivate for many consecutive years "faeces fields" near old habitation sites. Many rural Javanese latrines stand over fish ponds, whose muck is periodically spread over gardens and rice paddies.

MIXED GARDENS: TRADITIONAL AGRO-FORESTRY.

Mixtures of tree crops and annuals are often found near homes, less often away from them. Permanent, intercropped gardens generally incorporate trees for diverse uses. The term *mixed garden* is often and appropriately applied to the result. In well-developed forms, several stories range upward from a low ground cover to a high, open canopy. Gardens of this type lie hard by most rural houses in Java (Soemarwoto, et al., 1985b), where in 1980 they occupied 20.7% of the dryland agricultural area and their mean area was about 500 m² (Soemarwoto and Christanty, 1985). Similar gardens on the other Indonesian islands average 2,500 m² and have expanded rapidly in recent years, partly because of planting by transmigrating Javanese (Soemarwoto and Christanty, 1985). Other good examples of the system are reported from Papua New Guinea (Vasey, 1982, 1985); Kerala (Nair and Krishnakutty, 1985); Assam, southern Burma, southwestern Sri Lanka, northern Thailand, and Kampuchea (Terra, 1954); the Philippines (Penafiel, 1985); Yap (Falanruw, 1985); Ghana (Asare, Oppang, and Twum-Ampofo, 1985); Guatemala (Anderson, 1950); and Honduras (Anderson, 1954).

INFIELD-OUTFIELD SYSTEMS. Most mixed gardens are infields, but usually the words *infield* and *outfield* are applied to systems in which annual crops dominate both. Infield-outfield systems are reasonably abundant in the tropics, but particularly in the wet-dry zone of Africa. Folding, the confinement of stock in movable pens, is also widely used in Latin American highlands prior to planting, sometimes with the effect of creating an infield-outfield system, but the spatial differentiation of cropping systems is generally less systematic than in Africa; the folding is done into corrals, interestingly a word of African origin.

In Africa, cattle are often corralled at night near the settlement, giving rise to a series of concentric rings of land use, with cropping frequency declining away from the settlement. Permanent cultivation in these cases is really for the duration of the settlements, some of which shift at long intervals. Whatever manure is collected typically goes to sustain permanent cultivation, though the Fulani fallow for one or two years fields that were manured for a preceding crop (Allan, 1965:249–250), and the Kusani permanently cultivate both manured and unmanured fields (Allan, 1965:241–246, 249–250; Dumont, 1957:89–95; Friedrich, 1968; Ruthenberg, 1971). Mixed home gardens are common features immediately around the settlement, with a belt of permanently cultivated annual crops just beyond. In the wetter parts of the zone in East Africa, and possibly including some Am climates, constantly ratooned stands of banana dominate around the houses (Allan, 1965:392–400; Friedrich, 1968).

A semiurban version is reported in the Ethiopian highlands (Ahmad, 1960). An inner circle of city gardens surrounds a town of 20,000. Fruits, vegetables, and annual crops are permanently cultivated with the help of watering and manuring. Farther out, millet is cultivated in a rain-fed grass fallow system.

Van Parijs, in an experiment in the highlands of eastern Zaire, found that moderate yields could be sustained by applying manure from an area of native pasture three times as large (Sanchez, 1976:400). It is not known how that ratio compares with that for indigenous infield-outfield systems. A complication in the latter is that much of the grazing is on grass fallows that also function to build up biomass and soil reserves of nutrients for periods of cultivation.

WET RICE PADDIES, TARO POND-FIELDS, AND FISH PONDS. Among the permanent cultivation systems of the tropics, the greatest contribution to food supply comes from those that take advantage of flooded or waterlogged conditions.

Systems of this type will here be labeled wet, after wet rice, by far the most common sort. It might also be noted that organic soils of wetlands, once drained and thereby aerated, often grow upland crops for many years. In a sense these are dryland systems that benefit from their wet past, more specifically from the mineralization of organic matter accumulated over many centuries. Mineralization, which is especially rapid in the tropics, gradually consumes the organic matter and ultimately limits the useful lifetime (for example, Kawaguchi and Kyuma, 1977:204).

Rice fields are flooded either by impounding rainwater or runoff or by means of true irrigation. If the fields rely on rainfall, one or two crops are taken each year, depending on how long the rains last. Some rice is also sown in naturally flooded areas, in which case the planting of ordinary wet rice varieties must be timed with the water's rise, the harvest with its ebb. So-called floating rice, more accurately varieties that grow from the bottom soil on long stalks, is grown in Southeast Asia and parts of Africa on land where waters rise as high as 2 m.

Taro pond-fields of the Pacific resemble wet rice fields. They are found in subsistence agriculture and on fully commercial Hawaiian farms that employ a range of industrial inputs. Pond-fields do not dominate taro production as much as wet paddies dominate rice production. Dry taro cultivation everywhere contributes a substantial part of the supply, and there is another wet taro system, island bed cultivation (see Raised Fields, Drained Fields, and Island Beds, page 106).

Fish culture is prevalent in much of the tropics, especially in Southeast Asia. Included are herbivorous species such as grass carp and *Tilapia* spp., often cultured in fertilized ponds with little or no supplementary feeding, the wet equivalent of intensively managed pasture. Species that feed at higher trophic levels are also cultured. Bardach, Ryther, and McLarney (1972) give excellent descriptions of fish culture methods around the world and of wet cultivation of a few minor plants.

Periodic drainage, usually after each harvest, is typical of wet rice systems. Aeration of the soil is thought to be the primary function. The soil is usually plowed while drained, and an upland crop may be taken. Drainage is for two short periods (1 to 3 months apiece) or one long period (6 to 8 months) each year.

Taro requires the better part of a year to mature, and at harvest the pond-fields are drained briefly or not at all. But fallows are the rule every few years and are accompanied by drainage. The fallow may be short but is sometimes as long as or longer than the period of cultivation. In the latter case the field is not permanently cultivated in the usual meaning, but the average fallow:cultivation ratio is close to that of wet rice systems in which a single crop is taken every year.

Soil-plant relations have been studied with some thoroughness in wet rice fields. Findings pinpoint several benefits from both the flooded state and periodic drainage. Although research on pond-field taro cultivation has not been comparable, design and management sufficiently resemble wet rice practices to suggest the same benefits.

Nitrogen-fixing microorganisms identified in wet rice fields include numerous species of cyanobacteria and free-living bacteria. Fixation rates vary and are not always high, but under the right conditions the cyanobacterium *Anabaena azollae,* which grows in symbiotic association with a water fern (*Azolla* spp.), contributes combined nitrogen as rapidly as forage legumes do in any upland rotation. The fern and associated alga contribute more nitrogen in flooded fields prior to rice planting or transplanting than at other times.

Organic matter accumulates while the fields are flooded. Aeration during the drained period then increases mineralization and makes more nitrogen available. Any upland crops that are then planted benefit, as does the following wet rice crop.

The oxygen-deficient environment of inundated or waterlogged soils increases the availability of phosphorus (Patrick and Khalid, 1974; Patrick and Mahapatra, 1968). The effect is particularly marked in soils with a high proportion of hydrous iron-oxide clays, a condition often met in the tropics.

Incoming irrigation water has been shown to supply variable but often significant quantities of calcium, magnesium, and potassium in a sample of tropical Asian wet rice fields (Kawaguchi and Kyuma, 1977:58–59). The estimated contribution of potassium ranges from 8 to 45 kg/ha/crop.

Yields from wet systems are often high and sustained. Some Asian wet rice fields have been cropped once or more each year for hundreds of years, possibly thousands. Soil amendments are on the whole less used than in temperate Asian rice culture, though their use is well established in many areas. Reported yields mostly fall in the range of 1 to 3 t/ha/crop; by comparison, 1 t is probably above average for a cereal crop under preindustrial conditions. Taro pond-fields in Vanuatu yielded 32 to 52 t/ha/yr (Spriggs, 1981b: app. 5), a dry-weight yield close to that from rice paddies cropped two or three times a year.

RAISED FIELDS, DRAINED FIELDS, AND ISLAND BEDS. Large areas of the tropics that are seasonally flooded, permanently flooded, or waterlogged most of the year were once prepared for cultivation by removing earth to form ditches and placing it between the ditches to provide raised planting surfaces and a volume of drained and aerated soil. Water would have filled the ditches for at least the duration of the rainy season, in some places the whole year. Before their abandonment early in the colonial era, the largest tracts were in the wet-dry zone of the American tropics, with substantial expanses also in some lowland rain forests and semiarid highlands of the New World (Darch, 1983; Denevan, 1970, 1982) and throughout much of the Pacific (Spriggs, 1980, 1981b). Survivals include the chinampas of the central Mexican highlands and scattered plots in the Pacific. Old World prehistoric and historic examples have been listed (Denevan and Turner, 1974) but not yet closely investigated. Crop choice and the height of the planting surfaces above standing water divide these systems into two broad classes (Vasey et al., 1984): (1) low beds used for taro, and (2) higher surfaces planted in crops that are normally grown on well-drained soils.

The taro system is found in the Pacific from West Irian to Hawaii. The accepted description is *island bed,* reflecting the close proximity of crop and water. The beds are generally 0.1 to 0.3 m above high water, 1 to 6 m wide, and of variable length. Similar low beds are also planted in sago on Kolepom Island, West Irian (Serpenti, 1965) and reportedly in banana in some parts of Papua New Guinea.

Taro roots in waterlogged soils and if grown on low beds should benefit from the same fertility-enhancing mechanisms that are at work in wet rice or taro pond-field systems (Vasey et al., 1984). Indications are that each plant is situated so that its root system reaches both inundated soils, where phosphorus availability may be enhanced, and aerated soils, where mineralization of organic matter releases nitrogen. In an experiment, soils taken from an island bed just above the water table were kept underwater for some time, thereby raising their available phosphorus from almost nil to a level considered favorable to crop development (Vasey et al., 1984). Most island beds are built from wetland soils high in organic matter. Sometimes ditch sediments and a little green manure are incorporated in the beds. At Futuna (Kirch, 1975) and in historic cases on Hawaii (Earle, 1978), island beds are made from the bottom soils of pond-fields whose yields have declined, suggesting that additional nutrients become available when the soil is aerated.

Americanists describe raised fields or drained fields, typically higher surfaces than island beds. They come in many shapes and sizes, but planting surfaces are usually at least 0.5 m and often more than 1 m above high water. Similar raised fields are also reported in West Irian, planted in sweet potato in the Baliem valley (Heider, 1970) and assorted upland crops on Kolepom Island (Serpenti, 1965).

The typical crops of raised fields are generally unlikely to benefit from nutrients in surrounding water or in waterlogged soil horizons unless water, water plants, or sediments are applied to the planting surfaces. Nitrogen fixation in the surrounding water can be high, but upland crops are unlikely to root in the water, and if they did, they could not compete with algae for combined nitrogen (Vasey, 1983). Sediments and water plants are gathered and applied in contemporary cases, and the use of sediments is inferred in several prehistoric cases (Vasey et al., 1984). More-direct benefits are possible in semiarid lands; Wilken (1983) infers that chinampa crops benefit from an upward capillary movement of water and dissolved nutrients, but this would presumably involve bases and not phosphorus, which is less mobile, or nitrogen, which would not be abundant in lower horizons.

The cropping frequency is typically high on contemporary raised fields and island beds. The island beds of Kolepom Island, built in fairly deep water, are cultivated continuously until they deteriorate. Most taro island beds and the raised fields of the Baliem valley are fallowed but only after many years of cultivation. The chinampas are worked at a high frequency, at present with the help of a variety of organic and chemical soil amendments

FLOOD FALLOWING. A rare practice, but one that might repay investigation into possible mechanisms of nitrogen fixation and nutrient mobilization, is the temporary flooding of fields during seasonal fallows. Upland crops are grown shortly after drainage. Reported crops are sweet potato in the highlands of Papua New Guinea during the 1950s (Lacey, 1979) and sugarcane in Guyana.

SUMMARY. Systems of permanent cultivation make differing demands and offer differing rewards. At one extreme some soils support cultivation year after year without much use of soil amendments or ambitious modifications of the environment. On the best of these soils and in decrue cultivation the output may be excellent by preindustrial standards. But in many soils of the wet-dry tropics, though their bases are adequate for satisfactory sustained yields, their organic matter, the source of all the available nitrogen and sometimes much of the phosphorus, settles at a low equilibrium level, and crops are barely eked out each year. Nutrients may be imported, normally in organic matter, a process that may be very laborious, as on Ukara Island, or comparatively easy when domesticated animals do the carrying in their guts. Wet systems are a good example of environmental modifications that return a good output for many consecutive years once the initial investment of labor is made. Mixed gardens, from available evidence, offer good returns on favorable soils without demanding too much effort.

References

Ahmad, Y. (1960). *An Inquiry into Some Aspects of Harar and the Records of the Household Economy of the Amir of Harar.* University College of Addis Ababa, Ethnological Society, Bulletin no. 10, pp. 3–56. Addis Ababa.

Allan, W. (1965). *The African Husbandman.* Barnes and Noble, New York.

Anderson, E. (1950). An Indian garden at Santa Lucia, Guatemala. *Ceiba,* 1:97–103.

_____. (1954). Reflections on certain Honduran gardens. *Landscape,* 4:21–23.

Asare, E.O., S.K. Oppang, and K. Twum-Ampofo (1985). Homegardens (backyard gardens) in the humid tropics of Ghana. Paper presented at the First International Workshop on Tropical Home Gardens, Bandung, Indonesia, December 2–9.

Bardach, J.E., J.H. Ryther, and W.O. McLarney (1972). *Aquaculture.* Wiley Interscience, New York.

Bartlett, H.H. (1962). Fire, primitive agriculture, and grazing in the tropics. In *Man's Role in Changing the Face of the Earth* (W.L. Thomas et al., eds.), University of Chicago Press, Chicago, pp. 692–720.

Baum, E. (1968). Land use in the Kilombero valley: From shifting agriculture towards permanent farming. In *Smallholder Farming and Smallholder Development in Tanzania* (H. Ruthenberg, ed.), Weltforum Verlag, Munich, pp. 21–50.

Beckerman, S. (1987). Swidden in Amazonia and the Amazon rim. In *Comparative Farming Systems* (B.L. Turner II and S.B. Brush, eds.), Guilford, New York, pp. 55–94.

Brookfield, H.C. (1972). Intensification and disintensification in Pacific agriculture: A theoretical approach. *Pacific Viewpoint,* 15:30–48.

Chang Jen-Hu (1968). The agricultural potential of the humid tropics. *Geographical Review,* 58:333–361.

Clarke, W.C. (1971). *Place and People: An Ecology of a New Guinea Community.* University of California Press, Berkeley.

_____. (1976). Maintenance of agriculture and human habitats within the tropical forest ecosystem. *Human Ecology,* 4:247–259.

Darch, J.P. (1983). Drained fields in the Americas: An introduction. In *Drained Field Agriculture in Central and South America* (J.P. Darch, ed.), British Archaeological Reports, Oxford, pp. 1–10.

Denevan, W.M. (1970). Aboriginal drained-field cultivation in the Americas. *Science,* 169:647–654.

_____. (1976). The aboriginal population of Amazonia. In *The Native Popula-*

tions of the Americas in 1492 (W.M. Denevan, ed.), University of Wisconsin Press, Madison, pp. 205–234.

———. (1982). Hydraulic agriculture in the American tropics: Forms, measures, and recent research. In *Maya Subsistence* (K.V. Flannery, ed.), Academic Press, New York, pp. 181–203.

Denevan, W.M., and B.L. Turner II (1974). Forms, functions, and associations in the Old World tropics. *Journal of Tropical Geography,* 39:24–33.

Dumont, R. (1957). *Types of Rural Economy,* trans. D. Magnin. Methuen, London.

Earle, T. (1978). *Economic and Social Organization of a Complex Chiefdom: The Halelea District, Kaua'i, Hawaii.* University of Michigan, Anthropological Papers of the Museum of Anthropology, no. 63. Ann Arbor.

Falanruw, M.V.C. (1985). The traditional food production of Yap Islands. Paper presented at the First International Workshop on Tropical Home Gardens, Bandung, Indonesia, December 2–9.

Fong, N.K., T.C. Lian, and R. Wikkramatileke (1966). Three farmers of Singapore: An example of specialized food production in an urban unit. *Pacific Viewpoint,* 7:169–185.

Friedrich, K.H. (1968). Coffee-banana holdings at Bukoba. In *Smallholder Farming and Smallholder Development in Tanzania* (H. Ruthenberg, ed.), Weltforum Verlag, Munich, pp. 175–212.

Geddes, W.R. (1976). *Migrants of the Mountains: The Cultural Ecology of the Blue Miao (Hmung Njua).* Clarendon, Oxford, England.

Golley, F.B. (1975). Productivity and mineral cycling in tropical forests. In *Productivity of World Ecosystems,* National Academy of Sciences, Washington, D.C., pp. 106–115.

Gourou, P. (1947). *Les Pays Tropicaux: Principes d'une Geographie Humaine et Economique.* Presses Universitaires de France, Paris.

Greenland, D.J., and J.M.L. Kowal (1960). Nutrient content of a moist tropical forest of Ghana. *Plant and Soil,* 12:154–170.

Heider, K. (1970). *The Dugum Dani.* Aldine, Chicago.

Hoskins, M.W. (1984). Observations on indigenous and modern agro-forestry activities in West Africa. In *Social, Economic, and Institutional Aspects of Agro-forestry* (J.K. Jackson, ed.), United Nations University, Tokyo, pp. 46–50.

Kawaguchi, K., and K. Kyuma (1977). *Paddy Soils of Tropical Asia: Their Material Nature and Fertility.* University of Hawaii Press, Honolulu.

Kirch, P.V. (1975). Cultural adaptation and ecology in western Polynesia: An ethnoarchaeological study. Ph.D. dissertation, Yale University.

Kirchhoff, P. (1948). The Warrau. In *The Tropical Forest* (J.H. Steward, ed.), vol. 3 of *Handbook of South American Indians,* Smithsonian Institution, Bureau of American Ethnology, Bulletin no. 143, Washington, D.C., pp. 219–230.

Kjekshus, H. (1977). *Ecology Control and Economic Development in East African History: The Case of Tanganyika, 1850–1950.* University of California Press, Berkeley.

Kunstadter, P. (1987). Swiddeners in transition: Lua' farmers in northern

Thailand. In *Comparative Farming Systems* (B.L. Turner II and S.B. Brush, eds.), Guilford, New York, pp. 130–155.

Lacey, R.J. (1979). Evidence of the Enga economy: Extracts from early patrol reports, 1944–1954. Mimeo. History Department, University of Papua New Guinea, History of Agriculture Discussion Paper. Port Moresby.

Lambert, D.H. (1985). *Swamp Farming: The Indigenous Pahang Malay Agricultural System.* Westview, Boulder, Colo.

Laudelout, H. (1961). *Dynamics of Tropical Soils in Relation to Their Fallowing Techniques.* Food and Agricultural Organization, Rome.

Lea, D.A.M. (1965). The Abelam: A study in local differentiation. *Pacific Viewpoint,* 6:191–214.

_____. (1966). Yam growing in the Maprik area. *Papua and New Guinea Agricultural Journal,* 18:3–15.

Longman, K.A., and J. Jenik (1974). *Tropical Forest and Its Environment.* Longmans, London.

Ludwig, H.D. (1968). Permanent farming on Ukara: The impact of land shortage on husbandry practices. In *Smallholder Farming and Smallholder Development in Tanzania* (H. Ruthenberg, ed.), Weltforum Verlag, Munich, pp. 87–136.

Malinowski, B. (1935). *Coral Gardens and Their Magic.* Allen and Unwin, London.

_____. (1965). *Soil Tillage and Agricultural Rites in the Trobriand Islands.* Indiana University Press, Bloomington.

Miracle, M.P. (1967). *Agriculture in the Congo Basin.* University of Wisconsin Press, Madison.

Moss, R.P., and W.B. Morgan (1970). Soils, plants, and farmers in West Africa: A consideration of their relationships, with special reference to contiguous areas of forest and savanna in South-West Nigeria. In *Human Ecology in the Tropics* (J.P. Garlick and R.W.J. Keay, eds.), Pergamon, London, pp. 1–32.

Murphy, P.G. (1975). Net primary productivity in tropical and terrestrial ecosystems. In *Primary Productivity of the Biosphere* (H. Lieth and R.H. Whittaker, eds.), Springer-Verlag, New York, pp. 217–236.

Nair, C.T.S., and C.N. Krishnakutty (1985). Socio-economic factors influencing farm forestry: A case study of tree cropping in the homesteads of Kerala, India. In *Community Forestry: Socio-Economic Aspects* (Y.S. Rao, N.T. Vergara, and G.W. Lovelace, eds.), Food and Agricultural Organization, Rome, pp. 115–130.

Newton, K. (1960). Shifting cultivation and crop rotation in the tropics. *Papua and New Guinea Agricultural Journal,* 13:81–118.

Nishimoto, R.K., R.L. Fox, and P.E. Parvin (1977). Response of vegetable crops to phosphorus concentrations in soil solutions. *Journal of the American Society of Horticultural Sciences,* 102:705–709.

Nye, P.H., and D.J. Greenland (1960). *The Soil under Shifting Cultivation.* Commonwealth Bureau of Soils Technology, Harpenden, England.

Nye, P.H., and D. Stephens (1962). Soil fertility. In *Agriculture and Land Use in Ghana* (J.B. Wills, ed.), Oxford University Press, London, pp. 127–143.

Patrick, W.H., Jr., and R.A. Khalid (1974). Phosphate release and sorption by soil and sediments: Effect of aerobic and anaerobic conditions. *Science,* 186:53–55.

Patrick, W.H., Jr., and I.C. Mahapatra (1968). Transformation and availability to rice of nitrogen and phosphorus in waterlogged soils. *Advances in Agronomy,* 20: 323–359.

Penafiel, S.R. (1985). Homegardens: Prototype for expanding backyard agroforest gardens in sloping lands. Paper presented at the First International Workshop on Tropical Home Gardens, Bandung, Indonesia, December 2–9.

Peters, D.U. (1950). *Land Use in Serenje District.* Rhodes-Livingston Paper no. 19. Lusaka, Northern Rhodesia.

Richards, A.I. (1939). *Land, Labor, and Diet in Northern Rhodesia: An Economic Study of the Bemba Tribe.* Oxford University Press, London.

Richards, P.W. (1952). *The Tropical Rain Forest.* Cambridge University Press, Cambridge.

Rodin, L.E., N.I. Bazilevich, and N.N. Rozov (1975). *Production and Mineral Cycling in Terrestrial Vegetation.* Oliver and Boyd, Edinburgh.

Rooney, W. (n.d.). Changing food supply systems in eastern inland Manus. Mimeo. History Department, University of Papua New Guinea, History of Agriculture Discussion Paper. Port Moresby.

Ruthenberg, H. (1971). *Farming Systems in the Tropics.* Clarendon, London.

Sanchez, P.A. (1976). *Properties and Management of Soils in the Tropics.* Wiley, New York.

Schiefflin, E.L. (1975). Felling the trees on top of the crop: European contact and the subsistence ecology of the Great Papuan Plateau. *Oceania,* 46:25–39.

Schlippe, P. de (1956). *Shifting Agriculture in Africa.* Routledge and Kegan Paul, London.

Serpenti, L.M. (1965). *Cultivators in the Swamps.* Van Gorcum, Assen, Netherlands.

Snedaker, S.C., and J.F. Gamble (1969). Compositional analysis of selected second-growth species from lowland Guatemala and Panama. *Bioscience,* 19:536–538.

Soemarwoto, O., and L. Christanty (1985). Homegarden in the tropics. Paper presented at the First International Workshop on Tropical Home Gardens, Bandung, Indonesia, December 2–9.

Soemarwoto, O., L. Christanty, Henky, Y.H. Herri, J. Iskander, Hadyana, and Priyono (1985a). The talun-kebun: A man-made forest fitted to family needs. *Food and Nutrition Bulletin,* 7:48–51.

Soemarwoto, O., I. Soemarwoto, Karyono, E.M. Soekartadiredja, and A. Ramlan (1985b). The Javanese home garden as an integrated agro-ecosystem. *Food and Nutrition Bulletin,* 7:44–47.

Spriggs, M.J.T. (1980). Taro irrigation in the Pacific: A call for more research. *South Pacific Bulletin,* 30:15–18.

_____. (1981a). *Bombs and Butter: The Revival of Ancient Irrigation Techniques for a Market Economy, a Pacific Example.* Department of Prehistory, Research School of Pacific Studies, Occasional Papers in Prehistory, no. 2. Canberra.

_____. (1981b). Vegetable kingdom: Taro irrigation and Pacific prehistory. Ph.D. thesis, Australian National University, Canberra.

Stark, N. (1971). Nutrient cycling, II: Nutrient distribution in Amazonian vegetation. *Tropical Ecology,* 12:117–201.

Terra, G.J.A. (1954). Mixed garden horticulture in Java. *Malayan Journal of Tropical Geography,* 3:33.

Tothill, J.D. (1948). *Agriculture in the Sudan.* Oxford University Press, Oxford.

Trewartha, G. (1957). *Elements of Physical Geography.* McGraw-Hill, New York.

Vasey, D.E. (1981). Agricultural systems in Papua New Guinea. In *A Time to Plant and a Time to Uproot: A History of Agriculture in Papua New Guinea* (D. Denoon and C. Snowden, eds.), Institute of Papua New Guinea Studies, Port Moresby, pp. 17–32.

_____. (1982). Management of food gardens in the National Capital District. *Science in New Guinea,* 9:141–166.

_____. (1983). Plant growth on experimental island beds and nitrogen uptake from surrounding water. *Agriculture, Ecosystems and Environment,* 10:15–22.

_____. (1985) Household gardens and their niche in Port Moresby, Papua New Guinea. *Food and Nutrition Bulletin,* 7:37–43.

Vasey, D.E., D.R. Harris, G.W. Olson, M.J.T. Spriggs, and B.L. Turner II (1984). The role of standing water and water-logged soils in raised-field, drained-field, and island-bed agriculture. *Singapore Journal of Tropical Geography,* 5:63–72.

Vine, H. (1968). Developments in the study of soils and shifting agriculture in tropical agriculture. In *Soils Resources of Tropical Africa* (R.P. Moss, ed.), Cambridge University Press, Cambridge, pp. 89–119.

Waddell, E. (1972). *The Mound Builders: Agricultural Practices, Environment, and Society in the Central Highlands.* University of Washington Press, Seattle.

Walter, H. (1971). *Ecology of Tropical and Subtropical Vegetation,* trans. D. Mueller-Dombois. Van Nostrand Reinhold, New York.

Webster, C.C., and P.N. Wilson (1966). *Agriculture in the Tropics.* Longmans, London.

West, R.C. (1957). *The Pacific Lowlands of Colombia.* Louisiana State University Press, Baton Rouge.

Wilken, G.C. (1983). A note on buoyancy and other dubious characteristics of the "floating" chinampas of Mexico. In *Prehistoric Intensive Agriculture in the Tropics* (I.S. Farrington, ed.), British Archaeological Reports, International Series, no. 232, Oxford, pp. 31–48.

Wrigley, G. (1969). *Tropical Agriculture: The Development of Production.* Praeger, New York.

Zaag, P. van der (1979). The phosphorus requirements of root crops. Ph.D. dissertation, University of Hawaii, Honolulu.

6
Dry Lands and Dry Summer Lands

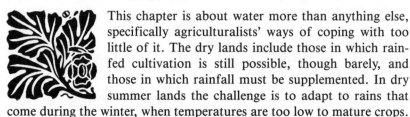 This chapter is about water more than anything else, specifically agriculturalists' ways of coping with too little of it. The dry lands include those in which rain-fed cultivation is still possible, though barely, and those in which rainfall must be supplemented. In dry summer lands the challenge is to adapt to rains that come during the winter, when temperatures are too low to mature crops.

The strategies described are, in order, farming that makes use of floodwaters; irrigation agriculture; and dry farming that depends on scant rainfall. Some treatment of industrial agriculture is included because many of its solutions to the problem of scarce water parallel those of preindustrial agriculture. The archaeological and historical evidence allows some time depth, because these regions take in many early civilizations and offer favorable conditions for the preservation of remains.

The chapter ends with a model of agricultural evolution under different degrees of population pressure and a related discussion of possible connections between the origins of civilization and the forms of agriculture in these lands. The latter is taken up briefly in the belief that theorists whose interests lie in the origins of civilization often misinterpret the demands of the agricultural systems that supported the first civilizations.

The Physical Environment

CLIMATES. The transition from the tropics through the dryland climates to the temperate zone is regular along continental west coasts. The wet-dry climates give way to Köppen's steppe (BS) and then to desert (BW) climates, also known respectively as semiarid and arid but lumped here as dry. Rainfall declines to almost nil, then rises again through another BS zone and the dry summer or mediterranean (Cs) climates to the humid temperate regions. The transition is similar inland in several regions: across northern Africa, from the western Indian Ocean into Southwest Asia, and across Australia as far east as the Great Dividing Range.

Rainfall peaks in summer near the tropics and in winter at the poleward end of the dry belt, near the mediterranean zone. Dual peaks, winter and summer, occur in parts of northwestern Mexico and central Western Australia. Near the middle of the great deserts any seasonal peak is a statistical nicety with little meaning for agriculture, because useful rainfall is so rare.

At higher latitudes, dry lands are found in the rain shadows of major mountain ranges. Unlike the climates of the subtropical deserts and steppes, these climates are not torrid. The dry lands of the Asian and North American interiors have hot summers but cold winters, a continental regime. Argentine Patagonia is kept cool at all times of the year by the strong westerlies that blow over the Andes from the southern reaches of the Pacific Ocean.

The aridity of a climate is calculated from its annual precipitation, the distribution of precipitation, and potential evaporation and transpiration under the prevailing temperatures and humidity. Because evaporation is reduced under cool winter temperatures, winter rainfall promotes plant growth more effectively than does summer rainfall; crops mature during winter and spring. The boundary between BS and BW climates is near the 450-millimeter isohyet in the hottest, summer rainfall areas of Africa's Sahel and north-central Australia, at about 250 mm in the winter rainfall belt of the Maghreb, and not far over 150 mm in some highlands of Central Asia and northwestern China.

The arid zone, on account of its distinctive natural vegetation and the virtual absence of rain-fed cultivation, is rightly distinguished from the semiarid, but the boundary is hard to define, because of the many factors that determine aridity. The boundaries in the two most often cited schemes, Köppen's and Thornthwaite's (1948), are nearly congruent in some places but not in others. Apart from the several variables of climate, other factors that affect the distribution of dry farming are soil type, agricultural technology, and the cultivators' capacity to cope with crop failures in the drier years. Dry farming in most regions dies out well within the semiarid zone, regardless of which classification scheme is used, but in isolated instances reaches into the arid zone, sometimes with help from groundwater. Hardship and struggle are common near the limits of dry farming—for example, among impoverished agriculturalists who must incur high risks of crop loss and famine or pastoralists whose herds barely survive dry years. Yet large commercial farms of the United States and Australia succeed by balancing low output with low costs and economies of scale.

Dry farming is risky because precipitation is not only near the lower limit for cultivation but also unreliable. As a rule the variability of precipitation from year to year becomes greater as mean annual precipitation declines. Rains are sporadic, and the onset of the rainy season is an uncertain event. Unpredictability of the change of the seasons causes losses when seedlings wilt or rains interfere with the harvest.

Droughts push the frontiers of cultivation back from areas whose mean rainfall is adequate. A run of drought years ended dry farming in parts of Arizona and New Mexico after the early years of post-Hispanic settlement. In Tunisia only sporadic cultivation is found in locations whose mean annual rainfall is at or about the 200 mm required for an adequate crop (Grigg, 1970:168). In that region any location with a mean of 200 mm would lie within the arid zone, indicating that rain-fed cultivation is precluded from the margins of the arid zone as much by the risk of drought as by the normal rainfall deficit.

This chapter includes dry summer lands with some reservations. Reckoned on the basis of annual precipitation and temperature, these climates are subhumid to humid, but the summer drought significantly limits crop growth and development. Agriculture shares some features with that of dry lands and shares others with that of humid temperate regions. The resemblance of field systems in the Mediterranean basin to those of humid temperate Europe is particularly strong, partly because of the historic diffusion of cereals sown in winter and early spring and the associated technology, cattle, sheep, and goats.

One feature of agriculture of the Mediterranean basin that is more distinctive than transitional is the prominence of tree and vine crops, a pattern that has partly spread to similar climates elsewhere. Orchards and vineyards give the landscape of the Mediterranean, not to mention the cuisine, much of its character. Olives are little grown in other climates. Grapes are prominent in some cooler, wetter lands, and figs, pistachio, carob, and pomegranate play a role in the humid subtropics, but all these crops attain their greatest importance around the Mediterranean and originated either in the basin or in Central Asia. Wild and domesticated chestnuts were until recently the main staple, *le pain d'arbre*, in parts of Corsica and southern France (Weber, 1976:129). Also prominent are stone fruits, nuts, and citrus fruits, all shared with other climates.

SOILS. Although soils of dry lands vary, some generalizations may be made about the effects of increasing aridity:

1. Leaching decreases. Soluble salts and alkalinity increase. Available mineral nutrient levels tend to be high, but so do those of sodium, often to the point of toxicity. Calcium and magnesium carbonates accumulate in subsurface horizons.

2. Equilibrium levels of humus decline. Limited plant growth reduces the accumulation of organic matter.

3. Bare soil is susceptible to erosion. The drier the climate, the barer the surface and the more that wind and water create physically inhospitable surfaces. Water carves the steep-sided rills, gullies, and canyons that give the landscape its look. Wind moves most readily the soil particles of intermediate size, that is, fine sand (0.1 mm); gravel is too large to blow easily, clay too cohesive. It thus leaves behind gravelly and bouldery lands (desert pavement) and builds shifting sand dunes. Agriculture, pastoralism, and the gathering of fuel wood speed the process by removing vegetation that had helped anchor the soil.

Extensive fertile soils are found in the temperate zone astride the boundary between semiarid and subhumid climates, in the eastern Great Plains of North America and the black soil belt of the Ukraine. These climates are dry enough that leaching is minimal but wet enough to support a good cover of grass. Cold winters bring on an annual addition of dead plant tissue in the root zone.

Groundwater moving to the surface evaporates and leaves behind accumulations of sodium, sometimes to the point that salts form surface crusts. Halophytic vegetation also transports sodium upward (Kovda, 1980:67). Salinity or alkalinity can be toxic to crops in poorly drained depressions even in the moister parts of the semiarid zone. A much larger proportion of arid lands is affected, including many hill and footslope soils.

Soil nitrogen falls with decreasing moisture and organic matter. Responses to added fertilizer nitrogen are thus more common in dry farming than responses to phosphorus or other mineral nutrients, though application rates are low because water limits crop growth. Animal manures have long been found useful for their nitrogen content and their favorable effect on soil physical properties, but high application rates are uncommon.

Irrigated land in arid regions is potentially exceptionally productive. More sunlight reaches the ground than in any other climate, and the growing season of the subtropical deserts is long. Appropriate management raises humus, nitrogen, and available phosphorus, and the reserves of other nutrients are often excellent or are replenished by incoming irrigation water. Most preindustrial cultivators use animal manures if available. Very high rates of nitrogen fertilization are common under industrial management, and rates of fertilization with mineral nutrients are high where bumper crops deplete reserves.

Only a small proportion of arid land is cultivable—about 20%, according to *The World Food Problem* (President's Science Advisory Committee, 1967)—but water, not land, is at present the limiting resource. Unless seawater can be economically desalted or used directly on crops (chapter 12), there will continue to be more cultivable land than there is water available to irrigate it.

NATURAL VEGETATION. So fragile is the vegetation of dry lands and dry summer lands that nearly all the present cover is anthropogenic. Trees were once scattered through all but the most arid areas but are now typically scarce. Cultivation and grazing take a toll, but the most ubiquitous damage results from the gathering of fuel wood. Overgrazing and cycles of cultivation destroy grass. Owing to these and other factors, the Mediterranean woodlands have given way to maquis scrub, steppe grasslands have replaced more-mixed communities, and arid lands are now deserts in every sense. Radical thinning of ground cover is documented in many regions, such as the American Southwest (Cloudsley-Thompson, 1970), North Africa, and the Arabian Desert (Kassas, 1970).

Seeming barrenness may thus be misleading. Dry farming presents the eye with patches of green dense growth surrounded by browner and thinner cover, but the contrast is as much a testimony to human destructiveness as it is to agricultural skill.

These lands are surprisingly bounteous in the wild foods they furnish. Wild food resources decline with increasing aridity—the population density of aboriginal Australian food collectors is negatively correlated with mean annual precipitation (Birdsell, 1953)—but the amount of available human nourishment is high in relation to biomass. Many ethnographic accounts belie the notion that food collectors in dry lands battle endlessly for survival (e.g., Fourie, 1966; Gould, 1969; Lee, 1968; Tindale, 1959; Woodburn, 1968). Dry summer lands, such as late precolonial California and the eastern Mediterranean basin during the first part of the Holocene, supported some of the densest known populations of food collectors. A large part of the annual food supply often came from a seasonal harvest of seeds: acorns in California (Gifford, 1967) and wild cereals around the Mediterranean.

Floodwater Farming

The term *floodwater farming* describes systems that utilize either water from seasonal floods or runoff from occasional rains (Bryan, 1929). Though irrigation farming often takes advantage of peak flows, in practice the difference is usually clear between irrigation systems and floodwater systems, which exploit only high water or runoff intercepted before it reaches permanent streams.

Floodwater farming systems are often technically simple in that little is done to direct or control water, but that does not necessarily make them primitive forms of irrigation. Irrigation takes some simple forms, and floodwater farming takes some fairly complex ones. Floodwater farming may be earlier than irrigation proper in some parts of the world, but its continuation is often soundly based on its advantages, and it has modern proponents.

DECRUE FARMING. The fundamentally simple technique of planting just above receding floodwaters diverges under varying local conditions: season of floods, their regularity, their rate of recession, and the slope of the floodplain. The growing crops extend their roots toward the falling water table and its overlying horizon of moist soil. Ideally, water recedes enough to furnish an adequate volume of aerated soil but slowly enough to supply moisture for the whole growing season. Early annuals are favored, because the root zone usually dries too fast for later sorts. Perennials are sometimes cultivated along the normal margins of the flood, not a true decrue technique.

Along the lower Colorado River, the Yuma (Castetter and Bell, 1951), Mojave, Cocopa, and Kamia (Gifford, 1931) planted summer crops following spring floods fed by Rocky Mountain snowmelt. The early onset of very hot, dry weather dictated the preeminence of tepary bean (*Phaseolus acutifolius*), an early heat-tolerant crop, and maize varieties selected for the same qualities. Cultivation of pumpkin and (postcolonial) watermelon may indicate that some soils stayed moist longer. Suitable locations were small and few, population densities low, and wild foods important. Little attempt was made to direct or control the flood, except that the Kamia sometimes dammed a small slough to encourage infiltration (Gifford, 1931:22). Floods were not completely dependable; Castetter and Bell (1951:7) list five years from 1775 to 1870 in which the flood failed and famine resulted. In this century, dams and irrigation networks have greatly curtailed the area on which the system can operate.

Decrue farming was the principal support of a dense precolonial population on the coastal plain of Mexico's Sinaloa and southern Sonora provinces (Armillas, 1961:264; Driver and Massey, 1957:225; Dunbier, 1968:219–230). The main crop followed summer rains in the nearby mountains. Less certain winter rains fed a second crop. The valleys are short, and floods tend to rise and fall rapidly and in intermittent surges, raising the risk of both inundation and drought. Short canals and temporary dams and weirs helped to control the floods. The methods persist today but are being displaced by irrigation schemes that incorporate water storage.

Some decrue farming was found near the southern limits of precolonial agriculture in South America along the Dulce and Salado rivers of Santiago del Estero, Argentina. The Andean grain quinoa (*Chenopodium quinoa*), not a cereal, was grown alongside the familiar New World trio of maize, beans, and pumpkin (Armillas, 1961:273).

In West Africa, advantage is taken of several rivers that carry rainy-season floods northward from the humid zone. Examples are found along the Senegal (Butzer, 1976:19) and Chari-Logone rivers (Erhart, Pias, and Leneuf, 1954). The crops are mainly drought-resistant millets and sorghum. Decrue farming along the Niger coexists with African rice (*Oryza glaberrima*) cultivated as the floods rise (Harlan, de Wet, and Stemler, 1976; McIntosh and McIntosh, 1980). The delta has a very low slope, and waters rise and fall slowly. No deliberate diversion or control is reported.

Decrue farming was the leading agricultural system of the arid sections of the Indus valley in the centuries prior to the start of canal irrigation, in 1859 (Bharadwaj, 1961:159). Its role during the florescence of Harappan culture from 2500 B.C. to 1700 B.C. is uncertain.

The winter rainfall regime of the Mediterranean basin and Southwest Asia limits the usefulness of decrue methods for the cultivation of the small grains traditionally planted in autumn or early spring. High water arrives in late winter or spring, and decrue crops would in most locations have to mature under hot conditions. The New World's maize or African millets and sorghum would be more suitable. Rivers rise and fall rapidly and in surges, because most of their courses are short. Consequently, most decrue farming of barley and spring wheat is found around the margins of lakes and swamps. Historic decrue cultivators of the lower Mesopotamian plain exploited depressions, not the Tigris and Euphrates rivers, which peak in April and May, respectively (Adams, 1981:4).

THE BASIN SYSTEM OF THE NILE. Decrue farming in the forms to which the term is normally applied involves either fairly simple works for water diversion or control, or none at all.

The basin system of the Nile (Butzer, 1976; Hamdan, 1961; O'Connor, 1972) is based on the same principle of postflood cultivation, but engineering works extend the inundated area. Basins furnished Egypt with most of its food from 3000 B.C. until recently. Their displacement by canal networks and true irrigation began in the nineteenth century and is nearly complete with the construction and filling of the Aswan High Dam.

Eons of alluvial deposition raised broad natural levees along the Nile, which now flows between them much like a stream channeled down the middle of a cambered road. Only the greatest floods reached the highest lands near the river. The Nile flood is a great annual event. Left to itself the river would repeatedly break through its retaining levees and flood the plains.

Basins eventually took up most of the lower-lying parts of the valley and much of the delta. They ran in lines diagonally away from the river, toward the northwest on the left bank where the valley was widest, and then due north parallel to the river. Basins were filled to a depth of 1.25 to 1.5 m, left for 40 to 60 days, and drained (Hamdan, 1961:122). The area of the individual basins ranged from 400 to 16,000 ha (Hamdan, 1961:121).

Planting followed drainage, in autumn because the floods originate in tropical rains of the northern summer. The main food crops were wheat, barley, lentils, and garbanzos, but flax was also important, an indication of adequate soil moisture reserves. Second crops required irrigation, however.

RUNOFF FARMING. Runoff varies with ground cover and rainfall intensity. Rainfall quickly infiltrates sandy and gravelly soils, but more runs off from clay, loess, and large rock surfaces, especially if it falls rapidly. Rainfall intensity tends to be greatest where the rainfall maximum occurs in summer, particularly where tropical depressions visit, but that has not prevented development of runoff farming in the arid southern margins of the Mediterranean winter rainfall zone.

The need for favorable topography further reduces the number and extent of suitable sites, but less so the more that cultivators are willing and able to divert and spread runoff. Choice locations are where runoff spreads across alluvial fans, but the general tendency in dry lands toward rill and gully erosion greatly restricts made-to-order locations. A little diversion is therefore the rule.

Runoff farming is most prominent in the Great Basin and the Sonoran Desert of North America (henceforth referred to as the Greater Sonoran Region) and in a belt across North Africa and into the northern

Arabian peninsula. Important runoff farming is also reported in Baluchistan (Leshnik, 1973:67; Raikes, 1964;). Examples are found in both arid and semiarid locations. The technique is ancient in both hemispheres, its extent less today than formerly, lending importance to archaeological and historical investigations.

A detailed analysis complete with trials of a reconstructed system grew out of archaeological work in Israel's Negev Desert (Evenari, Shanan, and Tadmor, 1971; Evenari et al., 1961). One goal of the project is to ascertain the potential of the system in an agroindustrial and commercial context.

Soviet scientists have also experimented with runoff farming and put sizable areas into production in Central Asia. Activity was at its height during the late 1930s and the Virgin Lands program of the 1950s (Kovda, 1961).

Within the semiarid zone, runoff that collects at the base of slopes, where groundwater may also be a factor, is often sufficient to support productive cultivation. Even the natural cover vegetation is denser within this belt. Though typically only a narrow strip benefits, Spanish settlers in the Greater Sonoran Region nonetheless took advantage, concentrating on locations below shale slopes (Bryan, 1929). Under the more arid conditions of the Negev, hillside runoff was further concentrated by channeling it into stone and earth conduits slanting down the slopes to farms in gullies below.

The Anasazi, people of a precolonial culture of the southwestern United States, made some use of hillside terraces, usually formed by letting soil collect behind shallow check dams. The dams also collected runoff. The best-known examples are at Mesa Verde, Colorado. The mean annual precipitation is 461 mm at the reporting station (Erdman, Douglas, and Marr, 1969:18–19) but varies with elevation and topography. Most sites are at elevations of about 2,100–2,200 m, where summer temperatures are warm but not hot and the moisture regime is semiarid; dry farming is presently successful on the nearby plains. Under this regime the ratio of catchment area to cropland need not be great. Three-quarters of the terraces have a northeast exposure, where snow lies longer in the spring (Erdman, Douglas, and Marr, 1969:57), possibly helping to close the gap between snowmelt and the onset of summer rains in July.

A structurally similar system, known as liman irrigation, has been in use in the trans-Volga steppes since the late nineteenth century and is "effective and cheap" (Kovda, 1961:194–195). Slopes are longer and gentler than those the Anasazi exploited, and earth ramparts 2.0 to 2.5 m high retain runoff.

The most frequently encountered method of runoff farming exploits natural watersheds. Favorite sites are alluvial fans at gully (wadi) mouths on the Mauritanian plateaus (Monod and Toupet, 1961:245) and gully floors in North Africa and the Negev. The floors offer little flat land, but if the slope is not too great, sediments accumulate behind dams built across them, resulting in a steplike series of terraces over which floodwaters move. Terraces are also found in some arroyos of the Greater Sonoran Region, notably at Mesa Verde and other Anasazi sites. Between 1909 and 1915 as much as 8,000 ha of gully floors was exploited on the Navajo reservation, often by building dams to spread the waters (Bryan, 1929). Most arroyos of the Greater Sonoran Region are etched into steep rocky slopes, and the fans at their mouths are the most common locations for farming. Probably the greatest present reliance on such fields is by the Papago of southern Arizona (Castetter and Bell, 1942; Hackenberg, 1974).

Valley bottoms and alluvial fans are inherently unstable sites for cultivation, because of the combined effects of siltation and erosion. Downcutting by uncontrolled floods may leave fields high and dry, a risk that increases the more that silt raises field surfaces. Soil lost from abandoned fields may be deposited a short distance downslope. Fields thus tend to shift. It is possible to add a little stability by building and maintaining retaining walls but not always for long; in the Negev, where ancient engineers made heroic efforts at conservation, several stages of use are often traceable in shifts of retaining walls and terraces.

Starting a runoff farm may be easy or may demand a considerable effort. Locations present different topography and degrees of aridity. Fields in the arid Negev require larger catchment areas than do fields of the same size at Mesa Verde, and many of the particular diversion methods used in the Negev would have been of little use on the high relief of the mesa. The Negev investigators attribute to population growth a gradual trend from exploitation of the most easily developed sites toward wider and more ambitious undertakings. Heaps of stones are one form of evidence. They grew as catchment slopes were cleared to increase runoff.

The precipitation patterns and the staple crops associated with runoff farming differ significantly between the two hemispheres. Winter rainfall in the Old World supports a typical Mediterranean mix of winter cereals and deeply rooted tree crops. Summer crops were tried in the Negev but failed. The Greater Sonoran Region has a double rainfall peak, winter and late summer, that allows the cultivation of summer crops, that is, maize, beans, and squash. Winter cereals are a successful postcolonial introduction. The summer rainfall peak is the greater in all past and present areas of indigenous agriculture except in the north near the Great Salt Lake, but useful soil moisture is everywhere normally at its height at the beginning of the growing season, because of lower evaporation over the winter months. The challenge in all rain-fed agricultural systems of the region is to see crops through to the often uncertain arrival of summer rains and then to gain and conserve as much moisture as possible.

MICROCATCHMENTS. Experiments in the Negev (Evenari, Shanan, and Tadmor, 1971) demonstrate that the efficiency of runoff capture improves the smaller the catchment. Over a seven-year period, ·mean runoff ranged from 5.0% to 12.2% of rainfall from watersheds of 10 to 7 ha and was 2.8% from one of 345 ha (p. 145).

The experimenters predicted that microcatchments might be yet more efficient and were certainly worth a trial, an inference that proved correct. Microcatchments of 80 m² with partial stone cover captured a mean runoff of 21.2% over a six-year period. On cleared 20 m² microcatchments the mean was 35.0%.

Microcatchment agriculture is not altogether new. Some preindustrial examples with designs similar to those of the Negev trials are reported from Tunisia (Evenari, 1975). Zuni pueblos in New Mexico make "waffle" patterns of sloped walls and planting floors (Spencer and Jennings, 1965:306). The ratio of catchment to cropping surface is low, but rainfall is higher than in the Negev, and pot irrigation sometimes supplements runoff.

DEPRESSION FARMING. Natural depressions often function as catchments in semiarid and dry summer climates. Small depressions are widely exploited and are popular for vines in many drier parts of the Mediterranean basin. Large depressions are often planted in cereals in the "dry steppes" of the Soviet Union, where Kovda (1961:194) estimates suitable ones cover 3% to 5% of the total area. Their size varies from 0.25 to 12 ha. Runoff of 300 to 500 mm supplements the annual precipitation of 250 to 300 mm.

THE PROS AND CONS OF FLOODWATER FARMING. Floodwater farming often uses the only available cultivable land, provided courtesy of the floods themselves. Floodplains used for decrue farming or the Nile basin system are all too often strips of alluvium amid vast tracts of desert pavement, alkaline soils, or other uninviting surfaces. Runoff farmers harness alluviation to build terraces, though maintaining them may be a struggle.

The annual addition of alluvium also contributes nutrients, a benefit that is often exaggerated. The Colorado is probably an especially favorable case, because its suspended matter is high, averaging 0.6% by volume (Castetter and Bell, 1951:12–15). If it flooded to the same depth as the Egyptian basins and half the solids were left behind, the Colorado would deposit 4 mm of solid matter, containing a significant but modest 12 kg of nitrogen per hectare (Castetter and Bell, 1951:12–15). The Nile basins gained about 1 mm of new soil each year (Hamdan, 1961:122). In general the sustained yield capacity of decrue fields and basins owes less to each year's flood than to the inherent fertility in deep layers built up over millennia.

Decrue and basin systems are apparently labor-efficient, their productivity generally good. The labor invested in water diversion and other capital works is slight or nil in some fortunately located runoff systems and is probably less in the basin systems than in the more ambitious irrigation works. Field operations are remarkably undemanding. The cycle of drying and inundation controls many weeds. Tillage is light or nonexistent. The Negev runoff trials gave excellent yields.

Most improvements increase the cultivated area. Along the Nile, where natural flooding would permit decrue farming on about two-thirds of the floodplain (Butzer, 1976:20), the basin system covered nearly all of it.

Because water, not land, most often limits food production from dry lands, floodwater farming and irrigation agriculture should be compared for their efficiency of water use. Decrue farming is disappearing in the face of demands for higher productivity, because most of the flood runs to the sea unused. Basins do a little better but have also given way to irrigation. Runoff watersheds, because they are small, collect water more efficiently than most irrigation watersheds and often intercept water before it is lost in a desert with neither surface drainage nor usable groundwater. Therefore, microcatchments can boost the productivity of dry lands (Evenari, Shanan, and Tadmor, 1971; Rosenberg, 1981), but runoff is sporadic and often not well matched to plant requirements. Water reaches the fields much as in flood irrigation, among the least efficient ways of directing water to the crop plants. Water storage could conceivably be adapted to microcatchments and combined with the most efficient means of applying water—whether such an arrangement would be called floodwater farming or irrigation is an academic question—but to do so economically is a challenge.

Seepage Areas, High Groundwater
Areas, and Sunken Gardens

In the miscellaneous groundwater systems to be discussed here, groundwater reaches crops without recourse to wells and irrigation. It is at the surface in seepage areas, and in other places it is near enough to be accessible to crop roots. If the water is a bit too deep, sunken gardens are excavated to lower the planting surface.

Sites where the water table lies near the surface are far more common and extensive than seepage areas. Ideally, upward capillary movement of water maintains a sufficiently deep layer of moist but aerated soil to support crops from planting to maturation. If not, mounds or ridges are built on ground that is too wet, planting holes are built on ground that is too dry, or young plants are watered from pots until their roots reach moist horizons.

Salinization often threatens continued cultivation. The nearer the water table is to the surface, the greater the risk. The problem is less if the salt content of the groundwater is low or precipitation periodically percolates downward, leaching salts. Adequate drainage favors downward movement and leaching.

The date palm (*Phoenix dactylifera*) is ideal for these situations. It benefits from dry weather, most of all when the fruit is ripening, but ironically the water requirement of this quintessential desert plant is high. It tolerates high salinity. Groundwater is sufficient to support growth at many oases of the North African and Southwest Asian deserts, though irrigated palms are often found nearby.

A few small sunken gardens are in use in Peru's coastal desert, survivors of a greater precolonial expanse. Remains of more than 10 km² have been described at Chilca, Chan Chan, and the Virú valley (Parsons, 1968). Knapp (1982) challenges the sunken-garden interpretation of Chilca in favor of an explanation that the works represent an elaborate system of floodwater farming. Smith (1985) concurs that the layout suggests flood capture but adds that floods are so rare their water was but an "occasional bonus" (p. 612), with groundwater being the main resource. In some locations, irrigation from wells may have supplemented groundwater, though it is not known whether the wells were present from the beginning or were added later (Smith, 1985).

Old World sunken gardens are reported in the Sinai Peninsula and southern Algeria (Hamdan, 1961:138). The date palm is the main crop, possibly alleviating the effects of salinization. In Peru, salt crusts are manually removed (Rowe, 1969), and figs and vines are preferred crops today.

Soviet agriculturalists in the 1930s developed related systems for mechanized farming (Kovda, 1961). Where built over a freshwater table, widely spaced trenches are excavated 1.5 to 3 m wide and 1.2 to 1.5 m deep. Another system exploits water that would be difficult to pump, a freshwater lens 2 to 3 cm deep atop a saltwater table 1 to 1.5 m below the surface. Locations lie mostly in a narrow strip along the eastern shore of the Caspian Sea. Fields are made up of alternating ridges and trenches of approximately equal width.

Sand dunes, so often a threat to cultivated land and pasture, are also efficient collectors of precipitation. Rainfall or snowmelt readily infiltrates, and the dune protects collected water at its base from evaporation. If dunes are stable, the hollows between them may be planted in date palms, a strategy most often found around the margins of the Sahara and near the Mediterranean coasts of Egypt and Libya. Springs and seepage areas near the base are also exploited, sometimes with diversion of water for irrigation (Hamdan, 1961:138). Holes for planting are dug into dunes in Turkmenistan (Kovda, 1961:195).

Irrigation Agriculture

The term *irrigation* here refers to the transportation of water to cropland by artificial means. Preindustrial and industrial forms of irrigation agriculture share many common solutions to common problems, but the differences should not be ignored. Industrial technology opens up new water resources, enhances storage capacity, and makes long-distance delivery more common. Modern science adds new and more efficient methods of applying water to crops.

SURFACE WATER RESOURCES. Surface water obviously decreases the more arid the climate. The major rivers that flow through dry lands begin either in distant, wetter lands or in mountains that intercept more moisture. Most lose volume during their traverse even if they are not diverted for irrigation and other uses. All dry summer lands except southwestern Australia also benefit from flows originating in wetter highlands.

The rivers' variable flows make their full exploitation difficult without adequate storage. The few streams that arise in semiarid lands or in small isolated mountain ranges have flows that vary markedly over short periods. Many streams are temporary. The major rivers display great seasonal variation. Those that flow from the tropics, like the Nile and the Niger, are at their peak in that hemisphere's summer. So is the Indus, because of the wet monsoon of the Himalayas. Winter or early spring maxima are typical of most rivers in subtropical dry lands, such as the Orange, Tigris-Euphrates, and Murray-Darling. Those flowing from high mountains or higher latitudes where snowmelt is the major source, like the Hwang-Ho, Volga, Dnieper, Amu Darya, Sir Darya, Colorado, Columbia, and Missouri, peak in late spring or early summer. Precipitation and the volume of peak flows vary markedly from year to year.

Few natural lakes in dry lands store large volumes of fresh water. Natural lakes are uncommon along the major rivers, and underground aquifers feeding the rivers are often the main buffer between high and low flows. In internal drainage basins all large bodies of water are more or less saline: the Caspian Sea, the Aral Sea, the Dead Sea, the Great Salt Lake, Lake Chad, and Lake Eyre.

Preindustrial engineers could only slightly smooth the variation of river flow. They built impressive distribution systems, including the Roman aqueducts and Incan canals that clung to the mighty Andes, but though many peoples built dams, the scale was very small by twentieth-century standards, and diversion was more the function than was storage.

Reasons are many to build storage capacity into a modern irrigation supply system, not all of them having to do with agriculture. Without storage, rivers whose flows are sporadic are of little use for irrigation. Reservoirs on the major rivers today serve both to store seasonal peaks and to even out downstream flows from year to year. Ample capacity sometimes permits crops to be taken in years in which there would otherwise be too little flow for irrigation. Storage from one season to another is useful to avoid wasting a peak flow that the distribution system could not handle, to allow cultivation of crops whose ideal temperature requirements do not coincide with high water, and to permit multicropping.

Storage usually entails dams and reservoirs in either the wetter headwaters or the drier lower courses. Dams and reservoirs are lately becoming controversial as their environmental impact becomes more evident. They also lose water. Evaporation from the surface is large in hot, dry conditions, and reservoirs lose water into underground aquifers, from which it may or may not be retrievable. Reservoirs on the Colorado River lose about 10% of the earlier, unimpeded flow (van Hylckama, 1971:140). Some research looks at films that reduce surface evaporation. Another approach already in use to a limited extent is to pump surface water into underground aquifers from which it may be withdrawn at nearby or more distant locations.

Diversions of water from one drainage basin to another are now common, often from a wetter side of a mountain range to a drier one, as in Australia's Snowy Mountains scheme. Soviet authorities have plans to divert water from rivers of the Arctic drainage southward into the Volga, an intensively exploited river that empties into the slowly subsiding Caspian Sea.

GROUNDWATER RESOURCES. Aquifers gain water through recharging and lose it through discharging. Sources of natural recharge are rainfall and snowmelt percolating from the surface, surface water, and higher aquifers, and in dry lands as a whole, aquifers receive more water than runs to the sea or inland lakes. Discharging occurs naturally into surface springs, rivers and lakes, and lower aquifers and to the atmosphere by upward capillary movement and evapotranspiration at the surface.

The only renewable discharge is that which is sooner or later matched by recharging, and most aquifers, if exploited at all, are being depleted. The Ogallala Aquifer is the main source of irrigation water in eight states of the North American Great Plains. Its water table is dropping an average of 3 m/yr over parts of Texas and very slowly in neighboring areas of New Mexico (van Hylckama, 1971:142–143), reflecting rates of depletion that vary with states' policies on water rights (Bittinger and Green, 1980). A problem in some places, particularly artesian basins (Kovda, 1980:193), is the increasing infiltration of saline water.

"Artificial" recharge—more precisely, measures undertaken to increase or augment natural recharge—takes the forms of injection of water into wells and construction of ponds and reservoirs to increase infiltration. The water ordinarily used is surface water, often excess flow that would otherwise go to the sea. Aquifers offer several advantages over surface reservoirs for storage: permanence, freedom from evaporation and sedimentation, lack of flood threat, high capacities, and their extent, which in part takes care of water distribution to consumers. On the negative side, though they are not especially prone to contamination, decontamination when needed is difficult (USDA, 1987:7–26).

Groundwater resources in dry lands are generally large in relation to surface water resources, making the volume of groundwater both tempting and deceptive. One indisputably nonrenewable resource is fossil aquifers of arid lands whose water derives from past periods when the climate was more humid. Their exploitation is important in some parts of the Sahara, though more to supply petroleum operations than for agriculture.

The greatest technical obstacle that preindustrial peoples face in their exploitation of groundwater is their limited ability to lift it. For most a bucket or water bag is the only means available, with only a rope to extend their reach. Some ancient improvements include the Egyptian shaduf, a bucket on a swing arm, reverse waterwheels driven by animal or human power, the Archimedean screw, and some endless-belt designs. The volume is small, and water can be lifted a few meters at best. The suction pump, a late design, relies on atmospheric pressure and, though the volume may be large, lifts water a maximum of 8 m. A bucket on a windlass can draw water from greater depths but requires a wide well, and the volume is slight.

Groundwater may be tapped at greater depths and in large volumes if it lies under a slope, by excavating a horizontal shaft into permeable, water-bearing strata. A chain of vertical shafts connects with the conduit, and through these, excavated material is removed and air reaches the workers (Fig. 6.1). In Iran these *qanats* have been known since the early first millennium B.C. and today supply about 75% of all delivered water (Wulff, 1968). Alluvial fans are a favored site. The system is also found across the breadth of North Africa, where it is known by the Arabic word *foggara,* and eastward to western China. Similar relict systems of possible precolonial origin are reported in Peru's coastal desert (English, 1968; Kobori, 1964).

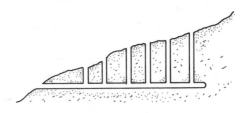

6.1. A *qanat* (foggara).

Industrial technology and artificial power make possible the exploitation of previously inaccessible water and the pumping of large volumes in many places where supplies had been scant. Wells can now be drilled to once-unimagined depths and through hard rock. Artesian wells are often common in the early stages of exploitation of an aquifer but tend after a time to need pumping, a sign of depletion. Force pumps with efficient mobile engines are a twentieth-century development that makes possible pumping from great depths. A depth of 1,000 m is now considered the economic limit for water exploitation (van Hylckama, 1971:140). About half of all groundwater resources lie deeper (p. 139), but deep aquifers have a low turnover and low sustained yield capacity. A great advantage of groundwater is its steady supply. Many shallow wells dry up seasonally, but that rarely curtails the length of cultivation. Serious crop failures and losses of livestock sometimes occur during a series of drought years, however. Droughts do not affect deep aquifers containing a large volume of water, because of their low rate of water turnover. Industrial technology in the form of tube wells and force pumps thus brings dependable water to places where old sources failed in droughts. The supply is dependable while the aquifer lasts.

WATER DISTRIBUTION AND APPLICATION. Modern methods of distributing and applying water differ from those of the past few thousand years mainly where conservation is a concern. True, all sorts of systems are now built with the help of earth-moving machinery, aluminum pipe, and concrete, but the basic elements of most systems are still dikes, weirs, ditches, gates, basins, and furrows. Agricultural science and industrial technology do afford new ways to conserve water in both distribution and end use. Irrigation ditches are sealed against percolation losses, using concrete, plastic films, and other materials. Closed pipes move water under pressure or in long siphon systems. Although Roman engineers understood water losses and the use of partially or wholly closed conduits, many modern systems are far beyond any ancient capabilities. At the delivery end, overhead sprinkler irrigation is virtually a new idea, and drip irrigation entirely so.

Flood and furrow irrigation methods long accounted for nearly all irrigated land and still occupy most. The least-managed variant, wild flooding, often uses irregular water supplies; the name describes it. Basin irrigation, in which water is impounded within dikes, and floating methods, in which a thin sheet of water flows over a carefully prepared field, more often exploit regular supplies. Furrow irrigation has long been the leading method of application and is adaptable to many situations. Both flood and furrow methods have been adapted to steep slopes; ancient peoples of the Yemen highlands and parts of the Andes built furrows on the contour and flooded terraces high on the mountainsides.

Today low-cost pipe with openings for water is sometimes laid underground in fields. The cost is more than for sprinkler systems, and upward movement can aggravate salinization problems. Sprinkler and drip irrigation systems are therefore receiving more attention.

Mass-produced pipe makes sprinkler irrigation practical on a large scale, though the principle has long been recognized and used in some special situations such as greenhouse cultivation. Use on a field scale in the United States began about 1900 and grew rapidly after the introduction of aluminum pipe about 1945 (Quackenbush and Shockley, 1955). Both sprinkler heads and perforated pipe are used to eject water, but farmers formerly had to use a lot of pipe or frequently shift pipe and sprinkler heads. That changed with center pivot systems, invented about 1942, patented in 1952, and thereafter widely adopted in the American Great Plains (Splinter, 1976). As the sprinkler pivots, the irrigated area assumes the shape of a circle, giving the fields a characteristic appearance from the air.

Drip, or trickle, irrigation (Shoji, 1977) was developed by S. Blass and associates in the late 1930s in Israel, where adoption was rapid after World War II. It then spread worldwide, reaching the United States after 1960. Water flows drop by drop from specially designed emitters onto individual plants or from perforated pipe or flexible hose onto rows. Distribution is carefully metered and adjusted for soil and crop requirements. Adequate moisture is maintained around the root zone, while soil beyond the root zone remains relatively dry.

The efficiency of an irrigation method is usually expressed in the percentage of water delivered to the field that is taken up and used by the crop. Shoji (1977:67) lists efficiencies of about 50% for furrow irrigation, 70% to 80% for sprinklers, and 80% to 95% for drip irrigation (Shoji, 1977:67). USDA (1987:7–15) estimates are 60% to 80% for flood irrigation, 75% to 80% for furrow, 65% to 82% for sprinklers (the high figure is for center-pivot systems), and 85% to 90% for drip. The high USDA estimates for flood and furrow methods are for those in which modern methods of field preparation are in place. These include careful leveling or grading prior to flood irrigation, now sometimes with the aid of laser beams to find the level, and the use of graded furrows or corrugations for furrow systems.

Both sprinkler and drip systems make frequent light irrigations feasible, which in turn make it easy to keep soil moisture levels within the optimum range of 80% to 100% of field capacity. Overhead sprinklers lose water in strong winds, however. Drip irrigation is an excellent example of the principle that information substitutes for matter-energy within a system. It reduces waste because just the amount of water the plants need is delivered to the right place at the right time.

Not all water that goes unused by the crop is lost. Some is lost through evaporation, spray drift, and other ways, but most runs off into surface waters or infiltrates lower soil horizons and enters aquifers or surface waters downstream. That water may be reused unless its salt content is too high. That which is irrecoverable amounts to about 13% of the water diverted for irrigation in the United States (USDA, 1987:7–17).

Dry Farming

The term *dry farming* has two related but distinct meanings. The one that will be used here refers to cropping systems that rely on precipitation in dry lands or during dry seasons. The other refers to the methods that make these systems practicable, what will here be referred to as *dry farming methods*. The two meanings are not synonymous, because dry farming methods prove useful in many situations in which other sources of soil moisture supplement precipitation. Groundwater often contributes to crop production in what appear to be "pure" dry farming systems. Moisture conservation techniques are essential to the success of much decrue farming. The use of dry farming methods is exceptional on irrigated fields, but known.

METHODS. Most moisture conservation techniques reduce either evaporation or transpiration. Others capture drifting snow or so improve infiltration that less precipitation runs off.

Transpiration is lessened mainly by reducing the number of plants. Planting densities of trees, vines, and annual crops decrease with growing aridity. Thus Tunisian cultivators sow 100 kg of barley per hectare in the mediterranean climate of the north but only 25 kg to the south near the margins of dry farming (Despois, 1961:221). Agricultural experiment stations recommend sowing rates and spacings based on climate and soil type. Weeds also transpire, and their control is crucial to successful dry farming.

The use of plowed fallows confines transpiration to the time that a field is in crops. The fallow year builds up a reserve of soil moisture that benefits the next year's crop. In the North American Great Plains and the Soviet steppes, wheat yields from fields that follow a fallow are often 1.5 to 2.0 times those from fields that follow another year of wheat (Brady, 1974:216; Kovda, 1980:118–119). The gain is usually greatest in dry years and on marginally arid lands and is often the difference between a crop that is worth the effort and expense and one that is not. Fallows are kept free of weeds. Plowed fallows are also common in Canada, Australia, and drier parts of the Mediterranean littoral. In the latter the practice is ancient; fallows kept bare by two or three plowings were the norm in the drier parts of Roman Italy (White, 1970).

Evaporation is attacked at the ground surface. Plastic films come close to eliminating it, though costs are prohibitive for most crops. Pre-industrial cultivators often cover part of the ground with stones. Sand, volcanic ash, and pumice are sometimes used on small areas. Pumice and ash are lighter and easier to transport; their application to vineyards and fields on the island of Lanzarote, Canary Islands, is best known. Organic mulches, though pervious, can be effective. A thin layer conserves a little moisture, a deep layer more. Organic mulch materials are hard to get in quantity in dry lands, so deep mulches are rare. More common are trash mulches, that is, those made up of crop and weed residues. Their use is old and is being revived, also because of interest in saving energy and controlling erosion. A new technique is to kill turf with herbicides. The crop is planted through the dead sod.

Deep planting conserves moisture by lowering the root zone below the surface horizon, a partial barrier to evaporative losses. The approach is most effective in at least moderately coarse-textured soils, in which water infiltrates rapidly, upward capillary movement is slight, and crops can emerge more easily from some depth. The Hopi and Zuni of the American Southwest have developed maize that can emerge from a depth of 30 cm (Carter, 1945:100–102), three times the maximum depth for most varieties.

Deep tillage is advocated to improve infiltration, but reported results are variable and the method controversial. Mechanization makes it available to most cultivators.

CROPS.   Cereals dominate the crop mix where rainfall is barely enough for dry farming. Legume crops virtually disappear, though some native tree legumes of the warmer regions show promise as fodder crops. Around the Mediterranean the vine and the olive usually disappear, though success has been gained in Tunisia near the limits of dry farming by spacing olive trees widely and implementing a combination of dry farming methods (Despois, 1961:221–222). The ash-mulched vines of Lanzarote are in the arid zone. Among the cereals, those with the C_4 photosynthetic pathway — maize, sugarcane, sorghum, millets, and amaranth — may produce up to 2.5 times as much dry matter from a given amount of water as a cereal with a C_3 pathway (Hodges, 1980:190). Sorghum and millets withstand prolonged drought better than maize does and are preferred in the summer-rainfall, semiarid zone of sub-Saharan Africa. In semiarid, winter-rainfall lands near the margins of mediterranean climates of North Africa, Asia, and Australia, wheat and barley are preferred for their growth in fairly cool weather, though interest in sorghum and millet is increasing. The dual precipitation peak of the Greater Sonoran Region supports in semiarid locations both maize and winter cereals, a postcolonial introduction.

The Evolution of Agriculture in
Dry Lands and Dry Summer Lands

The Boserup model of fallow and permanent cultivation systems (chapter 3) does not work well in dry lands and dry summer lands. Long fallow systems serve little if any function and are indeed rare, judging from Conklin's (1961) bibliography of "shifting cultivation." Short fallow systems abound in dry farming, and a few two- or three-year fallows are encountered, as in the *barbecho* system of Mexico, but in those cases in which the fallow serves to store moisture, it is difficult, and sometimes impossible, to change to annual cropping without irrigating. Rainfall generally limits dry farming to a maximum of one crop per year. Dry farming is thus confined to a narrow range of cropping frequencies. High cropping frequencies are the norm in irrigation agriculture and other systems in which surface water or groundwater supplement rainfall.

FALLOWS AND SOIL FERTILITY. Significant biomass accumulation is unlikely after the first year or two of a fallow. Studies of semiarid grasslands indicate that phytomass is less than twice the annual net primary production. Woody vegetation would accumulate biomass longer but is fragile and hard to reestablish in these regions. The original woody vegetation of dry summer climates accumulates more but tends under burning, heavy grazing, and fuel wood collection to degrade to scrub.

PERMANENT CULTIVATION, SOIL, AND SOIL AMENDMENTS. Soils that readily sustain good yields are most abundant in the more humid parts of the semiarid zone. There fallows are not likely to be needed to conserve moisture. Soils of sufficient quality are also fairly common on alluvial plains of the dry summer lands, though the total area is not great. Soils resting atop a high water table in these regions often have excellent nutrient status, because leaching of nutrients is slight, and abundant growth accumulates organic matter at a high rate.

Animal manure is far more important than green manure in these regions. The integration of animal husbandry with cultivation was an early phenomenon on the Eurasian steppes and is frequently reported in Africa's Sahel. Animal manure is in short supply in the Mediterranean basin in comparison with more-humid sections of Europe but has long been valued. Mixed farming and the use of animal manure spread with European settlement to semiarid parts of North and South America.

A GENERAL MODEL.   This general model is based on the assumption that cultivators would optimize returns on their invested labor. Both labor invested in building or creating the system and that spent cultivating the current crop are taken into account.

The best returns on labor at low population densities, given a preindustrial technology, are from decrue farming or the cultivation of sites watered naturally or with little effort: favorable seepage areas and land adjacent to bodies of water or above a high water table. The best locations provide a good sustained yield capacity. Weeding requirements are very low or nonexistent in decrue farming. Irrigation and runoff farming are nearly as attractive in locations blessed with particularly accessible irrigation water or runoff.

Credible responses to moderate increases in population pressure include dry farming, more-ambitious irrigation and runoff schemes, and an evolution of decrue farming first toward forms with more water control and finally to the basin system. Local conditions might greatly affect a choice among strategies. Farrington (1980), referring to Peru, issues a timely warning against generalizations that impressive irrigation works must demand a great deal of labor. Some do; others do not. Irrigation agriculture must eventually respond to high population pressure along involutionary paths, either highly labor-intensive field operations or the development of water supplies with diminishing returns.

Information is not available on the labor efficiency of sunken gardens, but one wonders how long it would take to repay the effort needed to excavate by hand the large volumes of earth. Hand removal of saline crusts and associated measures to build organic matter appear from the few descriptions to be laborious.

PREHISTORIC SEQUENCES.   One part of the above model can be safely assumed in arid lands, that early cultivators would work small areas at high cropping frequencies. Dry farming would be impossible, and low cropping frequencies would serve little purpose. Decrue farming preceded the basin system in the Nile valley (Butzer, 1976; Hamdan, 1961), and the valleys of the Peruvian coast would have also offered favorable situations for decrue farming. More needs to be learned about subsequent developments, but present evidence indicates in several places the predicted development of systems requiring increased investments of labor for their establishment. That trend was noted above in Negev runoff farming systems and has often been traced or inferred from the remains of irrigation systems.

One reconstruction of early agriculture in Southwest Asia and the eastern Mediterranean (Levy, 1983; Sherratt, 1980) fits the model. The earliest cultivation is found near lakes, rivers, and springs, where decrue farming or systems dependent on groundwater or simple irrigation would be practicable. It is also argued that the cultivars of wheat and barley were early varieties adapted to spring sowing, useful traits where floods recede rapidly in the spring. Sherratt believes that runoff and irrigation farming followed, but that complex canal irrigation systems and dry farming were later. Dry farming, dated by the use of plows, began in the late fourth and early third millennia B.C., but it should be noted again that rude implements can break sod.

Conversely, Smith and Young (1972) assume that most early systems included fallows of medium duration occupied by scrub vegetation, on the grounds that stone hoes are known from some early sites. Their association of hoes with bush fallows is an application of the Boserup model, probably one that is too literal. Bush fallows would be hard to sustain where woody vegetation is so fragile.

At Tehuacán, in the Mexican highlands, the picture is clouded by the small contribution of early agriculture to the food supply. This period falls into the Coxcatlán phase, ca. 5200–3400 B.C. (MacNeish, 1964). Many occupation sites were located to benefit from groundwater or runoff, but others were not. Woodbury and Neely (1972:150) argue that the crop mix—that is, squash, avocado, chilis, some maize, and possibly amaranth and cotton—would have needed additional moisture to supplement rainfall, though maize is dry-farmed in the area today (Mangelsdorf, 1974:166). In the next phase, settlements were more sedentary and more dependent on agriculture and had good access to farming sites with favorable runoff (Woodbury and Neely, 1972:150).

Reconstruction (Woodbury and Neely, 1972:150) suggests a long, simultaneous development of runoff farming and irrigation, especially after the abandonment of a large dam complex, which was in use from ca. 700 B.C. to A.D. 200. Diversion of perennial water sources probably increased toward the end of that period, and small, often temporary dams later became common. Walls and lines of boulders, evidence of runoff control and the buildup of terraces, were first built on hillsides and only later in gullies, a sequence taken to suggest "a need to control erosion and conserve moisture on slopes already being dry farmed, rather than a search for such water as would naturally collect in small drainage systems" (p. 151).

HISTORIC SEQUENCES IN THE MEDITERRA-NEAN. Diverse agricultural strategies have coexisted in those dry lands whose documented histories are long. Dry farming and irrigation agriculture are normal companions in semiarid and dry summer climates. Irrigation and the basin system coexisted along the Nile for 5,000 years.

Change can entail new technology or a shift of emphasis from one system to another. The abandonment of many irrigation works accompanied the end of the Roman era in North Africa, where the Arab conquest a few centuries later brought about an upsurge of nomadic pastoralism and some changes in dry farming methods. At no time in the alleged Dark Ages were the old methods everywhere forgotten. Roman methods, as described by White (1970), were much like those of the Mediterranean on the eve of industrial agriculture nearly two millennia later. Dry farming methods were similar. A few new wrinkles appeared in irrigation and drainage works in the late preindustrial period, though Roman engineers had set the standard for a very long time. The interplay of vine, olive, cereals, and pasture gave the landscape a timeless look. Marling, green manuring, and crop rotations, including legume rotations, were known and recommended in Roman and early modern times.

A hypothesis in line with the general model is that relief of population pressure or breakdown of central authority lead to abandonment not of major strategies but only of their more marginal expressions, such as dry farming in the driest locations, hard-to-maintain irrigation works, or cultivation of the poorer cultivable soils. Major historical events, such as conquests and revolutions, need to be studied with careful attention to their effects on population and on the distribution of agricultural systems.

Agricultural Evolution, Society, and Environment in Dry Lands

Food production in arid and semiarid lands can be extremely successful but operates under severe environmental constraints. Not only is water both limiting and in short supply, but aridity contributes to a fragile environment. Archaeologists trace serious damage to dry environments at least as far back as the first urban civilizations, probably earlier. Today science and technology furnish the means to wreak destruction on an unprecedented scale or alternatively to produce more while doing less harm.

The limitations and opportunities of the environment shape the history of society in dry lands. The first urban civilization appeared in lower Mesopotamia, and several other early states and urban civilizations were in dry lands. I shall argue that this is no coincidence. A sobering note on "progress" is that most of the land around the first Mesopotamian cities was long ago ruined for cultivation.

ENVIRONMENTAL PROBLEMS. Severe damage can come from any one of a number of causes. The cover vegetation is fragile. Damage from overgrazing, prolonged cultivation, and fuel wood gathering lasts long, reducing primary productivity and palatability to livestock. Erosion by wind and water is greatly speeded because so much ground is bare so much of the time. Dry farming or irrigation agriculture sometimes alters for the worse the physical properties of soils. Salinization is the bane of irrigated lands.

Accelerated soil erosion accompanies agriculture in nearly all dry lands. Irreversible damage is an old phenomenon renewed by the spread of dry farming in North America, Argentina, Australia, the Soviet Union, and China. Mechanization exacerbates the problem in the more developed areas; grazing, fuel wood cutting, and intensified food production, in the less developed areas.

Few subsoils in dry lands are cultivable. Some are cultivable loess, but the other common subsoils in dry lands are, in order of decreasing suitability, blocky-structured subsoils, calcareous zones, gypsum and saline horizons, hardpans, laterites, gravel, and rock. In arid lands the outcome of soil erosion is frequently the spread of desert pavement and dunes, and dry farming is spreading dunes to semiarid lands (Kovda, 1980:134ff.).

The more that water is diverted for irrigation, the greater is the risk of salinization. Salts left behind after evaporation and transpiration accumulate in soils, surface water, and groundwater. Nor is it only irrigated land that suffers damage. Dry farming increases infiltration into lower soil horizons if the crop uses less water than the natural vegetation or if summer fallows are used to store soil moisture. Under certain topography the water emerges downslope in a saline seep. An estimated 217,000 ha are thus affected in the western United States (USDA, 1987:5–8).

Soils are most adversely affected where the water table is near enough to the surface that capillary movement brings saline water upward. The high water table also prevents downward flushing of salts from being an effective control.

Salinization, like soil erosion, is an ancient problem aggravated by industrial agriculture. Soils salinized by irrigation hundreds or thousands of years ago are found in many regions, not only in lower Mesopotamia, but large tracts are found in the Nile Delta and the Indus valley as well. An FAO estimate holds that at least half the world's irrigated land is salinized so badly that yields are down or agriculture is no longer possible (Kovda, 1980:180).

The remedy is drainage. Although salinization occurs in well-drained soils, it is easy to prevent or correct if water that does not contain too much salt is available for irrigation and flushing. The harder it is to drain land, the more difficult control becomes. Unfortunately in arid lands, low-lying soils of river floodplains and internal drainage basins are usually good sites for irrigation agriculture, because of inherent fertility and ease of irrigation. Drainage can often be improved by building ditches and tile drains and occasionally by pumping out groundwater to keep the water table well below the surface.

The question arises of what to do with the drained water, which carries more salt than the incoming irrigation water. In internal drainage basins the only economic disposal may be in a lower portion of the basin from which it eventually reaches an aquifer. Drainage water most often finds its way into rivers, raising their salt concentration. The Colorado River's salt content rises steadily throughout its length (van Hylckama, 1971:147), reaching levels at the international border that evoke protests from Mexico. The politics of salty water will be heated for years to come along the lower Colorado and wherever rivers flow through dry lands and touch international boundaries.

Another vital part of salinization control is efficient use of irrigation water. A smaller volume brings in less salts and raises the water table less. Overuse of water is presently the norm. More applications and the sealing of ditches would save a great deal. Sprinkler irrigation and drip irrigation, by lowering the demand for water, are also useful. Drip irrigation moves salts horizontally within the surface horizon from the vicinity of the emitters and plants to the zone between the rows. Unusually saline water has been used in drip irrigation, perhaps offering relief, but the technology is new, and there must come a reckoning with the long-term consequences of continuing salt accumulation between rows.

The sum of dry land degradation from food production is commonly termed desertification. The destruction of cover vegetation, soil erosion, and the formation of dunes and desert pavements create a desert landscape from what had been grassland or scrubland. One hypothesis (Jackson et al., 1973) is that dramatic increases in atmospheric dust following the removal of cover vegetation depress precipitation. If the hypothesis is correct, positive feedback could augment desertification, as growing aridity and atmospheric dust levels reinforce one another.

Economic considerations hamper the control of desertification more than technical shortcomings do. Drainage of irrigated land, planting shelterbelts, terracing, and other control methods with proven value are resisted because of the short-term cost. The most effective erosion control measures, such as impervious soil covers, are prohibitively expensive, and much land now cultivated cannot with more-conventional methods withstand present erosion for many more years. Salinization of some irrigated areas has proven intractable with the best methods presently available.

DRY LANDS AND THE ORIGINS OF CIVILIZATION AND THE STATE.

Dry lands are prominent sites of early civilization. Those civilizations that sprang up with the least likelihood of influence from others already in existence were in Peru, Mesoamerica, and the earliest, lower Mesopotamia. Other important sites of early states or civilizations include Egypt, the Indus valley, and the plains of northern China. All are predominantly dry lands, with the partial exception of Mesoamerica, where formative stages are known in both semiarid highland basins and in humid lowlands.

The best-known causal connection with the dry environment is the hydraulic theory linking the emergence of highly centralized and despotic states to bureaucratic control over irrigation water (Steward, 1955; Wittfogel, 1957). Mitchell (1973) reviews pros and cons in the literature. Suffice it to say that irrigation on a large scale requiring central coordination is not by any means a demonstrated, consistent feature of early civilizations.

I suggest alternative connections. Pockets of dense population should accompany agriculture, very early if the general model is correct. Intensification takes place more by exploring expanded niches for agriculture than by increases of cropping frequency in existing field systems, and cultivators lose self-sufficiency when the expansion of intensive agriculture reduces access to resources or, less often, the time available for their exploitation.

References

Adams, R. M. (1981). *Heartland of Cities: Surveys of Ancient Settlement and Land Use on the Central Floodplains of the Euphrates.* University of Chicago Press, Chicago.

Armillas, P. (1961). Land use in pre-Columbian America. In *A History of Land Use in Arid Regions* (L.D. Stamp, ed.), UNESCO, Paris, pp. 255–276.

Bharadwaj, O.P. (1961). The arid zone of India and Pakistan. In *A History of Land Use in Arid Regions* (L.D. Stamp, ed.), UNESCO, Paris, pp. 143–174.

Birdsell, J.B. (1953). Some environmental and cultural factors influencing the structuring of Australian aboriginal populations. *American Naturalist,* 87(834):171–207.

Bittinger, M.W., and E.B. Green (1980). *You Never Miss the Water Till . . . (The Ogallala Story).* Resource Consultants, Fort Collins, Colo.

Brady, N.C. (1974). *The Nature and Properties of Soils,* 8th ed. Macmillan, New York.

Bryan, K. (1929). Flood water farming. *Geographical Review,* 19:444–456.

Butzer, K.W. (1976). *Early Hydraulic Civilizations in Egypt: A Study in Cultural Ecology.* University of Chicago Press, Chicago.

Carter, G.F. (1945). *Plant Geography and Culture History in the American Southwest.* Viking Fund Publications in Anthropology, no. 5, New York.

Castetter, E.F., and W.H. Bell (1942). *Pima and Papago Indian Agriculture.* University of New Mexico Press, Albuquerque.

———. (1951). *Yuman Indian Agriculture.* University of New Mexico Press, Albuquerque.

Cloudsley-Thompson, J.L. (1970). Animal utilization. In *Arid Lands in Transition* (H.E. Dregne, ed.), American Association for the Advancement of Science, Washington, D.C., pp. 57–72.

Conklin, H.C. (1961). The study of shifting cultivation. *Current Anthropology,* 2:27–59.

Despois, J. (1961). Development of land use in northern Africa. In *A History of Land Use in Arid Regions* (L.D. Stamp, ed.), UNESCO, Paris, pp. 219–238.

Driver, H.E., and W.C. Massey (1957). Comparative studies of North American Indians. *Transactions of the American Philosophical Society,* n.s. 48, pp. 167–456. Philadelphia.

Dunbier, R. (1968). *The Sonora Desert.* University of Arizona Press, Tucson.

English, P.W. (1968). The origin and spread of qanats in the Old World. *Proceedings of the American Philosophical Society,* 112:170–181.

Erdman, J.A., C.L. Douglas, and J.W. Marr (1969). *Environment of Mesa Verde, Colorado.* National Park Service, Archaeological Research Service, Washington, D.C.

Erhart, M.H., J. Pias, and G. Leneuf (1954). *Etude Pédologique de Bassin Alluvionaire du Logone-Chari.* Office des Recherches Scientifiques et Techniques d'Outre Mer, Paris.

Evenari, M. (1975). Ancient desert agriculture and civilizations: Do they point the way to the future? In *Arid Zone Development: Potentialities and Problems* (Y. Mundlak and S.F. Singer, eds.), Ballinger, Cambridge, Mass., pp. 83–98.

Evenari, M., L. Shanan, and N. Tadmor (1971). *The Negev: The Challenge of a Desert*. Harvard University Press, Cambridge.

Evenari, M., L. Shanan, N. Tadmor, and Y. Aharoni (1961). Ancient agriculture in the Negev. *Science*, 133:979–996.

Farrington, I.S. (1980). The archaeology of irrigation canals, with special reference to Peru. *World Archaeology*, 11:287–305.

Fourie, L. (1966). The Bushmen of South West Africa. In *The Native Tribes of South West Africa* (C.H.L. Hahn, H. Vedder, and L. Fourie, eds.), Barnes and Noble, New York, pp. 79–105.

Gifford, E.W. (1931). *The Kamia of Imperial Valley*. Smithsonian Institution, Bureau of American Ethnology, Bulletin no. 97. Washington, D.C.

_____. (1967). California balanophagy. In *The California Indians* (R.F. Heizer and M.A. Whipple, eds.), University of California Press, Berkeley, pp. 237–241.

Gould, R.A. (1969). *Yiwara: Foragers of the Australian Desert*. Charles Scribner's Sons, New York.

Grigg, D.B. (1970). *The Harsh Lands: A Study in Agricultural Development*. Macmillan, London.

Hackenberg, R. (1974). *Papago Indians, I*. Garland, New York.

Hamdan, G. (1961). Evolution of irrigation agriculture in Egypt. In *A History of Land Use in Arid Regions* (L.D. Stamp, ed.), UNESCO, Paris, pp. 119–139.

Harlan, J.R., J.M.J. de Wet, and A.B.L. Stemler (1976). Plant domestication and indigenous African agriculture. In *Origins of African Plant Domestication* (J.R. Harlan, J.M.J. de Wet, and A.B.L. Stemler, eds.), Mouton, The Hague, pp. 3–22.

Hodges, C.N. (1980). New options for climate-defensive food production. In *Climate's Impact on Food Supplies: Strategies and Technologies for Climate Defensive Food Production* (L.E. Slater and S.K. Levin, eds.), American Association for the Advancement of Science, Selected Symposium no. 62, Westview, Boulder, Colo., pp. 181–205.

Hylckama, T.E.A. van (1971). Water resources. In *Environment* (W.W. Murdoch, ed.), Sinauer Associates, Stamford, Conn., pp. 47–65.

Jackson, M.L., D.A. Gillette, E.F. Danielson, I.H. Blifford, R.A. Bryson, and J.K. Syers (1973). Global dustfall during the Quaternary as related to environment. *Soil Science*, 1161:135–145.

Kassas, M. (1970). Desertification versus potential for recovery in circum-Saharan territories. In *Arid Lands in Transition* (H.E. Dregne, ed.), American Association for the Advancement of Science, Washington, D.C., pp. 123–142.

Knapp, G. (1982). Prehistoric flood management on the Peruvian coast: Reinterpreting the "sunken fields" of Chilca. *American Antiquity*, 47:144–154.

Kobori, I. (1964). Human geography of methods of irrigation in the central Andes. In *Land Use in Semi-Arid Mediterranean Climates,* UNESCO, Paris, pp. 135–137.

Kovda, V.A. (1961). Land use development in the arid regions of the Russian plain, the Caucasus, and Central Asia. In *A History of Land Use in Arid Regions* (L.D. Stamp, ed.), UNESCO, Paris, pp. 175–218.

———. (1980). *Land Aridization and Drought Control.* Westview, Boulder, Colo.

Lee, R.B. (1968). What hunters do for a living, or how to make out on scarce resources. In *Man the Hunter* (R.B. Lee and I. DeVore, eds.), Aldine, Chicago, pp. 30–48.

Leshnik, L.I. (1973). Land-use and ecological factors in prehistoric north-west India. In *South Asian Archaeology* (N. Hammond, ed.), Noyes, London, pp. 62–84.

Levy, T.E. (1983). The emergence of specialized pastoralism in the southern Levant. *World Archaeology,* 15:15–36.

McIntosh, S.K., and R.J. McIntosh (1980). Initial perspectives on prehistoric subsistence in the inland Niger delta (Mali). *World Archaeology,* 11:227–244.

MacNeish, R.S. (1964). Ancient Mesoamerican civilization. *Science,* 143:531–537.

Mangelsdorf, P.C. (1974). *Corn: Its Origin, Evolution, and Improvement.* Harvard University Press, Cambridge.

Mitchell, W. (1973). The hydraulic hypothesis: A reappraisal. *Current Anthropology,* 4:532–534.

Monod, T., and C. Toupet (1961). Land use in the Sahara-Sahel region. In *A History of Land Use in Arid Regions* (L.D. Stamp, ed.), UNESCO, Paris, pp. 239–254.

O'Connor, D. (1972). A regional population in Egypt to circa 600 B.C. In *Population Growth: Anthropological Implications* (B. Spooner, ed.), MIT Press, Cambridge, pp. 78–100.

Parsons, J.R. (1968). The archaeological significance of *mahamaes* cultivation on the coast of Peru. *American Antiquity,* 33:80–85.

President's Science Advisory Committee, Panel on World Food Supply (1967). *The World Food Problem.* Vol. 2. The White House, Washington, D.C.

Quackenbush, T.H., and D.G. Shockley (1955). The use of sprinklers for irrigation. In *Water: Yearbook of Agriculture 1955,* USDA, Washington, D.C., pp. 267–273.

Raikes, R. (1964). The ancient gabarbands of Baluchistan. *East and West,* 15:26–35.

Rosenberg, N.J. (1981). Technologies and strategies in weatherproofing crop production. In *Climate's Impact on Food Supplies: Strategies and Technologies for Climate Defensive Food Production* (L.E. Slater and S.K. Levin, eds.), American Association for the Advancement of Science, Selected Symposium no. 62, Westview, Boulder, Colo., pp. 157–180.

Rowe, J.H. (1969). The sunken gardens of the Peruvian coast. *American Antiquity,* 34:320–325.

Sherratt, A. (1980). Water, soil, and seasonality in early cereal cultivation. *World Archaeology,* 11:313–330.

Shoji, K. (1977). Drip irrigation. *Scientific American,* 237 (5):62–68.

Smith, P.E.L., and T.C. Young (1972). Greater Mesopotamia: A trial model. In *Population Growth: Anthropological Implications* (B. Spooner, ed.), MIT Press, Cambridge, pp. 1–59.

Smith, R.T. (1985). Ground water and early agriculture in the Peruvian coastal zone. In *Prehistoric Intensive Agriculture in the Tropics* (I.S. Farrington, ed.), British Archaeological Reports, International Series, no. 232, Oxford, pp. 599–620.

Spencer, R.F., and J.D. Jennings (1965). *The Native Americans: Prehistory and Ethnology of the North American Indians.* Harper and Row, New York.

Splinter, W.E. (1976). Center-pivot irrigation. *Scientific American,* 2341 (6):90–99.

Steward, J.H. (1955). *Theory of Culture Change.* University of Illinois Press, Urbana.

Thornthwaite, C.W. (1948). An approach toward a rational classification of climate. *Geographical Review,* 38:55–94.

Tindale, N.B. (1959). Ecology of primitive aboriginal man in Australia. In *Biogeography and Ecology in Australia* (A. Keast, R.L. Crocker, and C.S. Christian, eds.), W. Junk, The Hague, pp. 36–51.

USDA (1987). *The Second RCA Appraisal: Soil, Water, and Related Resources on Nonfederal Land in the United States.* Review draft. U.S. Department of Agriculture, Washington, D.C.

Weber, E. (1976). *Peasants into Frenchmen: The Modernization of Rural France.* Stanford University Press, Stanford, Calif.

White, K.D. (1970). *Roman Farming.* Cornell University Press, Ithaca, N.Y.

Wittfogel, K. (1957). *Oriental Despotism: A Comparative Study of Total Power.* Yale University Press, New Haven, Conn.

Woodburn, J. (1968). An introduction to Hadza ecology. In *Man the Hunter* (R.B. Lee and I. DeVore, eds.), Aldine, Chicago, pp. 49–55.

Woodbury, R.B., and J.A. Neely (1972). Water control systems of the Tehuacan valley. In *The Prehistory of the Tehuacan Valley,* vol. 4 (F. Johnson, ed.), University of Texas Press, Austin, pp. 81–153.

Wulff, H.E. (1968). The qanats of Iran. *Scientific American,* 218 (4): 94–105.

7
Humid Temperate Lands

 Agriculture of middle latitudes includes the world's great granaries, where it takes its most characteristic forms, but grades toward the equator into those systems discussed in chapters 5 and 6 and reaches poleward into inhospitable territory. Subhumid climates, separate in some classifications from humid climates, are included here. So are some locations that are not temperate in either popular thinking or most classifications, such as the Yukon valley or some interior valleys of northeast Siberia.

Preindustrial agriculture follows divergent paths in the major humid temperate regions, and most of this chapter is therefore ordered geographically, not by system, as in the two previous chapters, which dealt with climatic zones in which developments are more parallel. The regions to be compared and contrasted are (precolonial) eastern North America, East Asia, and Europe. Concluding sections deal with postcolonial changes stemming from migrations of farmers and diffusion of crops and finally with food production at its poleward limits.

The Physical Environment

CLIMATES. We are mainly concerned with Köppen's C and D climates other than the Cs (dry summer) climates of chapter 6 and the warmest humid C climates lumped with the tropics in chapter 5. The C and D climates are distinguished from warmer ones and from one another on the basis of the mean temperature of the coldest month, between 18.0° and 0° C in C climates and less than 0° in D climates. The mean of the warmest month is less than 10° in E climates, where food production reaches its limits.

Continental and maritime climates offer very different agricultural possibilities. Where two areas have similar annual mean temperatures, the more continental location will offer more accumulated heat in the growing season but also obstacles of severe winter cold and a growing season limited by killing spring and autumn frosts. In the interiors of North America and Eurasia the difference between the mean temperatures of the warmest and coldest months is generally 25°to 35°, as much as 60° in the interior valleys of northeast Siberia. Oceanic influences along the eastern coastlines only slightly lessen the contrast, because the prevailing winds are westerly in these latitudes. The most maritime climates are thus found over the oceans and along the west coasts. The range between their highest and lowest monthly means is generally less than 15°, as low as 5° in some places.

Transitional climates, with intermediate temperature ranges, are found in several situations. Islands like Japan and Newfoundland lie off continental east coasts, and the intervening seas lessen the temperature range. A large part of the European landmass is transitional, open to both maritime and continental influences. In contrast the maritime climates of western North America lie in a narrow strip west of the cordillera, and transitional climates are few.

The frost-free season is long in maritime climates, but cool weather more or less limits growth. The predominant crops have a low threshold temperature and low to moderate accumulated heat requirements. Winters are not so cold that they kill winter wheat and rye, and livestock may feed through the winter on pasture and fodder crops that stay green though they make little growth. Too much moisture is a greater concern than too little, except where mountain ranges cast a rain shadow—for example, in the lee of New Zealand's Southern Alps or the state of Washington's Olympic Mountains.

The warm summers of continental climates allow rapid growth and maturation up to surprisingly high latitudes, particularly where moderating influences prevent frosts in late spring and early autumn. Fruits and nuts are especially susceptible to unseasonable frosts that occur after spring warming has brought them out of dormancy, and commercial production is clustered in the zones of transition between maritime and continental climates, in many southern areas of the United States and China that are less affected by cold-air outbreaks, along bodies of water, and in other locations where microclimatic influences reduce the hazard. Cold, snowy winters toward the poles increase the burden of winter feeding of livestock.

SOILS. In all three major regions the most productive soils are concentrated on alluvial land or astride the subhumid-semiarid boundary, where percolation and leaching are slight. Most of the black soil belt of European Russia and the Ukraine lies within the semiarid zone. The comparable belt in China, from parts of Ssu-chuan around the eastern margins of the steppes into some of the northern plains and most of Manchuria, includes large tracts of subhumid land. The same is true in North America, where the corn belt and the eastern-most parts of Canada's wheat belt are subhumid. Some belts of prime soil are nearly unbroken, but not all; the age and type of parent material, drainage, and other factors are as important as they are anywhere else.

The three regions differ significantly in the extent of alluvial land and the potential of uplands for cultivation. Each has its own plan.

Eastern China's eastward-flowing rivers have broad floodplains in their lower courses, but the intervening uplands have limited potential. From the Yangtze north, a vast alluvial plain is interrupted only by isolated, rugged limestone hills. Floodplains south of the Yangtze straddle short rivers and are narrow, but their aggregate area is still large. The intervening land is hilly, the slopes are often steep, and the most extensive cultivable soils are leached Ultisols of moderate nutrient status at best. A few better upland soils are found on more favorable parent material, most notably in the Red Basin of Ssu-chuan.

In eastern North America, inherently productive upland soils occupy much of the corn belt but are at a premium farther east. Except in the St. Lawrence valley, floodplains of rivers that flow eastward from the Appalachians to the Atlantic are short and narrow. For some distance west of the Appalachians, rivers of the Ohio and Tennessee systems cut down into plateaus before reaching their middle courses and wider floodplains. Upland soils from these plateaus to the Atlantic are with few exceptions mature and leached.

The value of river floodplains holds over most of Europe, but inherently productive upland soils are fairly extensive, including many formed over raised alluvium, chalk, loess, and basic volcanics. Much of the northern European plain is made up of gentle slopes. Leaching is not excessive under annual precipitation that is generally between 500 and 800 mm and well distributed throughout the year. The soil map of the plain is complex, and the best soils are often close by others that are useful for little other than coniferous woodland and rough pasture, but on the whole the region is better endowed with upland agricultural resources than either the eastern quarter of North America or China south of the Yangtze.

Each of the three regions is well suited to the kind of agriculture that actually evolved, but not to the point that alternative forms of land use could not have developed had historical circumstances been different. If drained, not flooded, most of East Asia's floodplains could grow maize or sweet potato instead of wet rice. Eastern North America's low population densities allowed careful selection of soils for maize growing, but then colonial-era importation of Old World small grains opened up large areas too dry or too cold for maize. Had the immigrants been Asian instead of European, they would surely have grown wet rice across much of the Southeast and farther north in the Mississippi valley than anyone now attempts. European mixed farming takes advantage of the frequent close association of lands with varying slope, drainage, nutrient status, and other qualities, but cultivation in the absence of livestock would have been feasible.

NATURAL VEGETATION. Forest is the predominant natural cover. In the more humid areas, trees are large, and the canopy is only a little less closed than in tropical rain forest. Species diversity is much less than in tropical forests. Toward the subhumid zone, woodlands are more open, and grasslands like the North American prairies are more in evidence. Much grassland is anthropogenic. The best forest soils are with few exceptions found under hardwood cover, not conifers, and stands of a particular tree often mark the best soil for a particular agricultural use.

Preagricultural populations enjoyed diverse sources of wild plant and animal food. Fruit and nut species abound in the forests. Hazelnut, walnut, and chestnut occur in clusters. Edible tubers are found in a variety of situations. Historical collectors make little use of the seeds of wild grasses; a notable exception was wildrice (*Zizania aquatica*) in eastern North America. The grasslands are more valuable to food collectors as feeding grounds for game. The many rivers supply fish.

CROPS. Crop choices differ from those of the zones already discussed but are neither consistent nor in close agreement with climatic boundaries. Major crops of dry lands and dry summer lands, except date palm and carob, are also important in wetter regions. Most important tropical annual crops thrive in middle latitudes wherever summers are long and hot. Of important temperate zone annuals, wheat and barley are found in the tropics mainly in drier climates, potato is found at higher elevations, and rye and oats are rare. Stone fruits—apples, pears, peaches, apricots, plums, and cherries—and many temperate zone nut trees are nearly absent from the tropics because of their need for cool winter temperatures and a period of dormancy. Tropical fruits reach only into middle latitudes in those locations where maritime influences exclude frost. Sheltered areas are found along the east coast of Australia in which commercial groves of banana, citrus, and apple are in proximity—a mix of a tropical fruit, a subtropical fruit, and a temperate zone fruit, but this is exceptional. In contrast the practical southern limits of peach and apple cultivation in central Georgia are well north of Florida's commercial citrus groves.

Eastern North America

This tale of three continents begins with precolonial agricultural systems of eastern North America. Population pressure is less here, the crop mix is distinct from that of Europe and East Asia, and domesticated animals are absent other than the dog (Driver, 1961:62), used primarily for hunting. The region is of interest in its own right but also because it places developments in the other two regions in strong relief.

NATIVE AMERICAN SYSTEMS IN THE ETHNO-GRAPHIC PRESENT. In spite of exceptions and often sketchy accounts, we may generalize that long fallow systems prevail in eastern North America. Abundant accounts from the early colonial period describe slashing and burning of well-developed forest. Day (1953) documents forest clearance in conjunction with moves of villages at long intervals in New England, New York, and New Jersey. Van der Donck (1841) in 1656 notes rapid woodland regrowth after cultivation in the Hudson valley. In the southeastern United States, trees are commonly girdled (Swanton, 1946), a sign that they are large. Trees are girdled farther west among the Caddo of Louisiana and east Texas (Swanton, 1942) and in several heavily wooded floodplains of rivers of the Great Plains: the Niobrara (Jablow, 1974), the Platte, and the Missouri (Will and Hyde, 1917). Cultivators of the Midwest prairies seek out patches of woodland (Driver and Massey, 1957:225), and so do the Seminole, postcolonial migrants from Alabama and Georgia to subtropical Florida (MacCauley, 1884). Throughout eastern North America the tools used for slashing forest are of stone and resemble those of tropical regions in which metal tools are absent. Alluvial floodplains and terraces are widely favored locations. They carry heavy forest, even in the semiarid plains, where tall cottonwoods grow in the moist soils along the rivers.

Most villages shift, but reported intervals and fragmentary descriptions of field management point toward longer periods of forest clearance than those prevailing in the humid tropics. Where villages are stationary, large areas are cultivated, 3 to 20 km across around Iroquois settlements (Day, 1953:333). Other villages in the east shift every 10 to 30 years. Shorter intervals may prevail in the prairie lands to the west, but the picture is complicated by widespread seasonal occupation of agricultural villages. In the river valleys of the plains, informants early in this century report, "Our fields the first year were quite small, for clearing the wooded bottomland was hard work. A family usually added to the clearing each year until their garden was as large as they cared to cultivate" (Wilson, 1917:6).

From clearance to abandonment, crops and grass alternate in the fields. In southern areas two crops of maize are sometimes taken in a single year from the same field (Swanton, 1942:129). On the other hand, early historic accounts there and in the Northeast frequently mention clearing of grass and weeds. According to Day (1953), fields and grasslands form a mosaic in cleared portions of the Northeast. In the valleys of the Great Plains the Hidatsa alternate two years of crops with an unstated period of fallow, after which grass had to be cut and burnt before recultivation. Grass fallows are probably easier to clear than the dense native sods; Hidatsa and other Missouri valley cultivators complain that weeds introduced by Europeans and carried in horse and cattle dung, which they remove, make clearing grass fallows and subsequent weeding more difficult (Will and Hyde, 1917; Wilson, 1917).

A complete cultivation and fallow cycle could easily take 50 to 100 years and possibly more, often outlasting several shifts of settlement. The average cropping frequency must be low despite prolonged periods of clearance. If clearance were for 10 years or longer, coppice regrowth would probably be suppressed. It must therefore take many years before there are once again hardwood trees large enough to require girdling.

Cultivation of upland soils and prairies is less common. Along the northeastern seaboard, fires are set to maintain upland prairies and pasture for deer, but according to most reconstructions, upland soils are little cultivated. However, introduced diseases precede most written accounts of native agriculture, and their awful mortality might have lessened population pressure on the river bottomlands. One agricultural historian (Russell, 1976) thinks that the ease with which coarser-textured soils of the eastern New England prairies can be worked makes them preferred over the finer-textured soils of the river bottoms. More-productive upland soils, Alfisols formed over limestone, are found farther west, in parts of eastern Pennsylvania and north and south of Lake Erie and Ontario. The powerful Iroquois, Huron, Neutral, and Erie nations spread settlement and agriculture across the lands near the Great Lakes outside the narrow confines of the river valleys. Prairie cultivation is occasionally reported farther west. The Great Plains, outside the valley bottoms, are mostly too dry for maize.

Maize, beans, and cucurbits (squash and pumpkin) dominate the crop mix. Fruits, nuts, and some fresh vegetables and tubers are gathered from the wild in quantity. Maize cultivation at its northernmost limit overlaps with the southern range of wildrice. Animal protein is obtained by hunting and fishing and sometimes from domesticated dogs (Driver, 1961:62).

Systematic use of soil amendments is not reliably reported among historic American Indians, apart from the old tradition that Squanto showed the Plymouth Pilgrims how to place a fish in each hill of maize. If it happened, either the fish were eschewed trash sorts or the settlers' benefactor was teaching them to convert high-quality protein into a lesser amount of low-quality protein.

PREHISTORIC SYSTEMS. Permanent settlements, many of impressive size, dotted a large area centered on the lower and middle Mississippi valley prior to Spanish entry into North America in the sixteenth century, when depopulation apparently led to dispersal. Introduced diseases must have been the cause, because contact with Europeans was not yet hostile. This Mississippian cultural phase began in the lower valley about A.D. 700 and had reached well up the valley and east to the Appalachian plateaus and southern Georgia by A.D. 900 (Dragoo, 1976). Much of the cultural tradition survived among such historic peoples as the Caddo, Natchez, and Chickasaw, but their villages were smaller and generally less permanent.

Mississippian agricultural fields are located from settlement sites and the remnants of ridges and furrows. Tillage was often more ambitious than that typical of later times—evidence, together with the size and permanence of settlements, of greater population pressure, but not severe pressure. Waselkov (1977) concludes that cultivation alternated with grass fallows, based on his assessment of what is possible without the use of soil amendments. Though some of the exploited soils later gave European settlers annual crops of maize for many years with little or no manuring, crops may still have responded to a fallow. The largest settlements were on the bottomlands of the Mississippi and Ohio valleys. Poorly drained land was not cultivated (Waselkov, 1977), but some uplands were. Relict ridged fields are found on uplands in southern Michigan, eastern Wisconsin, the middle Mississippi, and Georgia's Macon Plateau (Fowler, 1969, 1971; Riley and Freimuth, 1979; Waselkov,

1977). Ridgetops are usually less than 30 cm above the furrows, except in Michigan and Wisconsin, where the remaining height is 15 to 75 cm. Riley and Freimuth conducted experiments in some northern areas and conclude that the high ridges served to drain cold air at night and provide some frost protection.

Agriculture existed for some time in the eastern United States before the beginnings of the Mississippian phase, but methods of management are obscure. Much archaeological attention is given to the origins of the first domesticates, whether they were indigenous plants such as amaranths, chenopods, and *Iva* spp. or plants introduced from Mesoamerica, such as maize, beans, and cucurbits. Settlements were small in the early stages of agriculture, and wild foods were typically more important than crops.

East Asia

PREVAILING SYSTEMS OF THE LATE HISTORIC PERIOD. Documentation of East Asian agriculture is excellent for the early twentieth century and fairly good for some time before. Relevant statistics of varying reliability are available for several centuries. Buck's (1937) survey of nearly 17,000 Chinese farms from 1924 to 1933 is a comprehensive source of unusual depth and quality. King's (1911) earlier survey does not attempt as many statistical tasks but is full of insightful descriptions from Japan, Korea, and eastern China. Scholars find diverse historical sources. Japan is particularly well covered by histories that touch on specific technical developments.

Conspicuous features of East Asian agriculture are high cropping frequencies and high labor intensity. Buck (1937:33) finds that "idle" cropland, that lying fallow for a year or more, occupies only 0.2% to 1.0% of cropland in all Chinese regions, except in the spring-wheat region, where dry farming methods are in use and idle cropland reaches 9.3%. He reports a mean 1.49 crops per year, from 1.67 in the southern rice regions to 1.23 in the north (p. 44). Very high cropping frequencies are the rule in Japan early in this century; the importation of soybean cake for fertilizer encourages multicropping. In Korea the percentage of paddy that is double-cropped rises more recently, from 37.4% in 1955 to 60.0% in 1975 (Ban, Moon, and Perkins, 1980:119), the latter a mean of 1.6 crops per year.

Rice is emphasized wherever possible. It is virtually the only cereal in the valleys of southern Japan and in China south of the Yangtze, but farther north it alternates with winter cereals. Nursery techniques and the breeding of early varieties make its cultivation possible well to the north, where it is secondary to, variously, wheat, millet, sorghum, and, in Japan, buckwheat.

East Asia and Europe have long shared the same domesticated animals, but Asia has fewer per person and produces an even smaller proportion of animal products per person. Buck (1937:121) gives densities of animals per hectare (converted here from acres) of 0.84 in China, 0.47 in Japan, and 1.73 in Great Britain. Three-quarters of Chinese animals, calculated "in terms of animal units on the basis of food consumed per animal," are used for draft, a rate that would at that time probably be exceeded in Japan, where nearly all animal protein comes from fish. In central and southern China, draft animals do nearly all the grazing, and hogs, chickens, and ducks supply most animal products. Some sheep, raised for lamb meat, graze in northern China.

Perkins (1969:15) concludes from historical sources, including some sketchy statistics, that the number of meat and draft animals per capita changed little in China over the past five or six centuries. That this is so in spite of increasing cropping frequency and the bringing of hill lands into cultivation reveals the long-standing subordination of animal husbandry to cultivation.

The integration of farm activities impresses outside observers. Available organic matter is carefully recycled, so that many operations serve multiple functions, including the provision of manures and composts. Irrigation ditches supply sediments. In southern China, ponds are common and are used for fish culture, ducks, the growing of water chestnuts, and the supplying of sediments for application to the fields. Farmers recycle litter, thatch, and ashes and join in by contributing night soil.

It is perhaps surprising that more green matter is not cycled through livestock instead of being applied to fields directly or in composts. There are many leguminous green manure (cover) crops, most notably *Astragalus sinensis,* but much less use of fodder crop rotations. Grass and leaves from waste areas go into the compost heap or directly onto fields. Buck (1937:8) queries the direct use of soybean and oilseed cakes as amendments, arguing with some optimism that if they were instead used for feed, 80% of the fertilizing value would be retained in excreta.

A low return on labor is the price of high yields. Labor efficiency in China declines over several centuries (Perkins, 1969). Among the major field systems, wet rice is especially responsive to labor inputs, including hand weeding and transplanting from nurseries, trends that are evident in all densely populated rice-growing areas of East Asia by the nineteenth century.

ENVIRONMENTAL STRESS AND ITS MANAGEMENT. For all the success of supporting a dense population with preindustrial technology, symptoms of stress on the environment are widely apparent by the nineteenth century. Modern science and technology are now looked to for countermeasures, but their arrival coincides with accelerated rates of population increase and heightened environmental impact.

The use of night soil places human populations at risk for fecally transmitted disease. Careful composting can eliminate pathogens, but a sufficient standard is rarely achieved prior to modern promotions, and these diseases are endemic in much of East Asia. Night soil from urban populations once traveled no farther than the peri-urban market gardens but becomes more widely distributed as transportation improves. In Japan this was in the Tokugawa period (Smith, 1959:92). Pooling the donations of thousands might aggravate pathogen transmission.

Importing organic matter may stress the environment where it originates. Stripping hillsides of too much of the leaves and grass reduces their primary productivity and cover and increases soil erosion. Whatever rate is sustainable, it is widely exceeded by the early twentieth century. The amounts of foliage used are large. Cultivation on poor soils of Kitakami, northern Japan, is supported by grass and other foliage collected from land at least two-thirds the area of the cultivated fields (Eyre, 1962:245). An eighteenth-century Japanese source recommends 70 to 80 horseloads of grass per tan (about 0.4 ha) of paddy and 30 horseloads per tan of upland crops (Smith, 1959:93). The trend in recent centuries is toward replacement by purchased amendments, such as urban night soil and soybean cake, in China (Perkins, 1969) and Japan (Smith, 1959).

Soil erosion is the greatest threat to East Asian land. The leading causes are deforestation and the cultivation of highly erodible soils, both consequences of population pressure. The cumulative toll is enormous. A sixth of China's land areas is marked with surface and gully erosion (Kuo, 1972:125). By 1954 only 8% of China's land is forested (p. 127), mostly in remote mountainous areas. Probably the worst erosion is that of the loess lands along the middle Hwang-Ho of northern China, where deep gullies now etch the landscape and isolate cultivable fields like islands. Much of the eroded soil is deposited on the plains along the lower Hwang-Ho, formerly to their benefit, but increasingly the gullies are cutting through the loess and into sand and gravel, to the detriment of land downstream (Tuan, 1969:29–30). Japan retains much of its forests but still suffers some serious losses of soil.

Countermeasures have been in force for centuries, or the damage would surely be worse. Terracing nearly eliminates erosion. All rice land, as Buck (1937:7) points out, is in a sense terraced and erosion is nil, except from that minuscule area in upland rice. He finds that 24% of the land in his sample carries terraces built to hold soil on slopes (p. 37). Farmers in Ssu-chuan have for centuries hauled eroded soil back up slopes to build narrow terraces that are "20 to 30 feet wide and are surrounded by bare rock" (Tuan, 1969:30), rock that is itself a product of erosion, illustrating that control measures are sometimes initiated in the eleventh hour. Tuan contrasts the effective control of erosion in rice fields with the severe damage associated with upland crops, planted in south China "in neat rows up and down the cleared hillsides." As for afforestation, recent efforts in China have made headway, in part because of fossil fuel substitution for firewood, but demand for timber is still heavy, and progress is slow (Kuo, 1972:129).

WOODY FALLOW SYSTEMS. Swidden cultivation persists into this century mainly on steep hillsides, often adjacent to areas of intensive cultivation. At no historic time do swiddens contribute a large part of total production, but their existence and the methods employed are of interest both because they can be compared with those of eastern North America and because some prehistorians infer much wider use in the early phases of East Asian agriculture. Ethnographic descriptions come from northern Hokkaido (Eyre, 1962), Shikoku (Hall and Nok, 1953), and the Ryukyus (Nuttonson, 1952) in Japan; Korea (Lee, 1936; Stewart, 1956); and in China the Chekiang and Anhwei highlands (Buck, 1937:73) and the southwest (Anderson, 1876; Beauclair, 1956; Ho, 1959:145).

In Chekiang and Anhwei, methods are closer to agroforestry than to typical slash-and-burn farming. Maize is interplanted with wood oil and *Cunninghamia* trees. Cultivation stops after 2 or 3 years; then wood oil nuts are harvested for 7 years. Finally, *Cunninghamia* is allowed to "form a forest" for about 20 years, after which clearing begins a new cycle. Large wood is removed, and only the small wood is burnt. In Kitakami, northern Hokkaido, 5 years of crops alternate with 20 years under trees, and nothing is burnt; in a minor variant, the slash is burnt, and "several" years of crops alternate with forest.

The relegation of this system to marginal environments raises the question whether this was always the case or it is a survival of something once more widespread, a question that is not readily resolved. The most reliably documented instance of swiddening on a large scale was in the Yangtze highlands following the sixteenth-century introduction of maize, potato, sweet potato, and peanut. "Bumper crops during the first few years" were followed by continued cultivation until the land was badly eroded, at which time the settlement was shifted and new land cleared (Ho, 1959:145–148).

PREHISTORIC AND EARLY HISTORIC AGRICULTURE.

Two areas of early agriculture, possibly as early as 5000 B.C., are known in China: the Yangshao cultures of the middle Hwang-Ho and the Ch'ing-lien-Kang culture of the lower Yangtze, as well as a possible third area along the southeast coast (Pearson, 1983; Watson, 1974:9). Rice was the principal crop in the swampy lands of the lower Yangtze. Chang (1983) finds its initial cultivation was on land with a high water table, but not necessarily underwater, and infers that slash-and-burn methods were used. More reconstruction has been attempted of the Yangshao culture and its successors in northern China.

Reconstructions of Yangshao agriculture draw on scant evidence and vary greatly. Millet was the main crop, with possibly also wheat, rice, and sorghum as prominent crops in later phases. Some bones of domesticated animals have been recovered: dogs, pigs, cattle, sheep, and goats (Li, 1983). Settlements appear permanent. Watson (1974:9) estimates that one, Pan'po, had a population of about 400 to 500 and infers from its size that the cropping frequency was probably high. Chang (1963, 1964) observes that most Yangshao settlements are of modest size and scattered and adds that the layering of deposits points toward repeated occupations. From this evidence he argues that slash-and-burn methods prevailed, a conclusion reached more recently by Pearson (1983:120) and Li (1983), mainly on the grounds that the land was originally wooded. But deciduous forest is fragile in this area along the sub-humid-semiarid boundary. Ho (1977) argues from the pollen record that little of the landscape was wooded when the Yangshao phase began. Certainly by 4000 B.C., when settlement was denser, long fallow cultivation could not have supported the population.

In Japan the first heavy reliance on domesticated plants is associated with the Yayoi phase, beginning ca. 400 to 300 B.C., much later than in China. Yayoi agriculture appears to include wet rice cultivation. Regarding possible cultivation in the preceding Jomon phase, some evidence has been found of barley and rice near the end, and it has been inferred that cultivation was "probably of the slash-and-burn variety"

(Chard, 1974:139), because settlements were temporary and wild foods important.

Han Chinese expansion dominates Chinese history. The unwary risk confusing the best documented – the Han have left good records – with the most eventful, but unless ongoing archaeology greatly alters the picture, it appears that they carried with them higher population densities and cropping frequencies. That does not mean that Han land use was constant.

Available evidence offers only glimpses of the agriculture of the first (Shang) dynasty of the north China plain, but the subsequent spread of irrigation works and certain tools and techniques more surely indicates intensive methods during the succeeding Chou dynasty. Tuan (1969:60–62) infers that some kind of woody fallow system was in force in early (Western) Chou, but on thin evidence, that is, references to forest clearance in the *Shi Ching*. Subsequently, from 722 B.C. to 222 B.C. (Tuan, 1969:59), large-scale irrigation works appeared, and contemporary accounts mention the use of animal manures. Some iron plowshares have been found, though hoes and spades were far more numerous. A contemporary classification of land distinguished lands that could be cultivated every year, every other year, and one year in three (Hsü, 1956:11). Irrigation spread farther during the Ch'in and Han dynasties, up to A.D. 222. Contemporary writers recommended applying prepared composts, silkworm excrement, and night soil (Tuan, 1969:81–82). Plows were now more common and were often combined with seed drills. The *Ch'i Min Yao Shin,* a book of the sixth century A.D., mentions the moldboard plow and describes tree culture and a system of taking three crops of millet and wheat in two years (Tuan, 1969:90). Wet rice was subsequently much in evidence, at first confined to flat valley floors and later found on hillside terraces (Grigg, 1974:84–89; Tuan 1969:90). Double crops of rice in the south and of rice and winter upland cereals in central sections spread after the introduction of early rice varieties from India (Ho, 1956).

Under some circumstances the Han Chinese employed less intensive methods. The *Shi Chi* of Ssu-ma Chien (ca. 145–90 B.C.) refers to land "tilled with fire and hoed with water" in what was then a cultural frontier, the alluvial lands along the Yangtze (Tuan, 1969:38). Grigg (1974:84) reports evidence of swiddens in the Yangtze highlands during the early years of the Christian era.

Late in the first millennium A.D., intensity was greatest in and around the Yangtze valley and in northern China, Korea, and Japan. South of the Yangtze the scant available evidence is of wet rice cultivation in the valleys, without the elaborate irrigation works of later. Hill cultivation was apparently often of the swidden variety and in proximity to wet rice cultivation.

Europe

Outstanding features of historic European agriculture are cropping frequencies between those typical of the other two regions and mixed farming that incorporates animal husbandry as both a major source of food and a vital adjunct to cultivation. A distinctive feature is the widespread use of plowed fallows. Crops differ completely from those of eastern North America. A few East Asian cultivars are long absent from Europe—for example, the soybean came west rather late—but the greater difference is one of emphasis.

NUTRIENT FLOWS IN HISTORIC SYSTEMS. From the earliest historic accounts, European farmers rely on livestock to carry nutrients from uncultivated land to cropland, the carrying done more in the animals' guts than on their backs. Pastures and "meadows"—fields of grass and broadleaves for summer hay and winter grazing—are in medieval Europe considered as necessary to a community's survival as its cultivated land.

Low-lying, intermittently flooded plots, which would in East Asia be in rice, are in Europe the prized "water meadows." Intermittently flooded lands tend to be highly productive. They benefit from abundant moisture and presumably from high rates of biological nitrogen fixation, particularly where calcium, magnesium, and phosphorus in the soil or incoming water are available in good quantities. Water meadows in medieval and early modern Europe yield three times the hay taken from other, upland meadows (Kerridge, 1973:22–23): "They were the eyes of the land, like waterholes in the bush and artesian wells in the outback. No farmstead, no village could be built unless hard by them. They were much prized, but also scarce." Some communities in England (Thirsk, 1973:241) and France (Bloch, 1966:24) do without water meadows to their comparative disadvantage.

Stabling and folding at night concentrate the excreta of animals feeding over a larger area by day. This elegant method supplies most of the manure on some farms, particularly those with access to plenty of pasture. Stables are nonetheless the largest single source of animal manure on most medieval and early modern farms. The burden of transporting and spreading manure encourages its use near stables and byres.

One technique rivals East Asian green manuring for the bulk of organic matter moved. Turf manuring is the gathering of sod from peaty soils on which animals, mostly sheep, have grazed for several years. Turf and manure are spread heavily on permanently cultivated land, usually islands of sandy soils rising slightly above the peat lands, which after years of treatment become highly productive *plaggen* soils. From 40 to 150 horseloads of material are applied to each hectare of permanently cultivated land (Slicher van Bath, 1963:258). The main crop is rye. The system in the eighteenth century is found in the eastern Netherlands, adjacent parts of Germany, and some parts of Scandinavia (Slicher van Bath, 1963:58, 258–259).

Denshiring also concentrates available nutrients, because sod and grass are in most accounts gathered from a wide area, stacked, and burnt, and the ashes scattered over a lesser area. Denshiring in the eighteenth and nineteenth centuries is usually confined to marginal hill soils but is also found on some English chalk downs and was earlier more common in Ireland (Aalen, 1978:158) and Wales (Jones, 1972:341).

The recycling of night soil back to the land is known but is not as efficient or as prevalent as in East Asia. Urban wastes, including night soil and horse manure, find their way to peri-urban farms mostly on pastures (Dickinson, 1961).

MEDIEVAL AND EARLY MODERN SYSTEMS. The three-course system, also known as the three-field system, dominates much of the late medieval and early modern landscape. It is often described as a three-year cycle of winter grain, spring grain, and fallow. The winter grain is usually wheat or rye, the spring grain barley or oats, less often peas, broad beans, vetch, buckwheat, or spring wheat. As a rule, 12 to 14 months of fallow elapse between the spring grain harvest and the (autumn) sowing of winter grain. From winter grain harvest to sowing of spring grain, as little as 7 months passes, up to 10 months in warmer places where the crop matures early. Land is thus in fallow for more than half the cycle. Four-course systems, with a crop three years out of four, are an uncommon variation.

Two-course systems are widespread but predominant only in the far north, where winter cereals are not grown, and in dry summer areas of the south (chapter 6). The cycle includes a crop and about a year and a half of fallow.

In all of these systems, farmers plow the fallows during the summer, sometimes spreading and plowing under manure. Organic matter is thereby added throughout the period, first ungrazed stubble, then manure. The intervals between plowings are long enough to allow some regrowth of grasses and broadleaves but short enough to prevent the setting of seed or the formation of dense sod. Enough growth is left in winter to allow some grazing.

Loomis (1978) estimates sources of nitrogen and concludes that a two-course system could have a favorable nitrogen budget with the help of only modest inputs, none in favorable circumstances. A harvest of 1,000 kg of wheat, probably above average from a hectare, removes 20 kg of nitrogen. During an average cycle, 4 kg of nitrogen are added to each hectare in the seed sown, and 8 to 12 kg from rain, dust, and bird droppings. Free-living nitrogen-fixing bacteria add 4 to 10 kg, and cyanobacteria add a little more under some conditions. These sources together add 14 to 21 kg/ha/cycle, of which about 10% might be lost through denitrification, thus coming close to balancing crop removal. Loomis figures conservatively that animal manures, from animals mostly fed from other land, contribute 5 kg/ha/yr, an addition sufficient to sustain yields.

Nitrogen imports from pasture and meadow would obviously play a more critical role in the three-course system. If yields are the same as in a two-course system, nitrogen removal increases by a third, while in situ additions of nitrogen change slightly or not at all. Reduced yields might be tolerable so long as production over the whole period was raised. In a few areas the three-course system is tried but later dropped because of declining yields.

Spring grains include legumes that would contribute some nitrogen, but not much. Of the prominent legumes, only vetch would supply anywhere near as much nitrogen as would the East Asian soybean. Farmers of the later European agricultural revolution boost nitrogen fixation by adding the more effective fodder legumes to rotations, also improving the environment for nitrogen fixation by incorporating marl (a clay rich in lime and used on acid soils), a rare practice in medieval times.

Medieval estates practice permanent cultivation on a scale ranging from dooryard gardens to sizable fields, being largest where soils are exceptional or turf manuring is in use. Manuring is the rule, and it may be generalized that permanent cultivation, even more than the two- and three-course systems, relies on nutrient subsidies from pastures and meadows.

Medieval cultivation sometimes alternates with several years of pasture, in ways perhaps too irregular to be called ley systems. Sporadic cultivation of pasture is reported up to the eighteenth century in France (Bloch, 1966:28) and in some "marginal mountains of Ireland and Switzerland" (Evans, 1956:229). Denshiring, where practiced, allows occasional cultivation of marginal soils. During the agricultural depression of the late Middle Ages, some areas of south Germany and the Alps that had been regularly farmed are brought under long periods of pasture and brief periods of cultivation (Mayhew, 1973:115–116). I conclude that when demand is low, cycles of pasture and crops constitute an attractive system even on moderately productive soils.

The infield-outfield system is a strategy historically associated mainly with the Atlantic fringe of Europe, particularly Scotland, where it is the norm in the early modern period. Some of the cases of land division in nineteenth-century France into *terres chaudes* and *terres froides* (Bloch, 1966:78) seemingly refer to it. Infields and outfields in eighteenth-century Germany are found in the northwest and in a narrow belt eastward to Mecklenburg (Mayhew, 1973:169). A minor variation is the three-way partition of Rhineland holdings into manured and permanently cultivated *Dungland,* unmanured and frequently cultivated *Wildland,* and unmanured and occasionally cultivated *Rottland* (Slicher van Bath, 1963:58–59). Infields and outfields formerly existed in Norway and the Aegean region (McCourt, 1955:371).

Swiddens are a well-documented part of European agriculture as late as the mid- and late nineteenth century. They are then the mainstay of northern and eastern Great Russia (Ermolov, 1893) and important in Finland (Mead, 1953). Russian settlers carry swiddening to Siberia (Potapov, 1956:136). Communities of Old Believers in northern Russia and Karelia maintain them alongside the three-course system (Crummey, 1970:140–141). Pockets survive in the Vosges of France, southern Sweden (Darby, 1956), and parts of Germany (Darby, 1956; Pfeifer, 1956).

Earlier accounts place swiddening in wide areas of eastern Europe and scattered locations to the west. The distribution in the east takes in some productive soils, but most cases, including virtually all in the west, are on poor soils, often acid, leached, and formed under coniferous forest. Slash-and-burn methods are known in the sixteenth century in the Ardennes, Belgium (Pfeifer, 1956), and in the thirteenth century in the Eifel, Germany (Mayhew, 1973:86). The thirteenth-century Welsh *Book of Iorweth* prescribes no more than four years cultivation on cleared woodland (Jones, 1972:340). Swidden agriculture is common in the northeast Ukraine in the third and fourth centuries A.D. and throughout Great Russia until the sixteenth century (Darby, 1956).

Cropping periods in historic European swiddens are shorter than the periods of clearance in eastern North America, even including several years of grazing that normally follow cultivation. Finnish swiddeners use various cycles, but the average cropping period is four years, the same as that set by the Welsh laws. Periods are "a few years" in the

Ardennes and Vosges (Bloch, 1966:27) and "several years" in Siberia (Potapov, 1956:136). Fallows are 15 years in Siberia, about 30 years in Finland, and sufficient elsewhere to renew secondary forest after prolonged clearance.

CROPPING FREQUENCIES OF MEDIEVAL AND EARLY MODERN SYSTEMS. Average cropping frequencies may be roughly expressed as the ratio of cropping years to the total years of the cycle. Annual cropping has a ratio of 1.0, a two-course system 0.5, and a three-course system 0.67. In eighteenth-century Scots outfields, three to four years of crops alternate with five years of grazed fallow (Whittington, 1973). The infield is typically half the area of the outfield (Handley, 1953), so that the mean ratio of the whole infield-outfield system is 0.58 to 0.63. Infields on exceptional soils along the Tay are twice as large as outfields (Handley, 1953), indicating a ratio of 0.82. The ratio in swidden systems would be low, no more than 0.25 and in some cases closer to 0.10 or 0.15.

Inclusion of pasture and meadow in the calculations, because they provide manure, lowers all the ratios except that of swiddening, which gets no imports of manure. The mean ratio of turf farming when the peat lands are entered into the calculations is 0.11 to 0.33 (calculated from Slicher van Bath, 1963:258–259), a drastic reduction from the frequency of 1.0 of the manured *plaggen* lands alone. The low values are no better than those of swidden systems, but it should be added that the peat lands could not be cultivated without undertaking drainage.

HISTORIC CHANGES BEFORE THE EUROPEAN AGRICULTURAL REVOLUTION. The literature contains many a priori assumptions that particular systems are inherently primitive, but a moratorium on making such assumptions is long overdue. Except for swiddening and the rather special case of turf manuring, the similarities among systems are more striking than their differences. Tools and technology do not vary greatly. All create a landscape in which cultivated land, pasture, and meadow form a mosaic, along with tracts of woodland less fully integrated into the whole land use system. Cropping frequencies of infield-outfield systems mostly fall between those of the two- and three-course systems. One reason for the greater prevalence of the two- and three-course systems in medieval Europe may be the ease with which they are regulated, an advantage where tenure comprises a complex mix of ownership, usufruct, and sharecropping (Cooter, 1978).

Two- and three-course systems are coexisting options responsive to changes in population and the economy. The three-course system is not, pure and simply, a better idea that neatly supersedes two courses. Three courses become more common as the medieval period wears on, especially during the two centuries or so of population increase before the black death, but the trend is far from even. The three-course system is known in the seventh and eighth centuries in western Europe, whereas two courses are still in use in the eighteenth century in England (Thirsk, 1973:257), France (Bloch, 1966:33ff.), and Germany (Mayhew, 1973:85).

The origins and antiquity of the infield-outfield system are unclear. Bloch (1966) lists it among medieval French systems, though evidence prior to the early modern period is indirect. Jones (1972, 1973) traces the *tir corddlan* of northern Wales, permanently cultivated and well-manured "nucleal" lands, to the thirteenth century. Buchanan (1973) concludes that the Irish infield-outfield system is a late introduction from Scotland.

Premedieval agriculture in much of northwestern Europe appears to emphasize animal husbandry so much that many systems are best described as sedentary pastoralism with cultivation. In Ireland before the imposition of English rule the dominant role of cattle leaves its traces in the archaeological records and in epics like the *Tain Bo Cuailnge* (Cattle raid of Cooley). Irish Laws describe both pasture and cultivated land manured from byres (Buchanan, 1973). Combinations of pasture and infield therefore seem to precede infield-outfield, and Irish homesteads from ca. 300 B.C. to the Norman period are typically scattered and associated with small fields of about 0.4 ha (Buchanan, 1973).

PREHISTORIC SYSTEMS. The earliest agriculture of the northern European plain and the loess uplands to the immediate south was associated with the Linear Pottery culture of central Europe, beginning before 5000 B.C. (Bogucki and Grygiel, 1983; Milisaukas, 1978:46–47). Many settlements were on floodplains (Kruk, 1973). They seem to have had abundant cattle but left behind only a few remains of domesticated grains. Settlements a few hundred years later were more numerous and in more varied locations.

Arguments are made for and against swidden agriculture in the early phases. Some observers find signs of recurrent abandonment in Linear Pottery settlements, but Bogucki and Grygiel (1983) note that seasonal herding could account for them; small garden plots contributed a minor part of the diet, rendering the argument a bit moot. The pollen record in Poland is insufficient to test the swidden model in either the Linear Pottery phase or the phase that followed (Bogucki and Grygiel,

1983) but is sufficient in Denmark in the subsequent phase to indicate regular cycles of forest clearance, cultivation, grazing, and forest regrowth (Jensen, 1982; Welinder, 1975). Jarman, Bailey, and Jarman (1982) argue that the upland loessic soils of the central European areas sustain good yields without amendments, an assertion made by others for the floodplain soils (Dennell, 1983; Kruk, 1973; Sherratt, 1980). Jarman et al. wrongly assert that swiddens are not found today on good soils, but the authors make a good point that modern varieties of the primitive emmer and einkorn wheats grown at the time do not respond to high levels of available nutrients. That is unlike maize, the staple of eastern North American swiddens. A flawed argument is that wood ash contributes significant quantities only of potassium, which is not ordinarily limiting on these soils. In fact, substantial quantities of phosphorus are added in the ashes of leaves and smaller materials, and a little nitrogen in unburnt material.

Yields from experimental swiddens are low enough to cast doubt on their feasibility, though to my knowledge none of the trials have been on any of the major soil types associated with the early agriculturalists. Results were disappointing in a Danish hardwood forest on an acid soil low in several available nutrients (Steensberg, 1980). The best return on seed was threefold, and other harvests fell well short, though some problems encountered may not be representative. On chalk downs in England (Reynolds, 1977) a nearly threefold return of emmer seed was returned in the first year after clearing. Yields subsequently declined, but a drought in one test year obscures the picture. A threefold return of seed is comparable to that from some medieval European fields.

The thrust of subsequent events is better known, their association with population growth unmistakable. Clearing increased, and settlement spread onto a greater variety of soils. The foundations of European mixed farming were laid in the late fourth millennium and the third millennium B.C. Plow (ard) marks have been uncovered beneath barrows at several northern European sites dating from the late fourth millennium B.C.; alleged finds of earlier plows (Müller, 1964; Steensberg, 1973) are controversial. Sherratt (1981) argues that milk production was introduced from Southwest Asia as part of a "secondary products revolution," but the evidence is inferential; dairying is hard to trace archaeologically. By the third millennium B.C. most agricultural communities in Europe exploited a combination of cultivated land, pasture, and forest.

The roots of medieval agriculture are evident by the Iron Age. Forest clearance accelerated during the first millennium B.C. in much of the northern plain and early in the Christian era in Denmark (Jensen, 1982). Soils cultivated for the first time included many coarse-textured soils of moderate nutrient status as well as some highly productive soils previously avoided because they had heavy cover or were hard to plow. Plows were now heavier and may have been capable of turning soil over, though no moldboards are known until after the Roman period. Evidence of manuring is abundant for the Iron Age (Jensen, 1982:226; Phillips, 1980:228) but absent for earlier phases (Milisaukas, 1978:262). Small enclosed fields were common in much of central Europe and the Atlantic fringe, often rectangular fields suggesting cross-plowing with ards but also in less regular shapes (Bradley, 1978). Small enclosures were common, averaging 0.16 ha on the Continent and 0.25 ha in Britain (Bradley, 1978:270). The range in Denmark is 0.1 to 0.3 ha (Jensen, 1982:44). No direct evidence pins down their use.

A Comparison of Agricultural Systems of the Humid Temperate Zone

The agricultural paths of the three main regions diverged early. The outstanding contrast in land use is in the respective patterns of cultivation of uplands and bottomlands. Native North Americans prefer the bottomlands. Though East Asian agriculture develops early on both, bottomlands become especially valued for wet rice. Europeans cultivate both equally, exercising preferences according to soils, demand for food and fiber, and available tillage. East Asians extend wet rice cultivation across alluvial plains and then up the hillsides, making wet land from dry. Europeans exploit meadows for grazing and fodder but begin in the early modern period to make dry lands from wet, by poldering. The Mississippians drained a few wetlands, but other native Americans keep most cultivation on the better-drained alluvial soils.

In Europe, domesticated animals contribute more energy to cultivation than do humans and are conduits for nearly all organic matter and nutrients imported onto cropland. Farm animals are absent in eastern North America, and humans do all the field work. The domesticated animals of East Asia are as thoroughly integrated into crop production as in Europe, possibly more so in the thorough manner of utilizing wastes and the high proportion of animals that are principally kept for draft, but dairying is until very recently a rarity in East Asia south of the steppes.

Comparisons of yields show a large advantage of maize and wet rice cultivation. A ton from a hectare of cereals is a good yield under preindustrial conditions. Average yields of upland cereals in China (Buck,

1937:257) and Japan are about that, and those of medieval Europe probably slightly lower. Several estimates of Chinese rice yields made before World War II, including Buck's careful measurements, are 2 t/ha or better. Rice yields are 2.00 t/ha in Japan in 1880 and 1.82 t/ha in Korea in 1920 (Hayami and Ruttan, 1971), in either case before chemical fertilizers have much effect. Nakamura's (1966:92) estimate for Japan in the period 1878–1882 is much higher, 3.22 t/ha. Bennett (1955:391) cites historical evidence of maize yields on American Indian farms in New England of 40 bushels/acre, or about 2.5 t/ha. Later European settlers there and in the corn belt do as well or better without soil amendments.

American Indian cultivators are hardly to be pitied for their lack of milk, wool, and animal-drawn plows. The work of clearing a well-developed forest with stone axes is appreciable but amply repaid. The eastern North American diet would not be much improved by the addition of milk and meat from domesticated animals. Game and fish are plentiful and, along with beans, supply niacin and certain amino acids deficient in maize. Examinations of skeletons from this time reveal deficiencies of zinc and manganese (Waselkov, 1977:515), but modest additions of milk to the diet would not significantly improve matters.

Significant ethnographic parallels to eastern North American swiddening are to be found among the New Zealand Maori (Vayda, 1956) and the Chilean Mapuche (Cooper, 1946a). The main crops are sweet potato in New Zealand and maize and potato in Chile, crops whose old varieties can furnish high yields.

The ecological rationale for fallows is not the same in these latitudes as in the humid tropics. In the temperate zone, volunteer grasses effectively build soil organic matter and available nutrients. In forests and woodlands more of the mobile nutrients are in the soil, less in the biomass. Ashes and litter could still be beneficial to a new swidden—the value of ashes was understood on the fertile and nearly neutral soils of the Missouri valley (Will and Hyde, 1917:83)—but the long periods of clearance indicate that the burn was in no way essential. The alternation of crops and grass after clearance is a break with practice in the humid tropics but is explained by the favorable properties of these grasses, which in eastern North America may have included ease of tillage. Maori agriculture provides something of a contrast; as in the tropics from which the Maori migrated, cropping periods of 2 to 3 years alternate with fallows of 3 to 14 years (Vayda, 1956). Prehistorians should keep in mind the variety of temperate swidden systems when matching models with evidence of early agriculture.

Eastern North Americans benefit from low population pressure, only a little less so during the Mississippian phase, leaving to speculation what a denser population might have done. They could have cultivated more prairie lands, particularly in the Midwest, and used mounding and ridging to open up lands with a high water table. Because they lacked domesticated grazing animals, their only means to build soil organic matter and nutrients would have been to collect materials by hand. It is hard to imagine any strategies in this setting that would feed more people without diminishing labor efficiency.

East Asian and European agriculture diverge in association with differing degrees of population pressure. By late prehistoric and early historic times, China had more people on less cultivable land, although agriculture began at about the same time in both regions. Europe has 2.5 times as much cultivable land as China, about 3 million km² from the Urals west.[1] China is 90% as large, but much consists of mountains and desert. In the mid-1960s, 1.13 million km² were cultivated (Grigg, 1974:88), and it is generally conceded that little cultivable land remained uncultivated by that time. China's population in 400 B.C. was estimated as 30 million, and Europe's as 20 million (McEvedy and Jones, 1978:18). In A.D. 14, China's population reached 73 million, and Europe's 39.5 million (Clark, 1967:64). Neither population was evenly distributed, but the difference in average density speaks for itself.

The wide disparity in population density and pressure among the three continents poses a theoretical challenge. The low density of eastern North America might be due to late beginnings of agriculture, but the lateness itself demands explanation, particularly if we accept population pressure as a cause of agriculture. Alternatively, it might be argued that disincentives to intensify or expand the region's agriculture exerted a downward pressure on population through some fertility- or mortality-regulating mechanism.

Colonial Contact and the Agriculture of the Three Continents

The age of exploration and colonization most drastically affects the farmers of eastern North America. They are overrun. Another consequence, one that touches all three regions, is the diffusion of crop and livestock species. Some argue that American crops reached the Old World before Columbus, but if this did happen, the effect was minor in comparison with that in following centuries. Some colonial-era movement of varieties or species (the soybean) also occurs between East

Asia and Europe, but the impact is far less than that of transatlantic and transpacific diffusion.

European settlers in eastern North America fit maize and the other native crops into a mixed-farming template. Notwithstanding the adoption of native cultural practices, systems develop so strongly along European lines that any "Indian" phase of settler agriculture is largely a frontier expedient. Wessel's (1976:15) argument that frontier settlers well into the nineteenth century prefer clearing forests to plowing prairies and practice mostly "girdling trees and planting corn [maize] . . . what they knew best, the agriculture of the woodland Indian" is overstated. Settlers clear forest, often putting stump-jumper plows to good use, but from the start, they till grasslands or put them into pasture (Bidwell and Falcone, 1941:7; Day, 1953).

Settler agriculture after the frontier phase evolves distinctly toward the European mixed-farming model, though often with diminished attention to manuring or other improvements. Sometimes abandonment follows cultivation—some parts of New England have seen two or three cycles of cultivation and reforestation since the seventeenth century—but most settlers establish successful permanent cultivation or rotations of crops and pasture. German settlers in the eighteenth century plant grass or clover leys (Saloutos, 1976:48–50) and "float" water meadows (Bidwell and Falcone, 1941:103; Lemon, 1966:479). By 1820, settlers have the technology to devour the Midwest prairies that the Indians had but nibbled. Specialized operators use teams of oxen and heavy plows to break the sod (Schob, 1973).

Many American Indian communities, perhaps most notably the Cherokee, prove adept at mixed farming. Their success, by advertizing their land to the settlers, is often their undoing.

American crops, not American animals, alter European and East Asian farming. The crops at first blend into existing systems or remain garden curiosities, but when maize, potato, peanut, and sweet potato become important field crops, their distinctive requirements and potentialities bring about changes in field systems. The turkey, an American domesticate, assumes some importance in the Old World but has little effect on output and none on systems, because it occupies a feeding niche similar to that of the broiler chicken, with which it witlessly competes for much the same market.

Maize, sweet potato, and peanut become the main crops in the sixteenth and seventeenth centuries on hill land in the coastal and island areas of East Asia, where summers are warm and rainy. They open up new lands. The prevalence at first of swidden methods for their cultivation has been mentioned. In this century permanent cultivation and the use of soil amendments are the rule.

Maize becomes the main crop in large areas of southern Europe. It is the dominant staple for human consumption in parts of northern Italy and in much of Romania and the Caucasus, and its cultivation for stock feed spreads in this century wherever summer temperatures permit. The effect in the western part of this belt, where summers are dry, is to encourage irrigation. In the east, maize often replaces winter or spring small grains.

The potato is most popular in cooler areas. Particularly in such cool maritime areas as Iceland and the Scottish highlands, it often gives a profitable yield where cereals do not ripen. In slightly warmer locations, such as most of Ireland, it outproduces cereals on favorable soils. In the absence of mechanization, potato cultivation is more labor intensive than cereal cultivation.

Agriculture in Cool Lands

Food production earliest approached its historic pole-ward limits in Europe and along the west coast of South America (see climatic data in Table 7.1). In Europe, cultivation and animal husbandry reached the upper Bothnian coast, northern Sweden, after 2000 B.C. (Christiansen and Broadbent, 1975:49) and the central Norwegian coast in the first millennium A.D. Food production in the north was long secondary to food collecting, fishing, and sea-mammal hunting, until sedentary pastoralism gained in the last centuries before the Viking era. In precolonial southern Chile the potato replaces maize as the dominant staple and was cultivated down to Chiloé Island (Cooper, 1946b).

Native North Americans lacked the potato, and maize has a high threshold temperature and a fairly high accumulated heat requirement. The northern limit of agriculture crosses southern Ontario, the upper St. Lawrence valley, and the south-central coast of Maine, where maize cultivation is still spreading northward at the time of colonial contact (Bennett, 1955:379).

In East Asia, pastoralists range far to the north, and their military strength acts to contain the cultivators to the south. The Manchu dynasty, of pastoralist origins, long hold up Chinese settlement of the Manchurian plains. Later Russian settlers push cultivation into the forest (taiga).

Table 7.1. Climatic data for some Cc and Dc stations

Station	Mean temperature (°C)			Annual precipitation (cm)
	July	January	Annual	
Cc				
Thorshavn, Faeroe Islands	11	3	6	145
Punta Arenas, Chile	2	11	7	39
Dutch Harbor, Alaska	11	0	4	158
Dc				
Trondheim, Norway	14	−3	6	101
Verkhoyansk, USSR	16	−50	−16	13
Dawson, Yukon, Canada	15	−30	−5	34

Source: Trewartha (1954).

SOILS. The unique soils of the polar zones and high mountains are tundra soils formed over permafrost. They are exploited for reindeer pastoralism and on only an inconsequential scale for cultivation. The more agriculturally useful soils are in the same broad classes as those farther south.

Excessively wet soil conditions prevail and limit cultivation. Precipitation is well in excess of evaporation and transpiration not only in cool maritime regions but also over wide areas of the continental interiors. Seasonal freezing restricts drainage of many inland soils, and wet soil conditions slow the warming of ground in spring. No crops in these regions do well in waterlogged soils, though a few adapted wild plants are exploited. The most valued soils for cultivation are therefore those that are better drained, including some commercially valuable Alfisols of the Canadian Great Plains and western Siberia. Spring waterlogging can be a problem even on these soils, and artificial drainage is often essential.

The level of exchangeable bases tends to be low, particularly under the prevalent coniferous forest and where leaching is excessive. Calcium, magnesium, and potassium deficiencies often limit crop growth, and liming is widely used to counteract acidity. Seaweed, an excellent source of potassium, has long been a valued soil amendment around the northern coasts of Europe.

Though the content of organic matter, a product of slow decomposition in cold and wet conditions, tends to be high, nitrogen is often limiting. Organic matter content is usually 3% to 5% in the A horizon of forest soils, but the carbon:nitrogen ratio tends to be high. Nitrification is slow at low temperatures, and many native plants, such as the blueberry, take up nitrogen in the form of ammonia, not nitrate. Responses to manures and chemical fertilizers are widely reported. Except for lime, however, fertilizers are not as a rule applied at rates equivalent to those used on the same or similar crops in warmer locations. But yields and crop removal are also less.

THE DECLINING ROLE OF CULTIVATION. Toward the absolute limits of cultivation, crops are secondary to other sources of food or livelihood. Few crops ripen reliably. Soils with good drainage, a slope toward the sun, and favorable physical properties and nutrient status are preferred but hard to come by. Along the coasts, cultivation or animal husbandry is often a small supplement to food or income drawn from the sea. Because seaports are so often situated along rugged fjords, cultivation may be reduced to dooryard gardens on soil laboriously built up on rocky slopes. The husbandry of grazing animals often remains viable where cultivation is not, because the native grasses and broadleaves have low threshold temperatures. Cropland shrinks. In the subarctic interior of northwestern Canada and Alaska, a favorable region with warm summers, barley and spring wheat cover large areas, but ripe grain is harvested in fewer than half the years. In other seasons the crop is cut green for hay and silage.

Gardeners furnish warm soil by building labor-intensive raised beds that are well drained and readily warm in the sun. Icelanders use geothermal areas. The potato appears to respond particularly well to warm soils. Raised beds were already known on a small scale in Ireland and Scotland before the introduction of the potato but afterward become a common sight along the cool outer coasts and at higher elevations and somehow acquire the rather ironic name "lazy beds."

The transition from a primary dependence on cultivation to secondary and finally very little dependence is visible in a transect from Scotland northwest into the Atlantic. Infield-outfield cultivation in early nineteenth-century Scotland first gives way in the northern islands to systems in which cultivated land dwindles and uncultivated pasture replaces outfields. In 1808, 6.3% of land in the Orkneys is cultivated land, 15.6% first-class pasture and meadow, and 76.6% rough pasture (Fenton, 1978:57). In Funzie, Shetland, only 0.6% of the land is cultivated in 1829. Meadows are 14.5% of the productive area, and 13.8% of the productive area consists of manured and highly productive grassland (calculated from Fenton, 1978:46, 51). The Orkneys have more cultivable soil than the Shetlands, but climate must also be invoked to explain so great a contrast. Farther north, the Faeroes import about three-quarters of their grain (West, 1972:20). Inner, well-manured lands produce mostly hay, but on some of the land, barley alternates with grass (Williamson, 1948). In Iceland a little cereal is cultivated in the early years of settlement but not in the cooler period after 1200 until this century. Other crops occupy minute areas. The Norse press food production to its utmost limit in Greenland, named by Erik the Red with a touch of hyperbole. Hunting is vital to the Greenland colonists for food and a source of trade goods. Cattle and sheep, kept barely alive in their winter byres, supply hides, wool, and summer milk (Ingstad, 1966).

The potato is the ideal energy staple for these cool maritime lands, though it becomes prevalent only in the outer parts of northern Europe and the North Atlantic during the eighteenth century. Returns on potatoes are profitable where cereals yield little or not at all. The crop never rivals animal husbandry in overall importance nor has the dramatic effect on land holdings that it had in Ireland, but its introduction probably did much for nutrition. It is a source not only of carbohydrates but also of vitamin C, and tubers store well through winter and early spring, what was long the scurvy season in the north.

Russian settlers in the north of European Russia and in Siberia live in a cool continental climate. Livestock have from settlement ranked ahead of crops in spite of the difficulty of getting enough hay or other fodder for the long, severe winters. Few of the households subsist mainly from their crops. Just as the Atlantic islanders trade stockfish and hides for grain, so forestry, the fur trade, and forest products make the Russians' farms viable. Warm summers ripen barley, rye, and buckwheat almost to the northern limits of cattle and sheep, particularly in Siberia. The potato eventually becomes important but is still mostly grown alongside the grain crops, not in their stead (Symons, 1972).

New technology makes slight further extensions possible. Mechanization makes sedentary pastoralism commercially viable today in Siberia, Alaska, the Yukon, and southern Patagonia, largely because equipment allows ample haymaking during the long summer days. Scientific plant breeding and new methods of management that make better use of sunlight and heat slightly extend the limits of cereal and potato cultivation, and cucumbers ripen in Yakutia, sweet corn in Matanuska, but no green revolution is in the works so near the poles, because temperature is a less tractable limiting factor than nutrients or water. Thus far, scientific plant breeding has achieved mostly very early varieties or some with exceptional frost hardiness. Only slight success has been gained in lowering growth threshold temperatures.

Note

1. The authors of *The World Food Problem* (President's Science Advisory Committee, 1967) estimate 1.82 million km² are in Europe. The USSR is not counted in this statistic but is said to contain about twice as much cultivable land, and most other sources estimate that about a third of Soviet agricultural land resources are in its European part.

References

Aalen, F.H.A. (1978). *Man and the Landscape in Ireland.* Academic Press, London.

Anderson, J. (1876). *Mandalay to Momien.* Macmillan, London.

Ban, Sung Hwa, Pal Yang Moon, and D.H. Perkins (1980). *Rural Development: Studies in the Modernization of the Republic of Korea, 1945–1975.* Harvard University Press, Cambridge.

Beauclair, I. (1956). Culture traits of non-Chinese tribes in Kweichow province, southwest China. *Sinologica,* 5:20–35.

Bennett, M.K. (1955). The food economy of the New England Indians, 1605–75. *Journal of Political Economy,* 63:369–397.

Bidwell, P.W., and J.I. Falcone (1941). *History of Agriculture in the Northern United States 1620–1860.* Peter Smith, New York.

Bloch, M. (1966). *French Rural History: An Essay on Its Basic Characteristics,* trans. J. Sondheimer. University of California Press, Berkeley.

Bogucki, P., and R. Grygiel (1983). Early farmers of the north European plain. *Scientific American,* 248(4):104–112.

Bradley, R. (1978). Prehistoric field systems in Britain and north-west Europe—a review of some recent work. *World Archaeology,* 9:265–280.

Buchanan, R.H. (1973). Field systems of Ireland. In *Studies of Field Systems in the British Isles* (A.R.H. Baker and R.A. Butlin, eds.), Cambridge University Press, Cambridge, pp. 580–618.

Buck, J.L. (1937). *Land Utilization in China.* University of Chicago Press, Chicago.

Chang Kwang-chih (1963). *The Archaeology of Ancient China.* Yale University Press, New Haven, Conn.

———. (1964). China. In *Courses toward Urban Life* (R.J. Braidwood and G.R. Willey, eds.), Aldine, Chicago, pp. 177–192.

Chang Te-tzu (1983). The origins and early culture of the cereal grains and food legumes. In *The Origins of Chinese Civilization* (D.N. Keightley, ed.), University of California Press, Berkeley, pp. 65–94.

Chard, C.S. (1974). *Northeast Asia in Prehistory.* University of Wisconsin Press, Madison.

Christiansen, H., and N.D. Broadbent (1975). Prehistoric coastal settlement on the upper Bothnian coast. In *Prehistoric Maritime Adaptations of the Circumpolar Zone (W. Fitzhugh, ed.), Mouton, The Hague, pp. 47–56.

Clark, C. (1967). *Population Growth and Land Use*. Macmillan, London.

Cooper, J.M. (1946a). The Araucanians. In *The Andean Civilizations*, vol. 2 of *Handbook of South American Indians* (J.H. Steward, ed.), Smithsonian Institution, Bureau of American Ethnology, Bulletin no. 143, Washington, D.C., pp. 687–760.

_____ (1946b). The Chono. In *The Marginal Tribes*, vol. 1 of *Handbook of South American Indians* (J.H. Steward, ed.), Smithsonian Institution, Bureau of American Ethnology, Bulletin no. 143, Washington, D.C., pp. 47–54.

Cooter, W.S. (1978). Ecological dimensions of medieval agrarian systems. *Agricultural History*, 52:458–477.

Crummey, R.O. (1970). *The Old Believers and the World of Antichrist*. University of Wisconsin Press, Madison.

Darby, H.C. (1956). The clearing of the woodland in Europe. In *Man's Role in Changing the Face of the Earth* (W.L. Thomas et al., eds.), University of Chicago Press, Chicago, pp. 183–216.

Day, G.M. (1953). The Indian as an ecological factor in the northeastern forest. *Ecology*, 34:329–346.

Dennell, R.W. (1983). *European Economic Prehistory: A New Approach*. Academic Press, London.

Dickinson, R.E. (1961). *The West European City: A Geographical Interpretation*. Routledge and Kegan Paul, London.

Donck, A. van der (1841). A description of the New Netherlands. *New York Historical Society, Collectors Series*, 2:125–242.

Dragoo, D.W. (1976). Some aspects of eastern North American prehistory: A review 1975. *American Antiquity*, 41:3–27.

Driver, H.E. (1961). *Indians of North America*. University of Chicago Press, Chicago.

Driver, H.E., and W.C. Massey (1957). Comparative studies of North American Indians. *Transactions of the American Philosophical Society*, n.s. 48, pp. 167–456. Philadelphia.

Ermolov, A.S. (1893). Systems of agriculture and field rotation. In *The Industries of Russia*, pt. 3, Department of Trade and Industry, St. Petersburg, pp. 62–73.

Evans, E.E. (1956). The ecology of peasant life in Western Europe. In *Man's Role in Changing the Face of the Earth* (W.L. Thomas et al., eds.), University of Chicago Press, Chicago, pp. 217–239.

Eyre, J.D. (1962). Mountain land use in northern Japan. *Geographical Review*, 52:236–252.

Fenton, A. (1978). *The Northern Isles: Orkney and Shetland*. J. Donald, Edinburgh.

Fowler, M.L. (1969). Middle Mississippian agricultural fields. *American Antiquity*, 34:365–375.

_____. (1971). The origin of plant domestication in the central Mississippi valley: A hypothesis. In *Prehistoric Agriculture* (S. Struever, ed.), American Museum of Natural History, Garden City, N.Y. pp. 122–128.

Grigg, D.B. (1974). *The Agricultural Systems of the World.* Cambridge University Press, London.

Hall, R.B., and T. Nok (1953). Yakihata, burned-field agriculture in Japan, with its special characteristics in Shikoku. *Papers of the Michigan Academy of Sciences, Arts, and Letters,* 38:315–322.

Handley, J.E. (1953). *Scottish Farming in the Eighteenth Century.* Faber and Faber, London.

Hayami, Y., and V.W. Ruttan (1971). *Agricultural Development: An International Perspective.* Johns Hopkins University Press, Baltimore.

Ho Ping-ti (1956). Early ripening rice in Chinese history. *Economic History,* 9:200–218.

––––––. (1959). *Studies on the Population of China, 1368–1953.* Harvard University Press, Cambridge.

––––––. (1977). The indigenous origins of Chinese agriculture. In *Origins of Agriculture* (C.A. Reed, ed.), Mouton, The Hague, pp. 413–484.

Hsü Chung-shu (1956). The well-field system in Shang and Chan. In *Chinese Social History: Translations of Selected Studies* (E-tu Zen Sun and J. De Francis, eds.), Octagon, New York, pp. 3–17.

Ingstad, H.M. (1966). *Land under the Pole Star.* St. Martin's, New York.

Jablow, J. (1974). *Ponca Indians: Ethnohistory of the Ponca.* Garland, New York.

Jarman, M.R., G.N. Bailey, and H.N. Jarman, eds. for the British Academy Major Research Project in the Early History of Agriculture (1982). *Early European Agriculture: Its Foundations and Development.* Cambridge University Press, Cambridge.

Jensen, J. (1982). *The Prehistory of Denmark.* Methuen, London.

Jones, G.R.J. (1972). Post-Roman Wales. In *The Agrarian History of England and Wales* (H.P.R. Finberg, ed.), vol. 1, Cambridge University Press, Cambridge, pp. 283–384.

––––––. (1973). Field systems of north Wales. In *Studies of Field Systems in the British Isles* (A.R.H. Baker and R.A. Butlin, eds.), Cambridge University Press, Cambridge, pp. 430–479.

Kerridge, E. (1973). *The Farmers of Old England.* Rowman and Littlefield, Totowa, N.J.

King, F.H. ([1911] n.d.). *Farmers of Forty Centuries.* Reprint. Rodale Press, Emmaus, Pa.

Kruk, J. (1973). *Studia Osadnicze nad Neolitem Wyzym Lessowych.* Polska Akademii Nauk, Wroclaw, Poland.

––––––. (1975). Studies on the settlement of the loess uplands. *Polish Archaeological Abstracts,* 5:94/75.

Kuo, L.T.C. (1972). *The Technical Transformation of Agriculture in Communist China.* Praeger, New York.

Lee, Hoon K. (1936). *Land Utilization and Rural Economy in Korea.* University of Chicago Press, Chicago.

Lemon, J.T. (1966). The agricultural practices of national groups in eighteenth-century southeastern Pennsylvania. *Geographical Review,* 56:467–496.

Li Hui-lin (1983). The domestication of plants in China: Ecogeographical considerations. In *The Origins of Chinese Civilization* (D.N. Keightley, ed.), University of California Press, Berkeley, pp. 21–64.

Loomis, R.S. (1978). Ecological dimensions of medieval agrarian systems: An ecologist responds. *Agricultural History,* 52:478–483.

MacCauley, C. (1884). *The Seminole Indians of Florida.* Smithsonian Institution, Bureau of American Ethnology, Annual Report no. 5, pp. 469–538. Washington, D.C.

Mayhew, A. (1973). *Rural Settlement and Farming in Germany.* Barnes and Noble, New York.

McCourt, D. (1955). Infield and outfield in Ireland. *Economic History Review,* 7:369–376.

McEvedy, C., and R. Jones (1978). *Atlas of World Population History.* Harmondsworth, New York.

Mead, W.R. (1953). *Farming in Finland.* Athlone, London.

Milisaukas, S. (1978). *European Prehistory.* Academic Press, New York.

Müller, H.H. (1964). *Die Haustiere der Mitteldeutsche Bandkeramiker.* Akademie der Wissenschafts zu Berlin 17, Berlin.

Nakamura, J.I. (1966). *Agricultural Production and the Economic Development of Japan.* Princeton University Press, Princeton, N.J.

Nuttonson, M.Y. (1952). *Ecological Geography and Field Practices of the Ryukyu Islands.* Institute of Crop Ecology, Washington, D.C.

Pearson, R., with Shyh-Changho (1983). The Ch'ing-lien-kang culture and the Chinese neolithic. In *The Origins of Chinese Civilization* (D.N. Keightley, ed.), University of California Press, Berkeley, pp. 119–145.

Perkins, D. (1969). *Agricultural Development in China.* Aldine, Chicago.

Pfeifer, G. (1956). The quality of peasant living in central Europe. In *Man's Role in Changing the Face of the Earth* (W.L. Thomas et al., eds.), University of Chicago Press, Chicago, pp. 240–277.

Phillips, P. (1980). *The Prehistory of Europe.* Indiana University Press, Bloomington.

Potapov, L.P., with S.V. Ivanov, G.S. Maslova, and K.V. Sokolova (1956). Historical-ethnographic survey of the Russian population of Siberia in the prerevolutionary period. In *The Peoples of Siberia* (M.G. Levin and L.P. Potapov, eds.), University of Chicago Press, Chicago, pp. 105–202.

President's Science Advisory Committee, Panel on World Food Supply (1967). *The World Food Problem.* Vols. 1–3. The White House, Washington, D.C.

Reynolds, P.J. (1977). Slash and burn experiment. *Archaeological Journal,* 134:307–318.

Riley, T.J., and G. Freimuth (1979). Field systems and frost drainage in the prehistoric agriculture of the upper Great Lakes. *American Antiquity,* 44:271–284.

Russell, H.S. (1976). *A Long, Deep Furrow: Three Centuries of Farming in New England.* University Press of New England, Hanover, N.H.

Saloutos, T. (1976). The immigrant contribution to American agriculture. *Agricultural History,* 50:45–67.

Schob, D.E. (1973). Sodbusting on the upper midwestern frontier, 1820–1860. *Agricultural History,* 47:47–56.

Sherratt, A. (1980). Water, soil, and seasonality in early cereal cultivation. *World Archaeology,* 11:313–330.

———. (1981). Plough and pastoralism: Aspects of the secondary products revolution. In *Patterns of the Past: Studies in Honour of David Clarke* (I. Hodder, G. Isaac, and N. Hammond, eds.), Cambridge University Press, London, pp. 261–305.

Slicher van Bath, B.H. (1963). *The Agrarian History of Western Europe, A.D. 500–1850,* trans. O. Ordish. Arnold, London.

Smith, T.C. (1959). *The Agrarian Origins of Modern Japan.* Stanford University Press, Stanford, Calif.

Steensberg, A. (1973). A 6000 year old ploughing implement from Satrup Moor. *Tools and Tillage,* 2:105–118.

———. (1980). *Draved: An Experiment in Stone Age Agriculture.* National Museum of Denmark, Copenhagen.

Stewart, O.C. (1956). Fire as the first great force employed by man. In *Man's Role in Changing the Face of the Earth* (W.L. Thomas et al., eds.), University of Chicago Press, Chicago, pp. 115–133.

Swanton, J.R. (1942). *Source Material on the History and Ethnology of the Caddo.* Smithsonian Institution, Bureau of American Ethnology, Bulletin no. 132. Washington, D.C.

———. (1946). *The Indians of the Southeastern United States.* Smithsonian Institution, Bureau of American Ethnology, Bulletin no. 137. Washington, D.C.

Symons, L. (1972). *Russian Agriculture: A Geographic Survey.* Wiley, New York.

Thirsk, J. (1973). Field systems of the east Midlands. In *Studies of Field Systems in the British Isles* (A.R.H. Baker and R.A. Butlin, eds.), Cambridge University Press, Cambridge, pp. 232–280.

Trewartha, G.T. (1954). *An Introduction to Climate.* McGraw-Hill, New York.

Tuan Yi-fu (1969). *China.* Aldine, Chicago.

Vayda, A.P. (1956). Maori conquests in relation to the New Zealand environment. *Journal of the Polynesian Society,* 65:204–211.

Waselkov, G. (1977). Prehistoric agriculture in the central Mississippi valley. *Agricultural History,* 51:513–519.

Watson, W. (1974). *Ancient China: The Discoveries of Post-Liberation Archaeology.* New York Graphic Society, Greenwich, Conn.

Welinder, S. (1975). Agriculture, inland hunting, and sea hunting in the western and northern regions of the Baltic, 6000–2000 B.C. In *Prehistoric Maritime Adaptations of the Circumpolar Zone,* Mouton, The Hague, pp. 21–40.

Wessel, T.R. (1976). Agriculture, Indians, and American history. *Agricultural History,* 50:9–20.

West, J.F. (1972). *Faroe: The Emergence of a Nation.* C. Hurst, London.
Whittington, G. (1973). Field systems of Scotland. In *Studies of Field Systems in the British Isles* (A.R.H. Baker and R.A. Butlin, eds.), Cambridge University Press, Cambridge, pp. 530–579.
Will, G.F., and G.E. Hyde (1917). *Corn among the Indians of the Missouri Valley.* University of Nebraska Press, Lincoln.
Williamson, K. (1948). *The Atlantic Islands.* Collins, London.
Wilson, G.L. (1917). *Agriculture of the Hidatsa Indians: An Indian Interpretation.* University of Minnesota Studies in the Social Sciences, no. 9. Minneapolis.

8
Population and Agriculture

 Previous chapters touched on the association of population growth and agricultural intensification in preindustrial societies without separating cause and effect. This is the appropriate point at which to do so, before moving on to industrial agriculture. It is imperative to separate the short term from the long term. In the short term, population levels tend to compensate for a disturbance, moving toward equilibrium. The agricultural system that supports a population may be similarly conservative, yet changes in it can stimulate population growth. In the long term, population growth is so persistent that we must consider it the prime mover, a slow-acting but relentless engine of change.

This chapter first summarizes models of population growth and technical change, then draws on ethnographic sources to clarify the concept of population pressure. Treatments follow of pioneer populations and then of Holocene population growth after the origins of agriculture, illustrating how population levels respond to low population pressure. Self-regulation will then be demonstrated in historic cases, and finally explanations will be sought for the persistence of long-term change in the face of these mechanisms.

Models of Population and Agricultural Change

Malthus's legacy is lingering concern over our ability to keep pace with population growth. Much conventional wisdom, often labeled Malthusian with less than complete accuracy, holds that technical innovations or introductions cause population growth. A rejoinder, Boserup's *Conditions of Agricultural Growth* (1965), argues that population is the independent variable that shapes agricultural systems and technology. Each argument is supportable by simple yet significant illustrations. Boserup's introduction notes that the contemporary surge of world population is "autonomous" of innovations in agricultural production. Modern medicine and the resulting decline in mortality cause the population boom, growth that prompts agricultural intensification and research. Conversely, cases may be found in which population growth accelerates following some yield-raising innovation or introduction. Early Holocene population growth, following the advent of agriculture, is an excellent example.

These contrasting sequences of events may simply reflect different circumstances, but they are so prominent in world history that an attempt to reconcile them is in order. Some writers find Boserup's and Malthus's views compatible (Hammel and Howell, 1987; Pryor, 1982; Simon, 1978). I concur, beginning with the premise that populations are self-regulating. If regulating mechanisms were effective short of producing a persistent return to the same equilibrium level, population could respond to technical innovations or exogenous factors and still be a force for change.

Population regulation is a troublesome concept. Opinion varies widely over its effectiveness and the respective roles of fertility and mortality or of voluntary and involuntary curbs on births.

One view of food-collecting societies and some tribal agricultural societies is that their populations are in homeostasis, tending toward a level well below what the environment could support, a model pioneered by Carr-Saunders (1922) and embraced by many anthropologists in the 1960s and 1970s (Birdsell, 1968; Flannery, 1969; Hainline, 1965; Hayden, 1972; Lee, 1968; Lee and DeVore, 1968; Polgar, 1972; Schacht, 1980). As a consequence, collectors enjoy a measure of "primitive affluence."

A critique by Caldwell, Caldwell, and Caldwell (1987) is that primitive affluence rests on unrealistic notions of regulating mechanisms; the authors suggest instead that nothing "in the record can indisputably sustain population-equilibrium [steady-state] theories employing other than Malthusian means." They find proffered evidence of voluntary birth control thin or suspect and conclude that these and other preindustrial populations are close to "natural fertility," reputedly the pattern of births to women of various ages when no voluntary controls are in effect (Henry, 1961). Of the only control mechanisms left—involuntary fertility control and mortality—they stress mortality, presumably meaning that pressure on resources is the ultimate check on growth.

The Caldwells dispose too quickly of fertility regulation (Eversley, 1987). Netting (1987) observes that involuntary curbs on fertility are highly effective among San food collectors. Infanticide is fairly widespread among agricultural peoples and in several cases is sufficiently frequent to affect population levels significantly. In others it is practiced mainly by, variously, young mothers, old mothers, or those in uncertain economic circumstances, indicating likely responsiveness to any deterioration of living standards. Documented cases include eighteenth-century Japan (Dickemann, 1975; Smith, 1977), several provinces of nineteenth-century India (Dickemann, 1975), and the native South American Ayoreo (Bugos and McCarthy, 1984) and Tapirapé (Wagley, [1951] 1969). Several examples are from early colonial Polynesia (Firth, 1936; Kamakau, 1961; Oliver, 1974), not surprisingly, because malaria and many major epidemic diseases were absent from the region, and women were sexually active from an early age. Self-induced abortion is also well documented for the Micronesian island of Yap (Schneider, 1955). Coitus interruptus was prevalent in much of Polynesia and in some places had the force of authority behind it.

Certain preindustrial agriculturalists do benefit from low population pressure, regardless of how they arrived at that circumstance. I offer the precolonial population of eastern North America as a prime example.

The course will be steered here between the idyllic view that undisturbed populations remain comfortably well within limits and the gloomier alternative that numbers are chronically so near their limits that misery results, a course whose elucidation must await the introduction and development of several concepts. One concept is population pressure. To Boserup, pressure is generated by population growth but, because of the agricultural system's elasticity, is not ordinarily critical. In the darkest versions of Malthus's ideas, pressure is chronically severe, and any number of non-Malthusians have also come away assuming that pressure becomes significant only when a population is near its limit. The position shortly to be developed is that population pressure can impel intensification, population regulation, commonly both, at population levels well short of any limit.

MALTHUS. The ideas of Malthus — as presented in the first, second, and seventh editions of the *Essay on the Principle of Population* — are usefully separated into two components. In one component, population, food supply, and agricultural labor are conceived as interrelated parts of what would today be termed a self-regulating system. In the first *Essay,* Malthus (1959:11) describes what happens following an increase in population to levels that strain resources:

> During this season of distress, the discouragements to marriage, and the difficulty of rearing a family are so great that population is at a stand. In the mean time, the cheapness of labour, the plenty of labourers, and the necessity of an increased industry among them, encourage cultivators to employ more labour upon their land, to turn up fresh soil, and to manure and improve more completely what is already in tillage, till ultimately the means of subsistence become in the same proportion to the population as at the period from which we set out. The situation of the labourer being then again tolerably comfortable, the restraints to population are in some degree loosened, and the same retrograde and progressive movements with respect to happiness are repeated.

No better exposition of a tendency toward equilibrium can be found than in the return to the condition of "the period from which we set out." Malthus demonstrates his awareness of both mortality regulation and fertility regulation, especially the "discouragements to marriage." Boserup (1965:11) is incorrect in associating Malthus with the crude neo-Malthusian view that "population growth is seen as the dependent variable, determined by preceding changes in agricultural productivity which, in their turn, are explained as the result of extraneous factors, such as the fortuitous factor of technical invention and imitation."

Malthus in fact recognizes that population pressure stimulates innovation, which cannot therefore be fortuitous. He reaches the conclusion I have stressed, that population demonstrably tends toward equilibrium even where there is a long-term upward trend.

Self-regulation falls well short of producing anything like primitive affluence, so far short that pessimism is fairly described as the second component of Malthus's ideas. Populations tend toward equilibrium perilously close to the limits of their food-producing technology. His gloomy view of Irish poverty is justly infamous. If population growth does not act singly to wipe away the benefits gained through technical improvement, the early editions of the *Essay* tell us that is its eventual consequence. Petersen (1979) finds in later works more hope, a recognition that population growth might be checked short of producing general misery.

BOSERUP. If the intent of *The Conditions of Agricultural Growth* is to counter the notion that population growth depends on technical innovation, Boserup supplies a needed antidote. The remedy goes too far, though, by making agricultural systems wholly elastic.

Fairness requires separating Boserup's theory of population and agricultural intensification from the specific five-stage model she chooses for illustration (see chapter 3), a model acknowledged to be "arbitrary" and a "simplification" (Boserup, 1965:15). Boserup at times speaks separately of cropping frequency and intensity and is presumably aware that intensification takes other forms.

One part of Boserup's theory is dispensable, the principle that labor efficiency declines as cropping becomes more frequent, invoked to explain why cultivators under low population pressure do not intensify anyway. Bronson (1972) dubs this the "law of least effort," and so it will be called here. Boserup also recognizes that the large capital investment needed to establish certain more intensive systems might discourage cultivators, but she gives the law of least effort more attention, stress, and elaboration.

The law of least effort is independently supported (Barlett, 1976) and disputed (Bronson, 1972; Harris, 1975:239–246) and is difficult to test in a well-controlled fashion. Long-fallow cultivators in precolonial eastern North America probably achieve an exceptionally high labor efficiency, in company with many Amazonian swiddeners who manage with infrequent weeding (Beckerman, 1987:75–83), but so do some permanent cultivators, such as decrue farmers. Differences in crops, environment, and technology cloud comparisons. The work of clearing varies from forest to forest and grassland to grassland. It is easier to accomplish with metal axes than with stone axes. Draft animals may or may not be available. Soils vary in their capacity to support permanent cultivation without soil amendments. Not surprisingly, evidence of comparative labor efficiencies is conflicting and inconclusive (Vasey, 1979:278–279).

A comparison of Thai rice farming systems (Hanks, 1972) suggests that labor efficiency improves when fallow systems give way to permanent wet systems with low labor input (broadcasting), but most of the advantage is lost as the systems become more labor-intensive (transplanting). The latter are reminiscent of Geertz's (1963) "involuted" wet rice farming under high population pressure in Java.

Without the law of least effort, the elasticity of systems must be qualified. Brookfield (1972) speaks of "resistances" to intensification, including Boserup's bugbear—that is, a need for new technology—but also specific environmental conditions, investments required to establish the new system, and investments in the old system that are lost in the new. Brookfield proposes a model in which levels of intensification are in a hierarchy. As population pressure grows, labor efficiency first declines until resistances to transition to the next level are overcome; then it improves. The model fits Hanks's scheme for the evolution of rice farming, with broadcasting and transplanting being at the same level, but is hard to test widely with available historical or archaeological materials.

Boserup and others are probably right to argue that forest fallow systems would not persist were they very wasteful of effort, but an hour more or less of effort is a small price for the freedom they offer. The tools required are few and portable, and only the current crop is forfeit if war comes or tenure is lost.

Defining Population Pressure

Population pressure is evident to any farmer who confronts a crowded landscape and rising rents, but the concept is far more often invoked than clarified. The problem is how to take account of all those technical and environmental variables that exacerbate or relieve pressure.

One approach is to compare the actual population of a territory with its carrying capacity; the nearer that population comes to this limit, the greater the population pressure. But carrying capacity is a diffuse concept. It is also less powerful the more elastic the food production system is; before turning to carrying capacity, I shall show that subsistence strategies are only partly elastic and that, as population grows, their costs and risks tend to mount, but not at all evenly. This much hints that carrying capacity has some validity, but elasticity is typically sufficient to make its estimation difficult. We might instead try to deal more directly with population pressure by taking note of the increase in costs and risks as pressure mounts.

RISK MANAGEMENT AND POPULATION PRESSURE: A CASE STUDY. A combination of high costs and high risks is the best evidence of population pressure. Risk by itself is unconvincing, because most communities seem to accept avoidable risks. I know of no historic or ethnographic peoples who heed the biblical advice to store food for several years. Risks might be taken to alleviate the problems of severe population pressure or to avoid the costs of alternative strategies that could support as large or larger numbers. The price of taking risks may well be periodic famines, but if these episodes are sufficiently infrequent, the low population levels immediately following them are unrepresentative of long-term averages. The peasants of many preindustrial societies bear the risks and costs, while landowners or other elites exert more or less control over the choice of agricultural strategies. The peasantry may well experience famine even though they have many available options to raise yields or to maintain more reliable yields.

A look at the Motu and Koita of precolonial coastal Papua New Guinea, in the vicinity of modern Port Moresby, reveals the management of risks and, to some extent, of costs under moderate population pressure. The Motu trade for food, in effect allowing them to pursue some risky food-getting strategies. The population is not at its limit but would incur a significant penalty for being much more numerous. They would benefit from a lower population by incurring less risk. A more detailed analysis is in Vasey (1982).

The dry season is long, and the population density low for agriculturalists. The rainy season averages about 5 months, ranging from barely 3 to more than 10, according to records from 1954 to 1980. The Motu and Koita together number about 2,000 (Allen, 1976:442; Oram, 1977:96), or 17 per km². If they knew of cereals or manioc, a postcolonial introduction and a crop left in the ground for later harvest, far more people could be supported. Without these crops, if the Motu and Koita numbered 3,000, they would have to reorganize to maximize utilization of critical dry-season food resources and would pursue some highly risky strategies unless breakthroughs were made in local food storage.

Low-risk strategies available in the area are principally those involving cultivation of banana and coconut on soils that remain moist throughout the dry season. Fairly dependable wild food resources include cycad (*Cycas circinalis*) nuts, which must be processed to remove poison, and some minimum part of the fluctuating catch of fish and game. At their maximum dependable yields, these sources could together supply at least three-quarters of energy requirements, of which nearly half would be from banana, but a reduction by a third, to 1,000 kcal per diem (half the requirement), is reasonable to allow for less than maximum exploitation, for maximum exploitation is hard for any community to achieve. Cycad stands are scattered, and as the nuts ripen, they fall and quickly deteriorate on the ground, whereas coconut palms strung out along the strand would be subject to conflicting land claims and vulnerable to attack. The baseline year for determining low risk, 1980, was the driest in thirty years of record keeping, but it may or may not have been the driest year over a longer period.

Both peoples cultivate seasonally dry soils, and one crop, the long yam (*Dioscorea alata*), is stored, but relying too much on it is risky. Crops are subject to losses from dry spells during the rainy season, and in years of short rainy seasons the immature tubers that are produced do not store well, explaining historical accounts that yams are finished or have rotted less than six months after harvest (Groves, 1960:7), before the leanest period of the year.

To feed the actual population of 2,000, the Koita specialize in inland resources, including the better share of low-risk resources, whereas the Motu make more use of marine and coastal resources and undertake voyages up to 300 km westward to trade pots for sago starch and other foodstuffs. The Motu probably incur more risks than the Koita, as well as more costs. They make long, hazardous fishing forays (Oram, 1977, 1982). Their gardens climb steep coastal slopes whose soils drain and dry out quickly. They gather mangrove hypocotyls, a seasonal but variable resource.

CARRYING CAPACITY: AT LEAST THREE CONCEPTS.

Dewar (1984) finds in the literature two versions of carrying capacity: the equilibrium level of a population, k, and the technical and environmental limit of that population, Cc. These two versions are sometimes assumed to be the same (e.g., Maserang, 1977:483), an assumption that for human populations fails for want of empirical evidence. Population, as we shall see, may tend toward equilibrium well short of any absolute limit imposed by technology or environment.

More precisely, k is the standard symbol for the equilibrium level approached by an asymptotic growth curve. The most frequently used model of asymptotic growth is the logistic (Fig. 8.1), to the point that it is often taken to be the only model of asymptotic growth, but other

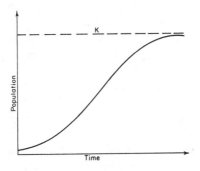

8.1. The logistic population growth curve. (After Keyfitz, 1968:213)

models are applied to human populations (Shryock et al., 1976:536), and in the cases to be taken up here the data are insufficient to cause any preference.

Dewar's Cc is usefully divided further into (1) the maximum population that a given technology can support in a given environment in the short term, herein the technical carrying capacity, or Ct, and (2) the highest level at which environmental degradation does not yet threaten loss of the productive base, herein the environmental carrying capacity, or Ce.

Allan (1965) and associates developed the concept of environmental carrying capacity, most often in connection with pastoralists or fallow cultivators. The value, though necessarily distinguished from Ct, may be altered by changes in technology. Implicit in the studies that use Ce is the assumption that Ct is greater than Ce, leading to environmental degradation as communities exploit their environments to the limits of their technology, but the principle does not always hold. Some systems — wet rice, for example — can be quite sustainable while giving the maximum technically feasible yields.

Some ethnographic accounts cast doubt on the utility of Ce, on the grounds that environmental damage occurs at fairly low population levels, increasing steadily as population pressure mounts. No threshold levels are readily identifiable (Dewar, 1984:606; Johnson, 1977; Montgomery and Johnson, 1977). Abundant historic evidence could also be cited of environmental destruction along thinly populated frontiers of European settlement.

But these cases may not be representative. Sometimes degradation does worsen markedly above a population threshold. A frontier of grass succession in the middle Sepik plains of Papua New Guinea is associated with growing numbers of cultivators (Reiner and Robbins, 1964; Robbins, 1960:328; Tuzin, 1976:13). Declining productivity (Lea, 1965:200) and depopulation often result. Regarding pastoralism, although experts do not always agree on how much stock a pasture can carry, the range of estimates is not cause to junk the concept.

Among agricultural populations, technical changes make Ct a moving target and may alter Ce as well (Brush, 1975; Street, 1969). Some methods of calculating carrying capacity leave no room for intensification, simply extrapolating from land that is in use to the total land area that could be used (Carneiro, 1960). Such an assumption of zero elasticity is obviously wrong. If Boserup's (1965) assumption of full elasticity is correct, Ct has no meaning until the stage of multicropping is reached, if then. In the Brookfield (1972) model of limited elasticity, Ct and possibly Ce shift as resistances are overcome and a breakthrough made to the next level of intensification.

The most convincing efforts to calculate Ct in agricultural communities are made where populations are dense, are isolated by physical barriers, and have few technical alternatives at hand. Even these calculations entail some extrapolation. Two particularly ambitious efforts by Bayliss-Smith deal with the Pacific atoll of Ontong Java (1974) and the island of Batiki, Fiji (1980). Only food production systems and an allowance for fishing enter into the calculations, but population densities and land productivity are high by preindustrial standards. The estimated Ct for Batiki is 871, which may be compared with the known precolonial peak of 500.

Estimates of Ct and Ce among nomadic pastoralists can be based on estimates of sustainable stocking rates. The ways available to raise productivity, apart from increasing cultivation, are limited: burning, scheduling of grazing, timing the slaughter of animals, and related forms of management. Most highly labor-intensive or capital-intensive methods, such as tilling or seeding pastures or making hay and silage, entail a sweeping change of subsistence strategy and settlement.

Asymptotic growth curves are often useful models of historic population trajectories, but k is never final. Real populations often stabilize for a time, then variously decline, grow at a slow rate, or even resume rapid growth.

Brookfield's stage model of agricultural intensification is appealing in this light, because it would explain cases in which populations seem to stabilize at irregular intervals but at levels that trend upward. At any given stage, the population does not have to reach Ct before ushering in the next stage. Rather, pressure mounts before the population reaches Ct and, by adding to costs and risks, stimulates innovations or investments in environmental modifications that create a new Ct and a new k. Population growth's stimulation of a transformation of production does not preclude its simultaneously acting on population-regulating mechanisms; however, that regulation is too little and too late to prevent intensification. But the model, for all its elegance, does not make the calculation of Ct any easier, and we cannot say for certain that technical changes tend to be innovated or diffused at such opportune times.

That population-regulating mechanisms directly related to subsistence output may operate at surprisingly low population densities is demonstrated among the Gainj of the central highlands of Papua New Guinea by Wood and Smouse (1982). They document density-dependent mortality, implicating nutritional factors, though the density in this well-watered area is 25 per km², well below that of other communities in similar and not too distant locations. Population has fluctuated somewhat around that level for at least three to five generations. The Gainj clear and cultivate primary and secondary forest and plant a variety of staple crops, whereas more densely settled neighbors rely heavily on grass fallow cultivation or continuous cropping of sweet potato. Judging by the availability of primary forest, the Gainj also have some leeway to shorten fallows without having to till grasslands. They have the same tools for tilling grasslands as their neighbors, should it be necessary to do so. The published findings do not provide a quantification of "resistances," but the presence of density-dependent regulation in a population that could be much denser if it changed its agricultural system supports some of Brookfield's premises.

Prehistoric Population Trajectories

PIONEER POPULATIONS. If population regulation is responsive to pressure on resources, pioneer populations should experience high initial growth rates, followed by leveling off as their density increases. Malthus reached this conclusion, and supporting evidence is strong. The Pitcairn Islanders are an often cited example. Their growth is explosive by any standard, at an annual rate of 3½% throughout much of the nineteenth century (Terrell, 1986:186–197). A prehistoric case, the peopling of Polynesia, is of particular interest for its time depth and the repetition, with variation, of a pattern in many islands and groups of islands.

A detailed study (Kirch, 1984) deals at length with Polynesian migrations, population histories of the islands, and the evolution of agriculture and other subsistence strategies. Another reconstruction of migrations is Finney's (1985).

The ancestors began about 1500 B.C. to move south and east from the Bismarck Archipelago east of the island of New Guinea, reaching the Marquesas Islands by the second century B.C. (Finney, 1985) and Hawaii and Easter Island not too long after, leaving only New Zealand and some outlying islands for later occupation. Linguistic and physical anthropological evidence suggest that the Polynesians originated from a small population. Finney's reconstruction of the sailing routes and their hazards gives weight to the view that the various island groups were in turn settled by small colonizing populations. Kirch's reconstruction has the colonists of new islands or island groups breaking off from their home islands well before populations reached their peaks.

What is most convincingly demonstrated is that population growth was initially high and subsequently tapered off, not that stabilization was permanent. Population pressure is evident in several ways as growth leveled off — for instance, in the settling of unpromising islands (Suggs, 1961). On Tonga, population growth leveled off a thousand years before European contact, and Kirch surmises that population over that millennium oscillated about equilibrium. The severe hurricanes to which the island group is prone would be a likely cause of depopulation. On certain other islands, population attained a level from which it subsequently plunged, not to recover during the precolonial era. Easter Island is the most renowned example.

The population trends best detailed and supported by Kirch are from the drier leeward parts of the Hawaiian group, settled in force later than the windward shores. In the west of the island of Hawaii, house sites nearly doubled each century until the increase slowed in the eighteenth century. A parallel rise on Kahoolawe precedes a steep fall before the eighteenth century, at which time sites number only 20% of the peak in the sixteenth century.

From ethnographic sources, Kirch concludes that the leveling off of population growth occurred through the regulation of both fertility and mortality by mechanisms that would respond to population pressure. Voluntary measures, as noted early in this chapter, included infanticide and coitus interruptus. The risk of mortality from hurricanes and other calamities increased as population pressure became severe.

Kirch makes population collapse the result of population rising well above carrying capacity, variously Ct or Ce. In some of his scenarios the peak levels simply reflect an insufficient margin in the event of a hurricane or other calamity, whereas in others, particularly leeward Hawaii and Kaho'olawe, signs of environmental degradation set in, indicating that Ce had been exceeded. Some other interpretations of Kirch's evidence are possible. A population could well tend toward a level below Ct and still incur unusual setbacks. Some environmental deterioration could occur at moderate pressure, because some more destructive options would be more attractive than less destructive ones. To give one possible example, it might be easier to rely more on short fallow cultivation on erodible slopes than on the more sustainable but more labor-intensive system of island-bed taro cultivation.

UPPER PLEISTOCENE POPULATION GROWTH.

The Pleistocene was before 10,000 B.C. but is worth examining to gain an appropriate perspective on subsequent population growth associated with early agriculture. Average Pleistocene growth rates were extremely slow, 0.0007% to 0.003% per year (Cohen, 1977:52). Such slow rates make events at the close of the Pleistocene appear remarkable, but local populations must have been less nearly static, and evidence suggests that populations of regions, possibly the world, were at times more dynamic.

The Upper Pleistocene (ca. 40,000 to 10,000 years ago) brought a spread of human occupation and a proliferation of cultural remains, so that the rate probably accelerated, possibly by quite a lot. If modern humans, *Homo sapiens sapiens,* who appeared in much of the Old World about 40,000 years ago, displaced Neanderthals and other earlier *H. sapiens* without much interbreeding, their numbers must have grown initially at a much higher rate than the Pleistocene norm. For example, if a population of 10,000 started growing 42,000 years ago at a mean annual rate of 0.1%, it would reach 1.5 million in 5,000 years. If the growth rate slowed to 0.02% over the next 5,000 years, the population would reach 4 million. That population would, by growing at an annual rate of 0.0046%, reach 10 million by 10,000 B.C., one rough estimate of the population of that time (Hassan, 1978). Rates would have been slower if *Homo sapiens* interbred a great deal with preexisting populations, whose numbers would then have to be taken into account.

If modern humans entered the Americas 30,000 to 40,000 years ago, a thesis advanced with more or less caution (for general discussions, see Bryan, 1969, and Carter, 1980), either the peopling of this hemisphere followed a most unusual trajectory, or accident or some unknown factor has concealed early sites of human occupation. Sites dated to before 13,000 to 14,000 B.C. are rare and subject to skepticism, but slightly later sites are common.

If modern humans entered the Americas 13,000 to 14,000 B.C., it was not long before the first signs of agriculture appeared in the New World, and subsequent population growth must have been quite rapid. Martin (1973) calculates that an original band entering 11,700 years ago would have reached the level of population at the time of Columbus by growing at an average annual rate of 0.1% but adds that growth was probably not even. Almost the whole of both continents was inhabited by 6000 B.C., after agriculture had begun in North and South America. Because much of the population gain had already taken place, the rate before 6000 B.C. would have been well above 0.1%. Martin believes that the early rate was explosive, pointing to the extinction of megafauna as a sign of an advancing human wave (also Haynes, 1966). On the other hand, Martin's entry date of 11,700 years ago now appears to be a few millennia too late.

THE FIRST DEMOGRAPHIC TRANSITION OF THE EARLY HOLOCENE. The world population growth rate reached about 0.1% during the early Holocene (Carneiro and Hilse, 1966; Cowgill, 1975; Hassan, 1973) and then slowed, though never again to the very low average rates of the Pleistocene. If it had not slowed, a world population of 10 million in 10,000 B.C. would have swelled to 86 billion by now, 17 times what it is. A mean rate of 0.04% from the late Holocene to the early modern period is likely. Later phases of rapid growth occurred in some places removed from the early centers, in Britain in the last two centuries B.C., long after the first agriculture there (Fowler, 1983:32–36).

The main growth surge is associated with the first primary reliance on agriculture and must have been its consequence, even if some kind of earlier growth had been a factor in agricultural origins (see chapter 2). The speeding and subsequent slowing of population growth are called the first demographic transition (Handwerker, 1983; Harpending, 1976:160). The analogy appropriately describes the growth curve, but the modern demographic transition (chapter 12) is a documented sequence of mortality and fertility changes, of which scholars know little in the first transition. Skeletal evidence of longevity is inconclusive; analyses show some gain from the late Pleistocene into the early Holocene, but bias and sampling error cannot be ruled out (Hassan, 1981:100–103). Explanations are varied and give different weights to fertility and mortality. Most draw substance from analogies with contemporary peoples. No dramatic shift must be invoked, however. Slight changes in fertility or mortality could account for the rise and fall of population growth rates.

Handwerker (1983) argues that the Holocene brought lower infant mortality, because children were more valuable to parents and hence infanticide declined, and because there were "improved health conditions at the initial period of settlement following from the relative abundance of resources." To cite improved health conditions without support or explanation is seemingly to return to older assumptions of struggling collectors. To the contrary, skeletal remains of early agriculturalists in southwestern Africa indicate they grew more slowly, had more disease, and lived shorter lives than food collectors in the same region (Kennedy, 1984).

Disease could be invoked, but it seems a better explanation of falling rates in the late Holocene than of rising rates in the early phases (Cohen, 1980:282). Dense settlements, which were often accompanied by appalling sanitation, may later on have bred the major epidemic diseases (Cockburn, 1971).

Most recent attention is to possible changes in fertility. Among most present-day food collectors, women average about 4 or 5 live births (Handwerker, 1983; Harpending, 1976; Howell, 1979; Jones, 1963). A rate of 5.76 among the Tiwi produces substantial population growth (Jones, 1963). The rate ranges from 6 to 9 among most historical agriculturalists not yet in the modern demographic transition (Handwerker, 1983). If modern food collectors are any indication, we should not assume that agriculture brought a better-quality diet and thereby improved fecundity. That leaves the quantity of food eaten and its effect on fecundity, motives for spacing births, and breast-feeding practices as the most likely explanations.

The so-called critical fat hypothesis (Frisch, 1974) correlates adult female body fat with fecundity. Several mechanisms are advanced (Frisch and McArthur, 1974). The least controversial is that subcritical fat levels delay menarche (Frisch and McArthur, 1974; Frisch and Revelle, 1970). Another suggested mechanism is competition for limited nutrition between breast milk formation and a potential fetus, delaying the postpartum resumption of menstruation. Statistical studies variously support or reject the hypothesis (Cohen, 1980:289).

Prolonged and frequent breast-feeding delays the resumption of menstruation. The effect is well documented among San collectors, whose women carry their children around the clock and nurse them frequently until a younger sibling is born, after an average interval of four years (Konnor and Worthman, 1980; Lee, 1980). Lee (1980) makes a comparison with Arnhem Land (Australia) aboriginal women, who leave children in camp while they gather and who have shorter birth intervals and rely more on infanticide to achieve spacing. One can only conjecture about the breast-feeding practices of Pleistocene food collectors.

Involuntary mechanisms could form a powerful combination with voluntary controls if motives can be established for spacing births. The burden of carrying children while gathering is one possibility (Lee, 1972, 1980; Sussman, 1972). In Lee's (1980:330) model of !Kung San women's schedules, the work of carrying children is reduced about 20% when the birth interval is cut from five years to four, another 22% if cut to three, and another 29% if cut to two. But Hassan (1973:535, 1981:222–223) disputes the contention that the burden is significantly greater for collector women than for those who do agricultural work, and Howell (1979) largely discounts voluntary measures by !Kung San women.

The prevalence of voluntary curbs is controversial. Birdsell (1968) concludes that natural fertility is so great that infanticide must account for 15% to 50% of Pleistocene births, an estimate the Caldwells (1987) contested and indeed one that takes insufficient account of the decline of fecundity in women as they age.

Ethnographic analogies may not be appropriate. Early Holocene collectors inhabited diverse environments, including many with a higher resource density than in the cited ethnographies. Pressure on resources would not thereby have to be less—that would depend on population density—but a good guess is that less walking would be needed between resource locations. An analogy from undernourished strata of modern populations, the primary basis for the critical fat hypothesis, to contemporary collectors and then to Holocene collectors is stretched.

The most often postulated cause of early Holocene population growth is not diet but the onset of sedentism (e.g., Binford, 1968; Lee, 1972; Polgar, 1972; Sussman, 1972). The timing of sedentism and the development of agriculture is not demonstrably the same everywhere (chapter 2), but we can generalize that permanent settlements proliferated during the period of population growth.

Relevant ethnographic evidence presents a mixed picture. Some recently settled !Kung San have a mean birth interval of 36.7 months, whereas groups that still collect and shift camps have a mean birth interval of 44.1 (Lee, 1980:336). A parallel is found in Inuit communities inhabiting of Arctic environments (Freeman, 1971; Schaefer, 1971), but Harpending (1976:160) found no increase among settled !Kung San. Birth intervals among semisedentary Pygmies, in groups whose women now do little gathering or shifting of camps, remained little changed (Cavalli-Sforza, 1973).

With so many questions unanswered and doubts as to the usefulness of ethnographic analogy, what regulating mechanisms were in play will likely remain unclear, but the surge in growth rates is really not surprising. The peak global rate of the early Holocene was well below that of many pioneer populations and may not have been greatly out of line with that of early *Homo sapiens sapiens*. It happened after a great expansion of food production, albeit not a sudden one. The analogy with pioneer populations is most appropriate where agriculture, already well developed, spread into areas that previously had none or only incipient forms.

Growth and Regulation of
Historic Preindustrial Populations

Historical demography relies on records that are far from precise prior to the development of census taking in eighteenth-century Europe. Most earlier recorded European and Chinese counts are of households or eligible taxpayers. Archaeologists make most of their population estimates from house counts. Household composition in some societies varies markedly from that of others, but these contrasts do not negate the use of house counts. Composition varies less in one culture over a modest period of time than from one culture or era to another, and an intriguing thesis that has been subjected to some cross-cultural testing is that house area is usually close to 10 m^2 per inhabitant (Naroll, 1962).

Available population data for large regions are generally not detailed enough to allow assessment of short-term responses to fluctuating population pressure. China and premodern Europe present somewhat inconclusive evidence but are worth reviewing for the stronger evidence of sustained, accelerated growth following prolonged periods of stagnant or falling population.

Two case studies of smaller populations provide surer evidence of short-term responses of fertility to changing population pressure. One famed case begins with the introduction of the potato into Ireland. Responses to drastic losses of life in eighteenth-century Iceland are of particular interest because the population is both well documented and decidedly preindustrial.

POPULATION TRAJECTORIES AND THEIR MODELS. Wide fluctuations in population are the historical norm. The effects of localized setbacks may be lost in a larger population, but epidemics, wars, and environmental disasters bring widespread depopulation. The rule already given of slow long-term growth must be balanced against the impact of such vast depopulating events as the great plague pandemics and colonial-era wars, enslavement, catastrophic displacements, and spread of diseases. China experienced a millennium of nearly stationary population; Iceland had almost as long a period of declining numbers. These instances do not fault the rule of slow growth but do beg explanation.

One common model of fluctuation — a series of wavelike oscillations (Fig. 8.2) that would be produced by a regular cycle of overadjustment — must be rejected in any sizable population. Population losses, to the contrary, are often abrupt and precipitous. Many are from exogenous

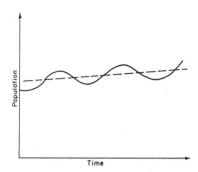

8.2. Wavelike population growth about a rising equilibrium level.

cause or act of God and may therefore occur at high or low population pressure. Among the worst epidemic diseases, cholera is more readily spread in dense populations, and malaria causes more deaths when it is accompanied by undernutrition, but plague and smallpox move easily through populations of a fairly low density and have not been convincingly shown to be more lethal among the undernourished.

We shall see that accelerated population growth has sometimes followed either sudden depopulating events or the end of long periods of exceptional mortality. That growth subsequently slows.

EUROPE AND THE PLAGUES.   The greatest population catastrophe in well-documented history is the black death of 1346–52. The plague fell on Europe at a time when population pressure was being felt on land resources, and some have suggested that the awful mortality stimulated fertility by relieving the pressure, though the evidence is found in records that chronicle only small parts of the population. Some point to earlier marriage and large families after the black death and later plague epidemics (Gies and Gies, 1987). Hatcher (1977) argues that the depopulation in England ought to have increased peasant incomes and certainly did lead to higher incomes among craft workers. McEvedy (1988:121) maintains that some sort of response allowed an equilibrium "between plague and people" by the beginning of the fifteenth century and led to population recovery thereafter.

Mortality is better known, and all indications are that it continued to be high for centuries, because of repeated plague outbreaks and other causes. Mortality peaked in Europe in the fifteenth century, even disregarding the black death proper, and decreased but slightly in the sixteenth and seventeenth centuries (Acsadi and Nemeskeri, 1970:256).

Some authorities believe that mortality in England decreased significantly during the sixteenth century, only to rise again in the seventeenth. What is more certain is that mortality fell during the eighteenth century in England and the Continent, ushering in a period of accelerated population growth.

The black death was not the first visitation of the plague upon Europe. Justinian's plague in the sixth century now appears to have been just as deadly. There followed more than 300 years of repeated population setbacks, often blamed on Moors and Vikings, but possibly due more to repeated epidemics of plague and other diseases. Then from the mid-eleventh century to the mid-fourteenth, the populations of England and France increased about 3.4 times (Petersen, 1975:427), at an annual rate of about 0.4%, which is comparable to late eighteenth-century rates.

Europe's preindustrial population thus twice demonstrated a capacity to recover after prolonged periods of high mortality, each time ultimately reaching historic high points. The first time, population again plunged when the plague returned. The second time it kept going upward under the exceptional circumstances of the industrial revolution.

China

Enough is known about Chinese population history to outline long-term trends. By the early centuries of the Christian era, growth had resulted in population densities and levels of agricultural intensity that exceeded Europe's by a wide margin. Subsequent settlement patterns, land use, and scanty official records show few signs of population growth until the thirteenth or fourteenth century (Grigg, 1974:86; Perkins, 1969:6), but people shifted southward on a vast scale. Then the population increased between 4½ and 7 times up to the mid-nineteenth century (Ho, 1959; Lee, 1982; Perkins, 1969:13).

China has suffered an awful assortment of disasters from natural and human causes, but the two worst events fell just before and after the period of population growth that ended in the mid-nineteenth century. China felt the plague of the fourteenth century as much as did Europe. The Taiping Rebellion of 1851–68 probably resulted in more loss of life than any other war anywhere except World War II.

Many sinologists, prompted by the factors of high population density and the labor intensity of historical agriculture, adopt the neo-Malthusian stance that agriculture strained against its limits. Population growth episodes are therefore interpreted as the result of technical innovations that lifted this ceiling, or Ct in the usage of this chapter. Ho (1959) attributes the resumption of growth in or about the fourteenth century first to the spread of early varieties of rice that permitted higher cropping frequencies and later to the introduction of New World crops that could be grown on the uplands.

The thesis that new crops and varieties spurred population growth is attractive, but to grant the point does not necessitate accepting the inference that population strained at its limits on the eve of introduction. That these populations were experiencing population pressure is evident, and it may even be granted that the pressure was exceptional, but not necessarily that Ct had been reached. Population had, after all, fallen in the northern plains.

IRISH PEASANTS, LANDLORDS, AND THE PO-TATO. Irish rural population growth before the potato blight and famine of 1845–48 is in most accounts a response to the introduction of the potato. The rate of population growth is quite slow until the mid-eighteenth century, when the new crop is widely adopted. Then the rate accelerates, peaks during the decades around 1800, and slows before the famine. By 1845 farmers are reduced to gaining their subsistence from small potato patches, in addition to producing various crops and animal products as rent for their landlords to export. Disputed points are the mechanisms by which the population spurt occurs and the respective roles of peasant fertility and landlords' policies in making tenants' livelihoods precarious.

A neo-Malthusian explanation of the famine is that the population increase had finally caught up with the higher yields of the potato. Catton (1980:247–250) thus blames both overreliance on a risky crop and the population's having exceeded its "carrying capacity." The famine obviously proves risk, and I concur with Catton that population pressure had risen on its eve, but the proof that the population had reached its ceiling has not been presented. We should suspect it had not; much of the productive land was devoted to export production and was worked less intensively than was potato land.

Connell (1950b) makes marriage age the principal regulating mechanism. When pressure on land resources is low, young men can acquire holdings, usually on leases, and thus meet a precondition of marriage. Fertility rises. Conversely, high population pressure leads to reduced opportunities, delayed marriages, and lower fertility. Accelerated population growth late in the eighteenth century follows a general shift from cereals to the potato. Some land that had been little used for food production, such as bog, is converted into potato land (Connell, 1950a, 1950b). The Napoleonic wars bring high grain prices, encouraging the plowing of pasture into cropland. These developments absorb additional agricultural labor and continue during the early nineteenth century along with growth of the population, which doubles in just over half a century preceding the famine (Connell, 1950b).

Early marriage peaks in the decades around 1800, when subdivision of holdings and colonization of hitherto uncultivated land make it easy for households to acquire adequate holdings for potato cultivation. Less land is needed than for the cereal plots their parents or grandparents had tended. Many women marry at the age of 17 or 18, and some at 13 or 14, much lower ages than previous norms.

Early marriage declines in the last years before the famine, when agrarian unrest and tight conditions on leaseholders reflect renewed pressure on land. Already by 1830, only 5.6% of women's first marriages are at age 17 or younger, a probable drop from the early years of the century, judging from contemporary accounts. The proportion is 3.5% by 1835 and 1.4% by 1840 (Connell, 1950b:41–42). Emigration is by this time also braking population growth.

The regulating mechanisms proposed by Connell, principally marriage age, are queried more than the population trajectory. Drake (1964) questions the sources on marriage age and concludes from an examination of the 1841 census that Irish fertility during the 1830s is not exceptional compared with that of England or Norway. However, a further examination of the 1841 census (Tucker, 1970) concludes that Irish fertility at the time is indeed higher than that of England and Wales, a finding consistent with Connell's interpretation; Drake does not take into account underreporting of children 12 months old and younger.

Other causes of population growth are possible, besides social mechanisms that stimulate fertility. Drake suggests that the potato improves nutrition and thereby lowers mortality and raises fecundity, though no more precise connection is given.

The famine relieves the pressure on the land, once the effects of the blight subside, but marriage age does not fall again, as should be expected if the pattern of small holdings and potato dependence continues. Instead holdings (often leases) are concentrated. Farms of one to five acres (0.4–2.0 ha) make up 43.6% of agricultural holdings in 1841, but only 15.0% in 1861 (Connell, 1957:77). Sons emigrate or acquire holdings of the new standard through inheritance or arranged marriages. Marriage rates between the famine and 1871 are lowest in eastern counties, where pressure arises from the conversion of cropland into pasture (Cousens, 1964). A distinctive pattern of marriage and fertility emerges after 1871. Though fertility within marriage is high, marriage age becomes higher and celibacy common (Walsh, 1970).

Ross (1985) cites English colonial policies for the rise and fall of Irish fertility. In this version, potatoes feed peasants and pigs (for export), aiding the profitable collection of rents. Landlords' policies, influenced by the colonial economy, do the most to encourage early marriage and other factors contributing to higher fertility. Land concentration takes place after the famine because the grain export trade dies.

The difference between Ross's treatment and some others is one of emphasis and where to lay blame, but fertility does seem to be regulated, no matter who were the regulators. Ross's culprit is the system of tenure and rent, not the prolific Irish peasant. Connell (1950a, 1950b) is quite clear that subdivision of land into small plots before the famine serves the interests of landowners, though the reasons he gives (1957) for post-famine concentration, namely an increased participation by leaseholders in the commercial economy and an unwillingness to risk potato monoculture, emphasize decision making by the Irish peasants and not the landlords. Cousens (1964) and Walsh (1970) also assign the landholders a leading role in determining land use after the famine.

ICELAND: FIRE, ICE, AND PESTILENCE. The population history of Iceland illustrates the regulation of population through adjustments in fertility, in this case in response to depopulating events. Iceland's location near the climatic limits of food production places its people in a precarious position. Over more than a thousand years of settlement, traditionally dated from 874, the productive base steadily declines, providing a test case of long-term population response to declining Ct. Population data are rough for early centuries but improve from the seventeenth century on. From the early centuries, men eligible for participation in parliament—that is, landholders—are sporadically counted, and some information may be gleaned from literary sources and archaeological surveys. The first national census is in 1703. Registers listing births, confirmation, marriages, and deaths are kept in a few parishes in the seventeenth century, though most records begin later, during the late eighteenth and early nineteenth centuries.

Soil erosion is the main cause of declining productivity, but not the only one. Erosion accelerates because of overgrazing and the removal of scrub until nearly half the vegetated land is left bare. The most fragile land is hill land of lesser productivity, and the loss of primary productivity is therefore only about a third (Fridriksson, 1972). Lava flows smother large areas. Cold summers, which reduce the hay harvest, become more frequent from the twelfth century on, and, save for a warm-ing during the fourteenth century, temperatures remain generally low until nearly 1900 (Bergthorsson, 1969).

Natural disasters other than epidemics kill more by inducing famine than by their direct effects. Natural disasters include lava flows, ashfalls, exceptionally cold summers, and floods, including a sort brought on with little warning when volcanoes erupt under ice caps. All of these disasters reduce the productivity of pastures and hayfields and cause losses of livestock. As for epidemics, the black death arrives later than on the European continent, from 1402 to 1404. Smallpox and other epidemic diseases visit from time to time.

Two reconstructions of Icelandic population history have a particu-lar bearing on population regulation and trends. Fridriksson (1972) con-nects the steady loss of productive land to a long-term downward trend in population. Tomasson (1977) chronicles the effects of natural disasters and analyzes fertility and mortality in the years for which census data are available.

According to Fridriksson, population fluctuates about an equilib-rium level (not his term) that rises slowly until the thirteenth century, falls slowly until about 1800, and then climbs sharply to the present. Although historians disagree on precensus population estimates, several grounds exist for accepting a value of about 80,000 in 1106, the year of the first parliamentary count. By the eighteenth century the population is barely 50,000 in the best years. Historical sources and archaeological surveys provide house and farm counts that corroborate the decline. Population at all times remains at least slightly below the supportable level that Fridriksson projects from the mean net primary productivity of natural pastures and meadows. The Icelanders, a scattered populace, would find it difficult to use all pastures to maximum benefit, but they supplement their diet with some fishing, bird hunting, and egg collect-ing. They cultivate barley in the early centuries but not after the climate cooled.

Tomasson's findings show clearly the tendency during the eighteenth century toward strong population recovery after depopulating events (Table 8.1). Fertility rises sharply in the decades that follow decades of high mortality. Growth is strong from 1708 to 1734, at a mean annual rate of 1.4%, following the smallpox epidemic of 1707, which kills a third of the population (Tomasson, 1977:410). After cold summers and disease in the 1750s bring high death rates, population growth and fertil-ity are high during the 1760s. The country's highest known crude birth rate, 41.4 per 1,000, high by any standard, is during the 1790s, following heavy loss of life from the great Laki eruption of 1783–84 and the

Table 8.1. Crude death and birth rates in Iceland, 1731–1830

Decade	Deaths per 1,000	Births per 1,000
1731–40	27.4	32.7
1741–50	25.3	34.4
1751–60	39.1	28.3
1761–70	28.0	37.0
1771–80	26.4	32.1
1781–90	48.6	27.3
1791–1800	24.4	41.4
1801–10	29.0	32.2
1811–20	25.3	24.6
1821–30	28.3	37.6

famine of the winter of 1784–85. In 1785 alone, 13.4% of the population dies. The annual rate of population growth is 1.5% from 1787 to 1801; a population bulge left over from the high birth rates of the 1760s accounts for only part of the surge.

The relationship between mortality and fertility changes during the nineteenth century. No population setbacks of the nineteenth century are comparable to those of the eighteenth, and what might be termed ordinary mortality begins to turn decisively downward after the 1860s. Fertility begins a lagged decline, part of Iceland's demographic transition.

Up to the nineteenth century, when circumstances change radically, regulating mechanisms are in effect, however much diminishing resources appear to confirm Malthus's worst fears. What is striking about the eighteenth century is that a population confronted by relentless deterioration of its productive base, in which fertility and mortality were already high, can at times increase its fertility.

The Icelanders' only means to relieve population pressure before the nineteenth century is to improve the management of grasslands. Potato cultivation begins in the eighteenth century but only on a dooryard scale.

Yields from native grasslands are greatly raised during the nineteenth and twentieth centuries. Methods that would be wholly unavailable to a preindustrial community, such as applications of chemical fertilizers, account for none of the nineteenth-century gain and surprisingly little in this century until after 1940. Well-known yield-raising techniques of the nineteenth century are the drainage of wetlands, stressed by Fridriksson, and the plowing and leveling of hayfields to encourage a dense sward. Drainage had been known to the Viking settlers, and plowing and leveling of hayfields in much of medieval northern Europe.

The flaw in viewing the earlier Icelanders with hindsight and assuming technical elasticity — that they could adopt later innovations — is that account must be taken of the severe demands placed on their labor and of the small returns from land improvements. Many modern hayfields are drained with the help of deep and extensive ditches dug with mechanical equipment. As for tillage, the earlier farms have ponies but no plows, little to fashion into plows, and limited capital for purchasing them. Haymaking takes extraordinarily long hours. Drainage of marshland in one experiment raised mean annual dry matter yields from 940 to 2,950 kg/ha (Fridriksson, 1972:794), an impressive-looking achievement, but one that means only three additional ewes could be carried per hectare, less than half the minimum support of one person. A drained or irrigated hectare of cropland in a warmer land could feed a family. Tillage is similarly unrewarding if undertaken to encourage slow-growing grass in a cool climate, rather than crops in a warm one. The season in Iceland for either improvement is short, between the spring thaw and the start of the frantic work of haymaking.

The effect of nineteenth-century improvements is hard to separate from other economic developments: a new fishing fleet, cooperative organization, and improved terms of trade for imported foods and consumer goods. Farmers of the time do not have tractors but do have improved horse-drawn plows, hay rakes, and other implements supplied by industries in other countries. They also have new commercial incentives to make investments in land, and some gain more secure tenure.

In another European population, a Swiss mountain community, Netting (1981) documents a pattern from the late eighteenth century through much of the nineteenth that is reminiscent in some ways of Iceland. Crude birth rates rise and fall with crude death rates, though in tandem, not lagging behind by a decade as in Iceland.

Summary and Conclusions

The population history of humans is unique among species, and so are its ecological consequences. Self-regulating mechanisms of humans and animals are analogous up to a point—work on animal populations, particularly by Wynne-Edwards (1962, 1965) impressed self-regulation on a generation of anthropologists—but through deer and lemming populations would repeatedly return to the same levels if we left them alone, our numbers long rose steadily and with great cumulative effect. We expand our numbers by preying on other species, but the predator-prey analogy (chapter 2) is only partly appropriate. If we are a predator, we are a singularly opportunistic one, expanding into nearly every type of ecosystem. And as well as being supertiger, we are also superbeaver, creator of an array of physically altered environments.

Existing theories that relate agriculture, food supply, and population have yet to come to grips with slow long-term growth, though many deal with short-term regulation. Regretfully, I can better criticize this shortcoming than develop an alternative theory that reconciles regulation and upward creep. At this point I can only offer some guidelines and a little speculation.

The association of population growth with the origins, spread, and intensification of agriculture is obvious. A parsimonious explanation may be had by reducing Malthus's ideas to the principle that technical innovation gradually lifts the ceiling on population level. Boserup's rejoinder that too many innovations are available before they are in general use is a good one, and I might add that contrasts in population pressure among regions, such as Europe, East Asia, and eastern North America (chapter 7), are not readily explained by differences in opportunity or inventiveness.

If innovation alone is a poor explanation of population growth, very slow innovation must be a worse explanation of very slow growth. Historical global growth rates are slight in comparison with local, short-term rates. They are trivial alongside the birth and death rates that generate them. Perfect regulation of population is impossible, and only by spreading the various rates of many smaller populations could very low rates of change be sustained (Hammel and Howell, 1987). That does not explain the persistent upward creep of population, however, or why imperfect regulation must tend to err on the high side.

To help explain this small but significant bias, I offer two principles as guidelines for enquiry:

1. Regulation must be examined as a regional phenomenon, possibly a global one, because of population redistribution. Though population may be redistributed from areas of higher population pressure to areas of lower pressure, redistribution operates whether population pressure is high or low.

2. Societies do not just replace their numbers; they replicate role players. Many roles are of peculiar demographic significance, and all roles are rooted in culturally transmitted values. We should therefore regard biased regulation as biased replication.

Redistribution of population is a historical norm. Two examples will demonstrate its operation at first lower and then higher levels of population pressure.

A medieval European manor with many large families in a single generation would end up with too many disinherited children if inheritance were restricted or with small, fragmented parcels if all inherited. Either outcome furnishes incentive to move to a less prolific village. Bound serfs do so as well as free men. Bloch (1961:263) ascribes the frequency of desertions of French estates to "the great abundance of virgin soil [that] made it useless to threaten with confiscation a fugitive who was almost always certain of finding a new place for himself elsewhere." Population pressure does not have to be severe and often is not.

Meggitt's (1977) study of the Mae Enga is revealing for its illustration of how responsive the recruitment in the clans is to both considerable population pressure, which they perceive, and to the rise or fall of their strength of numbers. Interclan warfare is rife, and clans must deal with fugitives from allied clans that have been defeated, often because their numbers had fallen too low to resist the attacks of a growing rival (Meggitt, 1977:25):

> If, as a result of war or sickness, a host clan is declining in population, its Big Men may well encourage newcomers to settle in order to enhance the clan's military and economic strength; to this end the clan may be generous in its concessions of usufruct. In most clans, however, the hosts are likely to consider their land resources barely adequate for their own needs, so that they are sparing in their generosity and wish to see the immigrants go home without delay. Accordingly, the Big Men of these clans take the lead in interceding with the victors, pressing for peace and the return of at least some land to the losers.

Communities everywhere have farm heirs, celibates, warriors with short life expectancies, and other role players whom we may expect to have more or less children. Recruitment rests on a wealth of social symbols and expectations: ideals of motherhood, piety, heroism, and more. The medieval European and Mae Enga cases reveal, besides population redistribution, the roughness of fit between replication of roles and renewal of population. Heirs were a variable quantity in medieval households, and the need for them was not precisely linked to any particular rate—positive, negative, or nil—of population growth. The Mae Enga perceive population pressure, but their need for warriors gives them incentive to gain population through birth or migration. This population gain is clearly in conflict with the need for enough land to feed their numbers, one reason they go to war. Population redistribution and role replication are imperfectly matched, and quite conceivably the need for warriors has the upper hand, whether operating through voluntary or involuntary mechanisms.

Possibly the demographic program of roles adjusts more readily to decreases of population pressure than to increases, though I admit this principle is speculative. Population pressure and opportunities are presumably inversely related, and it is at least credible that expectations are realized more quickly when population pressure lessens than when it increases.

References

Acsadi, G., and J. Nemeskeri (1970). *History of Human Life Span and Mortality.* Akademiai Kiado, Budapest.

Allan, W. (1965). *The African Husbandman.* Barnes and Noble, New York.

Allen, J. (1976). Fishing for wallabies: Trade as a mechanism for social interaction, integration, and elaboration on the central Papuan coast. In *The Evolution of Social Systems* (J. Friedman and M.J. Rowlands, eds.), Duckworth, London, pp. 419–456.

Barlett, P.F. (1976). Labor efficiency and the mechanism of agricultural evolution. *Journal of Anthropological Research,* 32:124–140.

Bayliss-Smith, T. (1974). Constraints on population growth: The case of the Polynesian outlier atolls in the pre-contact period. *Human Ecology,* 2:259–295.

———. (1980). Population pressure, resources: Towards a more realistic measure of carrying capacity. In *Population-Environmental Relations in Tropical Islands: The Case of Eastern Fiji* (H.C. Brookfield, ed.), MAB Technical Notes, no. 13, UNESCO, Paris, pp. 61–94.

Beckerman, S. (1987). Swidden in Amazonia and the Amazon rim. In *Comparative Farming Systems* (B.L. Turner II and S.B. Brush, eds.), Guilford, New York, pp. 55–94.

Bergthorsson, P. (1969). An estimate of drift ice and temperature in Iceland in 1,000 years. *Jokull,* 19:94–101.

Binford, L.R. (1968). Post-Pleistocene adaptations. In *New Perspectives in Archaeology* (S.R. Binford and L.R. Binford, eds.), Aldine, Chicago, pp. 313–341.

Birdsell, J.B. (1968). Some predictions for the Pleistocene based on equilibrium systems among recent hunter-gatherers. In *Man the Hunter* (R.B. Lee and I. DeVore, eds.), Aldine, Chicago, pp. 229–240.

Bloch, M. (1961). *Feudal Society,* trans. L.A. Manyon. University of Chicago Press, Chicago.

Boserup, E. (1965). *The Conditions of Agricultural Growth.* Aldine, Chicago.

Bronson, B. (1972). Farm labor and the evolution of food production. In *Population Growth: Anthropological Implications* (B. Spooner, ed.), MIT Press, Cambridge, pp. 190–218.

Brookfield, H.C. (1972). Intensification and disintensification in Pacific agriculture: A theoretical approach. *Pacific Viewpoint,* 15:30–48.

Brush, S.R. (1975). The concept of carrying capacity for systems of shifting cultivation. *American Anthropologist,* 75:799–811.

Bryan, A.L. (1969). Early man in America and the late Pleistocene chronology of western Canada and Alaska. *Current Anthropology,* 10:339–356.

Bugos, P.E., Jr., and L.M. McCarthy (1984). Ayoreo infanticide: A case study. In *Infanticide: Comparative and Evolutionary Perspectives* (G. Hausfater and S.B. Hrdy, eds.), Aldine, New York, pp. 503–520.

Caldwell, J., P. Caldwell, and B. Caldwell (1987). Anthropology and demography: The mutual reinforcement of speculation and research. *Current Anthropology,* 28:25–43.

Carneiro, R.C. (1960). Slash-and-burn agriculture: A closer look at its implications for settlement pattern. In *Selected Papers of the Fifth International Congress of Anthropological and Ethnological Sciences* (A.F.C. Wallace, ed.), University of Pennsylvania Press, Philadelphia, pp. 229–234.

Carneiro, R.F., and D.F. Hilse (1966). On determining the probable rate of population growth during the neolithic. *American Anthropologist,* 68:177–181.

Carr-Saunders, A.M. (1922). *The Population Problem: A Study in Human Evolution.* Oxford University Press, Oxford.

Carter, G.F. (1980). *Earlier than You Think: A Personal View of Man in America.* Texas A&M University Press, College Station.

Catton, W.R. (1980). *Overshoot, The Ecological Basis of Revolutionary Change.* University of Illinois Press, Urbana.

Cavalli-Sforza, L.L. (1973). Pygmies, an example of hunter-gatherers, and genetic consequences for man of domestication of plants and animals. In *Proceedings of the Fourth International Congress of Human Genetics,* Excerpta Medica, Amsterdam, pp. 80–95.

Cockburn, T.A. (1971). Infectious diseases in ancient populations. *Current Anthropology,* 12:45–62.

Cohen, M.N. (1977). *The Food Crisis in Prehistory.* Yale University Press, New Haven, Conn.

———. (1980). Speculations on the evolution of density measurement and population regulation in *Homo sapiens.* In *Biosocial Mechanisms of Population Regulation* (M.N. Cohen, R.S. Malpass, and H.G. Klein, eds.), Yale University Press, New Haven, Conn. pp. 275–304.

Connell, K.H. (1950a). The colonisation of waste land in Ireland 1780–1845. *Economic History Review,* 3:44–71.

———. (1950b). *The Population of Ireland 1750–1845.* Clarendon, Oxford, England.

———. (1957). Peasant marriage in Ireland after the great famine. *Past and Present,* 12:76–91.

Cousens, S.H. (1964). The regional variation in population changes in Ireland, 1861–1881. *Economic History Review,* 17:301–321.

Cowgill, G.L. (1975). Population pressure as a non-explanation. *American Antiquity,* 40:122–131.

Dewar, R.E. (1984). Environmental productivity, population regulation, and carrying capacity. *American Anthropologist,* 86:601–614.

Dickemann, M. (1975). Demographic consequences of infanticide in man. *Annual Review of Ecology and Systematics,* 6:107–137.

Drake, M. (1964). Marriage and population growth in Ireland, 1750–1845. *Economic History Review,* 16:301–313.

Eversley, D. (1987). [Comment on J. Caldwell et al., Anthropology and demography: The mutual reinforcement of speculation and research.] *Current Anthropology,* 28:34–35.

Finney, B.R. (1985). Anomalous westerlies, El Niño, and the colonization of Polynesia. *American Anthropologist,* 87:9–26.

Firth, R. (1936). *We, the Tikopia: A Sociological Study of Kinship in Primitive Polynesia.* Allen and Unwin, London.

Flannery, K.V. (1969). Origins and ecological effects of early domestication in Iran and the Near East. In *The Domestication and Exploitation of Plants and Animals* (P.J. Ucko and G.W. Dimbleby, eds.), Aldine, Chicago, pp. 73–100.

Fowler, P.J. (1983). *The Farming of Prehistoric Britain.* Cambridge University Press, Cambridge.

Freeman, M.R. (1971). The significance of demographic changes occurring in the Canadian East Arctic. *Anthropologica,* 13:215–236.

Fridriksson, S. (1972). Grass and grass utilization in Iceland. *Ecology,* 53:785–797.

Frisch, R.E. (1978). Population, food intake, and fertility. *Science,* 199:22–30.

Frisch, R.E., and J.W. McArthur (1974). Menstrual cycles: Fatness as a determinant of minimum weight for height necessary for their maintenance or onset. *Science,* 185:949–951.

Frisch, R.E., and R. Revelle (1970). Height and weight at menarche and a hypothesis of critical body weights and adolescent events. *Science,* 169:397–399.

Geertz, C. (1963). *Agricultural Involution: The Process of Ecological Change in Indonesia.* University of California Press, Berkeley.

Gies, F., and J. Gies (1987). *Marriage and Family in the Middle Ages.* Harper and Row, New York.

Grigg, D.B. (1974). *The Agricultural Systems of the World.* Cambridge University Press, London.

Groves, M. (1960). Motu pottery. *Journal of the Polynesian Society,* 69:3–22.

Hainline, J. (1965). Culture and biological adaptation. *American Anthropologist,* 67:45–85.

Hammel, E.A., and N. Howell (1987). Research in population and culture: An evolutionary framework. *Current Anthropology,* 28:141–160.

Handwerker, W.P. (1983). The first demographic transition: An analysis of subsistence choices and reproductive consequences. *American Anthropologist,* 85:5–27.

Hanks, L. (1972). *Rice and Man.* Aldine, Chicago.

Harpending, H. (1976). Regional variation in !Kung populations. In *Kalahari Hunter-Gatherers: Studies of the !Kung San and Their Neighbors* (R.B. Lee and I. DeVore, eds.), Harvard University Press, Cambridge, pp. 152–165.

Harris, M. (1975). *Culture, People, Nature: An Introduction to General Anthropology.* 2d ed. Crowell, New York.

Hassan, F.A. (1973). On mechanisms of population growth during the Holocene. *Current Anthropology,* 14:535–542.

_____. (1978). Prehistoric demography. In *Advances in Archaeological Method and Theory* (M. Schiffer, ed.), vol. 1, Academic Press, New York, pp. 41–48.

_____. (1981). *Demographic Archaeology.* Academic Press, New York.

Hatcher, J. (1977). *Plague, Population, and the English Economy, 1348–1530.* Macmillan, London.

Hayden, B. (1972). Population control among hunter-gatherers. *World Archaeology,* 4:205–221.

Haynes, C.V. (1966). Elephant hunting in North America. *Scientific American,* 214(3):104–112.

Henry, L. (1961). Some data on natural fertility. *Eugenics Quarterly.* 8:81–91.

Ho Ping-ti (1959). *Studies on the Population of China, 1368–1953.* Harvard University Press, Cambridge.

Howell, N. (1979). *Demography of the Dobe !Kung.* Academic Press, New York.

Johnson, A. (1977). The energy costs of technology in a changing environment: A Machiguenga case. In *Material Culture: Styles, Organization, and Dynamics of Technology,* 1975 Proceedings of the American Ethnological Society, West, St. Paul, Minn. pp. 155–167.

Jones, F.L. (1963). *A Demographic Survey of the Aboriginal Population of the Northern Territory, with Special Reference to Bathurst Island Mission.* Australian Institute of Aboriginal Studies, Occasional Papers in Aboriginal Studies, no. 1, Social Anthropology Series no. 1. Canberra.

Kamakau, S. (1961). *Ruling Chiefs of Hawaii.* Kamehameha Schools, Honolulu.

Kennedy, K.A.R. (1984). Growth, nutrition, and pathology in changing palaeodemographic settings in South Asia. In *Palaeopathology at the Origins of Agriculture* (M.N. Cohen and G.J. Armelagos, eds.), Academic Press, Orlando, Fla., pp. 169–192.

Keyfitz, N. (1968). *Introduction to the Mathematics of Population.* Addison-Wesley, Reading, Mass.

Kirch, P.V. (1984). *Evolution of Polynesian Chiefdoms.* Cambridge University Press, New York.

Konnor, M., and C. Worthman (1980). Nursing frequency, gonadal function, and birth spacing among !Kung hunter-gatherers. *Science,* 207:788–791.

Lea, D.A.M. (1965). The Abelam: A study in local differentiation. *Pacific Viewpoint,* 6:191–214.

Lee, J. (1982). Food supply and population growth in southwest China, 1250–1850. *Journal of Asian Studies,* 41:711–746.

Lee, R.B. (1968). What hunters do for a living, or how to make out on scarce resources. In *Man the Hunter* (R.B. Lee and I. DeVore, eds.), Aldine, Chicago, pp. 30–48.

———. (1972). Population growth and the beginnings of sedentary life among the !Kung Bushmen. In *Population Growth: Anthropological Implications* (B. Spooner, ed.), MIT Press, Cambridge, pp. 329–342.

———. (1980). Lactation, ovulation, infanticide, and women's work: A study of hunter-gatherer population regulation. In *Biosocial Mechanisms of Population Regulation* (M.N. Cohen, R.S. Malpass, and H.G. Klein, eds.), Yale University Press, New Haven, Conn., pp. 321–348.

Lee, R.B., and I. DeVore (1968). Problems in the study of hunters and gatherers. In *Man the Hunter* (R.B. Lee and I. DeVore, eds.), Aldine, Chicago, pp. 3–12.

McEvedy, C. (1988). The bubonic plague. *Scientific American,* 258(2):118–123.

Malthus, T.R. (1959). *Population: The First Essay.* Ann Arbor Paperbacks, Ann Arbor, Mich.

Martin, P.S. (1973). The discovery of America. *Science,* 179:969–974.

Maserang, C.H. (1977). Carrying capacities and low population growth. *Journal of Anthropological Research,* 33:479–492.

Meggitt, M. (1977). *Blood Is Their Argument: Warfare among the Mae Enga Tribesmen of the New Guinea Highlands.* Mayfield, Palo Alto, Calif.

Montgomery, E., and A. Johnson (1977). Machiguenga energy expenditure. *Ecology of Food and Nutrition,* 6:97–105.

Naroll, R.C. (1962). Floor area and settlement population. *American Antiquity,* 27:587–589.

Netting, R.M. (1981). *Balancing on an Alp: Ecological Change and Continuity in a Swiss Mountain Community.* Cambridge University Press, Cambridge.

———. (1987). On anthropology and demography. *Current Anthropology,* 28:202–203.

Oliver, D. (1974). *Ancient Tahitian Society.* Vol. 1. University of Hawaii Press, Honolulu.

Oram, N.D. (1977). Environment, migration, and site selection in the Port Moresby coastal area. In *The Melanesian Environment* (J.H. Winslow, ed.), Australian National University Press, Canberra, pp. 74–99.

———. (1982). Pots for sago: The *hiri* trading network. In *The Hiri in History* (T.E. Dutton, ed.), Development Studies Institute, Australian National University, Canberra, pp. 1–33.

Perkins, D. (1969). *Agricultural Development in China.* Aldine, Chicago.

Petersen, W. (1975). *Population.* 3d ed. Macmillan, New York.

———. (1979). *Malthus.* Harvard University Press, Cambridge.

Polgar, S. (1972). Population, history, and population policies from an anthropological perspective. *Current Anthropology,* 13:203–209.

Pryor, F. (1982). On induced economic change in precapitalist societies. *Journal of Development Economics,* 10:325–353.

Reiner, E.J., and R.G. Robbins (1964). The middle Sepik plains, New Guinea: A physiographic study. *Geographical Review,* 54:20–44.

Robbins, R.G. (1960). The anthropogenic grasslands of Papua and New Guinea. In *Symposium on the Impact of Man on Humid Tropical Vegetation,* UNESCO, Goroka, Papua New Guinea, pp. 313–329.

Ross, E.B. (1985). Potatoes, population, and the Irish famine: The political economy of demographic change. In *Culture and Reproduction: An Anthropological Critique of Demographic Transition Theory* (W.P. Handwerker, ed.), Westview, Boulder, Colo., pp. 196–220.

Schacht, R.M. (1980). Two models of population growth. *American Anthropologist,* 82:782–798.

Schaefer, O. (1971). When the Eskimo comes to town. *Nutrition Today,* 6(6).

Schneider, D.M. (1955). Abortion and depopulation on a Pacific island. In *Health, Culture, and Community* (B.D. Paul, ed.), Russell Sage, New York, pp. 211–235.

Shryock, H.S., S. Siegel, and associates (1976). *The Methods and Materials of Demography.* Academic Press, New York.

Simon, J.L. (1978). An integration of the invention-pull and population-push theories of economic-demographic history. *Research in Population Economics,* 1:165–187.

Smith, T.C. (1977). *Nakamura: Family Planning and Population in a Japanese Village, 1717–1830.* Stanford University Press, Stanford, Calif.

Street, J.M. (1969). An evaluation of the concept of carrying capacity. *Professional Geographer,* 21:104–107.

Suggs, R.C. (1961). *The archaeology of Nuku Hiva, Marquesas Islands, French Polynesia.* Anthropological Papers of the American Museum of Natural History, vol. 49, no. 1. Garden City, N.Y.

Sussman, R.W. (1972). Child transport, family size, and increase in human population during the Holocene. *Current Anthropology,* 13:258–259.

Terrell, J.E. (1986). *Prehistory in the Pacific Islands: A Study of Variation in Language, Customs, and Human Biology.* Cambridge University Press, Cambridge.

Tomasson, R. (1977). A millennium of misery: The demography of the Icelanders. *Population Studies,* 31:405–425.

Tucker, G.S.L. (1970). Irish fertility ratios before the famine. *Economic History Review,* 23:267–284.

Tuzin, D.F. (1976). *The Ilahita Arapesh: Dimensions of Unity.* University of California Press, Berkeley.

Vasey, D.E. (1979). Population and agricultural intensity in the humid tropics. *Human Ecology,* 7:269–283.

———. (1982). Subsistence potential of the pre-colonial Port Moresby area, with reference to the *hiri* trade. *Archaeology in Oceania,* 17:132–142.

Wagley, C. ([1951]1969). Cultural influences on population: A comparison of two Tupi tribes. Reprint. In *Environment and Cultural Behavior* (A.P. Vayda, ed.), Natural History Press, Garden City, N.Y., pp. 268–280.

Walsh, B.M. (1970). Marriage rates and population pressure: Ireland, 1871 and 1911. *Economic History Review,* 23:148–162.

Wood, J.W., and P.E. Smouse (1982). A method of analyzing density-dependent vital rates with an application to the Gainj of Papua New Guinea. *American Journal of Physical Anthropology,* 58:403–411.

Wynne-Edwards, V.C. (1962). *Animal Dispersion in Relation to Social Behaviour.* Oliver and Boyd, Edinburgh.

———. (1965). Self-regulating systems in populations of animals. *Science,* 147:1543–1547.

9

The Rise of
Industrial Agriculture

 This chapter and the next tell about the enormous impact of modern science, industrial technology, and industrial inputs upon agriculture. World War II divides the chapters, except that for the sake of continuity, this one follows some lines of scientific research up to the present. Plant breeding is taken to the eve of genetic engineering, presently a frontier of research, in order to follow the thread of its development. The chronicle begins with forerunning events, the European agricultural revolution of the sixteenth, seventeenth, and eighteenth centuries, before the use of industrial inputs in agriculture.

For a long time, improvements are largely biological and wrought by farmers with only a little help from scientists, who gradually make their mark. Scientists learn to apply genetics to breeding and begin to develop breeding programs that improve on those of amateurs and entrepreneurs. Agricultural chemistry is a recognized discipline by the mid-nineteenth century. Fertilizers and other products of the chemical industry are widely used early in the twentieth century and become essential for the yields subsequently obtained in western Europe and Japan.

Major Trends

The industrialization of food production enables a few farmers and ranchers to feed the masses and provide them with cloth. Agricultural workers' productivity increases dramatically, even if the supporting army of workers who make the inputs and process the output are taken into account (Teigen, 1982, re the United States). Average productivity of land substantially increases. Scientific breeders cannot yet bring about gross morphological changes in domesticates like those obtained by preindustrial peoples, but they effect equal or greater increases in yields in a far shorter span of time. Soil amendments appear in new forms and greater quantities than were available to preindustrial cultivators. Farm machinery does not yet perform any important new tasks nor all those done by hand, but it sharply reduces the need for human and animal effort and makes thorough land preparation the rule, where before many cultivators chronically lacked sufficient hands or draft animals.

What takes place is a massive escalation of human intervention in ecosystems. Formerly irrigation was the only means to raise net primary productivity, which in rain-fed preindustrial agricultural ecosystems is ordinarily about the same as or less than that of the natural ecosystems they replace. Preindustrial food producers' successes were their diversions of more of the ecosystems' production to feeding humans. Agricultural science continues that approach—in plant and animal breeding, for example—but goes beyond. Reseeding turns grasslands from sparse to lush, fertilization raises net primary productivity, and the irrigated area is greatly extended by means of large dams, deep wells, and powerful pumps that were not previously available. The primary productivity of the natural ecosystem cannot always be improved; rain forests are still not readily matched, let alone beaten.

Energy consumption by society had long risen, with agriculture usually contributing a share, and it surges with the advent of industrialization and industrial agriculture. Palaeolithic food collectors doubled their energy consumption when they added fire to food preparation (Cook, 1971). Early agriculture added to energy consumption, an increase due largely to the control of animals. The innovations of early modern Europe (A.D. 1300–1500), including stepped-up animal husbandry, the burning of coal, more travel and transport, and the harnessing of wind and water for power, bring about a further trebling (Cook, 1971). The quantum leap of the industrial revolution is primarily based on fossil fuels and is so great that, while the energy consumed in food production rises steadily, it declines relative to the energy used in producing other goods and services.

The age of coal and steam affects agriculture foremost by producing a revolution in transport, as well as in other ways. Coal fires heat barns and drying sheds. Steam engines pump out coal mines and later drain agricultural lands. A few steam tractors go to work before gasoline tractors push them out of existence.

Transport costs drop, encouraging the movement of more and bulkier goods over longer distances. Previously, sailing ships moved cereals from England to the Continent, and costlier commodities over longer distances: salted fish and sheepskins from Scandinavia to southern Europe, cotton from the American South to Manchester's mills, and wool from England to Flanders and later from Australia to England. But it is steamships and railways that really open up world markets, by the 1870s allowing cheap wheat from the North American Great Plains to flood Europe. Iced and insulated railway cars come into use in the 1880s, making California a major supplier of fresh fruit and vegetables to eastern cities. Steamships also begin to move commercial fertilizers — first Peruvian guano and later phosphate and Chilean nitrate, minerals mined with the help of dynamite and steam equipment. Sulfuric acid, made from sulfur in coal-burning factories, converts phosphate to superphosphate.

The age of petroleum and the internal combustion engine follow. Transport costs fall further, stimulating more movement of food and fiber. Tractors and chemical fertilizers become standard equipment. Both nitrogen fertilizers and a diverse array of agricultural chemicals are synthesized with the help of large inputs of fossil fuel energy. Petroleum becomes the feedstock for many new chemicals.

Industrialization, besides producing agricultural inputs, also generates the large urban markets to which ever more productive farmers sell. It stimulates modern experimental science.

Though agriculture, science, and industry have common roots and are today intimately linked pursuits, agricultural improvement and commercialization go a long way before industrialization has an effect. In England several centuries of infrastructure improvements, growing trade, and sweeping changes in farm management precede the industrial revolution. Experimental science as such plays little direct role at first, though many historians argue that science and technical change emerge together in a conducive atmosphere of challenge to orthodoxy.

This chronicle of agricultural change will begin with late preindustrial agriculture in Europe, what many European writers call the agricultural revolution. In this broad, global survey, the term *European agricultural revolution* is more apt, because the primary theater is western Europe. Eastern Europe and overseas settler colonies are late or peripheral participants, with Japan being a contrasting case.

What follows will be called the agroindustrial revolution. Up to World War II, this is an event of the developed countries but not peculiarly European. Indeed, little of the new technology is useful in only one specific region. A questioning and experimental frame of mind is behind the innovations of early industrial agriculture, but application of formal experimental science mostly comes later.

Late Preindustrial Agriculture

The European agricultural revolution is usually thought to be an event of postmedieval England, but it has its precedents, both in England and on the Continent during the late medieval era. Church estates belonging to the Cistercian order were particularly innovative. Slicher van Bath (1963:178) notes a reduction in fallows and increased planting of legumes in several parts of the Continent during the late Middle Ages.

The revolution also has no clear end. Trends in biological management merge in the nineteenth century with the adoption of industrial inputs.

EARLY INNOVATIONS IN THE LOW COUN-TRIES. The most significant early innovations are in the low countries. The planting of legumes, roots, and other fodder crops, as catch crops or to replace plowed fallows, is documented as early as 1278 and is common practice by the fifteenth century (Slicher van Bath, 1963:149). Dumont (1957:366) notes the disappearance of fallows and the increases in number of cattle in thirteenth-century Flanders. Ley farming is known at Ghent by 1323 and is common there by the seventeenth century. At first the ley is in grass, but planted clover later takes its place (Slicher van Bath, 1963:179). The influence of these developments on English farming, through the supply of seeds or the diffusion of methods of management, is controversial.

Poldering makes tidal flats into farmland during the Middle Ages in the Netherlands and Germany, on a large scale in the sixteenth-century Netherlands. Its widespread application illustrates both pressure upon land resources and an ability to mobilize and coordinate action to meet that pressure.

ENGLAND. Revision of older histories puts the major changes in English agriculture well ahead of the industrial revolution. Previously Ernle's influential *English Farming Past and Present* (1961, originally 1912) placed them in the same period as the industrial revolution, that is, the late eighteenth and early nineteenth centuries. Chambers and Mingay (1966) partly follow suit but note that ley farming and many new crops are common as early as the sixteenth century. Kerridge (1967) adds to the list of early innovations the "floating" of water meadows and various lesser innovations, stresses the breadth of earlier changes, and concludes that the sixteenth and early seventeenth centuries are the times of the most significant changes. He underplays the importance of certain rotations involving fodder crops, such as clover and turnip, that are loudly promoted in the eighteenth century and long thought to be the hallmark of the revolution in England. These fodder crops are now known to have been present long before the eighteenth century. John (1960) and Jones (1965) also support an early revolution.

The changes are primarily biological, though achieved by farmers, not scientists or natural philosophers. New crops lead to new cropping systems. Livestock feeding improves, increasing the supply of manure. Crop production and animal husbandry are better integrated, and more use is made of naturally occurring inorganic fertilizers such as marl (a clay rich in lime). Some later innovations, including the selection of pure livestock lines and improved iron and steel plowing implements, are simultaneous with the early industrial revolution but still antedate most use of industrial inputs in agriculture.

Substantial capital and labor go into marling and the floating of meadows. In floated meadows, water flows in a thin layer across a leveled grassland, thus imitating the valued water meadows. Enclosing open fields, most often with stone walls, is costly and laborious and in many cases a prerequisite for establishing annual cropping of food and fodder crops, though enclosure is not as ubiquitous as was once believed. Cropping frequency increases over large areas as summer-plowed fallows are eliminated, but other land is taken out of cultivation and put into pasture, floated meadows, or ley systems. Agricultural employment increases, if not always steadily, from the late sixteenth century through the eighteenth century. Productivity rises even more rapidly. For the country as a whole, the net return on labor rises a little. Improved management is the one consistent trend, with capital intensification and labor intensification both frequent but not inevitable accompaniments.

THE SPREAD OF THE EUROPEAN AGRI-CULTURAL REVOLUTION. Parallel changes away from England and the low countries come later, not too long before the adoption of industrial inputs. The lag is evident even in the British Isles. Scots farmers are conservative through most of the eighteenth century (Handley, 1953:33ff.) but in the next century are as innovative as those of England, at least where the environment is not so marginal that it discourages investment. Experiments are made with many types of horse-drawn equipment, forerunners of the machinery that later revolutionizes cultivation on the North American prairies and plains. The potato, widely adopted throughout the British Isles during the eighteenth century, demands greater labor intensity than was usual in cereal cultivation. Potatoes are often integrated into field systems, with some effect on rotations (Buchanan, 1973:586), but are more characteristically found on intensively worked patches, particularly in Ireland and the Scottish highlands.

Development trails in France outside Flanders, though authorities dispute how much. Faucher holds that the elimination of fallows and a "biological revolution" precede the "chemical revolution" of the mid-nineteenth century (Weber, 1976:119), but according to Weber (1976), methods remain unchanged in many areas until late in the nineteenth century, when chemical fertilizers, new field systems, and permanent cultivation are often adopted together (see also Jolas and Zonabend, 1977; Lefebvre, 1977).

Events also trail in southern and central Europe, except for some scattered patches of innovation and instances of proselytizing by publicists. In sixteenth-century Germany, Heresbach recommends a rotation of rape and root crops; Tarello's *Recorde d'Agricolture* of 1601 commends to Italian farmers a four-course rotation, including lucerne, clover, and sainfoin (Fussell, 1972:111); and lupine cover crops are grown in seventeenth-century Tuscany (Fussell, 1972:129). Sons of Danish aristocrats begin in the eighteenth century to study agronomy formally, usually in England, and by century's end, some Danish universities add the subject (Anderson, 1975:49–50). But these recommendations and pockets of interest remain isolated until after the mid-nineteenth century.

Parallel changes come late to eastern Europe, sometimes in advance of industrially based inputs, but only because the latter too arrive later than in western Europe. A belt of "progressive" agriculture—meaning that grass, timothy, or clover has replaced plowed fallows—extends in the late nineteenth century from Poland into parts of European Russia (Ermolov, 1893), though most authors (e.g., Pavlosky, 1968) minimize change in imperial Russian agriculture as a whole; little change is evident within the Ukrainian breadbasket.

The countries in which industrial inputs would soon play a major role in agriculture thus differ greatly in the degree to which systems are already transformed. Japan offers the greatest contrast with Europe. What is new in Europe is either old in Japan—legume rotations, for example – or of little use, as are most things involving mixed farming. The contrasts merit explanation.

SOCIAL AND ECONOMIC FACTORS IN EUROPE.

The lead of England and the low countries in the European agricultural revolution is a product of social and economic conditions, not a singularly favorable natural environment. Though many of the new methods are uniquely suited to the temperate maritime climate of northwestern Europe, others are eventually transferred to the continental climates of eastern Europe and eastern Northern America. What distinguishes the leaders from other countries is the early breakdown of feudalism, the development of infrastructure, and the rapid growth of internal and external markets. Population growth is substantial from the late seventeenth century on. Population pressure is also high in the low countries and no doubt a factor in the early elimination of fallows there.

Individualism and entrepreneurship play their part. Macfarlane (1978) argues that peasant society gives way in late medieval England to a rural entrepreneurial society in which land is individually owned. A farmer-entrepreneur class certainly drives the revolution in England. Most are tenant farmers, paying fixed rents instead of the shares that dampened incentive in medieval Europe. Others own their land or own some of the land and rent the rest. The role of great landowners is less. Habakkuk (1968), however, questions the common interpretation that they collect rent but manage little.

Over most of the continent the social class (or estate) structure and associated land tenure long discourage innovation. Only a handful of landed aristocrats write about the new methods, experiment with them, or send their sons to study agronomy.

Lingering feudal obligations still burden the French peasantry at the time of the revolution. They cling to their rights to uncultivated commons, and a few efforts in the last years of the monarchy to enclose and divide commons mainly benefit the wealthy landowners (Lefebvre, 1977:37ff.). Payments to the old landed classes persist long after the revolution (Soboul, 1977), and the holdings are so fragmented that they discourage better integration of cultivation and animal husbandry. Roads show little planning for the movement of agricultural goods before a massive corrective effort in the mid- and late nineteenth century (Weber, 1976:195–220).

Sharecropping and serfdom persist into the eighteenth and nineteenth centuries in central and eastern Europe. The Russian empire formally abolishes serfdom in 1861, but absentee landlords remain more the rule than those who take an active interest in management. The Prussian Junkers are generally the most innovative among the eastern aristocrats. Elsewhere in the German states, Amish smallholders introduce a four-course rotation, including clover, to the Palatinate in the seventeenth century (Schwieder and Schwieder, 1975) and subsequently take the system with them to other parts of Germany and to North America. Late and widespread innovations in central and eastern Europe, often accompanied by some adoption of industrial inputs, are often connected with land reforms, something best seen in the case of Denmark. There a rapid reorganization and technical transformation of agriculture takes place in the late nineteenth century, after remarkable grass-roots activity — including the free school and folk high school movements and the formation of powerful cooperatives — enables smallholders to take advantage of new methods and ready access to English markets.

JAPAN. Japanese farmers in the nineteenth century experience a dubious advance from a burdensome system of sharecropping to a burdensome system of tax payments. Peasants of the Tokugawa era turned over to their feudal lords 40% to 50% of the harvest, and in the late period as much as 70%, plus numerous other taxes and services (Hane, 1982:5–11). One official instructed his subordinates that the peasants "should be allowed to retain what they must actually consume during the year . . . what is essential but no more" (p. 9). After 1868 the new Meiji regime abolishes feudal obligations but refrains from making any sweeping land reform, though deeds are issued to many farmers. Peasants now pay to the government each year 3% of the assessed value of the land. The payment, in currency, fluctuates with the size of the harvest and the price of produce but averages about 33% of the yield (Hane, 1982:17). Many peasants fall into debt and lose the title they only recently gained.

Agriculture remains highly labor-intensive, a consequence in part of population pressure but also of new incentives. In the Meiji era the margin between income and rent is typically thin, and many peasants fall into debt or lose their land, but at least they are allowed to keep all production above their obligations.

The main improvements of the late nineteenth century are in plant breeding, labor-intensive cultural techniques, the use of organic manures at rates that are very high by European standards, and the beginnings of chemical fertilizer use. Irrigated rice farms cover much of the landscape, on holdings that average about a hectare. One task is to breed rice varieties that respond to high levels of available nutrients. Sources of nutrients are sought abroad. Before and after the adoption of chemical fertilizers, Japan imports large quantities of soybean press cake for use on rice fields.

NORTH AMERICA. North American farmers enjoy land that is cheap and abundant by European or Japanese standards, but agricultural labor is scarce and costly. The availability of frontier land may help keep agricultural wages up in older settlements. Slaves in the southern cotton plantations are the possible exception; their labor is cheap and their productivity enough to amply repay the investment (Fogel and Engerman, 1974). Everywhere, so long as frontier land is available, incentives for improvements on older lands are few, and land use remains more extensive than in Europe (Danhof, 1969).

The newer English methods have little impact on the British colonies in North America or on the fledgling United States. When change comes, it is at first in the eastern states and Canadian provinces, where "worn-out" soils are a recognized and growing problem by the 1830s. Remedies are sought, if at all, in imported soil amendments rather than in new field systems. Other farmland is simply abandoned to forest or rough pasture, as settlement shifts to the frontier.

Interest in labor-saving devices comes early, and the United States eventually becomes a leader in mechanized farming. Ironically, the invention of a labor-saving machine, the cotton gin, gives new life to slavery by making cotton more affordable to the new industrial mills.

Frontier opportunities dwindle in the late nineteenth century, rekindling interest in the restoration of worn-out lands in the eastern states and in maintaining the productivity of midwestern soils. New rotations and field systems and applications of chemical fertilizers increase, but compared with European practices the use of these land-saving methods, as many economists call them, still lags.

THE EVE OF INDUSTRIAL AGRICULTURE. The changes in late preindustrial agriculture in what are becoming the developed countries can be summed up: (1) Farm productivity grows impressively; (2) experimental science and industry contribute less to these gains than farmers' innovations and knowledge of how to manage such familiar inputs as seed, fodder, and manure; and (3) where feudal tenure existed, its breakdown is a precondition for change. In spite of these similarities, variation among countries cannot be overlooked. The timing of change varies with many factors, above all the social and political milieu. The new holding is the family farm in most countries, and some combination of renting and ownership in England.

Land-rich countries emphasize labor-saving techniques, whereas countries experiencing more population pressure do more to increase yields and save land.

The agroindustrial revolution begins slowly in the nineteenth century, if the measure is the use of industrial inputs, or at a crawl, if measured by the application of modern empirical science. The science of plant and animal breeding evolves slowly, beginning even while the European agricultural revolution is mostly confined to England and the low countries. Chemical fertilizers appear early in the nineteenth century and reach the North American frontier, albeit in small quantities. Agricultural experiment stations appear not long thereafter, and the odd steam tractor chugs past teams of horses.

Science and the Agroindustrial Revolution

Scientists through the first few decades of the nineteenth century get involved in agriculture largely through efforts to explain known successes. They are slow to assume leadership. Chemistry, though it received comparatively early attention, serves as a good example. First farmers try a growing array of already existing fertilizers, including mined products and industrial by-products. Chemists begin to evaluate commercial formulas and then, once the major fertilizer elements are identified, to suggest new compounds, identify industrial by-products whose value was previously overlooked, and develop syntheses for the purpose of fertilizer manufacture. Similarly, commercial plant breeders begin the systematic selection and production of hybrids. Scientists first step in to develop theories of inheritance and only later assume leadership in breeding.

By 1910, scientists are having an impact, though far from universally. The main chemical fertilizers are known, synthesis of chemical nitrogen fertilizers is an established industry, and Japanese breeders have cataloged specific traits in rice and wheat lines and are breeding these traits into the forerunners of modern high-yielding varieties. Scientifically tested insecticides and fungicides are on the market.

Hayami and Ruttan (1971:37) assert that much of the work on agricultural experiment stations well into the 1930s and 1940s is still directed toward "the testing and refinement of farmer innovations and to the testing and adaptation of existing crop varieties and animal species [races?]." The description is probably apt of most research, but not all. By that time scientists are making innovations that leave a clear mark on practice.

In the industrial revolution, the involvement of scientists in technical innovation is also largely after the fact, but they are quicker to assume a leading role, a contrast that gives us a better perspective on the peculiar relationship between farmer and scientist. Practical persons with mechanical and entrepreneurial skills lead the industrial revolution. A period after 1850, the "second industrial revolution," is generally thought to be the time during which science takes an increasing role in innovation. Eventually scientists predict inventions well in advance.

The development of electric communication is representative. Scientific interest in electricity stimulates the development of the telegraph in the 1830s, and scientists like Carl Friedrich Gauss and Wilhem Eduard Weber take part, but less lettered men devise the instruments and the codes. The first telephone (1875–76) is a more advanced instrument requiring some knowledge of acoustics and electromagnetism, though inventor Alexander Graham Bell is a teacher of the deaf and not a professional scientist. To develop the wireless (1895–96), an advance predicted by scientists, Guglielmo Marconi relies on knowledge of waves gained from experiments by a number of physicists. Television exists on paper a good half-century before the first workable sets of the late 1930s. The cathode ray, or picture, tube is a child of atomic physics.

If agricultural change is revolutionary as early as the sixteenth century, and the scientists' role is minor as late as 1850, then farmers led innovation much longer than did the mechanics and tinkerers of industry. Farmers have a long history of successful adaptation to changing social and physical environments. They deal with complex organisms and ecosystems. In many countries they remain suspicious of experiment stations long after the general public expects miracles from science. Premature hopes and subsequent disappointment often fuel farmers' skepticism of agricultural science; an excellent example is the early history of soil analysis in the United States (Rossiter, 1975).

AGRICULTURAL EXPERIMENT STATIONS.

Agricultural experiment stations germinate after 1850, following a heated discussion in the agricultural journals of the day over the conduct of field trials. Arguably the first station is established at Rothamsted, England, by philanthropist and accomplished amateur scientist J. B. Lawes. The first state-sponsored station begins at Mockern, Saxony, in 1852, and other German states follow suit. Connecticut starts the first United States station in 1876, quickly followed by several other states. The federal government in 1862 sets up the land grant system to help states fund agricultural colleges (Sanders, 1966:15), and the Hatch Act of 1887 establishes a network of experiment stations in conjunction with the agricultural colleges. Congress in 1890 mandates a second system of colleges and experiment stations for blacks in southern states and a few northern ones. *Separate* in this instance never means *equal.* U.S. Department of Agriculture funding of black colleges long averages 0.5% of allocations to white-only agricultural colleges in the same states (Hightower, 1973:11).

Experiment stations employ professional scientists, most often agricultural chemists in the early days, conduct more-rigorous and better-controlled experiments than those of most amateurs, and take on research that promises little immediate return. Their scientists build theories, a practice that many innovative farmers openly scorn in journals of the time. Rothamsted embodies all these features to a high degree. It is run from its start by Lawes and chemist J. H. Gilbert. Though a site of short-term and practical trials and a source of some recommendations accepted by farmers, Rothamsted also houses an admirable series of long-term experiments. A much cited soil exhaustion trial has today run for more than a century.

AGRICULTURAL CHEMISTRY AND SOIL SCIENCE. The publication simultaneously in German and English of Justus von Liebig's *Organic Chemistry in Its Applications to Agriculture and Physiology* (1840) draws attention to agricultural chemistry. It is also responsible for many heightened expectations of soil analysis that follow.

The most lasting contributions of early agricultural chemists are the identification of macronutrients and the analysis of fertilizers. Except for synthesizing superphosphate—the process of treating bones with sulfuric acid is developed by Lawes and Gilbert and later modified by others to use rock phosphate instead of bones—chemists through the middle decades of the nineteenth century do little formulating of chemical fertilizers. Liebig's single venture of the sort is a catastrophe (Rossiter, 1975:44). Entrepreneurs compound the commercial mixtures that are on the market. Quality varies. Chemists' main contribution, once the macronutrients are identified, is to assay products and detect shams. In recommending application rates, their judgments of soil quality are imprecise, and they cannot yet match soil, crop, and specific nutrient.

By the end of the century, chemists identify previously overlooked sources of fertilizer, notably Chilean nitrate and ammonium sulfate (from coal gas manufacture). Industrial chemists have the electric arc process of industrial nitrogen fixation on line by 1903, and the Haber ammonia synthesis during World War I.

No micronutrients are identified until the twentieth century, and then only through the work of scientists: iron by 1910; boron, manganese, and zinc by 1925; copper in 1931; and molybdenum in 1942 (Thompson and Troeh, 1973:325). Micronutrient deficiencies are widespread but particularly prevalent in soils formed on old geological formations, as in Western Australia; in organic soils of wetlands (copper, boron); and in alkaline soils (iron, zinc, manganese). Micronutrient research is a continuation of the lines of inquiry that revealed the macronutrients but also is a response to problems created by the success of macronutrient fertilization, an example of scientific discovery and technical innovation as dialectic response. As macronutrient fertilizers are used in large quantities, bumper crops remove more of the micronutrients, and the use of more-concentrated and more-refined fertilizers makes their accidental replacement less certain. In the United States, micronutrient research develops strongly in the 1960s, after the postwar boom in fertilizer use contributes to micronutrient deficiencies where none had previously existed.

Soil science gradually emerges as a recognized discipline, not just the dominant concern of agricultural chemists. Around 1850 J. T. Way in England investigates the capacity of soils to retain ions, and by 1870 S. W. Johnson in the United States is promoting soil physics (Rossiter, 1975:146–147). Soil microbiology is well established by 1900. Systematic soil classification is a critical step in the formation of a science of soils. The first comprehensive systems are usually credited to Dokuchayev, Sibirtzev, Kostychev, and other Russian scientists, from the early 1870s.

PLANT PROTECTION. Scientists add a few new methods of disease control to traditional ones. Microbiology and controlled experiments make possible the identification of plant pathogens and the substances that control them. The first effective new fungicides are not new substances — sulfur, for example, was known to the ancients — but chemistry is soon enlisted in the search for more effective agents. In a remarkable coincidence of ecological calamity, good luck, and perspicacity, when powdery mildew (oidium, *Uncinula necator*) of grapevines is introduced into Europe in 1848, it is in an experimental collection at Margate, England, where sulfur is being tried on a peach fungus. Tucker notices that sulfur appears to control the disease, then experimentally verifies his inference. The control follows the disease as it rampages through Europe's vineyards (Large, 1962:44–53). The next scourge of the vine, downy mildew (*Plasmopara viticola*), is fought with

Bordeaux mixture, made from two common substances, lime and copper sulfate. Bordeaux vignerons first spray the sticky, unattractive substance to discourage theft. Professor P. M. A. Millardet notices its apparent effect on downy mildew and follows up with experimentation and promotion (Dunegan and Doolittle, 1953; Evans, 1968).

Fungicides based on sulfur and copper subsequently prove effective on many other fungal diseases, are standard until the 1930s, and are in use today. Prevost ([1807] 1935) discovers copper fungicides in 1807 by identifying a fungal disorder of wheat and showing that copper destroys the spores. That his contemporaries ignore his work illustrates the importance in science of being timely.

Twentieth-century research in the field and in laboratories leads first to organometallic fungicides and then to organic agents (organic in the chemists' sense of compounds whose molecules contain carbon atoms) effective against fungi or bacteria. As the list of known compounds mushrooms, hit-or-miss trials are no longer good enough; scientists have to develop theories to guide the selection of compounds to screen for possible use as control agents.

The triumph of science also makes possible the improvement and refinement of old methods. Sanitation, as in the removal of infected animals or plant parts, is an old technique but is not always practiced. Knowledge of transmission and epidemiology provides surer means of knowing when sanitation is needed. Preindustrial agriculturalists select for phenotype in land races and apparently select for disease resistance — how consciously they do so is hard to say — but scientific breeders can develop resistant varieties far more quickly. Scientists also place crop rotation on a sound theoretical basis.

Before DDT the most widely used insecticides are either old substances discovered by preindustrial cultivators or slight improvements on them. Among plant extracts, sabadilla (from *Schoenocaulon* spp.) is in use in the sixteenth century, nicotine (from tobacco) in France before 1690, and pyrethrin (from *Pyrethrum* spp.) in Europe about 1828 (Crosby, 1966:2–3; Feinstein, 1952). Rotenone (from *Derris* spp.) is a fish poison also used to kill insects in parts of East Asia. A repellent, *Nicandra physalodes,* is known in India (Feinstein, 1952). Among inorganic substances, arsenic compounds are used to kill insects as early as 1681 in Europe, and the popular Paris green compound is on the market by 1870 (Carter, 1952).

Scientific experimentation in the late nineteenth and early twentieth centuries adds a few agents to the list. Where plants can be covered, fumigants are popular: naphthalene and carbon bisulfide in the nineteenth century, paradichlorobenzene after 1911 (Roark, 1952). Among field sprays, new arsenicals, petroleum fractions, dinitrophenol, and some zinc and thallium compounds gain acceptance, but not to the point that their use approaches that of plant extracts and older proprietary compounds. Much research in the United States just before World War II is aimed at isolating additional natural insecticides or at synthesizing and trying compounds related to natural insecticides.

In light of current debates over DDT and the whole generation of carbon-compound insecticides that follow, fairness demands pointing out that the leading insecticides of these earlier years are broad-spectrum types that affect most insects, not just selected target species. The plant extracts are quickly biodegraded, but the arsenicals are nonbiodegradable, as well as being infamous poisons.

Biological methods of disease control are far from neglected. Scientists by 1900, having learned that steamships are transferring pests and diseases to new environments, seek controls in the old environments. Biological control is later pushed into the background after DDT produces spectacular results, only to rise anew when problems surface with the "miracle" insecticides. Interest in biological controls therefore follows a pattern of dialectical response, first to the consequences of modern transport and then to the immunities and ecological disturbances brought on by pesticide use.

Viral diseases in crops are a particularly intractable threat and another one whose transmission by rapid international transport opens up a whole area of research directed toward control. The recognition of viral diseases, their eradication through heat treatment and other means, and the propagation of treated plants by means of meristem culture are recently developed preventatives to the buildup of exotic viruses in important fruit and nut clones.

The ideal method of insect and disease control is to breed for resistance, where this can be achieved without unacceptable side effects upon the plant or animal. Up to a point, breeding can also be used to help control weeds, usually by selecting for rapid production of ground cover.

Weed control is not plant protection, strictly speaking, because weeds do not attack plants, but the principle of controlling weeds to favor the crop is much the same as with controlling pests and diseases. Herbicides are the creation of modern science. Inorganic compounds are in use from the early 1900s, and "selective hormone-type" herbicides from the 1930s (Audus, 1964:13). Herbicides are essentially a substitute for labor and sometimes for tractor time and fuel. Yields may often be raised by applying herbicides when the only economic alternative is cultivation between crop rows, but hand control is equally or more effective when thoroughly done.

**BREEDING ANIMALS AND SEXUALLY REPRO-
DUCED PLANTS.** Plant and animal breeding is
gradually systematized over the eighteenth, nineteenth, and twentieth
centuries. Farmers and commercial seedsmen begin the work and for a
long time keep it going. Though not professional scientists, many of
them read natural history and natural philosophy and possess substantial capital. The new breeding methods are at first modest refinements of
old ones but lead in time to improved techniques of seed selection and
animal breeding that scientific programs still use. Some new crop hybrids come from breeding stock made available by transoceanic contacts
and the establishment of botanical collections. Systematic hybridization
comes later and is mostly a product of scientific programs.

Professional scientists enter slowly. T. A. Knight is often regarded
as the prototypical scientific breeder, because he publishes works on
heredity in peas and wheat and also develops useful field varieties. He is
credited with the first deliberate hybridization of wheat in Europe, in the
1820s (Smith, 1966:5). Later, mainly in the twentieth century, commercially important varieties emerge that owe their existence to the application of theory from heredity, plant physiology, and other formal scientific disciplines.

The method that most authorities believe long dominated the breeding of sexually reproduced plants is that of mass selection. Seeds are
selected, presumably by observing yields and other manifest traits
(phenotypes), then pooled before being planted the following season.
Mass selection results in land races (also called local races), in which
genetic composition varies somewhat, or quite a lot if the plant cross-
pollinates readily. A land race requires identification of a type. It is not a
hodgepodge of genes. Traditional cultivators have always recognized
separate varieties and segregated them; even the planters of complex
swiddens recognize distinct varieties and separate the seed stock. A land
race of a crop whose seeds are invariably from self-pollinated parent
plants would consist of a mixture of pure lines, but few, if any, major
crops are in fact always self-pollinated. Rice, barley, oats, tomato, and
lettuce probably come closest. As cross-pollination increases, the lines
become progressively less pure (strictly speaking, heterozygous pairs of
genes are found at more loci), until the land race does not consist of lines
at all.

Mass selection remains the main means of selection until the late
eighteenth century, when commercial grain buyers begin to demand
greater uniformity of type and when more varieties are named, factors
that encourage closer selection for type. The main crops of the European
agricultural revolution, apart from rye and some forage legumes, are

mainly self-pollinated, which would facilitate closer selection if this were desired.

Mass selection is also the main means by which preindustrial herders select domesticated animals, and land races again result. Because nearly all their keepers recognize sexual reproduction in animals, closer selection would always be possible, but more domesticated animals are free-ranging than confined, and inbreeding can result in the appearance of deleterious traits, possibly discouraging too-close selection for single traits.

To improve on mass selection of plants or animals, it is necessary to strike the right balance between inbreeding and outbreeding. Inbreeding offers the advantage that desirable traits already in the population can be incorporated into a uniform type. Outbreeding often affords hybrid vigor, more consistently in plants than in animals, and avoids the possible deleterious effects of inbreeding. Degradation, contrary to popular thinking, is not an inevitable consequence of inbreeding. Too-close inbreeding in animals tends to produce a decline in fertility after some generations, but some degree of inbreeding is usually practicable if the incidence of deleterious recessive genes in the breeding population is not too high. The situation in cross-pollinated plants is more variable. Some important crops, such as the cucurbits, tolerate inbreeding very well. At the other extreme, lines of lucerne (alfalfa, *Medicago sativa*) can barely be kept going after three generations of self-pollination (Allard, 1960:217). Normally, self-pollinated plants tolerate inbreeding the best, because deleterious genes have been selected out.

Backcrossing to create pure livestock lines becomes common practice in the eighteenth century, usually by breeding selected males with their daughters and granddaughters. The method is applied over successive generations, except that outcrosses are made when fertility declines or undesirable traits appear. Many now-familiar English sheep and cattle breeds are thus begun by eighteenth century farmers. In France the Rambouillet line is bred from the Spanish Merino race first in 1786, work begun under imperial sponsorship (Grigg, 1974:43). Today record keeping and knowledge of genetics permit better control of the detrimental effects of inbreeding.

The practical aim of plant breeding, to produce superior cultivars, only gradually converges with scientists' goals of gaining empirical knowledge and building theories. These paths are long set apart by the prevalence of crossbreeding in scientific work and of increasingly close selection for type in commercial breeding.

R. J. Camerarius's 1694 discovery of sex in plants spurs scientific interest. Inquiry focuses on the transmission of traits through successive crossbred generations. Allard (1960:434) notes that the first recognized, deliberate interspecific plant hybrid was from a 1717 cross between the carnation and the sweet william and states that through the early eighteenth century "the chief interest of botanists . . . not so much the production of better plants as the accumulation of evidence of sexuality in the plant kingdom."

Both commercial breeding and improvements on mass selection are first evident in the flower industry. During the seventeenth century, selection and propagation of tulips and hyacinths are an important business in the Netherlands (Krelage, 1946). Choice tulip bulbs sell for extraordinary prices. The small scale of the enterprises and the high value placed on some flower traits encourage inbreeding. One French enterprise, the family firm of Vilmorin, begins dealing in flower seeds and bulbs in 1727. Later generations of the family go on to breed many valuable field crop varieties and to contribute to method and theory.

Farmers of the late eighteenth century begin to select cereal lines more closely. British farmers apparently lead the trend and are naming and promoting selections by this time. P. Sherriff in Scotland, beginning in the 1820s, and Le Couteur in England recognize the value of selecting single plants and segregating their progeny, and each releases some useful varieties. Selection of wheat, barley, and oats develops toward the production of highly inbred lines. Louis de Vilmorin is credited with the first systematic progeny selection — progeny of possibly superior parent plants are grown and observed, and the lines are continued if the progeny plants are promising — but Sherriff is simultaneously working along a similar path (Smith, 1966:5).

Louis de Vilmorin applies progeny selection to sugar beets (Vilmorin, 1923), work of special historic note for the radical changes produced in a field crop in a few generations and for the knowledge gained of methods specific to cross-pollinated plants. The fodder beet, a normally cross-pollinated crop from which sugar beets are bred, averages about 6.2% sugar in its roots (Darlington, 1973:172). Philippe de Vilmorin and others raise the sugar content to 8.8% by 1838 (Allard, 1960:257) by means of mass selection, but progress is hindered by the biennial habit of beets, which produce their root the first year and seed the second. Louis de Vilmorin divides the progeny of a cross, saving some for evaluations of yield and quality and letting the rest produce seed. He achieves an average sugar content of 16% to 17%, whereas contemporary German breeders obtain only 9.8% to 11% (Coons, 1936). He finds that lines of sugar beet continue to exhibit variation and are capable of improvement over many generations.

Many breeding programs are well grounded in scientific method by the closing years of the nineteenth century. By this time, judgings of new crop varieties are a feature of fairs and shows in many countries. Much of the work is still in the hands of farmers, commercial breeders, and amateurs, but many of them have a sound knowledge of contemporary science. Commercial nurseries and amateur breeders to this day contribute useful fruit, vegetable, and especially flower varieties.

For all the contributions of persons other than professional scientists, many difficult challenges yield only to rigorous experimental work and applications of the theory of heredity, or genetics, as it is soon to be called. The development of hybrid maize is exemplary. Maize is perhaps the domesticated crop that ancient cultivators modified the most (Darlington, 1973:167). Scientific breeders cannot yet collapse comparable change within an acceptable time span, but they do obtain dramatic improvements by drawing upon germ plasm of far-flung origins. Among the traits selected to suit the conditions of industrial agriculture are many traits that the ancients would not have valued, such as the response to very high levels of available soil nitrogen or the absence of male inflorescences (tassels).

Success comes to scientists in the United States who apply theory to techniques that had given both promise and frustration. By 1812 J. Lorain produces maize hybrids of the major flint and dent races, and many exhibit marked vigor and high yields, but he cannot obtain consistently superior hybrids (Rasmussen, 1960:61). The problem, we now know, is that maize readily cross-pollinates, and his parent plants are from highly variable land races. The rest of the story is told in Allard (1960:263–278) and Mangelsdorf (1974:211–214). W. Beal works out the mass production technique of interplanting rows of two varieties and detasseling one, which can then be pollinated only by the other. After 1900, geneticist G. H. Shull develops inbred lines and crosses them. Hybrid progeny are consistent when bred from the same parent lines, but the seed is too expensive to produce, because inbreeding badly affects maize and thus plants in the inbred lines yield very poorly. Then D. F. Jones, in work that began in 1915, arrives at the solution of making a second cross. The first crosses, usually of separate pairs of inbred lines, produce costly seed but vigorous progeny, which are crossed to produce a second-generation (F_2) hybrid seed. It is abundant, and its cost is acceptable.

The scientists are in this instance years ahead of demand. Hybrid maize is not widely planted until World War II, when it is adopted in North America in association with high rates of fertilizer applications.

Twentieth-century plant breeding becomes a large and diverse enterprise. The century opens with the rediscovery of Mendel's genetics. Plant explorers travel to carefully selected locations looking for specific traits. Biogeography and the cataloging of traits become sciences in their own right. N. I. Vavilov and his associates begin in 1916 their lengthy and ambitious collection of cultivated plants from all over the world (Vavilov, 1951), work that contributes much to genetic theory and biogeography. Breeders from the 1920s on focus more on crossbreeding, both to obtain hybrid vigor and to transfer specific traits. Dwarf rice and wheat varieties, which respond well to high nitrogen levels without lodging (growing into a tangle or toppling), are selected first by Japanese farmers, then bred in lines at experiment stations, and finally used in crossbreeding as sources of the dwarfism trait. The new varieties are not much planted in Japan until after World War II (Hayami and Yamada, 1970:130–133), but the dwarfism trait is bred into the Taiwanese *ponlai* varieties widely planted in the 1930s, and later into the rice varieties of the green revolution (chapter 11).

The success of breeding programs threatens their raw material, the genetic resources scattered in local races around the world. Many authorities (e.g., Harlan, 1956, 1966; National Research Council, 1978) note with alarm that a single, attractive new variety often replaces several genetically diverse land races, and the green revolution now worsens matters by spreading uniform, high-yielding varieties in the regions where genetic diversity among land races is greatest. World collections are seen as the solution, though their adequacy and security are debated.

For most major crops the characteristics that contribute to higher yields have been mapped, and varieties carrying them are in collections, but omissions become evident from time to time, and many crops of little current importance but much potential value are not well mapped. Resistances to specific pathogens are also not completely mapped, one reason why good collections are essential, and attention is occasionally called to new traits.

The greatest yield increases of the future may come from emerging technologies that allow the transfer of genes between species that cannot be crossed to produce viable offspring. This so-called genetic engineering includes recombinant DNA techniques, in which the molecules that carry the genetic codes are transferred from the cell nuclei of one organism to the cell nuclei of another. The fusion of plant cells from two separate species is another technique. It has also become common practice to speed mutagenesis, the formation of new types through mutation, by use of irradiation and chemical means. Equally important, because the overwhelming majority of mutations are deleterious, are rapid screening methods that make it possible to reject a large number of mutations at an early stage, often while the plants are still in tissue cultures.

BREEDING ASEXUALLY REPRODUCED CROP PLANTS. Vegetatively propagated (asexually reproduced) crops present quite different possibilities to the breeder. A clonal variety, such as the Granny Smith apple or the Cabernet Sauvignon vine, should not be confused with an inbred line of a sexually reproduced plant, even though in either case each generation replicates its predecessor. The genes of the inbred line are predominantly in homozygous pairs, whereas most of the genes of the clone are in heterozygous pairs. If a clonal variety produces seed through self-fertilization, the seedling varies from type. Indeed the seedling is not true to type even if one plant is both its male and female parents.

Many clones are very old yet appear to be products of sexual reproduction and repeated cross-pollination. For example, many Andean potato varieties are products of several intraspecific and interspecific crosses. Modern breeders have the opportunity to create hybrids using stock from far-flung places and to propagate these hybrids in clones.

Propagation by seed of crops that are normally asexually reproduced is an important means of diversification. Creating a new variety may or may not be the grower's intent, and as a rule, useless seedlings greatly outnumber those worth saving. Despite the odds, this sort of variation is significant along distant frontiers of European settlement, to which seeds are more readily carried than plants or cuttings. Clones selected from seedlings form the basis of the North American apple industry. Along the United States frontier, John Chapman (Johnny Appleseed) in this fashion fosters diversity while spreading apple growing.

Mutation is another source of variation. Important phenotypic changes commonly result from long-accumulated mutations. Grapevine clones of the same name and ancestry often vary sharply in yield, flavor, and depth of color. Sudden dramatic changes are reported, for example, a change from black fruit to green on a single branch of a grapevine, one that was subsequently cloned to produce a new named variety (Popescu, Baditescu, and Popescu, 1974).

Before scientific breeding makes itself felt, hobbyists collect plants from remote parts of the globe and produce some useful hybrids accidentally. Modern domesticated strawberry varieties are descendants of an apparently accidental cross in France between the North American *Fragaria virginiana* and the South American *F. chiloensis,* from which Keen in England selects several clones (Darlington, 1973:172). Most of the commercial so-called "American" grapevines of eastern North America are hybrids of two or more indigenous species, and some also claim the European *Vitis vinifera* in their pedigree. Most are accidental progeny of wild and cultivated vines growing in proximity. Among those that are still grown commercially, Catawba is released in 1802, Isabella before 1816, and Clinton in 1821 (Pool et al., 1976).

This process of hybridization, propagation of the seedling, and vegetative propagation to establish a clone is gradually systematized. Grapevines are representative. Commercial breeders in France, beginning with G. Couderc in 1881, endeavor to save European vineyards from the ravages of vine pests and diseases introduced from North America by making successive crosses of *Vitis vinifera* with several North American species of *Vitis*. They succeed, and many of the hybrids become commercially important in Europe, North America, and as far away as New Zealand. Experiment stations today perform much of the vine breeding work, but private breeders are still active. Soviet, Canadian, and Chinese breeders also incorporate *V. amurensis,* a wild vine of northern Asia, in their programs.

The transfer of a trait is usually fairly easy in asexually reproduced plants that normally produce seed. Only one seed is the progenitor of the clone, making mass seed production techniques unnecessary. Female flowers or plants are protected from undesirable pollen. If the plant is self-fertile, the male parts of the flowers are removed. Those flowers that exclude outside pollen are opened.

Breeders are today inducing seed production in many crops that do not normally produce seed. Only a few of the major crops, such as the banana (Simmonds, 1966), still prove exceedingly hard to hybridize.

Plenty of scope remains for hybridizing asexually reproduced plants. Progress is slow through the tedious process of making crosses and evaluating progeny, leaving plenty of work yet to be done. The typical variety, a group of related clones, with each carrying many recessive traits that may become manifest in hybrids, is a gene mine.

Techniques of rapid vegetative propagation promise to speed the distribution of advantageous varieties. Faster production of progeny also makes them more quickly available in quantity for evaluation. Obtaining a few thousand plants from the original seedling typically takes years with the older methods, less than a year using mist propagation, and as little as two to three months using tissue culture. In the 1940s, researchers and commercial nursery managers develop mist propagation: Short stem cuttings, root cuttings, or leaf cuttings are kept on a soillike medium under intermittent mist until they form roots. Because the mist prevents drying, green parts from growing plants can be used, and growing plants are divided at short intervals, sometimes every few weeks. Methods of using very small plant parts are more recent but are in common use. Tissue culture is one; the plant part, usually the meristem (growing stem tip), is kept on a sterile medium that contains carbohydrates and various substances that promote growth or rooting, encouraging the rapid production of small plants.

Another promising approach is to change from vegetative propagation to propagation by seed. If the plant does not already produce viable seed, it must be induced to do so, and inbreeding must be used to produce a line with minimum variation in type. The most progress on a major crop to date has been made with the potato. Some varieties often produce viable seed, and selection and hybridization programs are going on at several centers to produce "true potato seed" that grows into consistent and useful plants.

BREEDING AND PLANT PROTECTION. The main protection of any crop from disease and pests is its own resistance, and that is as true now as ever. The history of plant breeding for disease and pest resistance is summarized by Painter (1951). Cook and Baker (1983) survey breeding for disease resistance, mainly in this century. An update of breeding for insect resistance is in Maxwell and Jennings (1980).

A strong stimulus to breeding for disease resistance is the rash of exotic plagues carried by the steamship, which is fast enough that pests and diseases survive on planting stock. The potato blight is one such disease, and resistant potato varieties are being selected by the late 1860s. As for grapevine breeding, the North American vine stocks imported as sources of resistance to powdery mildew and downy mildew are themselves the carriers of an even worse scourge, the phylloxera root louse, whose depredations stimulate both interspecific breeding and the grafting of traditional European varieties onto resistant (hybrid) rootstocks, eventually the more widely adopted preventative.

Two crucial steps are the development of adequate methods of evaluation and the elucidation of inheritance. Dominant and recessive genes for specific resistances are soon being identified, but some years elapse before the complexities posed by racial variation in pathogenic organisms can be confronted. Evaluation of resistance improves through careful experimental control of infection or infestation. Experimental control is more difficult to achieve with insect resistance than with disease resistance (Fitzgerald, 1966).

The prevailing conditions of industrial agriculture increase the risk of serious losses. Though some pests and diseases are mobile and attack most varieties of a crop, thus posing an equal threat to most anyone's fields, others that are less mobile and comparatively specialized do damage mainly where high planting density combines with low genetic diversity. A fungal blight, *Helminthosporium maydis,* which decimates United States maize fields, is a good example. Introduced from the Philippines, it seriously damages only plants carrying a particular gene, one for male sterility that allows growing hybrid seed without detasseling plants. Losses in 1970 amount to 15% of the crop (Perelman, 1977:47).

New problems continually arise, underlining the importance of retaining genetic diversity in collections. Many disease organisms quickly evolve new variants. External conditions change, making new threats of what had previously been given little thought. For example, the use of insecticides causes some herbivorous insects and mites to emerge as serious agricultural threats when their natural enemies are killed.

The solution is to identify resistant varieties, breed the trait or traits into desirable seed lines, and distribute the new planting material in time. Responses to new threats are not always in time, as the taro blight reminds us, but sometimes suitable stock is available within a year after a threat is detected, because resistant lines were already known and the crop produces seed in abundance. The new propagation techniques make possible the almost as rapid distribution of resistant varieties of asexually reproduced crops.

Breeders can combat new threats only if they have access to diverse breeding stock. Maize with resistance to *Helminthosporium* is widely available for planting the season after the worst losses are suffered. Resistances to various pests and diseases are now often combined in single varieties. Single tomato varieties are now available that are resistant to fusarium wilt, verticillium wilt, crown wilt, tobacco mosaic virus, and root-knot nematodes.

Mechanization

The most important of the machines that plow, cultivate, and cut first appear behind horses. They replace human labor with that of animals and later with that of tractors.

The steel plow should be counted, though it lacks essential moving parts, because it is a product of the same advance in technological competence and industrial productivity. All-iron plows are in use by the 1770s in England (Grigg, 1974:54), where they subsequently replace iron-shared wooden plows. In the United States, production of John

Deere's steel plow begins in 1839. Other early mechanical inventions, the cotton gin among them, add to the capacity to handle large quantities of food and fiber.

Mechanized harvesting is especially significant, because harvesting by hand absorbs as much as half the labor of the whole season where animals or tractors aid plowing. Stationary threshing machines are in use in England before 1800 and shortly thereafter in the United States. Cereals are cut by hand until successful reapers are developed, beginning with some Scots designs. Commercial production of reapers the United States gets under way based on C. McCormick's 1847 prototype. J. F. Appleby's grain binder, which ties sheaves, follows in 1879 (Kelly, 1967:52), combines and mechanical hay mowers come after that. Sugar beets are lifted mechanically in the United States by the 1920s (Kelly, 1967:50), potatoes in Europe a little earlier. The Rust brothers have a working cotton picker in 1927 (Kelly, 1967:57).

Some innovations in farm machinery are specifically tailored for use with tractors. These include the mechanical harvesters developed for fruits and soft vegetables, mainly since the 1960s.

Existing machinery is improved and adapted to tractor farming. Plows, harrows, seed drills, and other implements grow steadily wider, particularly in countries where large holdings prevail. Wider equipment does the job faster and with less labor but requires more tractor power.

Tractors are around for some time before they became affordable or practical for most farmers. The first steam plows appear in the United States and Great Britain in the 1850s and see limited use on large farms through the last half of the century. Most of them are pulled by cables from stationary engines, a method also used with electric engines in Germany (Fraser, 1973:9). Mobile but heavy steam tractors and threshers gradually make their appearance. Annual tractor production in the United States is nearly 6,000 by 1890 (Dieffenbach and Gray, 1960:28). Development of somewhat lighter engines partly overcomes earlier difficulties with cumbersome handling and soil compaction, and steam tractors vie with internal combustion engines until about 1920. The first gasoline tractor is built in 1892 (Grigg, 1974:53), and several commercial designs are on the market in Great Britain and the United States by 1910. The United States leads in tractor adoption (Fig. 10.1). Other land-rich, developed countries are not far behind. Even in the Soviet Union, where investment in agriculture receives a low priority before World War II, large collective farms and open expanses favor tractors, and agricultural planners allocate a large share of scarce funds to them. By 1940, 531,000 tractors are in use, a sixfold increase from 1932 (Symons, 1972:51).

Social Impact of
Pre–World War II Changes

Many prewar innovations save labor, yet reductions in the farm work force are slight in most countries. Most analyses point toward a modest but significant reduction in labor for the task performed, but growing demand offsets the savings. Harvesting with a reaper about doubles workers' productivity, which doubles again with the adoption of the binder (Rogin, 1931). In the United States, where tractors are fairly common by the 1930s, the total hours of farm labor fall slightly from a peak in the 1920s, for which the Depression is also a likely factor. Fertilizers are usually classed as land savers rather than labor savers, but Nghiep (1979) presents evidence that they supplant labor in prewar Japan, because purchased fertilizers replace composts prepared on the farm. Population in the developed countries grows fairly rapidly through most of this period until the Depression, absorbing most increases in productivity. Markets also expand because of higher per capita demand for meat, dairy, and other land-consuming products.

Trends in farm employment vary. The settler countries of North America and Australasia absorb labor by expanding the area in farms. In the United States, agricultural land per worker nearly doubles from 1880 to 1940 (Hayami and Ruttan, 1971:338), but so does farmland (USDA, 1966). The farm work force in both France and Germany increases somewhat from the mid-nineteenth century to World War I, but in the United Kingdom it declines 38% from 1861 to 1911 (Tracey, 1964). In all three European countries, change is negligible in the interwar years. Net change in Japan is slight despite a high density of farm workers; in the midst of concerted efforts to raise productivity, labor saved by one innovation is usually absorbed by intensification in other ways.

No consistent pattern of land concentration is evident. Apparently, technical innovations do not impel much concentration. The mean size of farms varies sixtyfold from Japan to the United States. It changes little in Japan and grows slowly in the United States until the 1930s (USDA, Statistical Reporting Service, 1966; Fig. 10.4). The strongest trend, mandated by collectivization, is in the Soviet Union. In other places, such as Prussia, land reform actually decreases concentration by breaking up large holdings.

References

Allard, R.B. (1960). *Principles of Plant Breeding*. Wiley, New York.

Anderson, R.T. (1975). *Denmark: Success of a Developing Nation*. Schenkman, Cambridge, Mass.

Audus, L.J. (1964). *The Physiology and Biochemistry of Herbicides*. Academic Press, London.

Buchanan, R.H. (1973). Field systems of Ireland. In *Studies of Field Systems in the British Isles* (A.R.H. Baker and R.A. Butlin, eds.), Cambridge University Press, Cambridge, pp. 580–618.

Carter, R.H. (1952). The inorganic insecticides. In *Insects: The Yearbook of Agriculture 1952,* U.S. Department of Agriculture, Washington, D.C., pp. 218–222.

Chambers, J.D., and G.E. Mingay (1966). *The Agricultural Revolution, 1750–1880*. Schocken, New York.

Cook, E. (1971). The flow of energy in an industrial society. *Scientific American,* 224(3):134–147.

Cook, R.J., and K.F. Baker (1983). *The Nature and Practice of Biological Control of Plant Pathogens*. American Phytopathological Society, St. Paul.

Coons, G.H. (1936). Improvement of the sugar beet. In *The Yearbook of Agriculture 1936,* U.S. Department of Agriculture, Washington, D.C., pp. 625–651.

Crosby, D.G. (1966). Natural pest control agents. In *Natural Pest Control Agents,* American Chemical Society, Washington, D.C, pp. 1–17.

Danhof, C.H. (1969). *Change in Agriculture: The Northern United States, 1820–1870*. Harvard University Press, Cambridge.

Darlington, C.D. (1973). *Chromosome Botany and the Origins of Cultivated Plants*. 3d ed. Allen and Unwin, London.

Dieffenbach, E.M., and R.B. Gray (1960). The development of the tractor. In *Power to Produce: The Yearbook of Agriculture 1960,* U.S. Department of Agriculture, Washington, D.C., pp. 25–45.

Dumont, R. (1957). *Types of Rural Economy,* trans. D. Magnin. Methuen, London.

Dunegan, J., and S.P. Doolittle (1953). How fungicides have been developed. In *Plant Disease: The Yearbook of Agriculture 1953,* U.S. Department of Agriculture, Washington, D.C., pp. 115–120.

Ermolov, A.S. (1893). Systems of agriculture and field rotation. In *The Industries of Russia,* pt. 3, Department of Trade and Industry, St. Petersburg, pp. 62–73.

Ernle, R.E.P. (1961). *English Farming Past and Present*. 6th ed. Heinemann, London.

Evans, E. (1968). *Plant Diseases and Their Chemical Control*. Basil Blackwell, Oxford, England.

Feinstein, L. (1952). Insecticides from plants. In *Insects: The Yearbook of Agriculture 1952,* U.S. Department of Agriculture, Washington, D.C., pp. 222–228.

Fitzgerald, P.J. (1966). Discussion on "The role of pest resistance in new varieties." In *Plant Breeding: A Symposium Held at Iowa State University* (K.J. Frey, ed.), Iowa State University Press, Ames, pp. 231–233.

Fogel, R.W., and S.L. Engerman (1974). *Time on the Cross: The Economics of American Negro Slavery.* Little, Brown, Boston.

Fraser, C. (1973). *Tractor Pioneer: The Life of Harry Ferguson.* Ohio State University Press, Columbus.

Fussell, G.E. (1972). *The Classical Tradition in West European Farming.* Fairleigh Dickinson Press, East Rutherford, N.J.

Grigg, D.B. (1974). *The Agricultural Systems of the World.* Cambridge University Press, London.

Habakkuk, H.J.C. (1968). Economic functions of English landowners in the seventeenth and eighteenth centuries. In *Essays in Agrarian History* (W.E. Minchinton, ed.), Augustus M. Kelley, New York, pp. 187–202.

Handley, J.E. (1953). *Scottish Farming in the Eighteenth Century.* Faber and Faber, London.

Hane, M. (1982). *Peasants, Rebels, and Outcasts: The Underside of Modern Japan.* Pantheon, New York.

Harlan, J.R. (1956). Distribution and utilization of natural variability in cultivated plants. *Brookhaven Symposia in Biology,* 9:191–208.

——. (1966). Plant introduction and biosystematics. In *Plant Breeding: A Symposium Held at Iowa State University* (K.J. Frey, ed.), Iowa State University Press, Ames, pp. 55–68.

Hayami, Y., and V.W. Ruttan (1971). *Agricultural Development: An International Perspective.* Johns Hopkins University Press, Baltimore.

Hayami, Y., and S. Yamada (1970). Agricultural productivity at the beginning of industrialization. In *Agriculture and Economic Growth: Japan's Experience* (K. Ohkawa, B.F. Johnston, and H. Kaneda, eds.), Princeton University Press, Princeton, N.J., pp. 105–135.

Hightower, J. (1973). *Hard Tomatoes, Hard Times.* Schenkman, Cambridge, Mass.

John, A.H. (1960). The course of agricultural change 1660–1760. In *Studies in the Industrial Revolution* (C.S. Presnell, ed.), Athlone, London, pp. 125–155.

Jolas, T., and F. Zonabend (1977). Tillers of the fields and woodspeople. In *Rural Society in France: Selections from the Annales: Economies, Societies, Civilizations* (R. Forster and O. Ranum, eds.; E. Forster and P.M. Ranum, trans.), Johns Hopkins University Press, Baltimore, pp. 126–151.

Jones, E.L. (1965). Agriculture and economic growth in England, 1660–1750: Agricultural change. *Journal of Economic History,* 25:1–18.

Kelly, C.F. (1967). Mechanical harvesting. *Scientific American,* 217(2):50–59.

Kerridge, E. (1967). *The Agricultural Revolution.* Augustus M. Kelley, New York.

Krelage, E.H. (1946). *Drie Eeuwen Bloembollenexport: De Geschiedenis van den Bloembollenhandel en der Hollandsche Bloembollen Tot 1938.* Rijksuitgeverij, Dienst van de Nederlandsche Staatscourant, The Hague.

Large, E.C. (1962). *The Advance of the Fungi*. Dover, New York.

Lefebvre, G. (1977). The place of the revolution in the agrarian history of France. In *Rural Society in France: Selections from the Annales: Economies, Societes, Civilisations* (R. Forster and O. Ranum, eds.; E. Forster and P.M. Ranum, trans.), Johns Hopkins University Press, Baltimore, pp. 31–49.

Macfarlane, A. (1978). *The Origins of English Individualism*. Basil Blackwell, Oxford, England.

Mangelsdorf, P.C. (1974). *Corn: Its Origin, Evolution, and Improvement*. Harvard University Press, Cambridge.

Maxwell, F.G., and P.R. Jennings, eds. (1980). *Breeding Plants Resistant to Insects*. Wiley, New York.

National Research Council, Committee on Germplasm Resources (1978). *Conservation of Germplasm Resources*. National Academy of Sciences, Washington, D.C.

Nghiep, L.T. (1979). The structure of changes of technology in prewar Japanese agriculture. *American Journal of Agricultural Economics*, 61:687–693.

Painter, R.H. (1951). *Insect Resistance in Crop Plants*. Macmillan, New York.

Pavlosky, G.P. (1968). *Agricultural Russia on the Eve of the Revolution*. Howard Fertig, New York.

Perelman, M. (1977). *Farming for Profit: Capital and the Crisis in Agriculture*. Universe, New York.

Pool, R.M., J. Einset, K.H. Kimball, J.P. Watson, W.B. Robinson, and J.J. Bertino (1976). *1958–1973 Vineyard and Cellar Notes*. New York State Agricultural Experiment Station, Special Report no. 22. Geneva, N.Y.

Popescu, Gh., M. Baditescu, and T. Popescu (1974). Mutantă naturale Babească Gri, soi de perspectivă pentru podgoria Odobeşti. *Analele Institutului de Cercetari Pentru Viticultura si Vinificatie*, 5:69–80.

Prevost, B. ([1807] 1935). *Memoir on the immediate cause of burst or smut on wheat, and of several other diseases of plants, and the prevention of burst*. Reprint. Phytopathological Classics, no. 6. American Phytological Society, St. Paul.

Rasmussen, W.D. (1960). *Readings in the History of American Agriculture*. University of Illinois Press, Urbana.

Roark, R.C. (1952). How insecticides are developed. In *Insects: The Yearbook of Agriculture 1952*, U.S. Department of Agriculture, Washington, D.C., pp. 200–202.

Rogin, L. (1931). *The Introduction of Farm Machinery*. University of California Press, Berkeley.

Rossiter, M.W. (1975). *The Emergence of Agricultural Science: Justus Liebig and the Americans: 1840–1880*. Yale University Press, New Haven, Conn.

Sanders, H.C. (1966). A brief history. In *The Cooperative Extension Service* (H.C. Sanders, ed.), Prentice-Hall, Englewood Cliffs, N.J., pp. 13–25.

Schwieder, E., and D. Schwieder (1975). *A Peculiar People: Iowa's Old Order Amish*. Iowa State University Press, Ames.

Simmonds, N.W. (1966). *Bananas.* Longmans, London.

Slicher van Bath, B.H. (1963). *The Agrarian History of Western Europe, A.D. 500–1850,* trans. O. Ordish. Arnold, London.

Smith, D.C. (1966). Plant breeding—development and success. In *Plant Breeding: A Symposium Held at Iowa State University* (K.J. Frey, ed.), Iowa State University Press, Ames, pp. 3–54.

Soboul, A. (1977). Persistence of "feudalism" in the rural society of nineteenth-century France. In *Rural Society in France: Selections from the Annales: Economies, Societies, Civilizations* (R. Forster and O. Ranum, eds.; E. Forster and P.M. Ranum, trans.), Johns Hopkins University Press, Baltimore, pp. 50–71.

Symons, L. (1972). *Russian Agriculture: A Geographic Survey.* Wiley, New York.

Teigen, L.D. (1982). Productivity and the cost of food. In *Food—From Farm to Table: The Yearbook of Agriculture 1982,* U.S. Department of Agriculture, Washington, D.C., pp. 52–58.

Thompson, L.M., and F.R. Troeh (1973). *Soils and Soil Fertility.* McGraw-Hill, New York.

Tracey, M. (1964). *Agriculture in Western Europe.* Praeger, New York.

USDA, Statistical Reporting Service (1966). *A Century of Agriculture in Charts and Tables.* U.S. Department of Agriculture, Washington, D.C.

Vavilov, N.I. (1949–50). *The origin, variation, immunity, and breeding of cultivated plants,* trans. K. Starr Chester. Chronica Botanica, vol. 13. Waltham, Mass.

Vilmorin, J.L. (1923). *L'Heredité chez la Betterave Cultivée.* Gauthier-Villars, Paris.

Weber, E. (1976). *Peasants into Frenchmen: The Modernization of Rural France.* Stanford University Press, Stanford, Calif.

10

Industrial Agriculture to the Present

 World War II is a watershed, and events thereafter deserve to have their own chapter. The pace of agricultural change in the developed countries picks up dramatically: New types of equipment and agricultural chemicals are introduced, tractors and chemical fertilizers are used far more, and land concentration and farm labor reduction occur at a much faster pace. This account will give special attention to the United States, the largest producer among a group of countries—including Australia, Canada, New Zealand, Argentina, and lately Brazil—whose postwar farming develops with few constraints on large-scale methods. These countries are also major exporters and along with the European Community are caught up in a spiral of subsidies, commodity gluts, and fierce competition for world markets. The United States farm crisis of the mid-1980s, though exacerbated by circumstances peculiar to that country, is part of a painful process of readjustment of world agriculture brought on by the success of postwar technical change.

The last part of the chapter takes up critiques of some major technical trends in industrial agriculture. One is the advocacy of "alternative agriculture," which more or less rejects chemical fertilizers and pesticides. Another approach more in the scientific mainstream is research on the substitution of biological controls for pesticides.

Major Trends

The use of industrial inputs in agriculture grows everywhere during this period. The trend continues in countries in which their use grew rapidly before the war, while other countries close the gap where they had lagged. The use of chemical fertilizer surges in the United States and the Soviet Union, where prewar growth was slower than in western Europe or Japan. Conversely, tractors are for the first time typical fixtures of European farms, as are power tillers on Japanese farms.

Before World War II, agricultural science made major progress on the things whose subsequent effect is the greatest. Among the main classes of industrial inputs, only in pesticides and herbicides is there a quantum postwar leap in the range of available products or in their effectiveness. Fertilizers are not new, save for some micronutrients, and mechanization continues along prewar lines. Plant and animal breeding is stepped up—the number of new crop varieties grows every year, and livestock breeding enters a world of frozen-sperm banks and genetic data bases—but the fundamental techniques of selection and hybridization are old, with genetic engineering still on the horizon.

What really sets off postwar agricultural science is its vigor. Experiment stations proliferate worldwide and are in effective communication with one another. Farmers more quickly adopt new methods, because of expanded extension services and a large increase in research directed toward specific local needs. Thus fertilizer recommendations become highly specific, taking into account crop choice, soil, fertilizer costs, and commodity prices. Plant breeding is directed toward local conditions, so that individual crop varieties tend to be adopted over smaller areas than before but sometimes to the virtual exclusion of other varieties.

Technical Change

MECHANIZATION.　In the United States, already a prewar leader in mechanization, the total number of farm machines goes from 300,000 in 1940 to 3 million in 1960 (Kelly, 1967). The variety of implements grows. Especially significant is mechanized harvesting of crops previously picked or dug by hand. As late as 1950, only 8% of United States cotton was mechanically picked, but 52% is mechanically picked in 1962 and 89% by 1966 (Marshall and Godwin, 1971:8). Mechanization of sugar beet harvesting—cutting the tops and loading the roots—takes place between 1944 and 1957 (Kelly, 1967:55). Tomato harvesters are adopted during the 1960s after breeders provide custom-made varieties whose fruit ripens all at the same time. Lettuce, grape, and tree fruit harvesting are partly mechanized in the 1970s and early 1980s.

Tractor numbers increase a little less dramatically (Fig. 10.1). Ex-

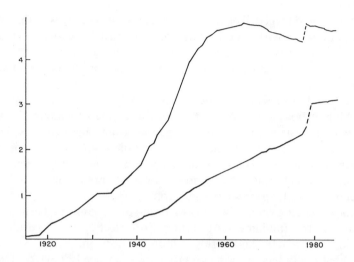

10.1. Tractors on U.S. farms, 1915–85. *Upper line,* millions of tractors; *lower line,* rated tractor horsepower in hundred millions. A change of data-gathering methods in 1978 slightly inflates data from that year on relative to earlier years. (*Agricultural Statistics,* 1985; USDA, Economic Research Service, 1976)

cept for a hiatus during the Depression, the growth curve is fairly steadily upward from 1918 until the early 1950s, when it begins to level off. When the sharp postwar decline in the number of farms is taken into account, it is apparent that the number of tractors per farm leaps upward for a time after 1940. The average exceeds 1 tractor per farm by 1955 and is close to 1.5 by 1965. The averages reflect multiple tractors on large farms, presumably some maintenance of old units to back up new ones, and the virtual end of horse-powered operations. Tractors, once used primarily for tillage, are increasingly used in spraying and dusting, to pull harvest machinery, and in other operations that extend their use over the entire season.

The increase in total rated tractor horsepower continues even after the climb in tractor numbers levels off. More-powerful tractors are needed to pull larger equipment, particularly wider equipment that can work more rows.

In Europe, where before the war tractors were common only in the Soviet Union and a few parts of Great Britain and the northern Continent, tractor numbers grow explosively. The implements used in western Europe were never very different from those in the United States, but the use of horses limited their application. North American tractor manufacturers open factories in Great Britain shortly after the war, and the main spurt is earlier than on the Continent, where much of the manufacturing capacity is set up during the 1950s. There are 422,000 farm tractors in the United Kingdom in 1955 and only few more, bringing the total to 470,000, by 1968. Over the same period, farm tractors in the Six—the original countries of the European Economic Community (EEC, now the EC, or European Community)—increase from 1,067,000 to 3,242,000, and in the former European Free Trade Association from 732,000 to 1,304,000 (Johnson, 1973:74).[1]

Renewed growth in the number of Soviet tractors follows recovery from the war. The rate of their production, half that of the United States in 1955, is doubled by 1975. Still, only about half as many tractors are in operation as in the United States, partly because of a high retirement rate in the Soviet Union (Clark, 1977:32), for which heavy use on vast collective farms, engineering deficiencies, and poor management are to blame. Despite tractor numbers, the breadth of mechanization lags in the Soviet Union, and agriculture in general remains more labor-intensive than in the United States. Harvesting machinery is less diverse, particularly for fruits and vegetables. Milking machines are a recent innovation on many farms. The direction of change is today toward more diversified machinery, however.

Power implements come late to Japan, mainly in the form of the power tiller or "walk behind" tractor. A handful of power tillers are on Japanese farms before 1950, 89,000 in 1955, 517,000 in 1960, and 2,500,000 in 1965 (Tsuchiya, 1970:155). Their horsepower is today typically less than 10, whereas that of the average United States farm tractor is about 60. Most are used in rice paddies and not on hillside fields. Tillers do not pull planting or harvesting equipment. Riding tractors are found on a few large farms, particularly on the northern island of Hokkaido.

FERTILIZER USE. Prewar United States fertilizer use was conservative. Pasture was rarely fertilized, and hayfields were fertilized at low rates or not at all. The rule on cropland, judging from published recommendations and national rates, was to maintain native fertility or at most to raise nutrient levels to those inherent in first-rate soil. Application rates were greatest on poor and depleted soils of the Northeast, but other depleted soils received little or no fertilizer, and mining of nutrients was common, at its worst in southern tobacco lands.

The adoption of hybrid maize, which responds to exceptional nutrient levels, is often credited with most of the postwar boom in fertilizer use, but that increase is actually general. Hybrids occupy 2.5% of all maize acreage in 1935, 30.7% in 1940, 63.5% in 1945, and 95.5% in 1960 (Hayami and Ruttan, 1971:339). Hybrid wheat varieties, common after 1950, account for another sizable part of increased fertilizer use. At first the effect is greatest on irrigated or well-watered lands, but moderate fertilization eventually becomes common even on lands with moisture limitations. The area under fodder crops, including silage maize, expands to supply feedlots. These crops respond well to high nutrient levels, as do many vegetables, and all tend to receive higher doses than before. Land prices after 1940 climb out of their Depression slump, raising equity capital for farm investment. The real cost of nitrogen fertilizer in the United States falls by about 30% from 1936 to 1960 (Sahota, 1968), making it economic on many farms to replace fodder legume rotations with more maize, applying fertilizer nitrogen to make up the loss of biologically fixed nitrogen.

United States fertilizer use rises throughout the twentieth century, except during the Depression, but much more rapidly after 1940. Figures 10.2 and 10.3 chart farm consumption of nitrogen, phosphorus, and potassium. The growth curves are steeper after about 1940 and steepest during the 1960s. Lime use follows a different curve: a steady upward trend until just after World War II, then little change (USDA, Economic

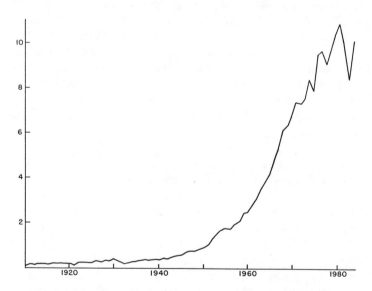

10.2. Nitrogen applied to U.S. farmland, 1910–84, in million metric tons. (*Agricultural Statistics*, 1985; USDA, Economic Research Service, 1976)

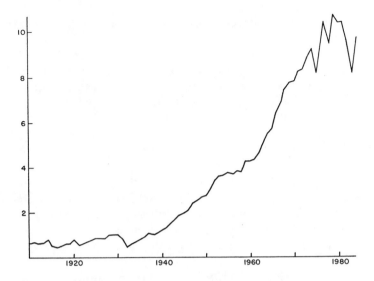

10.3. Phosphorus and potassium applied to U.S. farmland, 1910–85, in million metric tons of P$_2$O$_5$ and K$_2$O, combined. (*Agricultural Statistics*, 1985; USDA, Economic Research Service, 1976)

Research Service, 1976). Apparently most of the needed adjustments of soil acidity were made by that time, and previously treated soils need only small applications.

Fertilization rates in the United States after the war move upward to near those of the leaders, despite a continuing climb in the European and Japanese rates. Not coincidentally, land prices also rise in the United States, though they do not approach so closely those of Japan and Western Europe.

Use of chemical fertilizers was long retarded in the Soviet Union, partly because large areas of cultivable land were still underutilized, but also because industrial capacity was diverted to other priorities. Rapid development of munitions was regarded as a necessity during the 1930s, a judgment borne out by the Nazi invasion. Stalin was convinced that grass ley rotations could meet immediate fertility needs and diverted capital to tractor manufacture and to industry in general. Tractor factories offered the advantage of being readily convertible to military production.

During the early Khrushchev years, increases in agricultural production are mainly attempted by plowing virgin lands, practicing grass and clover rotations, and implementing an ambitious program to increase maize planting. Fertilizer production doubles during the 1950s, but from a low initial level.

By the early 1960s the effect of mining soil nutrients is evident, and the Soviets make a major effort in chemical fertilizers, trebling production from 1962 to 1969 (Symons, 1972:279). Subsequent performance is also impressive, and some published recommended application rates are near those of the West for the same crops under similar conditions, but the prevalence of severe environmental limitations on cultivated land should for the foreseeable future keep average application rates from catching up.

Postwar use of chemical fertilizers other than lime rises in all developed countries, nitrogen the most so. Cereal breeding programs produce varieties particularly responsive to high nitrogen levels. Nitrogen fertilizers increasingly replace legume rotations or cover crops. Their real world market price improves more than that of other fertilizers.

ENERGETICS. Energy inputs into food production mushroom, because of the use of tractors, chemical fertilizers, petrochemical pesticides, power pumping for irrigation and drainage, artificial crop drying, and more. The net effect of herbicide use is unclear and probably variable; energy enters into the production, distribution, and application of herbicides but may be more than compensated if their use substitutes for tractor tillage.

Estimates show the growth of energy inputs into United States maize production (Pimentel et al., 1973). Inputs per hectare are 2,286,000 kcal in 1945 and 7,155,100 kcal in 1970. Energy expended to construct, maintain, and fuel machinery increases 68%. Application of N-P-K fertilizer, expressed as energy, grows 1300% to become the largest single energy input, accounting for 36.5% of the 1970 total for maize production; nitrogen alone accounts for 32.5%. Maize is the leading crop in the United States, and the figures are probably roughly representative of energy use in crop production as a whole; take away a little for soybean, a major crop that typically receives little or no nitrogen fertilizer, and add some for expanded irrigation and increased finishing of cattle with grain and silage.

Energy use grows more slowly after 1970. Inputs into agriculture rise at an annual rate of 4.5% from 1945 to 1970, and 1.4% from 1974 to 1978 (Torgerson and Cooper, 1980).

Food distribution, processing, and preparation together use more energy than does production. Pimentel and Pimentel (1979) estimate that of all energy used in the United States, 6% is spent in food production, and another 11% in getting the food onto the table. Agricultural fiber production and processing also account for a share.

LIVESTOCK FEEDING. The most distinctive new agricultural operation is the factory-style livestock feeding operation. Broilers, laying hens, turkeys, pigs, and beef and dairy cattle are widely reared and maintained in confined quarters. Beef cattle fatten in feedlots, beginning with steers raised on pasture. None of these enterprises are entirely new to the postwar era, but only in recent decades do they take a major share of the animal products market.

Operations of this sort develop first in the United States and remain particularly dominant there. Concentration in large enterprises is greatest in poultry and eggs. During 1954, 69% of broilers come from farms selling less than 16,000, and virtually none from operations selling 100,000 or more. By 1974 the respective figures are 29% and 30% (Reimund and Moore, 1981:3). Small scale production of dairy, beef, pigs, and sheep survives better, some operators using the new confinement methods, but there is still a concentration at the top end. By 1969 seven percent of the producers of cattle-calves and of sheep-lambs make half the sales (USDA, Economics, Statistics, and Cooperatives Service, 1978).

Factory-style feeding saves labor and improves the conversion efficiency of feed into useful product. Tasks are rationalized, most clearly in egg production, where hens lay in cubicles from which eggs roll onto conveyors. Labor savings are bought with capital investment, and conversion efficiencies are improved by reducing the animals' movement and by close monitoring of feeding and either weight gain or production. Ingenious techniques of egg production include lighting schemes that speed up day and night cycles.

The new operations are in most ways more energy-intensive than farmyard production. More efficient utilization of feed affords some energy savings, but equipment and housing must often be built and feeds must often be transported from a distance. Manure too is returned some distance back to the fields, or an equivalent amount of chemical fertilizers must be substituted, in which case disposal of the manure is a problem whose solution consumes energy. Finally the confining of beef and dairy cattle encourages some shift from pasture to fodder production, which then receives more passes of the tractor and, in the United States, more fertilizer.

Adoption of similar confining methods in other countries varies with the scale of existing farms and with government policies. Mostly

252

eggs and broilers are produced this way in Europe. Some pigs are confined, but small herds are the rule. Feeding of concentrated feedstuffs to dairy and beef cattle remains mostly a supplement to grazing, though the practice is steadily growing. Broiler production leads a trend after 1950 toward large operations in the United Kingdom, and egg production follows suit in the late 1950s. In spite of parallel developments in France, as late as the mid-1960s half the eggs marketed are from "hens of uncertain age and breeding" that scratch in farmyards for much of their food (Butterwick and Rolfe, 1968:162).

The Soviet Union's large farms appear well suited to vertical integration and to feeding operations of this sort, and that is the trend, particularly on the state farms (sovkhozy), but mechanized operations lag. The large role of personal plots in livestock operations complicates the picture. They are normally less than 0.30 ha, and their owners must use labor-intensive methods to gain any appreciable income, but incentives to keep livestock are excellent. Owners buy feed grains at close to world market prices and sell animal products at high, controlled prices. In 1967 the ratio of animal product prices to feed grain price reaches three times the ratios prevailing in the Western market economies (Wadekin, 1973:217).

Social Transformation

Social changes in all developed countries are parallel to a point, beyond which contrasts reflect government policies and differences in the preexisting structure of rural society. Land concentration and the replacement of labor by mechanization are both variable trends, though mechanization is universal and land concentration nearly so. The base farm size from which concentration begins varies radically and affects opportunities for mechanization. Government policies and the ways that farmers organize provide more or less protection from land concentration.

LAND CONCENTRATION AND THE FARM WORK FORCE. Both the pace of land concentration and farm size at its start vary greatly among the developed countries, but the trend is manifest in all except Japan. Large farms, it is suggested, tend to better utilize new machinery and other technology to the full (technical economies of scale), buy at quantity discounts, manage more competitively in a changing economic environment, and better meet operators' aspirations to higher incomes at a time when the rate of return on farm investment is declining.

The number of United States farms peaked at nearly 7 million in the mid-1930s. There are 5.6 million in 1950, 4.0 million in 1960, 2.9 million in 1970, and 2.7 million in 1978 (Schertz, 1980:13). The trend slows in the 1970s and reverses in the early 1980s. Even after an increase in foreclosures during the ensuing farm crisis, the reduction in farm numbers is less in the 1980s than in any decade since the 1940s (Westphal, 1988). Before 1940 the size of farms crept upward though their numbers rose, because new land was going into production. Faster growth begins during the war and continues through the 1950s and 1960s (Fig. 10.4).

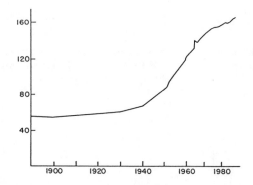

10.4. Mean size of U.S. farms, 1890–1985, in hectares. (*Agricultural Statistics*, **1982; USDA, Economic Research Service, 1976**)

The farm work force peaks earlier than the number of farms and falls more rapidly, as shown by the trend in labor inputs on farms (Fig. 10.5). Sharp fluctuations during the 1930s mirrored the economy. Then a steep and comparatively steady decline begins about 1942. Machines only slowly displaced workers until the 1930s, an effect compensated by other trends, including the expansion of cultivation. Hired laborers' share of the work declined from the late nineteenth century on, possibly reflecting a loss of seasonal employment to mechanization. The dramatic change after 1940 is obviously attributable to labor-saving technical innovations and mechanization in the main, but also to herbicides and the development of factory-style livestock operations.

Workers' productivity leaps upward after 1940 (Fig. 10.6), but so

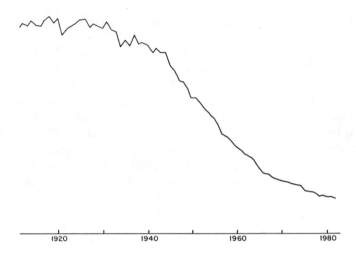

1920 1940 1960 1980

10.5. Labor inputs into U.S. farms, 1910–82, in billion hours. (*Agricultural Statistics,* 1982; USDA, Economic Research Service, 1976)

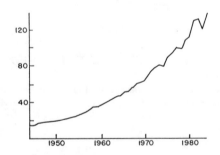

120

80

40

1950 1960 1970 1980

10.6. Indexed productivity of U.S. farm labor, 1944–84 (1977 = 100). (*Agricultural Statistics,* 1960, 1966, 1982, 1985)

does production per hectare (Fig. 10.7), if not quite so sharply. Higher yields are obviously associated with greater use of chemical fertilizers (Figs. 10.2, 10.3, and 10.7). The use of chemical fertilizers can demand more labor per hectare, particularly if little was done previously to maintain soil nutrient levels, but a net reduction in labor is to be expected where chemical nitrogen fertilizers replace legume cover crops.

These trends in the United States farm work force are paralleled in the other land-rich countries – Canada, New Zealand, Australia, and

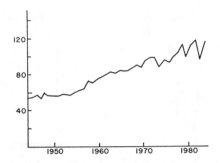

10.7. Indexed U.S. crop production/unit of area under crops, 1944–84 (1977 = 100). The criteria were changed in 1977 to exclude farms with sales of less than $1,000 per year. To make the graph consistent, figures from 1977 on have been multiplied by a correction factor of 0.924. (*Agricultural Statistics*, 1982, 1985; USDA, Economic Research Service, 1976)

Argentina—except that most farms were already quite large in Argentina and in most of Australia.

Japanese agriculture remains labor-intensive even in the face of heavy use of agricultural chemicals and a modest degree of mechanization. The number of workers per hectare of cultivated land is 3.09 in 1880, 2.40 in 1945, 2.73 in 1950 (after land reform), and 2.21 in 1960 (calculated from Hayami and Ruttan, 1971:340). The ratios in the United States are 0.12 in 1880, 0.05 in 1930, and 0.02 in 1960 (Hayami and Ruttan, 1971:338). Thus Japanese workers were initially more numerous upon the land, and their numbers subsequently fall more slowly. The fastest decline in Japan, during the 1950s, coincides with widespread adoption of power tillers (Tsuchiya, 1970). Annual net out-migration from the farm work force reaches 4% at times during the 1960s, in response to opportunities in industry and the cities (Yamada and Hayami, 1979:56).

Individual farms average between 1 and 1.5 ha from the Meiji restoration (1868) to the present. The lowest mean size is 1.04 ha in 1950 (Kawano, 1969). Subsequent growth is slow despite the rapid outflow of workers. Because the farms are almost wholly family farms, and the role of hired labor is slight, we may conclude that most families reduce their members' net participation. A high proportion of Japanese farms are within commuting distance of urban workplaces, which employ growing numbers of farm residents.

Western European farms fall between Japanese and United States farms in both average size and labor intensity. Mean farm size in the Six is 13 hectares in 1970 (Herlitska, Malve, and Winegarten, 1974:76), about 10 times the Japanese mean. Farms at that time in the eastern United States, where there is no dry land to drive up farm size, average 64 ha (*Agricultural Statistics,* 1971), nearly 5 times as great as the mean for the Six. Continental farms are predominantly family operations, and the number of workers per hectare not surprisingly lies between United States and Japanese levels.

Land concentration was slight on the European continent before 1950. The number of farms in the EC countries (the original six, plus Greece, Spain, and Britain) falls 21.3% during the 1960s, almost as fast as in the United States (25.4%), but falls only 0.9% in the 1970s, when the United States decline is 17.8% (Friend and Trostle, 1985:85).

Consolidation of holdings is a goal of EC policy, one not yet entirely realized. As late as 1950 most holdings are fragmented into small parcels, because of the long-standing custom of dividing inheritance among male children. French holdings in 1882 averaged 22 parcels apiece (Tracey, 1964:611). Fragmentation slowed mechanization. Tractors could not work parcels that were too small or whose access lay along narrow paths and field borders.

The rate of subsequent out-migration from Continental farms is comparable to that of Japan and peaks at about the same time. The farm work force in the Six falls 3% to 4% each year from 1958 to 1970 (Herlitska, Malve, and Winegarten, 1974:67).

Farms in the United Kingdom throughout the modern era were considerably larger than those of the Continent. Their mean size was 57 ha in 1870 (Tracey, 1964), slightly larger than the United States average at that time. However, an exceptionally high proportion of hired workers distinguishes the work force and gives British farming a labor intensity closer to the Continent's than to that of the United States.

Soviet farms had been collectivized and consolidated in the late 1920s and early 1930s, becoming large by any standard, to meet both managerial and ideological objectives. In 1940, collectives proper (kolkhozy) averaged 1,600 ha, of which a third was cropland. By 1968 the mean size of kolkhozy is up to 10,730 ha (Symons, 1972:51). State farms (sovkhozy) are larger still, averaging 40,310 ha (Clark, 1977:9). These operations are far beyond the sizes considered necessary in a market economy to take advantage of economies of scale, even if the marginal character of much of the land is taken into consideration.

IS LAND CONCENTRATION INEVITABLE?

The viability of small farms in an industrial society is controversial. Some see the small farm as an anachronism or a hobby for the self-indulgent wage earner. Such farms, it is said, can meet a substantial part of a modern nation's food and fiber needs only if supported by burdensome subsidies. Other voices tell us that small farms can survive and contribute more than their share of commodities, and only modest support is needed from government and private institutions. Indeed it is argued that United States farm subsidy and taxation policies, far from buoying up small farms, actually speed their demise.

The absence of any consistent and meaningful definition of *small* and *large* hinders analysis. The physical environment and the type of operation make a great difference. A well-watered 10-hectare orchard or vineyard may have the same gross sales as a 20,000-hectare beef ranch in an arid region. Gross or net sales can be the distinguishing criterion, a method that partly controls for differences in productivity, but a farm may then be made "larger" by installing irrigation, applying more fertilizer, or adopting more labor-intensive management. Making a farm larger in economic scale without expanding its physical boundaries usually entails an increase in capital investment, itself a sometimes encountered criterion of scale. All these criteria are applied arbitrarily. National standards vary with mean values; a 10-hectare rice farm is small in the United States but large in Japan.

Most problems of definition are circumvented if the rate of land concentration is the basis for comparison, not the scale of farms per se. Using that rate also provides a useful measure of the success or failure of efforts to counter land concentration.

In every developed country, strong sentiments and organized movements may be found in favor of stopping or slowing land concentration. That preservation of the status quo in Australia would keep farms vastly larger than what an advocate of consolidation could conceive in Japan does not fault the parallel. A holding action is more often advocated than a freeze on farm size. Few propose reversing the trend; the back-to-the-landers of the 1960s made small homesteads in the United States, Australia, and elsewhere, but only the odd zealot believed the movement would reform the landscape.

Land concentration is today opposed for its perceived threat to rural culture. Agrarianist ideals persist of maintaining an independent yeomanry. Accordingly, the structure of farming, especially corporate involvement, is an attendant issue. Losses of farm population erode the economic base of rural communities. Land concentration can in theory proceed without reducing the farm work force, but as farms grow larger, they usually employ fewer workers per hectare, and rural towns lose business and finally people.

The issue of land concentration is so bound up with nationalism that its worldwide manifestation is often overlooked. We have outgrown the penchant among pre–World War II militarists to view farm and rural populations as the ideal stuff from which to build armies, but the idea survives that those populations carry and transmit a vital part of the national identity. Jeffersonian ideals and the image of the rugged individual color United States thinking. Icelandic informants repeatedly informed me that a thousand years of history rests in the farms, but barely a hundred in the cities. The same sense of history contributes to Japanese agrarianism (Havens, 1974).

Economies of scale may help a farmer toward the goal of increasing income, but growth alone can also do so without there being any gains in efficiency. We cannot therefore assume that land consolidation is in each case a response to a need for economies of scale. Rising wages in a growing economy and the lure of higher urban incomes provide incentives for farm expansion—keeping up with the urban Joneses, in short.

Land concentration in the United States is only partly attributable to economies of scale. Several studies find that the largest farms are well beyond any optimum. One review (Miller, Rodevall, and McElroy, 1981) concludes that farms with gross annual sales of $41,000 to $76,000 achieve the significant technical economies of scale. In 1978, 7.0% of United States farms have gross sales of $100,000 or more, and 2.4% have sales of $200,000 or more. The latter group accounts for 39% of the total gross sales for all farms (Schertz, 1980:18–19). Madden (1967) earlier concludes that one- or two-person operations achieve the major economies of scale in crop production. These studies do not deal with possible marketing advantages of large operations, but gains should not be assumed.

Doubling a farm's size does not necessarily double net income. In fact a lesser gain is usual. Additional labor may have to be drawn from the family work force or else hired, or capital may have to be invested in machinery to replace labor. The first strategy is likely if the operation has already achieved technical economies of scale; the second, if it has not.

Capital earnings, principally from rising land values, are another incentive to expand. United States farms between 1970 and 1978 return an average of 4.69% per year on investment. Any number of easier and safer investments would pay more. But capital earnings are 11.5% per year, giving a very healthy total return of 16.14% (Schertz, 1980:39). The period is one of exceptional inflation of land values, but capital earnings also exceed profits from 1960 to 1969 and during many other earlier decades. Farmers can control their investment and enhance their borrowing power if they invest available capital on the farm. Declining land values, brought on by declining profits and often by speculation in the 1970s, aggravate the farm crisis of the mid-1980s. Farmers lose both equity and a major source of deferred income.

Government policy in the United States fosters concentration. Most farm supports are based on either the area under a particular crop or the volume of sales, a practice that favors large farms or, as Heady (1975:5) notes, "large landholders, whose central occupation was not farming" (also see Boehlje and Griffin, 1979). Many use the subsidized income to finance expansion (Nelson and Cochrane, 1976). The use of farms as tax shelters is another peculiarity of the United States. Some legislation of the mid-1970s and the 1987 tax reform law aim to discourage this so-called tax farming, but the ingenuity of the tax avoiders must not be underestimated.

Internationally, very large holdings are most often encountered in the former settler colonies, including both more and less developed countries. Well-known examples include the latifundios of Latin America and the vast grazing operations of Australia. Crop and mixed farms in Canada, New Zealand, and Australia share a history of family ownership and recent concentration, though Australian farms have long tended to be larger than the others. Corporate farms are nearly absent from all three countries.

In the older developed, capitalist countries the prevalence of smaller operations makes the achievement of economies of scale a believably ubiquitous motive for land concentration. Volumes of sales reach North American proportions mainly in specialized operations, such as broiler houses.

Small farms are by no means an endangered species. Land concentration is slow in Western Europe and almost negligible in Japan. Even within the United States, small farms show no sign of dying out altogether. One projection (Lin, Coffman, and Penn, 1980) is of an increasingly bimodal distribution of farm size, because the attrition of small farms is much less than that of medium-sized ones, a prediction borne out during the farm crisis. Not all large farms escape foreclosure; Campbell (1985) observes that the farmers most likely to be in trouble in the 1980s are those who borrowed heavily in the 1970s in order to expand. The more conservatively managed farms, medium or large, are surviving better, though their disposable income may now be below the standards of the wage economy.

Some small farms survive by finding a highly specialized market that larger farmers cannot exploit or have not yet found. Luxury commodity production often fits into this category. The growth of the economy often provides expanding opportunities for specialty crops, unusual livestock, or innovative nursery operations. Some small greenhouses and fish farms cut costs by utilizing hot water effluent from local power plants. A drawback of this kind of niche seeking is that profitable lines tend to expand and attract big capital. A prime example is that of mushroom culture in the United States, which began as a virtual cottage industry and an adjunct to manure recycling but is now an industry dominated by large firms.

The market for major farm commodities is nearly stagnant in the developed countries, affording only limited opportunities for the creative entrepreneur and seeker of profitable specialties. For most farmers, smallholder survival is sought in three ways: cooperation, off-farm employment, and subsidization.

Cooperation. Cooperation can offer economies of scale to smallholders, but not equally in all economies and in all circumstances. In the developed countries as a whole, excluding those that have collectivized agriculture, cooperation is most successful in the borrowing and banking of capital through credit unions and cooperative banks. Group purchases of inputs and sales of products are also widely successful. Some cooperatives own and operate fertilizer plants, rural electrification networks, packing plants, slaughterhouses, dairies, and the like, thereby gaining the advantage of volume transactions. Stationary equipment such as irrigation pumps is sometimes cooperatively owned, but cooperation in the use of mobile farm machinery is exceptional.

Cooperatives are not a specific antidote for land concentration. They do not play that part in the United States, despite some past expectations, but they do in some other countries, notably Denmark, Yugoslavia, and Israel, which apply cooperation in very different ways. For all their past success, all three now show the effects of renewed pressures for concentration.

Denmark furnishes the outstanding case whereby cooperation shores up small farms with little help from government. The number of farms was nearly constant from the late nineteenth century, when Danish land was reformed and agriculture reorganized around cooperatives, until World War II. Most holdings were in the 10–60 hectare range, with the mean 15 or 16 ha (Larsen, 1970), fairly small sizes for what were predominantly dairy and pig farms in an advanced economy, yet income from farming kept pace with nonfarm income at least as well as in the other developed countries. Unlike most of its neighbors, Denmark provided virtually no subsidies or protection from foreign competition. Most of the produce was sold in Great Britain at world market prices. Productivity rose steadily, and use was made of the full range of industrial inputs, except that tractors were common only on large farms.

Denmark does not entirely escape postwar concentration trends, but the impact thus far is less than in most developed countries. Farm numbers fall from about 200,000 in 1939 to 153,000 in 1968, when the mean size reaches 19 ha. The farm work force declines by nearly a third over the same period, losing mostly hired workers; family members supply 50% of farm labor before 1940 and 80% by 1968 (Larsen, 1970). Postwar changes accompany a general adoption of tractors, milking machines, and other dairy equipment.

Danish cooperatives improve the profit margins from small and medium-sized farms (Jensen, 1937; Larsen, 1970). Their first major impact was in operating creameries, which established a reputation for high quality. Cooperatives of all sorts now dominate the economic networks in which Danish farmers participate. They are active in extension. Marketing networks display a high degree of vertical integration, and dairy products and bacon are sold abroad under established brand names.

Yugoslavia is a socialist nation whose stated postwar goal is steady expansion of collective farming, yet cooperatives working under state planning and direction support small private farms. Though not as industrialized as most economies discussed in this section, Yugoslavia nonetheless experiences strong postwar growth, out-migration of the rural work force, and mechanization. Private farms average 3.2 ha (World Bank, 1983) and by law cannot exceed 10 ha for most types of operations, a limitation now under review. Cooperative and collective features mingle under state auspices (Hamilton, 1968; World Bank, 1975), though most development funds are allocated to state farms (World Bank, 1983). Some noteworthy features include cooperation between state farms and private farms, persistence of fragmented private holdings, and the importance of machinery cooperatives. The latter is attributable to state intervention. The number of privately owned tractors rises sharply after 1965, when preexisting restrictions are relaxed (World Bank, 1975:156–157).

Israel's moshavim are villages of cooperating farmers, organized in some respects more like the kibbutzim, or communes, than cooperatives of other countries. Members' holdings are usually contiguous. The size of individual holdings is standardized in each moshav when the moshav is founded, which for most occurs before independence and most mechanization. The subsequent adoption of tractors provides an incentive to combine blocks, and out-migration of heirs is a concern, but the average holding grows little. Baldwin (1972) furnishes an account of conflict between the egalitarian ideology set by the founders and the drive for modernization.

A pertinent contrast between the moshavim founded by European emigrants and newer ones of so-called oriental Jews has to do with the outlets they provide for personal ambition (Sadan and Weintraub, 1980). Many members of older, "Western" moshavim "have become overattached to their customary dairy and mixed farming pattern" (p. 504), and their more ambitious children seek opportunities outside farming. The oriental settlers of necessity develop newer farming strategies, and the moshav is for them and their children a preferred outlet for entrepreneurship.

Off-Farm Employment. The growth of part-time farming is one of the most significant social developments. By the mid-1970s the proportion of farm households that derive more than half their income from nonfarm sources is close to 40% in Austria, Norway, Switzerland, the United States, and West Germany (Benetiere, 1978). The numbers in the United States illustrate that the trend is not restricted to countries in which mean farm size is small, but its part-time farms are smaller than full-time farms, and their contribution to total farm production smaller still.

Part-time farming in many places benefits from the expansion of industrial employment into farming areas and from favorable government policy. Benetiere (1978) notes that German government policies allow supports for part-time farmers, whereas France's do not; only 16.8% of French farm households derive more than half their income from nonfarm sources.

Japan is the best example among the developed countries. The official Japanese definition of a part-time farm is one in which a member of the household works at an off-farm job. By 1965, 78.5% of Japanese farms are part-time, and on 41.7%, off-farm income exceeds that from farming (Misawa, 1970:252). In 1975, slightly fewer, 77.5%, of the farms are part-time, but off-farm income exceeds farm income on 62% of the farms (Benetiere, 1978). What most of all distinguishes Japan is the large role of part-time farms in total agricultural land use and production, owing to the small size of nearly all farms.

Dense settlement combines with rapid economic growth and full employment to afford Japanese farm residents unusual opportunities for off-farm employment. Few farm households had significant off-farm income until the late 1930s (Misawa, 1970:251), but the postwar economic "miracle" follows, and with it comes the rise of part-time farming. Today most off-farm income is earned by household members who commute to urban workplaces. Former members who move to the cities frequently send income back to the farm households, income not counted in official statistics. Japanese farms, it should be noted, benefit from a strong system of cooperatives.

Off-farm employment has long been significant in the United States and emerges after the war as the crucial factor in small-farm survival. Most farm households have appreciable off-farm income, according to Lewis (1980), but he makes no distinction between wages and investment income. Statistics show the necessity of outside income. Two-thirds of United States farms in 1978 have gross sales of less than $20,000, and most of these are "part-time" farms, defined as households that contribute 200 or more workdays a year to off-farm work. On nearly all farms in this group, some member of the household has a nonfarm job.

Direct marketing to consumers is not classed as off-farm employment but plays much the same role in keeping small farms going. Henderson and Linstrom (1982) report that part-time farmers manage two-thirds of direct marketing enterprises in a sample of states and conclude: "Direct marketing may be the primary outlet for small full-time or part-time farmers who do not produce in sufficient quantities to attract large-volume commercial buyers" (p. 12).

Handicrafts and other cottage industries also provide significant income, probably more so in Europe than in the United States. Many households process farm products, and the product is often marketed directly. The products frequently draw a premium price because of a reputation for high quality. The weaving of wool sweaters is a familiar example in northern regions. Some of the products are normally associated with larger enterprises, such as the fruit brandies of Alsace and "country" wines of much of France.

Subsidization. Subsidization, including price supports, protection from import competition, and direct payments, is often advocated to keep farmers in business and thereby slow land concentration. As noted above, the effect in the United States is often the reverse, but where the protected farms are too small to achieve full economies of scale, the effect can be to negate competitive forces favoring land concentration. Capital-intensive and moderately labor-intensive methods may be rendered profitable. Small farms become extremely productive, because subsidies meet the marginal costs of inputs and encourage their use where they might not otherwise be economic.

The goals of the EEC's Common Agricultural Policy (CAP) are to slow, not halt, concentration; to preserve rural communities; and to ease the transition toward concentration for individual smallholders (Herlitska, Malve, and Winegarten, 1974:75). The costs of the CAP to the present EC are so burdensome that proposals to bring commodity prices nearer to market levels are considered in late 1983 (Dunne, 1983), only to be dropped amid the pressures of intense competition for world markets. At present the EC appears ready to incur continuing high costs rather than lose its share of world markets or return to the rates of land concentration of the 1960s.

Japan represents the best case whereby price supports help keep small farmers' incomes at acceptable levels. Of several forms of support, that with the greatest impact is the "production cost and income determination formula" calculated to meet the production costs of the least profitable rice farms and thereby assure a profit for the remainder (Yamada and Hayami, 1979). Rice prices are first fixed to the formula in 1960 and subsequently remain several times world market levels. Other types of Japanese farms, notably those that produce fruits and vegetables and more readily achieve economies of scale at a small size, receive less generous supports. Livestock operations, small by Western standards, are protected and receive high prices, though farmers' groups and policymakers in Japan and competing countries contest the extent of protection.

THE STRUCTURE OF UNITED STATES FARM- ING. The issues of land concentration and farm ownership are related but should not be merged. Proponents of family farms advocate them over corporate ownership, but many, at least in the United States, also favor measures to restrict the size of all farms, regardless of ownership. Land concentration by definition takes families off the land but does not necessarily signal the end of family farms, which can be quite large.

That family farms under the present highly mechanized state of United States agriculture are technically efficient at a moderate scale makes it evident that corporate farms are not explicable with reference only to agricultural technology. Clearly the economy must be invoked, the political economy in fact, because government is so much caught up in the process.

We should steer clear of stereotypes, which are all too common in discussions of this value-loaded subject. For instance, tenant farmers are popularly thought to be poor and dependent on landowners. Impoverished southern sharecroppers come to mind, but many medium to large family farms now rent land, and the tenants are frequently better off than the owners, many of whom are former farmers now dependent on other income.

In *The Myth of the Family Farm,* Vogeler (1981) argues, correctly in my view, that definitions of "corporate" and "family" farms used in presentations of census data obscure the decline of full-time farms that are family owned and operated, but he goes on to display an aggressively egalitarian concept of the family farm, more a matter of judgment than of analysis. He wants family farms to be preserved without their growing to what he regards as large scale, equating farms whose gross sales are $100,000 or more with "industrial farmers" or "larger-than-family farmers . . . enroute to becoming industrial farmers" (pp. 27–30). Gross sales of $100,000 are above the national farm mean at that time but would not normally provide a net income out of line with the national household median income.

Opposing camps muddy the issues. Agribusiness boosters often confound technical factors that increase economies of scale with economic policies that promote concentration, such as absentee ownership and corporate ownership. Critics of current trends sometimes simultaneously condemn corporate farms and large family farms without making any distinction between them.

Given the passions the subject excites, the term *corporate farm* should be reserved for farms owned and operated by corporations as corporations are commonly understood, not just legally incorporated entities. Under United States law, advantages of incorporation often accrue to farmers who run family operations. Bona fide corporate farms are fewer than many imagine but are prevalent where opportunities abound for vertical integration. In 1974 legally incorporated farms constitute 1.7% of all United States farms and account for 18% of gross sales, a sure indication of large average size. They are concentrated in certain states, above all California, and to some degree in fruits and vegetables, nurseries, greenhouses, cattle feedlots, and sugarcane (Schertz, 1980:23–25). But families own 77% of these legal corporations, accounting for about one-half of sales by corporations. Many of the remaining corporate farms are held by nonfamily private corporations of varied form. A small number, 0.06% of all farms, are held by publicly owned corporations and account for 3.4% of sales. An unknown number of corporate partners are also to be found among the 145,000 farming partners.

Families still own a large majority of United States farms and make a majority of sales. Their market share is frequently cited to downplay the role of corporate farming, a line of argument protested on the grounds that many family-owned farms have absentee owners, hired managers, or nonfamily workers (Rodefeld, 1973). Absentee owners and hired managers do not fit the traditional picture of a family farm, and they are also features of many bona fide corporate farms. Unfortunately, published national statistics do not break down family-owned farms into categories that allow much relevant analysis. Rodefeld, like Vogeler, argues that large-scale family-owned farms most resemble corporate farms in their reliance on hired labor, and hired labor since 1950 does decline more slowly than family labor (Schertz, 1980:27). This trend is a reversal of the trend up to 1940 (USDA, Statistical Reporting Service, 1966), but how much of the reversal is due to replacement of family labor and how much to a slower pace of mechanization are not precisely known.

Another issue is corporate influence over family farming. Critics of agribusiness are more unanimous on this issue than over direct ownership. Vogeler (1981) and Shover (1976) argue that family farmers are losing their independence of action to creditors and contracting firms. Growing indebtedness, it is maintained, also encourages land concentration, because banks are reluctant to lend to small producers. Few agribusiness advocates dispute the contention that banks and contractors are making managerial decisions, but the advocates look on that role as assistance to the farmer at a time when management is increasingly complex and the risks of wrong decisions are high. Private firms' expenditures on extension now nearly equal those of the federal and state governments.

RELATED ISSUES IN OTHER DEVELOPED MARKET ECONOMIES. Corporate farming hardly exists in Europe or Japan, except that in Europe a few processors, notably wineries, own part of their supply network, and some broiler houses and egg-producing operations are corporate owned. Vertical integration and contract farming are issues, however, particularly in the case of European sugar beet farms. Contract farming in the sugar industry (from beet or cane) is also strong in the United States and Australia.

Alternative Agriculture

A look at alternative agriculture is timely. Rapport between the movement's advocates and mainstream agricultural scientists, once poor, is on the whole much better than it was a decade or two ago. Professional scientists more widely profess concern over undesirable effects of uncontrolled agroindustrial technology, while the standards of experimentation and verification in alternative agriculture are improving. Some alternative agriculturalists give qualified endorsements to less restrictive approaches such as integrated pest management. "Low-input" agriculture, receiving attention at a number of experiment stations and land grant colleges of agriculture, is not too far removed from "regenerative agriculture" endorsed by the Rodale organization, long the principal North American advocates of "organic" methods; and the editor of the magazine *Organic Gardening* (Rodale, 1987) urges readers to support research on low-input methods.

BIOLOGICAL CONTROL AND INTEGRATED PEST MANAGEMENT. Biological control and integrated pest management (IPM), as approaches to the control of pests and diseases, fall squarely within the scientific mainstream. They are nevertheless alternatives to the present level of use of chemical pesticides.

The term *biological control* most often refers to the introduction or management of natural enemies of target populations, usually insects and other macrofaunal pests, less often weeds and plant diseases. We already know that biological checks are the main means of pest control. That the absence of natural enemies in an introduced pest's new environment allows calamitous proliferation is proof. When we speak of deliberate measures, then, we mean giving nature a hand.

Deliberate introductions of natural enemies go back to the colonial era or earlier (Doutt, 1964; Simmonds, Franz, and Sailer, 1976). Intercontinental transport moved exotic pests, creating a need for controls often met by introducing natural enemies from the pests' endemic regions. A landmark was the introduction of the vedalia beetle (*Rodolia cardinalis*) from Australia into California to control cottony-cushion scale (*Icerya purchasi*) on citrus trees. The control was spectacularly successful and was achieved through systematic scientific work, entailing identification of both the beetle's home and its natural enemy. Biological controls were prominent for several decades thereafter, until the postwar advent of DDT and other insecticides dampens enthusiasm. Research never dies out altogether, and the pace picks up again after about 1960 because of the recognition of spreading immunities to pesticides and of damage from previously insignificant pests. Concern about pesticide pollution is another factor.

Methods of control are becoming more varied. Management of native control species receives more attention. A broader definition of *biological control* now takes in ecosystem management, including both new developments and such old techniques as crop rotation. Other new techniques are the introduction of sterile males to produce unfruitful matings, the introduction of deleterious genes into the pest population, and disturbances of pest behavior.

Reviews of biological control point to many successes, and commercial firms have clienteles despite the experimental nature of the most promising lines of research. Summaries cover research on entomophagous parasites (van Lenteren, 1983), the control of fungal disorders by means of antagonistic microorganisms (Brown and Beringer, 1983), predators of pests (Luff, 1983), ecosystem management (Speight, 1983), the compatibility of pesticides with biological control (Stevenson and Walters, 1983), and the use of chemicals that alter target insects' behavior, including pheromones and other substances secreted by the insects themselves (Kydoneius and Beroza, 1982; Mitchell, 1981; Nordlund, Jones, and Lewis, 1981). General surveys of biological control include Coppel and Mertins (1977), DeBach (1964, 1974), and Huffaker and Messenger (1976).

The essence of integrated pest management is that the agricultural ecosystem is analyzed in its entirety, controls are aimed selectively and with restraint at specific target species, and account is taken of the whole set of interrelationships within the ecosystem. Chemical pesticides are frequently used at present, but preferably they are narrow-spectrum agents that disturb a minimum of species other than the target. Improved knowledge should lead to less need for pesticides, which might eventually be eliminated (DeBach, 1974).

IPM is widely hailed as the only realistic long-term solution to pest and disease problems. A USDA report (USDA, Office of Environmental Quality, 1980:51) endorses it as "the best approach to controlling pests without damaging the environment," though some critics think that the USDA should give it more attention and funding.

Many of modern agriculture's trends make effective use of IPM more difficult. Speight (1983) lists monoculture and the introduction of high-yielding exotics. Cosmetic use of pesticides, aimed at giving consumers a blemish-free product, demands heavier or more frequent sprayings or dustings than the protection of yields requires.

In spite of these and other obstacles, IPM succeeds in many situations. The use of pesticides is radically reduced in some crop ecosystems that were threatened by diverse pests. Crops thus protected include alfalfa in California, where several IPM firms have found clients since the 1960s, and apples in Nova Scotia, beginning in the 1940s, before IPM was a familiar concept. Hoy and Herzog (1985) furnish a status report for North America.

Insecticide use in the United States is off since 1976 (USDA, 1987) after decades of dramatic increase. Little of the decline is attributable to IPM programs as such; more is attributable to selective application of agents, a modest step in the same direction.

Historically, IPM is an intriguing phenomenon. The advent of broad-spectrum insecticides encourages simplification of control measures after World War II to the point that many farmers spray prophylactically. Then second thoughts set in, not only among alternative agriculturalists or advocates of IPM. More and more farmers are moving toward restraint and selectivity in the use of pesticides. If they go further and embrace IPM, they resume their ancient role of ecologist but may now consult with professionals.

THE ALTERNATIVE AGRICULTURE MOVEMENT. Advocates of alternative agriculture propose alternatives to the use of most industrial inputs in agriculture. Chemical fertilizers and pesticides excite the greatest reaction; few alternative agriculturalists object in principle to mechanization. The two schools with the most adherents worldwide are Biodynamic Agriculture, based on ideas first expressed by Rudolf Steiner in 1924 (Steiner, 1958), and organic (biological, on the European Continent) agriculture, which originated in Albert Howard's compost experiments in India during the 1930s. These schools attract followers after World War II, they are joined by several others, and numerous journals begin.[2] Some movements are less restrictive, such as ANOG agriculture (Arbeitsgemeinschaft für naturgemässen Qualitätsanbau von Obst und Gemüse, or "Working Group for the Natural Cultivation of Fruits and Vegetables"), Howard-Balfour agriculture, and particularly eco-agriculture, the offspring of soil scientist William Albrecht, which allows limited use of chemical fertilizers and low-toxicity pesticides.

Alternative farms are nowhere numerous. The USDA Study Team on Organic Farming (1980:10) estimates that about 24,000 organic farms are in the United States, or about 1% of all farms. Many of the farms studied are small, but a few very large ones are noted. In 1972 the various forms of alternative agriculture occupy in 1972 0.03% of the total agricultural area of Belgium, 0.04% in the Netherlands and West Germany, 0.24% in France, and 0.1% in England (Boeringa, 1980:21). The Tasmanian movement is especially active, and informants in 1977 documented an assertion that about 2% of the island's farms are organic.

The various schools all prefer manures and composts to industrially produced chemical fertilizers, hand or mechanical weed control to herbicides, and hand or biological pest control to chemical pesticides, but the strength of their preference and their attitudes toward specific substances often vary. Most practitioners accept naturally occurring mineral fertilizers, such as rock phosphate and greensand (glauconite), though the USDA Study Team found that their actual use is very limited, except for lime (as ground limestone). Most practitioners restrict the use of synthesized compounds and chemically treated minerals, such as superphosphate, though I have encountered, particularly in Australia, organic farmers who use superphosphate fertilizer. In principle the familiar chemical N, P, and K fertilizers are permitted only in ANOG agriculture and eco-agriculture, though use is reported on a few organic farms of the USDA sample. If allowed or practiced, application rates are low, and slow-acting forms are preferred to quickly solubilized forms. Attitudes toward chemical nitrogen fertilizers are generally the most negative, because biological nitrogen fixation can meet requirements or because high application rates are believed to overstimulate crops. Some limited use of herbicides is allowed in ANOG agriculture and Howard-Balfour agriculture (Boeringa, 1980:126) but is otherwise exceptional.

Pest control recommendations and practices are particularly variable. Alternative agriculturalists frequently insist that appropriate crop rotations or interplanting schemes, soil rich in organic matter, and practices peculiar to each school keep pests in check.

Many of the claims clash with agricultural science, but others do not. The claims for organic matter tend to be a sore point, at least as stated. Possible control benefits from interplanting are the subject of scientific research, though some of the rationale, particularly in Biodynamic Agriculture, is mysticism to most scientists. Rotations are a long-accepted method of control.

Biological control methods of all sorts are normally approved by alternative agriculturalists, making them prospective consumers of all research along those lines. Regarding integrated pest management, no solid consensus is yet apparent.

Three major surveys are useful sources on alternative agriculture. Two are primarily concerned with organic agriculture in the United States. Oelhaf (1978) is a general review by an advocate noteworthy for its analysis of cost factors in organic farming. The report of the USDA Study Team on Organic Farming (1980) is particularly useful for its findings on pest control and methods of maintaining soil fertility. A parallel survey by a Netherlands group covers the more diverse forms of alternative agriculture in Europe (Boeringa, 1980). A 1981 symposium on organic farming brought together researchers associated with the movement and others working within the mainstream United States land grant colleges, and the proceedings (Bezdicek et al., 1984) update many of the conclusions of the three surveys.

Expressions of the philosophy of alternative agriculture often exhibit vitalism; that is, an active role is ascribed to some life force. This is particularly true of some European schools: Biodynamic Agriculture, grounded in the philosophy of anthroposophy; Lemaire-Boucher agriculture, based in part on L. Kervran's idea that biological organisms can transmute the elements; and Macrobiotic Agriculture, rooted in concepts of yin and yang, and a balance of the living and nonliving. A critical review of experiments purported to back the vitalistic claims is in Boeringa (1980). None of this facilitates dialogue with mainstream scientists, but many advocates of alternative agriculture, including most spokespeople for organic methods, do not rely on vitalistic justifications and should not be burdened with a need to prove them.

The potential role of alternative agriculture will here be assessed in purely material terms. For example, the benefits of manure are sought in empirically verifiable effects, above all its nutrient content. The claim is ignored that ammonia from a manure pile possesses a vital force that ammonia from a factory lacks.

FEEDING THE WORLD WITH FEWER INDUSTRIAL INPUTS. Could alternative agriculture feed the world? The question is rhetorical, given the small number of alternative farmers, but answering it helps us understand how much we presently rely on industrial inputs into agriculture. It is not enough to compare present-day and preindustrial agriculture, because alternative forms can and do benefit from continuing advances in breeding and other biological measures. Some varieties of alternative agriculture can utilize mineral fertilizers that were little used in the past, and low-input agriculture is a compromise that would selectively reduce, not eliminate, industrial inputs.

On a small scale, gardeners can adhere to the rules of the strictest schools of alternative agriculture and obtain yields at or very near the maximum obtained by any means, relying on additions of organic matter and varied means of pest control. We need to ask if larger field operations can do as well, or, if not, whether that matters. Answering these questions necessitates looking at the factors that might limit alternative agriculture, then at global agriculture in its entirety to see if those limits would impose a penalty on a world that adopted alternative methods. A good place to begin is with nitrogen, because such a clear choice is presented between biologically fixed nitrogen and that from industrial synthesis.

Organic farmers obtain most of their nitrogen from in situ biological fixation, not from imported organic matter. Organic farmers in a magazine readership survey apply 3 to 11 metric tons (wet weight) of organic matter per hectare (Power and Doran, 1984). Both this survey and the USDA Study Team report that most of the organic matter applied is in the forms of animal manure and crop residues drawn from cultivated fields and pasture. Some use is made of animal manure from other farms and of high-nitrogen fertilizers such as leather dust and cottonseed meal, in effect a small subsidy of nutrients from industrial agriculture, a point also made about alternative and industrial farms in the Netherlands (Boeringa, 1980:36–37). With these exceptions the nitrogen supplied to crops on the organic farms studied in the United States comes from biological fixation on these farms. Legume rotations are important. Wastes from uncultivated, unpastured land are not.

Organic wastes applied to United States farmlands contain about 9.6 million t of nitrogen (calculated from USDA Study Team, 1980:36–37), about equal to that supplied by chemical fertilizers in most years since 1976 (Fig. 10.2). Unused organic wastes contain 4.3 million t, but much would be lost in transit to the fields if they were used, and some are not accessible to farms. These wastes thus constitute an unused resource but not one that could come close to completely replacing industrially fixed nitrogen.

A legume grown in rotation can substitute for much of the combined nitrogen needed by a following, high-yielding nonlegume crop, provided that the legume is itself high-yielding and conditions are favorable (Voss and Shrader, 1984), but the ideal is not always realized. Although some fodder legumes annually fix several hundred kilograms of nitrogen per hectare, comparable to the quantity removed in the most productive systems, recovery by crops is incomplete (Heichel and Barnes, 1984). Biological nitrogen fixation also ceases when inorganic combined nitrogen reaches about 100 kg/ha (Wittwer, 1975), a level that is reached in some highly productive systems and might be required by more-productive crop varieties yet to be developed. Ways to circumvent this obstacle, such as modifying the nitrogen-fixing microorganisms, are foreseen by some researchers and are given a high priority by the Office of Technology Assessment (1977) in the United States.

If aggregate yields are to be as high as those from systems that incorporate only high-yielding cereals, legume yields must be increased, but to date breeders have obtained much less improvement with these than with most cereals. Some workers anticipate that gains from either conventional breeding of legumes or genetic engineering may yet be dramatic, but not all are so optimistic. Efforts with lucerne have not furnished any varieties to rival the most productive cereals (Barnes et al., 1981). Another promising area of research, also far from application, is the transfer to cereal crops of the property of association with nitrogen-fixing microorganisms.

Mineral nutrients to replace those the harvest removes cannot, like nitrogen, come out of the air. The USDA Study Team found that adequacy of biological nitrogen fixation probably contributes to steady depletion of phosphorus and potassium reserves. Depletion occurs in spite of careful return of crop residues to the soil. No mineral fertilizers are used to any great extent, and low-input farming research accordingly concentrates on efficient use of mineral fertilizers, not their replacement.

How hard it is to supply alternative agriculture with sufficient mineral nutrients varies with nutrient, soil, and how much modification of natural mineral amendments is acceptable. Calcium and magnesium are no problem, because of the acceptance of limestone and dolomite. Micronutrients can be supplied in many ways in the small quantities needed. Rock phosphate can be an effective source of phosphorus. Factors that increase its availability are acid soils and the use of rock that is finely ground and low in chlorine and fluorine. Other options might be silicated rock phosphate prepared by fusing rock phosphate and sand, or aluminum phosphate ores prepared by heating, but no policy or attitude toward these fertilizers is yet evident among alternative agriculturalists. Potassium is abundant in the earth's crust. Mineral deposits range from highly soluble desert salt deposits to greensand and granite, a source recommended in some alternative agricultural literature but generally discounted in industrial agriculture. Sulfur is readily available in elemental form or pyrites. On the whole, it appears that a little flexibility would go a long way. More information is needed on what happens over many years when cultivators apply slowly available forms.

Another obstacle to matching the yields of industrial agriculture may be the restriction on herbicides. Other means exist to eliminate any weed now controlled chemically, but under present conditions the only economic substitute in highly productive industrial agricultural systems is mechanical cultivation, which is not always equally effective. The thick mulches used by many alternative gardeners are clearly not feasible on a large scale. Organic farmers widely perceive a weed control problem (McLeod and Swezey, 1979; USDA Study Team, 1980). Andres and Clement (1984) express some optimism that "integrated weed management" in a favorable social and economic climate could entail substantially reduced use of chemical herbicides.

The USDA Study Team and the Netherlands group both report few problems with pests and diseases, but much of the area surveyed is under cereals, grass, or fodder crops. Both teams and Oelhaf report greater problems in fruits and vegetables.

If today's most productive agriculture had to do without industrial inputs, some part of its yield would be sacrificed, but projections of the decrease differ substantially. In the United States corn belt, yields of maize and other crops on organic farms are reportedly 6% to 17% less than on industrial farms (Lockeretz et al., 1984). Aldrich (1979, 1980), in response to an earlier report of that same research and as part of a vehement critique of organic farming, argues that the sacrifice would be greater. The comparison by Lockeretz et al. uses a farm survey, not experiments, and differences in conditions, particularly the skill of management, are not controlled. The organic farms include substantial areas of permanent pasture, the industrial farms very little. Aldrich argues that the yields from the pasture (more exactly, their value) should be averaged in, certainly a valid point if pasture supplies manure to cultivated land. He concludes from the results of controlled experiments at the University of Illinois, after allowing for the land in pasture or hay in the organic rotation, that aggregate yields from organic farms would be at least 20% less than from industrial farms in the corn belt. Other corn belt comparisons (Oelhaf, 1978; USDA Study Team, 1980) agree more closely with those of Lockeretz's group than with Aldrich's, but they too are based on whole-farm comparisons and in addition rely on farmers' memories of yields; Lockeretz's group also measured yields from sample plots.

The differing methods of reaching comparisons are not easily reconciled. Aldrich makes a good point about the need to control for management and other variables. On the other side, the director of the Rodale organization's experimental effort argues that whole systems must be tested and complains that trials of organic methods have often really used "no treatment check plots" that virtually assure poor yields (Harwood, 1984:2). A similar complaint by Oelhaf (1978) indicts the same trials used by Aldrich for comparison, on the grounds that they set up an "organic plot" managed by methods that would not pass muster on any actual organic farm. The argument is therefore in part between holistic and analytical research designs. Several researchers are interested in finding a way out of the impasse and are therefore trying to develop trials in which controlled comparisons can be made of organic and industrial methods in spite of the multiple management variables involved (Harwood, 1984).

If we take a worst-case scenario and assume that Aldrich is correct about corn belt yields, strict alternative methods could still feed the world. If farmers in the United State wanted to support livestock industries at their present level and keep their market share, they would have to press more marginal land into production, but we should not expect the substitution of biological nitrogen fixation for chemical nitrogen fertilizers to be equally daunting everywhere. With regard to the other major exporting countries, much of the grain production of Canada, New Zealand, and Australia and a significant though shrinking part of that from the EC countries comes from land on which industrial farming systems include the same fodder or pasture crop rotations found on alternative farms. Sacrifices would presumably be less, even using Aldrich's assumptions. Some production could be reallocated and intensive alternative methods used on presently uncultivated or extensively cultivated land.

What is technically possible is of course a different matter from what is achievable under existing or likely future economic constraints. Although any shortfall created by Iowa's going organic might in theory be eliminated by plowing more of Australia's north, where some ambitious agricultural development projects have failed for lack of markets, it is not about to happen.

Low-input agriculture would necessitate less reallocation, possibly very little. Agricultural commodities are presently in surplus. Interested parties agree that fertilizer and pesticide use is commonly excessive in advanced industrial agriculture; better matching of applications to needs can readily result in major savings. In less developed regions, the tropics in particular, great opportunities exist for low-input systems (chapter 11). A low-input, very high-yield agriculture, adequate to feed more than the present world population, may become feasible if three conditions are met: (1) breakthroughs in facilitating biological nitrogen fixation, (2) efficient use of mineral fertilizers, and (3) continuing improvement of IPM.

EFFICIENCY OF ALTERNATIVE AGRICULTURE.

Alternative agriculture combines old and new practices, but its effect is to partly reverse the historic trend toward less labor and more energy. The effect is most evident in small gardens relying on hand labor and compost making but is documented in field systems. Pimentel, Berardi, and Fast (1983, 1984) find organic maize production to be 29% to 70% more energy-efficient than industrial methods at a cost of a drop in labor efficiency of 22% to 43%. Findings are similar for spring wheat production, but organic potato and apple production is 95% less labor-efficient and 10% to 90% less energy-efficient, a poor performance attributed mainly to projected losses from pests and diseases, and in apples to a struggle to meet consumers' standards for appearance of fruit.

Here, too, low-input agriculture is worth inserting into the comparison. Excessive and wasteful use of inputs—above all, fertilizers—contributes to low energy efficiency on many farms. In the economic climate of the 1980s, many farmers are cutting down on their use of inputs, paralleling the rise of research into low-input methods.

Notes

1. The original six EEC members were Belgium, France, Italy, Luxembourg, the Netherlands, and West Germany. The EFTA members were Austria, Denmark, Norway, Portugal, Sweden, Switzerland, and the United Kingdom.

2. Oelhaf (1978:256–258) lists the following alternative agriculture journals: *Acres, U.S.A.; Biodynamics; Biodynamic Farming; Compost Science; Lebendige Erde; Organic Gardening and Farming* (now Rodale's *Organic Gardening*), *Soil Association Quarterly Review;* and *Henry Doubleday Research Association Newsletter*. To these may be added *Mother Earth News*, Rodale's *New Farmer*, and *Organic Gardener and Farmer* (Hobart, Tasmania).

References

Agricultural Statistics (1960, 1966, 1971, 1982, 1985). U.S. Department of Agriculture, Washington, D.C.

Aldrich, S.R. (1979). Organic farming can't feed the world. *World Agriculture,* 27(1):17–19.

———. (1980). *Nitrogen in Relation to Food, Environment, and Energy.* University of Illinois Press, Urbana.

Andres, L.A., and S.L. Clement (1984). Opportunities for reducing chemical inputs for weed control. In *Organic Farming: Current Technology and Its Role in a Sustainable Agriculture* (D. Bezdicek et al., eds.) American Society of Agronomy, Madison, Wis., pp. 129–140.

Baldwin, E. (1972). *Differentiation and Co-operation in an Israeli Veteran Moshav.* Manchester University Press, Manchester, England.

Barnes, D.K., G.H. Heichel, C.P. Vance, D.R. Viands, and G. Handanson (1981). Successes and failures while breeding for enhanced nitrogen fixation in alfalfa. In *Genetic Engineering of Symbiotic Nitrogen Fixation* (J.M. Lyons, R.C. Valentine, D.A. Philips, D.W. Rains, and R.C. Huffaker, eds.), Plenum, New York, pp. 233–248.

Benetiere, J.J. (1978). Main problems posed by part-time farming. *World Agriculture,* 26(4):21–24.

Bezdicek, D.F. et al., eds. (1984). *Organic Farming: Current Technology and Its Role in a Sustainable Agriculture.* American Society of Agronomy, Madison, Wis.

Boehlje, M., and S. Griffin (1979). Financial impact of government support price programs. *American Journal of Agricultural Economics,* 61:285–296.

Boeringa, R., ed. (1980). Alternative methods of agriculture: Description, evaluation, and recommendations for research. *Agriculture and Environment,* special issue, vol. 5.

Brown, M.E., and J.E. Beringer (1983). The potential of antagonists for fungal control. *Agriculture, Ecosystems, and Environment,* 10:127–141.

Butterwick, M., and E.N. Rolfe (1968). *Food, Farming, and the Common Market.* Oxford University Press, London.

Campbell, R.R. (1985). Some observations on the deflation of the farm assets in the Midwest. *Culture and Agriculture,* 3 (Summer–Fall): 1–5.

Clark, G. (1977). Soviet agricultural policy. In *Soviet Agriculture: An Assessment of Its Contributions to Economic Development* (H.G. Shaffer, ed.), Praeger, New York, pp. 1–55.

Coppel, H.C., and J.W. Mertins (1977). *Biological Insect Pest Suppression.* Springer-Verlag, Berlin.

DeBach, P., ed. (1964). *Biological Control of Insect Pests and Weeds.* Reinhold, New York.

DeBach, P. (1974). Biological Control by Natural Enemies. Cambridge University Press, Cambridge.

Doutt, R.L. (1964). The historical development of biological control. In *Biological Control of Insect Pests and Weeds* (P. DeBach, ed.), Reinhold, New York, pp. 21–44.

Dunne, N. (1983). Shall they beat their plowshares into swords? *Europe,* no. 239 (September–October): 10–12.

Friend, R.E., and R. Trostle (1985). Agriculture in Western Europe. In *U.S. Agriculture in a Global Context: The Yearbook of Agriculture 1985* (L.B. Marton, ed.), U.S. Department of Agriculture, Washington, D.C., pp. 81–99.

Hamilton, F.E. (1968). *Yugoslavia: Patterns of Economic Activity.* Praeger, New York.

Harwood, R.R. (1984). Organic farming research at the Rodale Research Center. In *Organic Farming: Current Technology and Its Role in a Sustainable Agriculture* (D.F. Bezdicek et al., eds.), American Society of Agronomy, Madison, Wis., pp. 1–18.

Havens, T.R.H. (1974). *Farm and Nation in Modern Japan: Agrarian Nationalism, 1870–1949.* Princeton University Press, Princeton, N.J.

Hayami, Y., and V.W. Ruttan (1971). *Agricultural Development: An International Perspective.* Johns Hopkins University Press, Baltimore.

Heady, E.O. (1975). The basic equity problem. In *Externalities in the Transformation of Agriculture* (E.O. Heady and L. Whiting, eds.), Iowa State University Press, Ames, pp. 3–21.

Heichel, G.H., and D.K. Barnes (1984). Opportunities for meeting crop nitrogen needs from symbiotic nitrogen fixation. In *Organic Farming: Current Technology and Its Role in a Sustainable Agriculture* (D.F. Bezdicek et al., eds.), American Society of Agronomy, Madison, Wis., pp. 49–60.

Henderson, P.L., and H.R. Linstrom (1982). *Farmer-to-Consumer Direct Marketing, Selected States, 1979–1980.* U.S. Department of Agriculture, National Economic Division, Economic Research Service, Statistical Bulletin no. 681. Washington, D.C.

Herlitska, A., P. Malve, and A. Winegarten (1974). European agricultural policy. In *U.S. Agriculture in a Global Context: Policies and Approaches for the Next Decade* (D.G. Johnson and J.A. Schnittker, eds.), Praeger, New York, pp. 62–102.

Hoy, M.A., and D.C. Herzog, eds. (1985). *Biological Control in Agricultural IPM Systems.* Academic Press, New York.

Huffaker, C.B., and P.S. Messenger, eds. (1976). *Theory and Practice of Biological Control.* Academic Press, New York.

Jensen, E. (1937). *Danish Agriculture: Its Economic Development.* J.H. Schultz, Copenhagen.

Johnson, D.G. (1973). *World Agriculture in Disarray.* Macmillan, London.

Kawano, S. (1969). Effects of the land reform on consumption and investment of farmers. In *Agriculture and Economic Growth: Japan's Experience* (K. Ohkawa, B.F. Johnston, and H. Kaneda, eds.), Princeton University Press, Princeton, N.J., pp. 374–397.

Kelly, C.F. (1967). Mechanical harvesting. *Scientific American,* 217(2):50–59.

Kydoneius, A.F., and M. Beroza, eds. (1982). *Insect Suppression with Controlled Release Pheromone Systems.* 2 vols. CRC Press, Boca Raton, Fla.

Larsen, P. (1970). Agriculture. In *Denmark: An Official Handbook,* Royal Danish Ministry of Foreign Affairs, Copenhagen, pp. 409–422.

Lenteren, J.C. van (1983). The potential of entomophagous parasites for pest control. *Agriculture, Ecosystems, and Environment,* 10:143–158.

Lewis, J.A. (1980). *Landownership in the United States.* U.S. Department of Agriculture; Economics, Statistics, and Cooperatives Service, Agriculture Information Bulletin no. 435. Washington, D.C.

Lin, W., G. Coffman, and J.B. Penn (1980). *U.S. Farm Numbers, Size, and Related Structural Dimensions: Projections to Year 2000.* U.S. Department of Agriculture; Economics, Statistics, and Cooperatives Service, Technical Bulletin no. 1625. Washington, D.C.

Lockeretz, W., G. Shearer, D.H. Kohl, and R.W. Klepper (1984). Comparison of organic and conventional farming in the corn belt. In *Organic Farming: Current Technology and Its Role in a Sustainable Agriculture* (D.F. Bezdicek et al., eds.), American Society of Agronomy, Madison, Wis., pp. 37–48.

Luff, M.L. (1983). The potential of predators for pest control. *Agriculture, Ecosystems, and Environment,* 10:159–181.

Madden, J.P. (1967). *Economies of Size in Farming.* U.S. Department of Agriculture, Economic Research Service, Agricultural Economics Report no. 107. Washington, D.C.

Marshall, R., and L. Godwin (1971). *Cooperatives and Rural Poverty in the South.* Johns Hopkins University Press, Baltimore.

McLeod, E.J., and S.L. Swezey (1979). Survey of weed problems and management technologies in organic agriculture. Mimeo. Appropriate Technology Program, University of California, Berkeley.

Miller, T.A., G.E. Rodevall, and R.G. McElroy (1981). *Economies of Size in U.S. Field Crop Farming*. U.S. Department of Agriculture, National Economics Division, Economics and Statistics Service, Agricultural Economics Report no. 472. Washington, D.C.

Misawa, T. (1970). An analysis of part-time farming in the post-war period. In *Agriculture and Economic Growth: Japan's Experience* (K. Ohkawa, B.F. Johnston, and H. Kaneda, eds.), Princeton University Press, Princeton, N.J., pp. 250–269.

Mitchell, E.R., ed. (1981). *Management of Insect Pests with Semiochemicals*. Plenum, New York.

Nelson, F.J., and W.W. Cochrane (1976). Economic consequences of federal farm commodity programs. *Agricultural Economic Research*, 28(2):52–64.

Nordlund, D.A., R.L. Jones, and W.J. Lewis, eds. (1981). *Semiochemicals: Their Role in Pest Control*. Wiley, New York.

Oelhaf, R.C. (1978). *Organic Agriculture: Economic and Ecological Comparisons with Conventional Methods*. Allanheld, Osmun, and Co., Montclair, N.J.

Office of Technology Assessment (1977). *Organizing and Financing Basic Research to Increase Food Production*. Office of Technology Assessment, Washington, D.C.

Pimentel, D., and M. Pimentel (1979). *Food, Energy, and Society*. Edward Arnold, London.

Pimentel, D., G. Berardi, and S. Fast (1983). Energy efficiency and conventional agriculture. *Agriculture, Ecosystems, and Environment*, 9:359–372.

_____. (1984). Energy efficiencies of farming wheat, corn, and potatoes organically. In *Organic Farming: Current Technology and Its Role in a Sustainable Agriculture* (D.F. Bezdicek et al., eds.), American Society of Agronomy, Madison, Wis., pp. 151–162.

Pimentel, D., L.E. Hurd, A.C. Bellotti, M.J. Forster, I.N. Oka, O.D. Shola, and R.J. Whitman (1973). Food production and the energy crisis. *Science*, 182:443–449.

Power, J.F., and J.W. Doran (1984). Nitrogen use in organic farming. In *Nitrogen in Crop Production* (R.D. Hauck, ed.), American Society of Agronomy, Madison, Wis., pp. 585–598.

Reimund, J.R.M., and C.V. Moore (1981). *Structural Changes in Agriculture: The Experience of Broilers, Fed Cattle, and Processing Vegetables*. U.S. Department of Agriculture, Economics and Statistics Service, Technical Bulletin no. 1648. Washington, D.C.

Rodale, R. (1987). You can help turn the toxic tide. *Organic Gardening*, July, pp. 20–22.

Rodefeld, R.D. (1973). A reassessment of the status and trends in "family" and "corporate" farms in U.S. society. *Congressional Record*, 93d Congress, 1st session, May 31, p. S10056.

Sadan, E., and D. Weintraub (1980). Ethnicity, nativity, and economic performance of cooperative smallholding farms in Israel. *Economic Development and Cultural Change,* 28:487–507.

Sahota, G.S. (1968). *Fertilizer in Economic Development: An Economic Perspective.* Praeger, New York.

Schertz, L. (1980). *Another Revolution in U.S. Farming?* U.S. Department of Agriculture, Washington, D.C.

Shover, J.L. (1976). *First Majority, Last Minority: The Transforming of Rural Life in America.* Northern Illinois University Press, De Kalb.

Simmonds, F.J., J.M. Franz, and R.I. Sailer (1976). History of biological control. In *Theory and Practice of Biological Control* (C.B. Huffaker and P.S. Messenger, eds.), Academic Press, New York, pp. 17–41.

Speight, M.R. (1983). The potential of ecosystem management for pest control. *Agriculture, Ecosystems, and Environment,* 10:183–199.

Steiner, R. (1958). *Agriculture.* Biodynamic Agricultural Association, London.

Stevenson, J.H., and J.H.H. Walters (1983). Evaluation of pesticides for use with biological control. *Agriculture, Ecosystems, and Environment,* 10:201–215.

Symons, L. (1972). *Russian Agriculture: A Geographic Survey.* Wiley, New York.

Torgerson, D., and H. Cooper (1980). *Energy and U.S. Agriculture: 1974 and 1978.* U.S. Department of Agriculture; Economics, Statistics, and Cooperatives Service , Statistical Bulletin No. 632. Washington, D.C.

Tracey, M. (1964). *Agriculture in Western Europe.* Praeger, New York.

Tsuchiya, K. (1970). Economies of mechanization in small scale agriculture. In *Agriculture and Economic Growth: Japan's Experience* (K. Ohkawa, B.F. Johnston, and H. Kaneda, eds.), Princeton University Press, Princeton, N.J., pp. 155–174.

USDA (1987). *The Second RCA Appraisal: Soil, Water, and Related Resources on Nonfederal Land in the United States.* Review draft. U.S. Department of Agriculture, Washington, D.C.

USDA, Economic Research Service (1976). *Change in Farm Production and Efficiency: A Special Issue Featuring Historical Series.* Statistical Bulletin no. 561. U.S. Department of Agriculture, Washington, D.C.

USDA, Economics, Statistics, and Cooperatives Service (1978). *The Future Role of Cooperatives in the Red Meats Industry.* U.S. Department of Agriculture, Washington, D.C.

USDA, Office of Environmental Quality (1980). *Annual Report on Agriculture's Contribution to a Better Environment.* U.S. Department of Agriculture, Washington, D.C.

USDA, Statistical Reporting Service (1966). *A Century of Agriculture in Charts and Tables.* U.S. Department of Agriculture, Washington, D.C.

USDA Study Team on Organic Farming (1980). *Report and Recommendations on Organic Farming.* U.S. Department of Agriculture, Washington, D.C.

Vogeler, I. (1981). *The Myth of the Family Farm: Agribusiness Domination of U.S. Agriculture.* Westview, Boulder, Colo.

Voss, R.D., and W.D. Shrader (1984). Opportunities for meeting crop nitrogen needs from symbiotic nitrogen fixation. In *Organic Farming: Current Technology and Its Role in a Sustainable Agriculture* (D.F. Bezdicek et al., eds.) American Society of Agronomy, Madison, Wis., pp. 61–68.

Wadekin, K.E. (1973). *The Private Sector in Soviet Agriculture.* University of California Press, Berkeley.

Westphal, D. (1988). Iowans flee state from urban areas faster than rural. *Des Moines Register,* March 8, p. 1.

Wittwer, S.H. (1975). Food production: Technology and the resource base. *Science,* 188:579–584.

World Bank (1975). *Yugoslavia: Development with Decentralization.* Johns Hopkins University Press, Baltimore.

_____. (1983). *Yugoslavia: Adjustment Policies and Development Perspectives.* World Bank, Washington, D.C.

Yamada, S., and Y. Hayami (1979). Agricultural growth in Japan, 1880–1970. In *Agricultural Growth in Japan, Taiwan, Korea, and the Philippines* (Y. Hayami, V.W. Ruttan, and H.M. Southworth, eds.), East-West Center, Honolulu, pp 33–58.

11

Agriculture for Development

 Agriculture in the less developed countries must feed growing populations and assist economic development. Agriculture cannot absorb many more workers but can provide capital for development of the whole economy and in this way contribute more to employment than it does directly. Appropriate models must be found for technical and social innovation in agriculture, whether the changes are directed or are spontaneous outgrowths of development. The persistent technical question is the appropriateness of the model of industrial agriculture in the developed countries.

This chapter will first survey the special problems of these countries and then move on to the possible role of agriculture in solving them. Three main approaches to agricultural development will be treated: (1) the green revolution, a parallel to much of the main course of industrial agriculture in the developed countries, though not a duplicate; (2) innovative systems that come out of modern scientific research but rely more on the management of tropical ecosystems than on heavy capital and energy inputs; and (3) the likely impact of such high technology as tissue culture and genetic engineering.

Many of the issues raised about the direction of agricultural development in the less developed countries are the same as in the developed countries—for example, ownership and scale of holdings—but one critical issue is peculiar to the less developed countries. Although popular sentiment and political rhetoric often are in favor of spreading development across the rural populace, most development tends to occur in the cities and in a few rural enclaves. The process is a manifestation of a dual economy; one sector replicates many of the features of the developed countries, while the other gains technical innovations and new capital more slowly.

Economic gains are real but uneven from country to country and within countries, and disparities are as great in agriculture as in anything else. Fortunately, several signs point to improvement in many countries that have lagged in agricultural production, those in sub-Saharan Africa in particular. A less tractable problem may prove to be the persistence in many countries of the "poorest," an underclass whose lot, if anything, is getting worse (Loup, 1983).

Indigenous cultivators have long had to adapt their methods to feed growing populations, and in many places they still enjoy room for maneuver. In other areas where population pressure mounts, they face diminishing returns on their labor, or worse. And though the populations of most less developed countries are growing more slowly than before, at present rates they will still double once or more in a lifetime, and nearly everywhere urban populations that produce little food are booming.[1]

Development Past and Present

The less developed countries of today are not replicas of the presently developed countries when they first embarked on industrialization and industrial agriculture. Social and economic conditions are only partly comparable. As for the physical environment, much of the less developed world lies within the tropics and subtropics. Even where the climates do resemble those of regions in which industrial agriculture is well established, the interplay of environment and society creates unique challenges. Thus the agricultural landscapes of the Himalayan valleys, China, and the Koreas evolved quite differently from those of the other humid temperate regions. In places, nomads still drive their herds.

The less developed countries share many common experiences but must not be casually lumped together. A rural community of Haiti is not cut from the same cloth as its counterparts in Bangladesh or Zaire. Colonial experience varied. Scientific and technical advances that have transformed the world touch the remotest backwaters of the Third World, but the less developed countries vary among themselves in economic growth and their adoption of modern technology.

POPULATION GROWTH. During the population explosion of the 1950s and 1960s, annual growth rates in most of the less developed countries reached between 2% and 4%. The mean rate remains greater than 2% in spite of recent rate decreases in all but a few countries. The developed countries' historic peaks were substantially lower, generally between 0.5% and 2%.

The rapid population growth rates of the less developed countries, following so soon upon much slower rates, result in exceptional age structures. By the 1970s the older and younger halves of most populations are divided at between 15 to 29 years of age. By contrast, immigrants of working age accounted for much of the growth at its peak in the United States and Australia, whose populations therefore never became so young.

The less developed countries are faced with the tasks of keeping economic growth above rapid population growth and of maintaining a large, young, dependent population. Slowing growth rates now ease these burdens, but unemployment often increases as the population bulge reaches adulthood. In coming decades many countries, most notably those that have achieved the most rapid decreases in fertility, will strain to support a large elderly population.

Opinion regarding the economic advantages and disadvantages of rapid population growth swings several times. After nationalistic support for pronatal policies wanes in the less developed countries, the most prominent opinion worldwide (e.g., Kuznets, 1966, 1975) is that the developed countries benefited from their past growth, but the higher rates of the less developed countries are detrimental. Pronatalism then makes a comeback, beginning perhaps with Boserup's (1981) argument that population growth consistently fosters economic growth, particularly through its favorable effects on the domestic market and on the development of infrastructure. Others find no relation between population growth and economic growth, leading the United States delegation to the 1984 United Nations Conference on Population (Mexico City) to assert that the population growth rate has neither positive nor negative effects on economic growth.

Coale's (1986) careful rejoinder emphasizes the deleterious effects of high fertility and distorted age structures. Although granting that economic growth is not apparently associated with the annual growth rate per se, he adds that per capita income tends to rise fastest in countries with less of a bulge in the younger age categories and with lower total fertility (mean number of live births in a woman's lifetime), particularly in those countries whose total fertility declines the most from mid-1952 to mid-1982. These seemingly contradictory findings, suggesting that the economy is burdened by too many births but the burden's effect is lost in comparisons of population growth and economic growth, are in part explained by the variable effects of mortality, which tends to remain the highest (though well down from historical levels) in the poorest countries.

Although a country that vigorously and successfully enters world trade may be little hampered by a need to import food—Singapore imports nearly all its food, and other fast-developing countries of East Asia are net importers—purchased imports tie up capital, which is scarce in most less developed countries. Many less developed countries up to the mid-1960s take advantage of food aid in order to allocate resources to industrial development that might otherwise go to agriculture. Optimism about the green revolution in the late 1960s and early 1970s coincides with a renewed emphasis on agricultural development and in some countries, notably India and Pakistan, with disillusionment over the dependability and long-term desirability of massive food-aid programs.

If food production and population of the less developed countries may be portrayed as competitors in a race, food production speeds ahead during the peak years of the green revolution. Since then the race is more even, and population may even gain slightly around 1980 and again in the mid-1980s.

The worst news comes from sub-Saharan Africa, where food production per capita falls from the late 1960s on. The droughts of the Sahel and the wars in Sudan, Ethiopia, and Somalia contribute to the drop, but most countries experience some relative decline. Some observers cite government mismanagement and a continuing tendency to divert capital to industrial development as the causes, but the particular circumstances of sub-Saharan African farmers should also be noted.

At the start of the population boom, long fallow cultivation systems prevail more in sub-Saharan Africa than in any region of equivalent size. Africans thus contend with high population growth rates, progressive shortening or elimination of fallows, attendant problems of soil erosion and deterioration, and long-established preferences for staple crops that do not receive much early attention from scientific breeders and researchers.

Those less developed countries that have the densest populations in 1950 achieve the greatest agricultural productivity gains. They already have stable, sustainable systems of permanent cultivation over much of their territory, and adoption of new methods and inputs is for them a less radical departure than it is for fallow cultivators. Productivity gains are most striking in the rapidly developing East Asian countries but are impressive as well in densely populated parts of Indonesia (Java) and the Philippines. Even in Bangladesh, where the combination of a dense and growing population, sluggish economic growth, underemployment, and declining real rural incomes portend to some the fulfillment of the worst neo-Malthusian forecasts, agricultural production is a bright part of the picture, more than keeping up with population growth from 1970 to 1982 (World Bank, 1984).

THE WORLD ECONOMIC ORDER. The less developed countries enter a world market dominated by the developed countries, which by their economic and political power exert a degree of control that the newcomers cannot hope to match at this time. Not coincidentally, trade in tropical products is largely free of the combination of internal protection and export subsidization that accompanies the major agricultural commodities of the temperate zone. Efforts by producers' cartels to control the prices of tropical commodities, notably coffee and cacao, achieve no lasting success.

The less developed countries face protected internal markets and subsidized exports when they export products in competition with the agriculture or industry of the developed countries. Sugar is the best example. The sugar beet industry has never been competitive with the tropical and subtropical industry based on cane, yet large expanses under sugar beet are to be found in North America, the Soviet Union, and Australia, and the EC exports heavily subsidized beet sugar.

A frequent assertion is that the economies of scale achieved in the developed countries, most of all those in industry, have lowered real prices, making newcomers' entry into the world market more difficult. Kravis (1970), however, argues that world economic growth more than offsets these disadvantages by opening up new opportunities. Real world market prices for agricultural commodities too have fallen over the years, in large part because of productivity gains (though not necessarily economies of scale), and the decline affects less developed countries that have the potential to export wheat, feed grains, and beef.

The Green Revolution

TECHNICAL CHANGES. The high-yielding varieties (HYVs) of wheat and rice share a dwarfism trait, which prevents excessive top growth and lodging under high rates of nitrogen fertilization. Wheat varieties brought from Japan are used in breeding work in the northwestern United States after World War II, and Norman Borlaug at the Rockefeller Foundation station in northern Mexico uses some of this stock in crosses with lines selected from subtropical land races. Breeders at another Rockefeller station, the International Rice Research

Institute (IRRI) in the Philippines, work with a collection of world germ plasm, including the Taiwanese *ponlai* varieties, the source of the dwarfism gene. Breeding programs follow in other less developed countries, some to develop wheat and rice HYVs specially suited to local conditions, others to work on other cereals.

HYV adoption is rapid in particularly favorable areas. By 1970 roughly 12% of rice land in the less developed countries (excluding China) and a slightly higher percentage of wheat land is planted in the new varieties (Chandler, 1973:30–31). Subsequent spread is slower but steady, despite setbacks caused by adoption in some places that were unsuitable and by diseases to which some releases prove highly susceptible.

The impact on productivity is great. Food-importing countries become exporters, such as Mexico in the 1950s and several Asian countries in the late 1960s. Productivity gains in cereals lead those in other crops. The annual increase in root and tuber crop production in the less developed countries is about 1.1% from 1969 to 1981, about half that of cereals (USDA, Economic Research Service, 1981). The rate of growth of cereal production is close to the population growth rate over the same period, and higher if sub-Saharan Africa is excluded.

Without the needed inputs, the HYVs often yield less or hardly better than local races. The HYVs respond to fertilizer nitrogen on some of the best soils, and high application rates are usual. The need for other fertilizers is more variable, but they are often used in large quantities, and rates of application will presumably tend to increase after years of nutrient removal in the bumper crops. Seed usually must be purchased, and purchased in quantity, because dense planting is necessary to maximize gains. A dense stand requires more water than a thin one, and the water supply must be dependable. Wheat yields increase the most on irrigated land, necessitating the expansion and improvement of irrigation works. Owing to pest and disease susceptibilities, spraying is often added to the list of field operations, though breeding of resistant HYVs is now a research priority.

SOCIAL CHANGES: PROS AND CONS. The cost of joining the green revolution is a concern because the farmers have so little capital. The high yields that may be obtained often repay debts in a space of time that farmers in the developed countries would envy, but credit is hard to obtain in most of the less developed countries and was in the past often a source of peonage. The investment required to adopt the HYVs is sometimes quite small, particularly where irrigation is already adequate or natural rainfall unusually reliable, but the costs of installing irrigation are usually high in wheat fields that had been rain-fed, and they can be high in rice fields that are already irrigated. Rice fields may have to be leveled to allow control of water depth within narrow limits, because the plant does not tolerate having its head underwater for long. Regardless of starting costs, the flow of capital is greatly increased as inputs and outputs both grow. Villagers who previously subsisted, possibly made payments in kind for the use of land, and sold a little surplus now become entrepreneurs and keep books.

Farm operations need not be mechanized to gain the increased yields, but mechanization accompanies the green revolution in enough places that some commentators claim a general association (Griffin, 1974), thereby touching off a debate over cause. Mechanization is especially advanced in northern Mexico and the Punjab-Haryana, the early showcases of HYV wheat production, but in the rice lands of Southeast Asia it is generally missing or confined to small power tillers. Freebairn (1973:107) attributes mechanization to the demands that multiple cropping makes upon the scheduling of operations and to the demonstration effect from agriculture of the developed countries. Hayami (1981) avers that government policy decisions rather than the demands of the HYVs contribute to mechanization in those areas where the process is most evident, and that the process was already under way before HYV adoption. Ruttan and Binswanger (1978) acknowledge some effects on mechanization but attribute them to an increased demand for labor created by HYV adoption.

The main concern about mechanization is over its effect on employment, because few of the countries in question have a nonagricultural sector that is expanding fast enough to absorb their growing working-age population. Larger farms are better able to mechanize, so that the issue is also tied up with a controversy over the green revolution's effect upon land concentration, tenure, and farm structure. Equity is a recurring theme in all the arguments.

Mechanization notwithstanding, the new technology increases the demand for labor in its vicinity (Hayami, 1981; Ruttan and Binswanger, 1978; Sudhir Sen, 1975). Demand rises in 34 of 36 villages adopting rice HYVs in a sample drawn across tropical Asia, with the increases ranging from 10% to 50%, a trend found even in those villages where significant numbers of tractors are in use (IRRI, 1975).

The catch is that average production comes close to doubling. If the market for food remains constant, farm employment over the wider supply area should fall. Countries in fact find expanded markets through import substitution, exports, and the feeding of growing populations, but falling grain prices depress agricultural incomes in communities that continue to rely on older varieties and methods. Preexisting income gaps therefore widen between northern and southern Mexico and between the Punjab and many other parts of India and Pakistan. Higher productivity is what development is all about, and cost-price squeezes are as yet small compared with those experienced by farmers in the developed countries, but the green revolution will in hindsight look best in those countries that couple successful adoption of the new technology with enough other economic gains that the less successful participants are not pauperized.

Agricultural wages may rise with the demand for labor, as in the Punjab (Ladejinsky, 1970; Wesley, 1986) and northern Mexico. Employers and landlords do not always accept this situation gracefully, and unrest and violence follow in parts of India in the late 1960s, as workers' unions struggle against landlords' associations. The gains of hired workers and tenant smallholders are not equal to those of landowning farmers and landowners, and income gaps tend to widen (Ruttan and Binswanger, 1978). Hayami (1981), however, attributes the widening to continuing population growth and the resulting devaluation of labor.

Land concentration and land reform are issues of social design as much as of economic policy. Adoption of HYVs does not thus far cause land concentration. Apart from Chinese and North Korean communes and the latifundios of parts of Latin America, the size of holdings in most less developed countries is closer to that of Japan than of the other developed countries. Concentration is not evident after 20 years of HYV adoption in the Punjab-Haryana (Wesley, 1986) and many rice-growing areas. Land reform is of interest for its possible effect on HYV adoption, which may in turn affect the landlords' power over tenants, but evidence for the effect is thin. Generalization is difficult because of the profuse forms of smallholder tenure, including sharecropping, tenancy, customary tenure, and customary landlord-tenant obligations reminiscent of feudal Europe.

Potential sources of unequal benefit are many. Rights to water are an advantage that is not adequately documented. Access to credit is also important and has received more attention. Differences are bound to emerge in the ability to manage new technology and cash flows. Access to extension services and other forms of assistance is often unequal (Feder and O'Mara, 1981). The potential advantage of possessing substantial capital is obvious. For all these possible sources of inequality, benefits in Punjab-Haryana, though unequal, are not radically so, and absolute income increases across the board (Wesley, 1986).

One possible source of inequality that can be discounted is size of holding per se, though larger holdings may in some cases allow better access to certain critical resources, notably water. Economies of scale are insignificant in HYV wheat production in the Indian Punjab (Surjit Sidhu, 1974). Cross-national surveys of events through much of the 1970s (Hayami, 1981; Ruttan and Binswanger, 1978) find little difference between large and small farms in their rate of adoption of HYVs and associated technology. Access to water is an important and parallel issue, because large farms may be better able than small ones to benefit (Grabowski, 1981). A great increase in tube wells in the Punjab (Ladejinsky, 1970:760) allows a high proportion of farmers to benefit (Azam, 1973; Surjit Sidhu, 1974), but in the basins of northern Mexico, omitted from both of the above surveys, most adoption is indeed by large farmers who could exploit water diversions, and the slight benefit to the poor ejidos is a frequent complaint (Wellhausen, 1976).

TAIWAN: ANOTHER VIEW OF SMALLHOLDER DEVELOPMENT. Taiwan merits special attention because smallholdings survive there in the face of high and sustained economic growth. Both HYV rice and the forerunning *ponlai* varieties are widely adopted, and other forms of production are growing, particularly fruit and vegetable production for domestic and export markets.

Factors contributing to smallholder survival in Taiwan are reminiscent of Japan. The cooperative structure is strong. A propensity exists to save and invest in farms (Grant, 1972–73). Above all, unusual opportunities may be found for off-farm employment, so that part-time farming is the rule, and income derived off the farm gives farming households incomes close to those of the cities (Chinn, 1979; Griffin, 1976:269–271). Taiwanese industry comes to the farmers; decentralized industry complements agriculture, because food processing is one of the major enterprises. Farm development follows a series of land reform measures between 1949 and 1953 (Lee and Chin, 1979:86–87) that leaves most farmland in owner-operated parcels, averaging 1.26 ha in 1952 (Chinn, 1979:300). Mechanization is mainly confined to power tillers.

Repeating the Taiwanese experience would not be easy in most less developed countries. Very few have so high a rate of economic growth or such a strong cooperative structure. Off-farm employment is important in many of the countries but not often in rapidly growing, conveniently located industries. A survey of off-farm employment (Anderson and Leiserson, 1980) finds that 20% to 30% of the rural work forces of most less developed countries is primarily employed outside agriculture. The low is 12% in Brazil; the high, 49% in Taiwan. Worldwide, nearly as many rural workers draw seasonal employment in remote locations as work at nearby off-farm employment. Low's (1981) report on off-farm work in Swaziland and Lesotho concludes that distant work in South African mines suppresses agricultural productivity by drawing away needed labor.

Developing Innovative Tropical Systems

The tropical agricultural systems about to be described use industrial inputs in only moderate amounts. Up to a point, they resemble systems of the European agricultural revolution more than they resemble those of the agroindustrial revolution. In comparison with the green revolution, they are less like the grain fields of the developed countries and more something peculiar to their environment.

Before describing these alternatives, note should be taken of research strategies that could moderate the capital and energy demands of all systems, including those belonging to the green revolution. HYVs are increasingly bred for specific environmental requirements. Fertilizer management is a major research topic, with one goal being the achievement of savings across the board. Economic means of using fertilizer phosphorus are particularly needed because soils with a high capacity to immobilize phosphorus are common in the tropics and subtropics. Very high rates of nitrogen fixation have been recorded in association with several tropical legumes and might prove useful in rotations or interplanting plans.

Four broad approaches will be surveyed here: agroforestry; intercropping; the revival of raised fields, drained fields, and island beds; and pasture improvement.

Agroforestry

Agroforestry, an old strategy, is only lately a subject of scientific scrutiny, with impressive results. It is actively promoted, often as an alternative to capital-intensive and energy-intensive systems. A journal, *Agroforestry Systems,* is published.

The concept embraces two broad classes of preindustrial systems described in previous chapters: those in which crops are interplanted among trees (mixed gardens), and those in which annual crops alternate with planted fallows or tree crops. The two strategies are sometimes combined. The trees may be primarily timber or fuel-wood species, or they may produce fruit, nuts, or other foods. If the garden or field in question consists largely of food-producing perennials, *permaculture* (chapter 3) would be a more specific label than *agroforestry;* similar ecological and economic arguments are put forward under either label.

Agroforestry is often advocated as part of a development strategy emphasizing technologies of intermediate scale, on grounds that these systems are sustainable in the absence of chemical fertilizers or other costly inputs. At least some of the mixed garden systems are quite old. Those in Java go back at least 500 years (Terra, 1954), and their extent has increased greatly in the past few decades. They are thus an indigenous solution to the problem of maintaining a sustainable permanent system.

The literature frequently asserts that mixed gardens replicate the structure, or "architecture" (Michon et al., 1983), of tropical forests, which are obviously sustainable. A study of Javanese mixed gardens (Christanty and Priyono, 1979) found light interception to be almost as good as in a well-developed rain forest; only a little more light reached the ground. The common mixing of deep- and shallow-rooted species, and the high net primary productivity reported in some mixed gardens, support the assumption that the recycling of nutrients and their upward movement from lower soil horizons are sufficient to sustain the system, though these nutrient cycles are not yet well known, let alone shown to equal those of the rain forests. Javanese mixed gardens sometimes receive organic manures, which could contribute to their long history, though it is typically applied in small quantities and only around selected plants.

Agroforestry systems in general should derive some degree of sustainability from their well-established root systems and a good ground cover that reduces erosion. Inclusion of legumes and other tropical tree species associated with nitrogen-fixing bacteria might help. Some very high annual nitrogen-fixation rates are reported in association with tropical tree or shrub legumes: 904 kg/ha with *Leucaena leucocephala* (Whitney, 1975) and 897 kg/ha with *Sesbania cannabinus* (Nutman, 1976:231). Some colonial-era tree plantations were maintained for many decades without benefit of soil amendments in spite of their lack of species diversity. That agroforestry systems are sustainable in the absence or near absence of soil amendments does not necessarily rule out profitable use of amendments in larger quantities, but it is unlikely that such systems would respond to added nutrients at the levels used on HYV cereals.

The emphasis thus far in demonstration plots and promotions is more on forestry than on agriculture. Often crops are taken only between rows of young trees while a forest is established. That strategy was often used to establish rubber plantations in Southeast Asia and was developed by villagers in Pahang, Malaysia, out of forest fallow systems (Lambert, 1985). A project well beyond the demonstration stage in Lae, Papua New Guinea (Siki, 1980), aims to provide a growing urban population with fuel wood.

Systems that more permanently incorporate agriculture are attracting more attention, and United Nations University has cosponsored two international workshops on tropical home gardens, dealing in large part with the mixed home garden as a model for development in areas experiencing population pressure and a need for permanent agriculture. Given the present state of knowledge, promotion of the mixed garden in these situations is mostly a matter of transferring indigenous technology, though scientists might well have a role—for example, in choosing locations for trial and demonstration and obtaining appropriate planting material.

INTERCROPPING. Intercropping is ancient, not a casualty of agricultural modernization but a practice that makes as much ecological sense now as ever. New knowledge is needed to accommodate intercropping to mechanization and production for market. Among indigenous tropical examples, the crop mix tends to be most complex in land cleared from woody fallows, where stumps protrude and microenvironments vary, and least complex in annually cropped fields, though exceptions are readily found on both scores. One might therefore expect only monocropping on fields geared to continuous commercial production, and that has been the norm, but experiments (Nnko and Doto, 1982) show that intercropped fields under many types of management, including chemical fertilization, are more productive. When properly designed, the intercrops are less susceptible to pest and disease losses (Keswani, 1982).

Preferences for intermediate technology prompt some of the resurgence of interest in intercropping, and these systems do offer modest savings in fertilizer and pesticide costs. Row intercropping, in which rows of crops alternate, is potentially adaptable to mechanization of cultivation and harvesting and appears to be nearly as efficient as other forms.

RAISED FIELDS, DRAINED FIELDS, AND ISLAND BEDS. Efforts to reconstruct and revive the old systems of raised fields, drained fields, and island beds follow their description and mapping by geographers and archaeologists. The known area of abandoned fields is far larger than that of the few surviving examples (chapter 5). Reconstructions on Aneityum, Vanuatu (Spriggs, 1980), in the Titicaca basin of Bolivia (Mullen, 1986), and in the Mexican lowlands (Gomez-Pompa, 1978; Maier, 1979) are aimed at ascertaining the productivity of ancient systems and the potential for modern applications.

Yields, though gained without benefit of chemical fertilizers, are very high by the standards of preindustrial agriculture and compare reasonably well with those for the same crops obtained in industrial agriculture. Clark Erickson obtained a respectable harvest of 16 t/ha of potatoes at Titicaca using the muck from the ditches as the only soil amendment; nearby, dryland methods achieved yields of 2 to 3 t/ha (Mullen, 1986). Spriggs (1980) got 46 to 52 t/ha/yr of taro from island beds. These systems benefit from optimal placement of the root systems and water tables, and from nitrogen fixation and organic-matter production in the water-filled ditches if muck is moved onto the beds (chapter 5). None of the trials have run long enough to provide information on the long-term effects on nutrient levels. The Mexican chinampas have been under cultivation for centuries, but chemical fertilizers are used today and presumably account for some part of the high yields obtained.

The original systems were labor-intensive, though the amount of required labor would vary with soil, the amount of material to be moved, and other conditions. Hand labor not only maintained the fields but also built them by moving mud or clay. In the Titicaca basin a cobblestone base was laid. Denevan and Mathewson (1983) estimate that the systems of the Guayas basin, Ecuador, capable of feeding between 160,000 and 190,000 people, required 38.5 million labor days to build, or better than 200 workdays per man, woman, and child to be supported. Possibly their maintenance was no longer worthwhile once population pressure was relieved. On the other hand, descriptions of the construction of taro island beds (Spriggs, 1980) and the higher beds of the Kolepom Island swamps (Serpenti, 1965) are much less daunting. Abandonment of the precolonial systems might instead have resulted more from the breakdown of the social and political order that coordinated their development than from farmers following the law of least effort. Some past systems involved coordination of efforts over a large area, that surrounding Lake Titicaca in particular (Lennon, 1983). As for modern applications, operations could presumably be mechanized, not the least the preparation of the fields and beds themselves.

These systems could not be extended as readily as agroforestry or pasture development but could be built in many wetlands that would otherwise not be used for the same crops. The effort required to establish them probably mitigates against their rapid adoption, but trials are slowly getting larger in scale.

PASTURE DEVELOPMENT. Natural grasslands of the tropics are adapted to a lean nitrogen cycle. Fixation rates are not high relative to net primary productivity, and protein content is generally low as a result. The dominant grasses also fail to respond well to high levels of inorganic combined nitrogen, and nitrogen fertilization is not usually economical (Sanchez, 1976:540).

Yet net primary productivity is high in natural grasslands, particularly if rainfall is not limiting for too much of the year. Pasture improvement is often highly profitable, but sustainability is hard to achieve, especially in the most humid areas where the potential is greatest. Degradation of pasture, even serious soil loss, is a frequent price of development. Stable and productive systems are therefore an important research goal.

The emerging technology of pasture improvement is largely in the hands of entrepreneurs who control large tracts of land and possess substantial capital, but some of the techniques were pioneered by family farmers of the Queensland, Australia, tablelands, and smallholders use similar methods in the highlands of Kenya. The level of investment needed to establish the systems and maintain those that are sustainable varies with the environment and the strategy chosen. Initial investments are very high — and prohibitive for smallholders of the less developed countries — if forest is converted directly into pasture, but are more acceptable, though again variable, if existing grassland is upgraded. In short, a wide range of possibilities is emerging, from systems that demand moderate capital and energy to those that, if not as costly per unit of land area as the green revolution technology, are costly for the value of output and must be undertaken by large enterprises or perhaps cooperatives.

Large-scale clearance of rain forest, often by dragging a heavy chain between two construction tractors of great power, makes its conversion to beef production economically attractive, though it takes a few years to repay the initial investment. As a rule, these areas are initially more productive than grasslands produced by overcultivation and burning. Until recently, the most extensive clearance of rain forest for pasture was on the Queensland tablelands during the 1920s and 1930s, mainly for dairy production. Conversion for beef production is now widespread in Amazonia and other Latin American rain forests. Queensland's family farmers usually contracted out land clearance, but in present-day

Latin America, large estates and corporate entrepreneurs finance the task, which has been scaled up through the use of very large and expensive equipment. Forest conversion thus frequently becomes a political issue, particularly where peasant or tribal long fallow cultivators are "displaced" (a euphemism in many instances).

The humid tropics presents apposite examples of destructive exploitation and possibly also of productive, sustainable pasture systems. Numerous experiments at stations in the humid zone show that good stands can be established and maintained but thus far point to the importance of moderate to high rates of fertilization (Sanchez, 1976:550–553) and of seeding grasses that will respond. Much of the activity in Amazonia is exploitative. Seeding is the rule, but fertilizer application is a rarity. Evidence of pasture degradation abounds, and plots are typically abandoned after some years; little is yet known about forest regeneration, or lack of it, after these episodes. In Queensland's Atherton Tableland, most farmers apply superphosphate and plant grass-legume mixtures. Some pastures are thriving and productive after more than a half century of grazing, whereas others are degraded and dominated by coarse, unpalatable growth (field observations, 1980).

Techniques of improving pastures in the wet-dry tropics are better known and widely applied. The potential productivity is less than in the humid zone, but so are initial investments. Sustained production is achievable at moderate continuing cost. Application has gone far in developed countries, as in tropical Australia and some leeward areas of the Hawaiian Islands, and research is active in Brazil, Kenya, and elsewhere. One technique is oversowing grasslands with legumes; another, eradicating the stand and sowing selected grasses or grass-legume mixtures. Planted grasses are selected for their nutritive value, palatability, and response to high levels of combined nitrogen, and nitrogen fertilization is needed to maintain pure stands. If a high enough proportion of legume is present, often 20% to 30% of the cover, fertilizer nitrogen is not needed, though productivity may not be as high as from fertilized stands of grass. Requirements for other fertilizer elements vary with the soil and the efficiency with which manure is recycled if grass is removed for fodder. Superphosphate is widely applied, and molybdenum in much of northern Australia. A summary of fertilization practices is in Sanchez (1976).

Some emerging systems combine agroforestry and pasture improvement. A tree legume, *Leucaena leucocephala,* is planted in some grasslands in northern Australia. Cattle browse the lower leaves, a good source of protein. Pods fall to the ground and are eaten.

Various supplements are fed to cattle to improve weight gains. Calcium, magnesium, phosphorus, and micronutrients are often fed in small quantities in lieu of much larger quantities going on the pastures. The practice does not improve the productivity of the pastures but is often an inexpensive way to gain modest improvements in beef production. Urea, from which bacteria in the stomachs of cattle synthesize amino acids, can take the place of some protein and is then a cheap alternative to upgrading the protein content of pastures. Because efficient utilization of urea requires a diet that is high in carbohydrates relative to roughage, carbohydrates must often be fed if cattle are on rough pasture. Molasses and sugarcane tops are used for this purpose.

From a conservationist point of view, the improvement of existing grasslands, whether of the wet-dry or humid zones, is preferable to clearing rain forest or woodland. Even though productive grasslands can be carved from rain forest and maintained through fertilization, present economics makes continued maintenance after a number of years less attractive than clearing more forest, at least where forests are still extensive and land costs low. In the Queensland tablelands and the Kenya highlands, where productive grasslands have been sustained with more or less success, the climates are cooler and the industry is dairy, which repays painstaking management more than beef production does.

The holdings of graziers must necessarily be larger than those of small cultivators but need not be too large in lowland beef production, at least not in the wet-dry tropics. Oversowing legumes, sowing grass-legume mixtures, and feeding supplements are techniques of only moderate capital intensity if rents are not too high. Even more capital-intensive methods, involving heavy fertilization of high-yielding, high-protein grasses, might not confront smallholders with a much more difficult problem of management than does the green revolution. There just has not yet been much experience with this sort of development.

Research challenges are many. We need to know the long-term effects on rain forest. If and where clearance is destructive, various technical, economic, or legal means must be found to make it less attractive than establishing a sustainable, productive grassland or leaving the forest alone. Alternatively the patches of coarse *Imperata* and other grasses that dot the humid tropics, testimony to past exploitative agriculture, might be upgraded, if the process can be made sufficiently attractive.

SETTLING THE NOMADS. Governments today have two main reasons to settle nomadic pastoralists. One is political, to integrate traditionally independent peoples into the nation, a goal many researchers of development support or accept as inevitable, but one that also draws criticism (Bodley, 1982:12–122). The other motive, one cited in proposals for research and aid, is to increase productivity and income. The second motive really hinges on the first, because meaningful increases in productivity can be made only by increasing economic dependence and thereby reducing social and de facto political autonomy. Without judging these motives, this section will project what settling means for the nomadic pastoral strategy. Many case studies of sedentarization may be found in the literature, including the collections edited by the Equipe Ecologie (1979) and Salzman (1980).

Sedentarization is not new: "Nomads have been settling and resettling themselves repeatedly throughout history" (Aronson, 1980:173). Recent studies of nomadic pastoralists emphasize the strategy's flexibility, so changes should be expected. Many of the methods of settling now used by governments were tried in the 1930s on the Karimojong of the then British colony of Uganda (Dyson-Hudson, 1962) and on Siberian reindeer herders by the Soviet government. What is different today is that so much settling is going on, and little if any "desettling," and that so many governments and international agencies are involved. Wherever the nations involved are striving for unity and face mounting population pressure on land resources, pastoralists and their lands are bound to be square in the path of development efforts.

Industrial technology reaches the pastoralists' communities to a varying degree but often with minor effect on herd management and almost no effect on pasture management. Trucks can move animals whose owners adopt sedentary ways (Chatty, 1980). Same reindeer herders move themselves on snowmobiles and may relinquish control over the herds to the point that they nearly revert to a herding-hunting strategy (Pelto, 1973). Portable yurts may be found near high-rise apartments in Mongolia. How the herders can afford these products of modern industrial technology, let alone consumer goods and schools, is another matter. Reindeer herders sometimes sell meat for premium prices, and some pastoralists either find employment in the national economy or obtain some kind of subsidy, possible strategies for many in northern countries or in Southwest Asian countries that have oil revenues, but in sub-Saharan Africa or North African and Southwest Asian countries that have more Bedouins than revenues to spend on services and subsidies, efforts to settle nomads rest on a change in the pastoral strategy itself.

Intensification of production almost invariably entails sweeping changes in the nomads' relationship with the land and the herds. Sedentarization is only one of these changes. It is problematic whether or not extension agencies can bring about much change in productivity by gradually introducing new breeds or making other piecemeal changes. Past attempts to reduce the number of cattle or of male calves encountered intense cultural resistance and achieved at best only modest productivity gains.

Many yield-increasing measures favor sedentism. Because lean-season grazing limits the productivity of a herd, and sometimes dry-season water does too, tube wells and irrigated pastures can greatly increase productivity. To date, this is the main technical approach taken toward settling nomads. Silage can be made from tropical grasses early in the rainy season when their feeding quality is at its peak, and some ways have been found to make hay under certain conditions, but these techniques are in the tropics mainly promoted among mixed farmers. Mechanized haymaking is part of the settling process in areas of the USSR. Fertilization might become practical and economical under certain circumstances, though it is not a part of settling programs to date in the less developed countries. Finally, crop cultivation can be increased, something encouraged in several programs.

Where sedentarization has been brought about, reports can be chosen to demonstrate satisfactory or unsatisfactory outcomes. Most accounts indicate difficulty in introducing modest changes without effecting far-reaching social or environmental changes. For example, land around tube wells is often severely overgrazed.

If sub-Saharan African countries that have large nomadic pastoralist populations wish to achieve yields from pasturelands comparable to those obtained in the developed countries or on their own experiment stations, it is hard to imagine nomads remaining as owners and managers without prerequisite radical culture change. For one thing, the level of capital investment would be too great. The capital requirements of even modest pasture improvement are beyond the means of the nomads of the Sudan and Sahel. Irrigated pastures or hayfields are costlier still. It remains to be seen whether African pastoralists will learn entrepreneurship and evolve some form of ownership and management in which they retain control or will become workers for cattle companies, migrants to the cities, or sedentary mixed farmers.

Beyond the Green Revolution

The green revolution is being extended. High-yielding maize and sorghum varieties are among the new hybrids, a turn of great significance for sub-Saharan Africa, where there is also an expansion of wet rice cultivation. How effectively the green revolution will penetrate those large areas in Africa and elsewhere in which land tenure is still customary and with what social consequences remain to be seen. HYVs are being developed for a wider range of conditions. Much of the present focus is on varieties that achieve somewhat lesser yield increases but are more resistant to pests and diseases and less demanding of water and soil nutrients.

Genetic engineering and other advanced biotechnologies now entering the less developed countries may loom large in the near future. Their potential impact on the organization of agriculture is as yet hard to predict.

Vegetative propagation techniques already in use multiply small plant parts and promise large yield increases in root crops and some perennials, often with the help of only moderate increases in capital inputs. Improved clones and planting materials can be freed of harmful viruses by heat treatment or by culturing shoot tips and can be rapidly made available. Rapid propagation of manioc from green internode cuttings and leaf-petiole cuttings was developed at the Centro Internacional de Agricultura Tropical, Cali, Colombia (Cock, 1985). A related technique, "miniset" production of yam planting materials, developed by Nigeria's National Root Crops Research Institute and improved by the International Institute of Tropical Agriculture (IITA), is now in use by Nigerian farmers, providing gross incomes as high as $3,000 to $4,400 (U.S.) per hectare (B. Okigbo, pers. com.). Micropropagation techniques are used at IITA for the production of "virus-free" material of yam, taro, *Xanthosoma,* and sweet potato (IITA, 1985). These advances in root crops, together with some of the new maize and sorghum hybrids, could be as timely for sub-Saharan Africa as HYV wheat was for the Punjab in the 1960s. They would be appropriate for farmers who are newly turning to permanent cultivation and have some experience with fertilizers and other purchased inputs but have only limited access to capital—a description that fits many below the Sahara.

A contrasting prospect (Buttel, Kenney, and Kloppenburg, 1985) is that genetic engineering will have a major impact on Third World agriculture within the next 10 years, but major corporations will monopolize much of the technology. Emerging technologies include recombinant DNA techniques, plant cell fusion, rapid techniques of mutagenesis, and tissue culture. Possible benefits include yield increases, transfer of nitrogen fixation capabilities, enhancement of photosynthesis, and disease resistance. That micropropagation procedures are already having an effect would appear to back this part of the forecast, and all these methods are research topics at experiment stations in the less developed countries.

But the authors go on to note that the worldwide role of private companies in research of this type is very large and increasing, both directly through in-house research and indirectly through arrangements with universities. They conclude: "It is very likely that less developed countries will become increasingly dependent on technology located in developed countries" (p. 49).

The successes obtained thus far do not point in the predicted direction. One wonders how much control could be gained by being ahead in developments pursued by so many public and private agencies or how enforceable patent rights will be. It is likely, however, that Buttel et al. have raised an issue destined to be as controversial as the green revolution was 15 to 20 years ago.

Note

1. The contribution of urban home gardens to urban food supply is generally a few percent in less developed countries, though recent work (Niñez, 1985) notes their importance to many individual households as a source of cash and a source of foods that nutritionally complement purchased bulk staples.

References

Anderson, D., and M.W. Leiserson (1980). Rural nonfarm employment in developing countries. *Economic Development and Cultural Change,* 28:227–245.

Aronson, D.R. (1980). Must nomads settle? Some notes toward policy on the future of pastoralism. In *When Nomads Settle: Processes of Sedentarization as Adaptation and Response* (P.C. Salzman, ed.), Praeger, New York, pp. 173–184.

Azam, K.M. (1973). The future of the green revolution in West Pakistan: A choice of strategy. *International Journal of Agrarian Affairs,* 5:404–429.

Bodley, J.H. (1982). *Victims of Progress.* 2d ed. Mayfield, Palo Alto, Calif.

Boserup, E. (1981). *Population and Technological Change: A Study of Long-term Trends.* University of Chicago Press, Chicago.

Buttel, F.H., M. Kenney, and J. Kloppenburg, Jr. (1985). From green revolution to biorevolution: Some observations on the changing technological bases of economic transformation in the Third World. *Economic Development and Cultural Change,* 34:31–56.

Chandler, R.F. (1973). The scientific basis for the increased yield capacity of rice and wheat, and its present and potential impact on food production in the developing countries. In *Food, Population, and Employment: The Impact of the Green Revolution* (D.K. Poleman and T.T. Freebairn, eds.), Praeger, New York, pp. 25–43.

Chatty, D. (1980). The pastoral family and the truck. In *When Nomads Settle: Processes of Sedentarization as Adaptation and Response* (P.C. Salzman, ed.), Praeger, New York, pp. 80–94.

Chinn, D.L. (1979). Rural poverty and the structure of farm household income in developing countries: Evidence from Taiwan. *Economic Development and Cultural Change*, 27:283–301.

Christanty, L., and Priyono (1979). Measurement of photosynthesis in home-garden plants. Paper presented at the Fifth International Symposium of Tropical Ecology, Kuala Lumpur, Malaysia, April 16–21.

Coale, A.J. (1986). Population trends and economic development. In *World Population and U.S. Policy: The Choices Ahead* (J. Menken, ed.), W.W. Norton, New York, pp. 96–104.

Cock, J.H. (1985). *Cassava: New Potential for a Neglected Crop*. Westview, Boulder, Colo.

Denevan, W.M., and K. Mathewson (1983). Preliminary results of the Samborondon raised field project, Guayas basin, Ecuador. In *Drained Field Agriculture in Central and South America* (J.P. Darch, ed.), British Archaeological Reports, International Series, no. 189, Oxford, pp. 167–182.

Dyson-Hudson, N. (1962). Factors inhibiting change in an African pastoral society. *Transactions of the New York Academy of Sciences*, ser. 2, vol. 24, pp. 771–801.

Equipe Ecologie et Anthropologie des Societés Pastorales, eds. (1979). *Pastoral Production and Society: Proceedings of the International Meeting on Nomadic Pastoralism*. Cambridge University Press, New York.

Feder, G., and G.T. O'Mara (1981). Farm size and the diffusion of green revolution technology. *Economic Development and Cultural Change*, 30:59–76.

Freebairn, T.T. (1973). Income disparities in the agricultural sector: Regional and institutional stresses. In *Food, Population, and Employment: The Impact of the Green Revolution* (D.K. Poleman and T.T. Freebairn, eds.), Praeger, New York, pp. 97–119.

Gomez-Pompa, A. (1978). An old answer to the future. *Mazingira*, 5:7.

Grabowski, R. (1981). Induced innovation, green revolution, and income: Reply. *Economic Development and Cultural Change*, 30:177–182.

Grant, J.P. (1972–73). Accelerating progress through social justice. *International Development Review*, pp. 2–9.

Griffin, K. (1974). *The Political Economy of Agrarian Change: An Essay on the Green Revolution*. Harvard University Press, Cambridge.

———. (1976). *Land Concentration and Rural Poverty*. Holmes and Meier, New York.

Hayami, Y. (1981). Induced innovation, green revolution, and income distribution: Comment. *Economic Development and Cultural Change*, 30:169–176.

IITA (1985). *IITA Annual Report 1985*. International Institute of Tropical Agriculture, Ibadan, Nigeria.

IRRI (1975). *Changes in Rice Farming in Selected Areas of Asia*. International Rice Research Institute, Laguna, Philippines.

Keswani, C.L. (1982). Summary and conclusions [of papers on plant protection]. In *Intercropping: Proceedings of the Second Symposium on Intercropping in Semi-arid Areas, Held at Morogoro, Tanzania, 4–7 August 1980* (C.L. Keswani and B.J. Ndunguru, eds.), International Development Research Centre, Ottawa, Canada, p. 94.

Kravis, I.B. (1970). Trade as a handmaiden of growth: Similarities between the nineteenth and twentieth centuries. *Economic Journal,* 80:850–871.

Kuznets, S. (1966). *Modern Economic Growth: Rate, Structure, and Spread.* Yale University Press, New Haven, Conn.

———. (1975). Population trends and modern economic growth—notes toward a historical perspective. In *The Population Debate: Dimensions and Perspectives,* vol. 1, United Nations, New York, pp. 425–433.

Ladejinsky, W. (1970). Ironies of India's green revolution. *Foreign Affairs,* 48:758–768.

Lambert, D.H. (1985). *Swamp Rice Farming: The Indigenous Pahang Malay Agricultural System.* Westview, Boulder, Colo.

Lee Teng-hui, and Chin Yueh-eh (1979). Agricultural growth in Taiwan, 1911–1972. In *Agricultural Growth in Japan, Taiwan, Korea, and the Philippines* (Y. Hayami, V.W. Ruttan, and H.M. Southworth, eds.), East-West Center, Honolulu, pp. 59–89.

Lennon, T.J. (1983). Pattern analysis of prehistoric raised fields of Lake Titicaca, Peru. In *Drained Field Agriculture in Central and South America* (J.P. Darch, ed.), British Archaeologica l Reports, International Series, no. 189, Oxford, pp. 183–201.

Loup, J. (1983). *Can the Third World Survive?* Johns Hopkins University Press, Baltimore.

Low, A.R.C. (1981). Effect of off-farm employment on farm income and production: Taiwan contrasted with southern Africa. *Economic Development and Cultural Change,* 29:741–747.

Maier, E. (1979). *Chinampa Tropicale: Una Primera Evaluación.* Centro de Ecodesarrollo, Mexico, D.F.

Michon, G., J. Bompard, P. Hecketsweiler, and C. Ducatillion (1983). Tropical forest architectural analysis as applied to agroforests in the humid tropics: The example of traditional village-agroforests in West Java. *Agroforestry Systems,* 1:117–129.

Mullen, W. (1986). Secrets of Tiwanaku. *Sunday: The Chicago Tribune Magazine,* November 23, pp. 10–32.

Niñez, V., ed. (1985). *Food and Nutrition Bulletin,* vol. 7, no. 3.

Nnko, E.N., and A.L. Doto (1982). Intercropping maize or millet with soybean, with particular reference to planting schedule. In *Intercropping : Proceedings of the Second Symposium on Intercropping in Semi-arid Areas, Held at Morogoro, Tanzania, 4–7 August 1980* (C.L. Keswani and B.J. Ndunguru, eds.), International Development Research Centre, Ottawa, Canada, pp. 33–36.

Nutman, P. (1976). *Symbiotic Nitrogen-Fixation in Plants.* Cambridge University Press, London.

Pelto, P.J. (1973). *The Snowmobile Revolution: Technology and Social Change in the Arctic.* Cummings, Menlo Park, Calif.

Ruttan, V.W., and H.P. Binswanger (1978). Induced innovation and the green revolution. In *Induced Innovation: Technology, Institutions, and Development* (H.P. Binswanger and V.W. Ruttan, eds.), Johns Hopkins University Press, Baltimore, pp. 358–408.

Salzman, P.C., ed. (1980). *When Nomads Settle: Processes of Sedentarization as Adaptation and Response.* Praeger, New York.

Sanchez, P.A. (1976). *Properties and Management of Soils in the Tropics.* Wiley, New York.

Serpenti, L.M. (1965). *Cultivators in the Swamps.* Van Gorcum, Assen, Netherlands.

Siki, B. (1980). Food production in Lae. In *Urbanisation and Its Problems in Papua New Guinea* (R. Jackson, J. Odongo, and P. Batho, eds.), University of Papua New Guinea, Port Moresby, pp. 173–184.

Spriggs, M.J.T. (1980). Taro irrigation in the Pacific: A call for more research. *South Pacific Bulletin,* 30:15–18.

Sudhir Sen (1975). *The Green Revolution: Food and Jobs for All.* Tata McGraw-Hill, New Delhi.

Surjit S. Sidhu (1974). Economies of technological change in wheat production in the Indian Punjab. *American Journal of Agricultural Economics,* 56:217–226.

Terra, G.J.A. (1954). Mixed garden horticulture in Java. *Malayan Journal of Tropical Geography,* 3:33.

USDA, Economic Research Service (1981). *World Agricultural Situation.* U.S. Department of Agriculture, Washington, D.C.

Wellhausen, E.J. (1976). The agriculture of Mexico. *Scientific American,* 235(3):128–153.

Wesley, J.R. (1986). *Agriculture and Equitable Growth: The Case of Punjab-Haryana.* Westview, Boulder, Colo.

Whitney, A.S. (1975). Symbiotic and non-symbiotic nitrogen-fixation as viewed by an agronomist. In *Proceedings of the Soil and Water Management Workshop,* Agency for International Development, Washington, D.C., pp. 51–75.

World Bank (1984). *World Development Report 1984.* Oxford University Press, New York.

12

The Future

 Predicting the future is at once hazardous and safe, because predictions must surely be more wrong than right, but no one can now prove they err. A fun pastime, forecasting has a serious purpose. We base policy decisions on our ideas of what the future holds, ideas heavily influenced by current events. In the atmosphere of the 1970s, when world population growth seemed to portend famine, increasing crop yields was a lauded research goal, but policymakers now want a rationale, in the light of projections that agricultural commodity surpluses will be with us for some time. The best reason for predictions is that vague, unarticulated assumptions about the future flourish in their absence.

The forecaster's task is approached with trepidation. From the same clues of what the future holds, some see terrors and the collapse of society as we know it, whereas others are Panglossian. I shall be timid and present a range of possible outcomes, an approach that will not satisfy optimists, pessimists, or many specialists closely identified with particular population, energy, or food futures but will perhaps be informative.

On Optimism and Pessimism

Forecasters even more than historians owe it to their readers to state the predispositions that may color their perspective. I find optimism and fatalism plausible companions. I see the nuclear apocalypse, though perhaps not for thousands of years. Today's silos and submarines may rust away and never launch their missiles. We may ban the bomb but not the knowledge that it can be made, not likely even the blueprint. Just as I would reject a choice between imminent destruction and a permanent ban, so I would reject the restriction of future growth scenarios to the two most often proclaimed: unlimited growth or imminent curtailment.

Catastrophists caught the public's attention 20 years ago with their gloomy milestones. We have passed some by, like *Famine—1975* (Paddocke and Paddocke, 1967), and others do not now loom so large, but we should not overreact to false gloom with false cheer. The catastrophists might someday be honored for sounding the alarm but condemned for seeing only the dark side of coming decades. Many pessimists fail to recognize the breadth of options we have for feeding present or greater populations or the opportunities we have to substitute better biological management for continuing overdrafts on soil and energy resources. The optimists, particularly those quartered in economics, recognize no limits whatsoever but create paper utopias in which the laws of science are no obstacle if the price is right. We have the ability to solve present problems of population and resources, and those of maldistribution of resources and wealth, but the world is still finite. We must soon achieve a sustainable society.

The Issues

Food futures hinge on population and energy futures. Population sets energy's agenda. Worries are that population growth will outstrip renewable resources while speeding the exhaustion of nonrenewable resources, and that growing energy demand will leave insufficient time to change over to a renewable resource economy when that becomes imperative.

Apparently nonrenewable resources may in future be recycled or otherwise extended for many more years than we now envision, a plausible argument against restricting population growth or resource use, but vast amounts of energy would be required. The economy, like an organism, presently consumes low-entropy matter-energy, such as high-grade ores. Low-grade ores, dispersed wastes, and the products of wear and corrosion are high-entropy matter-energy, and much energy must be spent to exploit them.[1] Space-age solutions, exporting people to other planets or importing ores from them, would require truly fantastic amounts of energy. Nearly four decades ago, *The Next Million Years* (Darwin, 1952) made clear how much the shape of future society rests on what substitute is found for fossil fuels. Nothing today contradicts that judgment.

Population

Advocates of population control ably demonstrate that present growth rates would before too long reach impossible levels. A 2% growth rate, just over the current world rate, would in a thousand years put 1,440 people on every square meter of land and sea and would in a few thousand years more fill the known universe with a solid mass of human beings expanding at the speed of light (Ehrlich and Ehrlich, 1970:41–42). We must conclude that population has its limit.

None of this means that we are now near the absolute limit. The rate of present population growth is an immediate concern for its effect on developing economies, but some of the worst effects are in countries whose population density is low.

We could guess at the wars, famines, and draconian police-state measures that might ultimately restrain runaway population growth. Fortunately for analysis and probably for humanity, growth is slowing enough that many anticipate a stabilization of population in the next century or so. We can therefore focus our concerns by projecting various population levels at the point at which stabilization occurs. What relative stabilization will mean in the longer term—no growth, negative growth, or the historical norm of very slow growth—is another question.

THE DEMOGRAPHIC TRANSITION. The course of the demographic transition over the coming decades will determine the level at which stabilization occurs and the circumstances surrounding that stabilization. Demographers commonly portray three stages: (1) High death rates more or less balance high birth rates; (2) death rates fall, while birth rates remain high, causing growth rates to soar; and (3) birth rates fall. A fourth stage is sometimes stated and usually implied, in which low birth rates and low death rates more or less balance.

The transition is not nearly so regular when examined in particular times and places. Death rates in preindustrial populations are indeed relatively high but also variable. Mortality declines over more than 200 hundred years in Europe but falls much more sharply in the less developed countries when modern medicine reaches them in advanced form. Birth rates in many European countries begin to decline not long after death rates start down, and much later in other countries. Birth rates in some less developed countries actually rise at about the same time that mortality begins its decline, as customs of sexual abstinence and prolonged breast-feeding weaken. We are now witnessing a drop in birth rates in most less developed countries that is early in time, having begun 25 to 35 years after medicine's impact was first felt, but late in its effect, because it follows unprecedented growth. The third stage of the transition is far from complete in most less developed countries, and its completion cannot always be assumed.

POPULATION PROJECTIONS. We should approach population projections with caution. Past projections have repeatedly been wide of the mark, usually being too low.

Most projections of United States population arrive at a fairly stable level of 300 million to 350 million by the middle of the next century. The data are sound, except for probable errors in the numbers of illegal immigrants, and projection mainly involves following through indicated changes in the age structure of the population. Unknown factors that could affect numbers include future immigration policies and the course of a recent upswing in births to older women, many of whom had long delayed motherhood.

Earlier zero population growth (ZPG) is projected in most developed countries, whose "baby boom" was much less pronounced than that of the United States. East Germany's births are below the replacement rate, and the United Kingdom is barely above it (U.S. Department of Commerce, 1983). In Italy the birth rate, after falling comparatively slowly for much of this century, has nearly halved in the past 20 years. Birth rates are below replacement levels in Japan and in European Russia. Austria, Denmark, Hungary, and Germany already have decreasing populations.

A consequence of recent declines is the renewal of pronatalism, often of the nationalistic variety, in the developed countries (e.g., Wattenberg, 1987; see Teitelbaum and Winter, 1985, for a historical review), even as it abates in most of the less developed countries. The city of Paris now pays parents a monthly stipend after the birth of their third child. Italy's health minister warns, "If this trend continues, Italians will be a lost race in the next century" (*Telegraph Herald,* 1986:7E).

The downward trend in population growth in the less developed countries presently ranges from barely noticeable to a decline nearly as great as in the developed countries. For these countries as a group, population growth falls from a peak annual rate of 2.4% in 1965 to about 2% in 1984 (World Bank, 1984:63).

Forecasts of the future course of the transition depend on what influences we assign it. Contraceptive technology is generally slower to be accepted than lifesaving technology, and it follows that death rates would decline before birth rates. No population has balanced modern low death rates without contraception, and the rate of fertility decline in the less developed countries is strongly associated with the promotion of family planning by government agencies (Simmons, 1986). However, limiting births requires motive as well as means.

In the original rendering of "transition theory" (Notestein, 1945, 1953), social institutions and customs that act to maintain high fertility in the face of high mortality survive the first impact of modern medicine on mortality but gradually crumble as society modernizes. How much of the change is due to industrialization and how much to changed expectations of mortality is not always clear.

Economic development is an often cited cause of declining birth rates. One line of reasoning is that children are valued in traditional farming households for their labor contribution, with that value sometimes contingent on prevailing land use and tenure (Boserup, 1981:179–182). Development converts children into more of a financial liability than an asset (Caldwell, 1977, 1981; see Mueller, 1976, for an opposing point of view). Numerous community studies support the connection between income and conscious limitation of births, but national comparisons give a more ambiguous picture. Several countries have lowered birth rates well below the previous norm at their level of per capita income: The World Bank (1984:69) lists China, Colombia, India, Indonesia, [South] Korea, Thailand, and Sri Lanka. Reports on Thailand (Knodel, Chamratrithirong, and Debavalya, 1987) and Kerala (Mahadevan and Sumangala, 1987) in the mid-1980s reveal fertility declines across income and social class lines.

Given the many uncertainties, forecasts of future global population could hardly be expected to agree. The World Bank (1984:74–75) projects stabilization of the population of less developed countries at between 6.9 and 10.0 billion by 2100, to which might be added another 2 billion for the presently developed countries. A gloomier scenario (Meadows et al., 1972) is similar until world population reaches 7 billion in 2025, after which it declines to 4 billion by 2100, because of food shortages and higher death rates. Some projections are above 15 billion.

The world now holds 5 billion people, so the problem at stabilization will be to feed 1½ to 3 times as many. Even the ability to support 5 billion must be demonstrated and not assumed. Arguments are made (Spengler, 1971) and debated (Singer, 1971) that we are already above the population that would allow both preservation of the environment and a satisfactory living for all.

POPULATION GROWTH AND FUTURE ECONO-MIES. Some forecasters anticipate economic benefits from ZPG or very low population growth rates, but others foresee ill. Contrasting assessments of resources dominate the debate, which is as old as the industrial revolution (Spengler, 1978). What is in question is the availability and cost of resources by the time population growth stabilizes in the less developed countries. Pessimists (Meadows et al., 1972) believe that early ZPG and limits to economic growth are essential to head off a reckoning with finite resources. Optimists look forward to ready technological solutions (Kahn and Wiener, 1967). Clark (1973) and Weber (1977) argue that the demographic transition will save us from crushing togetherness, and that until then the benefits of population growth outweigh the costs.

Energy

Industry and industrial agriculture are built on fossil fuels. When these run out or we choose not to burn them, the form that energy harnessing and distribution takes will have much to do with the shape of agriculture, industry, and society. It matters how abundant energy will be, how costly, and whether we will capture it in vast reactors or dispersed solar collectors.

FOSSIL FUELS. We have burned in 200 years a sizable part of fossil fuel deposits that took tens of millions of years to accumulate. The Ford Foundation Study Group (1979:248) estimates that recoverable resources will be all but gone by the end of the twenty-second century. The study group assumes a 2% annual increase in energy consumption, which may underestimate conservation. Other estimates of resources range from about a third as great as the study group's (Hubbert, 1975) to several times larger.

Coal makes up at least two-thirds of all known fossil fuel reserves and may regain its dominant role in industry as petroleum becomes scarce. A possible wild card is oil shale; it is barely explored, but some forecasts are that ultimately recoverable resources of it might exceed those of coal. The cost of energy will probably tend to rise as the more easily won deposits are used up and if synfuels manufacture, thermal electric generation, and other conversions increase.

Continuing to burn fossil fuels has serious implications for the environment. Coal is a notoriously dirty fuel, and future use of emerging clean-burning technologies should not be assumed if past experience is any guide. Oil shale exploitation may create large spoil heaps and its own share of air and water pollution. Carbon dioxide, unavoidably released when any fossil fuel is burnt, is the worst culprit in the greenhouse effect.

The implications of the greenhouse effect for agriculture are serious.

Melting ice caps would raise sea levels and flood low-lying land. Climatic belts would shift. The worst news from the many computer projections is that climates in the next century will fluctuate wildly, making it hard for farmers to adjust; long-range weather forecasters, if accurate, could be our gurus.

A brighter side may be found. Affluence is compatible with conservation of energy and fossil fuels, raising the possibility of changing to alternative resources before we feel the worst effects of not doing so (Lovins et al., 1981). Cultivation could expand in high latitudes, though the proportion of suitable soils is small. Higher carbon dioxide levels could themselves boost crop yields (see Raising Yields, p. 320).

NUCLEAR FISSION. Breeder reactors may offer abundant energy for many thousands of years. That energy would probably be costly, and we may not really want vast number of reactors operating for that long.

The potential energy to be gained from the present generation of reactors amounts to only a few decades of world energy use. About 1% of the uranium mined for nuclear reactors presently undergoes fission. Breeder reactors would use most of the natural uranium and alternatively would use thorium. Thorium reserves and resources are often roughly equated with those of uranium, though the estimates are as much from lack of knowledge as from anything else. Breeders would multiply resources not by hundreds but by thousands, because by using more of the uranium and thorium, they would make it economical to exploit abundant low-grade ores (Weinberg, 1986) and possibly even seawater (Lidsky, 1983:35).

All the current arguments over reactors and radioactive waste disposal must be expanded several hundred times in contemplating a future breeder economy, if only because so many more reactors would be on-line. Experts disagree over the relative operational safety of present-day reactors and breeders and whether the recycling of fuel in the breeder cycle would afford special opportunities to official or clandestine makers of nuclear weapons (Willrich and Taylor, 1970).

The promise of cheap energy from nuclear reactors has faded. Breeder power might be abundant but not cheap. Even a veteran advocate of nuclear energy and breeders (Weinberg, 1986:114–115) estimates that breeder reactors, once in commercial operation, would cost half again as much as present reactors for the power produced.

The traditional defense of nuclear energy—that technology will resolve technical obstacles to the point that costs and risks are acceptable—must be geared up for the prospect of a breeder economy. Weinberg (1986:122) concludes: "[The breeder] is flawed because it is costly and may be proliferation-prone . . . but . . . these flaws cannot be overcome by human ingenuity—this I can never concede." I would only reply that human ingenuity would be taxed, and that the cost of a lapse of managerial judgment could be great.

THERMONUCLEAR FUSION. After decades of effort, informed opinion falls into two camps: one that anticipates fusion's rise to dominance in the next century, and another that doubts it will ever supply energy at acceptable cost. Reactors that might come from the main research programs would require very large, heavily capitalized installations, in order to meet the technical challenge of containing reaction temperatures of 100 million degrees Celsius. Hopes for smaller installations hinge on disposable reactors (Bussard, 1981; McColm, 1981) and the controversial "cold fusion" announced by S. Pons and M. Fleischmann.

Possible resources are almost limitless. At least their lifetime might approach that of our planet. One possible reaction would use only deuterium, which makes up 0.01% of ordinary water—a tiny proportion but a vast resource.

Compared with nuclear fission, fusion would meet with fewer valid safety or environmental objections. The cost is hard to predict amid all the uncertainties.

LESSER RESOURCES: GEOTHERMAL ENERGY, TIDES, HYDROPOWER, AND WIND. Geothermal technology traps heat that would take eons to replace, making the resource nonrenewable for all practical purposes. Foreseeable technology could produce as much energy as the world's potential coal resources (Muffler and White, 1975).

Tidal energy and hydropower cannot expand enough to meet even present needs. The tides' potential is slight except in a few favored sites (Hubbert, 1975; Merriam, 1978). Hydropower is proven, cheap at the best locations, and attractive if your lands or sacred burial places are not behind the dam. Potential generated output is about 30% to 40% of the present rate of world energy consumption (Edmonds and Reilly, 1983; Hubbert, 1975:362). Much future development will be in small generating plants, whose possibilities have not been explored as much as those of large installations.

Windpower is abundant but dispersed and variable. The World Meteorological Organization estimates resources of about 20×10^9 kilowatts on land (Ford Foundation Study Group, 1979:488), more than twice the present world energy consumption rate. The amount of useful energy that can be delivered is much smaller. Away from the most favorable sites and those where other energy sources are unusually costly, the cost of equipment and the need to store energy lead many authorities to cast windpower in a subordinate role, supplying at best a tenth of the power in a supply grid.

SOLAR ENERGY. Solar energy, which must loom large in any nonnuclear future, is tremendously abundant but dilute. That which reaches the earth's surface is more than 10,000 times 1985 world energy consumption. Values are impressive even in high latitudes, though poorly distributed through the year. The efficiency of harnessing solar energy is greatest, and the cost already competitive, where low-grade heat meets the end use. Low-grade heat is no small part of the energy budget; half the energy used in West Germany is heat at less than 100°C (Lovins et al., 1981:xxix).

Surprisingly then, most projections of a future solar energy economy feature central electrical generation, involving conversion of energy and more or less its concentration, sacrificing thermodynamic efficiency to meet end use needs for high-grade energy. Methods in comparatively advanced stages of development include photovoltaic generation, as in the familiar solar cells, and power generation from solar boilers. Less developed methods include ocean thermal electric generation, which would exploit high temperature gradients at a few tropical locations, and production of chemicals by means of photochemical reactions. The cost of delivered solar electricity is presently higher than that of low-grade solar heat, but proponents look forward to breakthroughs.

BIOMASS ENERGY AND AGRICULTURE.
Biomass energy—really solar energy captured by plants—is often put in a class apart. The efficiency of conversion is low, but so is the cost of installation. Biomass energy will here be treated at some length because of its possible special connection with agriculture. Biomass energy production could compete with food production for land and other resources, and one fear is that rich buyers of energy might outbid poor buyers of food (Brown, 1980). But usable biomass can be produced on land ill suited to food crops, say, because it is too cold or too erodible.

Photosynthesis captures about five times as much energy as the world consumes. The part of the resulting biomass that might be fuel must be reduced by excluding that which is inaccessible, below-ground growth, and grass, which is better fodder than fuel. Food, fiber, and timber uses take their share. Nutrients would have to be replaced in order to sustain maximum yields. For these reasons, estimates of potentially usable biomass-energy resources generally fall well short of meeting present or projected needs.

Research on biomass energy resources will be summarized with particular reference to the United States, a well-documented and heavy consumer of energy, whose per capita endowment of potential biomass resources is in the middle range between the haves and have-nots. Brazil and Sweden are particularly well-endowed countries strongly committed to biomass energy development.

Estimates of the amount of biomass energy that could be extracted annually in the United States by the year 2000 are 1.4×10^{15} kcal (Tillman, 1978) and 2.5×10^{15} kcal (Hewett et al., 1981:143). The latter is nearly 14% of 1983 national energy consumption. The estimations assume sustained-yield harvesting of fuel wood and widespread exploitation of municipal wastes and timber by-products but not intensively managed tree farms or the growing of starch and sugar crops for ethanol production (which is done now). Tillman estimates that the equivalent of 0.17×10^{15} kcal is available from agricultural wastes alone.

Ethanol production is attractive where pressure on agricultural resources is not too great, as in Brazil, or where new markets are needed to reduce crop surpluses, as in the United States. Some interest and experimentation in Papua New Guinea has also focused on the use of wild sago stands not presently exploited for food. Projections of the amount of ethanol that the United States can produce without harmfully detracting from food production are modest, on the order of 0.00005×10^{15} kcal per year (Flaim and Hertzmark, 1981; Meekhoff, Tyner, and Holland, 1980).

Ethanol production converts solid fuel to liquid at some cost in energy. In fermenting sugars and starches to alcohol, 11% to 14% of their energy value is lost. Distilling the ethanol may take as much energy as it contains, though advanced processes use only a fourth as much (Flaim and Hertzmark, 1981:93–94). Crop wastes are often burnt for the purpose, and solar energy could be used; low-grade heat at $80°–90°C$ is all that is needed.

A complete energy budget of ethanol production should include energy that goes into growing the feedstock. Maize production in the corn belt yields for every kilocalorie of input energy about 3.5 kcal in the form of carbohydrates that can be converted to ethanol (Pimentel, Berardi, and Fast, 1983). The by-product (spent) grains that remain after fermentation are a high-protein feedstock that can replace other feeds. Spent grains from a given volume of original maize replace 0.19 volumes of soybeans (Meekhoff, Tyner, and Holland, 1980). If the energy efficiency of soybean production is close to that of maize, and stover or waste heat fuels the ethanol stills, the gain in energy efficiency from feeding the spent grains would more than offset fermentation losses, and about 3.75 as much energy would be produced as used.

Intensively managed tree farms could achieve much higher efficiencies than ethanol production without competing for cropland. A study of United States standing forests (Garret, 1980) concludes that with better management they could yield twice the present harvest, and energy output would be 2,000 times the input. Land for this purpose cannot be too steep or too rough but need not be tillable. Competition with grazing might be more serious, especially on rough pasture. A model of intensive tree farms in Wisconsin and Louisiana (Fege, 1981) projects fuel wood energy yields of 10 to 15 times energy inputs, assuming fertilization and irrigation.

Forests and tree farms can supply liquid fuels. Industrial processes similar to those used to synthesize liquid fuels from coal can use wood instead, though not as efficiently. Ethanol can be produced from wood pulp and other materials rich in cellulose, and some researchers believe that genetically engineered fermentative microorganisms might make the process competitive with ethanol production from conventional feedstocks. Some tropical tree legumes produce sap that may be used directly in diesel engines.

Nutrients in the ash or other residues from biomass energy production might be recycled, a step that would stretch fertilizer resources and save energy. Bhagat, Davitian, and Paredes (1979) find that ash retains 21% to 32% of the potassium and 51% to 75% of the phosphorus in maize, wheat, and soybean residues. Nitrogen and sulfur are lost in burning but are mostly retained when manure and other nitrogenous organic matter are anaeorobically fermented to generate methane.

ENERGY PATHS. The choice of energy paths to be taken is nothing less than a choice of the kind of society that will exist. Lovins (1976, 1977) distinguishes between hard and soft energy paths and prefers the soft. Detractors find that preference to be out of touch with presently abundant oil supplies, or worse: technically impractical, economically ruinous, and socially utopian (Nash, 1979). Without taking sides, I would argue that the hard-soft dichotomy provides a framework in which to project alternative futures after fossil fuels.

Soft energy paths stress energy conservation and match resources and technology with end use in scale, location, and the form in which the energy is delivered. Transfers of energy are minimized. The emphasis is on renewable resources, but not all technologies that harness them belong. Lovins particularly dislikes the use of centrally generated electricity where other energy sources would be more direct, as in space heating or vehicle fueling. He would radically conserve fossil fuels and virtually do away with nuclear fission, thermonuclear fusion, solar thermal electric, solar power satellites, and intensive biomass farms.

Most portraits of a future breeder or fusion economy epitomize the hard path, as much because of the heavy reliance on electricity as the energy sources themselves. The picture is familiar from futurist projections. Electricity provides low-grade and high-grade heat, electrolytic hydrogen to power vehicles, and an endless array of synthesized electrochemicals.

Forecasts made before the 1970s assumed that hard paths must dominate energy futures. Projections of energy demand began with the premises that consumption would grow with the economy and that electricity would command an ever-increasing share of the market.

Quite the contrary happens following the oil crises. Electric generation grows substantially only where it was previously little developed. The first solar energy application to go commercial is low-grade heat supply. Energy consumption in the United States declines slightly from 1979 to 1983 (Energy Information Administration, 1986). European Community consumption rises slightly. Japan's consumption is nearly constant during the 1970s, while its gross national product grows at an annual rate of 4% (Lovins et al., 1981:xxxvi). Present world consumption rates are well below those projected in "low-growth scenarios" forecast a few years ago.

Most analysts agree that consumption can be further cut without jeopardizing economic growth. Yergin (1979) estimates worldwide cuts of 30% to 40% would not be harmful. Lovins et al. (1981) go further, arguing that even an economy as advanced as Germany's could absorb cuts of 80%. Besides conservation and so-called passive uses of solar energy, which are included as energy consumption in some accounts but as conservation in others, another factor contributing to relative savings is that per capita energy demand shows signs of saturation. New energy-using inventions continue to come out, but many new consumer items, notably microwave ovens and computers, use surprisingly little energy.

The soft path in agriculture calls for energy conservation on the farm, including low-input methods and the use wherever feasible of solar, wind, and biomass resources at hand. The hard path is a continuation of the mainstream of the agroindustrial revolution, with energy-using inputs to be applied in ever-larger quantities and eventually to be supplied through some mix of renewable resources and breeder or fusion reactors.

Contrary to an opinion of Lovins, soft and hard energy paths are not mutually exclusive, at least not in agriculture. Biological fixation might supply crops with nitrogen, clearly a soft path, while high-grade energy is spent extracting phosphorus and other mineral nutrients from low-grade ores, a situation that could come about if energy, though plentiful, were costly.

Ways to Increase Food Production

This section deals with yield-raising technology that is on the drawing boards and takes only a glance at more-distant prospects. An assumption is that the food chain still begins with crops and photosynthesis. We may someday harness fusion or solar energy to bypass photosynthesis, feeding nutrient solutions to cultures of fruiting parts of plants programmed to yield seductively aromatic melons or grapes for indescribably richly flavored wines. Then again, all that may be totally unnecessary, except to prove at great cost the virtuosity of science.

Energy must always be kept in mind while evaluating agricultural futures. We must ask not only how we can raise yields but also what it will cost. The odd plea that food production absorbs only a few percent of world energy and is somehow exempt from energy policy considerations is plainly bankrupt, because all users contribute to depletion and must pay the costs and penalties.

THE ADEQUACY OF PRESENT FOOD PRODUC-TION. Enough food is now produced to feed everyone. The hundreds of millions of chronically hungry are not a sign that we are near a limit but rather inform us of the maldistribution of wealth, and no technical breakthrough will eliminate hunger unless social conditions are improved. In 1980, a year of moderately favorable weather, world production of cereals, pulses (excluding soybeans), protein meal, edible oil, roots and tubers, sugar, apples, citrus, and bananas amounts to 4,540 kcal and 143 g protein per person per day.[2] We could add some fruits, vegetables, and nuts not in the tally, as well as honey, game, and the edible portion of about 33 g of fish per person per day.

Livestock consume about 27% of the food energy and a third of the protein in the above crops. With the help of pasture and fodder crops not counted above, they produce 89 g of dressed meat, 290 g of milk, and 18 g of eggs per person per day. The net amount thus available to humans amounts to at least 1,000 kcal and 26 g of protein per person per day.

After subtracting the net effect of animal industries and adding the uncounted food sources, the per diem food production should be more than 4,000 kcal per person,[3] about twice the minimum requirement, and 120 g protein. The discrepancy between that amount and consumption is accounted for by seed carried forward for planting, storage losses to vermin, losses in processing, and, at the consumer end, pet feeding, industrial uses, and waste. Storage losses are especially serious but are considered reducible by available means.

The best-seller *Diet for a Small Planet* (Lappe, 1975) argues that we could meet our nutritional needs with fewer livestock and consume most crops directly. The strategy, much like the soft energy path, is a product of 1970s concerns over limited resources and rising world population. Though the 1980s push *Small Planet* out of the public consciousness, the strategy is a future option.

PUTTING MORE LAND INTO PRODUCTION.

About half the world's cultivable land was cultivated a few years ago (Buringh, Van Heemst, and Staring, 1978; Foin, 1976:120; President's Science Advisory Committee, 1967). Somewhat more is now under cultivation, though estimates differ.

If we could double the area of cultivated land, duplicating the existing cropping pattern, production would increase but not double. Food now obtained by hunting, collecting, and grazing on the additional land would have to be foregone; in Australia and New Zealand nearly 98% of the cultivable but presently uncultivated land is used for grazing. Presently cultivated land tends to be better land. Little credence can be given to the uncorroborated inference of Kahn, Brown, and Martel (1976:115–116) that presently cultivated land in its raw, unimproved state was comparable to the uncultivated land of today. The history of land use shows that farmers first exploit that land which is more productive or more easily brought into production, and examples have been given throughout this book.

The cited land-use surveys count fallow land as uncultivated, and the reduction of fallows probably accounts for much of the subsequent expansion of cultivated area. We should anticipate that fallow reduction will create a demand for chemical fertilizers and other energy-using inputs. Most previously fallowed land or land formerly in fallow longer is not going into wet rice, permaculture, or other systems that readily give moderate, sustained yields without the use of soil amendments.

Much of the uncultivated but cultivable land consists of Oxisols, Vertisols, and highly leached Ultisols, soils that are prevalent in the tropics and subtropics and often present special problems of management for high yields, including the heavy traction required to till Vertisols and the capacity of many of the remaining soils to immobilize fertilizer phosphorus. The additional costs are probably not prohibitive for farmers who already use tractors or fertilizers but may be prohibitive for essentially preindustrial cultivators.

Water conservation measures and new supplies of irrigation water could increase cultivated land. Not all the added land would now be classed as cultivable, a classification that is partly based on evaluations of presently available rainfall or irrigation.

Present water-conserving techniques can be expanded (chapter 6), but the energy costs vary. Microcatchment techniques exploiting runoff would allow a limited extension of rain-fed agriculture at low energy cost. Drip (trickle) irrigation fits well with soft energy paths, at least in comparison with alternative methods of irrigation, because it conserves water without requiring too much energy to install the system. Plastic mulch films curb evaporation but are at present synthesized from petrochemicals, and their capital cost, which is prohibitive for field crop production, probably indicates that their energy costs are also high. Methods of reducing leaf transpiration are under investigation, though in an early stage. Their effect on energy demand is unknown.

The development of energy resources may cause some highly productive land to come out of cultivation. Agriculturalists in arid and semiarid lands face growing competition for water from nonagricultural users. Not the least of likely future competing uses is energy resource development. Oil shale, coal, and tar sands development in the western United States, if it goes ahead, will almost certainly divert water away from agriculture (Pimentel et al., 1982). Experience tells us that industrial water consumers outbid agricultural users.

Desalted seawater could add to cultivated dry lands but only by multiplying energy costs. Proponents (Weinberg and Hammond, 1970) assert that capital costs will be acceptable for the production of staple field crops, a judgment based on a prediction of cheap and abundant energy, apparently from breeder or fusion reactors. Using their estimate of the highest attainable energy efficiencies in the desalting process and well-known minimum water requirements for grain production, I calculate that 1.71 to 2.15 kcal would be added to the cost — now a fraction of a kilocalorie—of producing each kilocalorie of grain. The water would then be pumped, a staggering escalation of energy costs if inland basins were exploited. Growing crops for fuel would of course be counterproductive.

Irrigating with seawater would demand much less energy. Onshore mariculture has a checkered history, but progress is being made. Algae culture is feasible, but for the immediate future, fish or other secondary producers are more acceptable products. An ideal soft-energy, biotechnic approach would be to irrigate croplands with seawater, either by growing familiar crops modified for salt tolerance or by developing salt-tolerant (halophilic) desert plants for food or livestock feed (Hodges, 1980). Some promising halophiles have been identified.

RAISING YIELDS. Presently available means of increasing yields are not used to the fullest possible extent. In much of the less developed world large yield increases are still obtainable with present technology or minor adaptations thereof. That farm subsidies boost productivity in the developed countries is evidence that means are at hand to raise yields.

A productivity gap exists within the developed world between land-rich and land-poor countries and between average farm and test plot. Methods like intercropping, multicropping, catch crops, and relay intercropping, which are widely adopted in Japan and some less developed countries of East Asia, are utilized less in Europe and hardly at all in North America and Australasia. Most of the present discrepancy between United States and EC fertilization rates is due to differences in the use of fertilizers on pastures and hayfields; grassland productivity in North America and Australasia could be substantially higher.

Several reports list promising technologies that are under active development or foreshadowed by present research (Avery, 1985a,b; Frey, 1984; National Academy of Sciences, 1975; Office of Technology Assessment, 1977, 1986; Paarlberg, 1985; Revelle, 1976; Touchberry, 1984; Wittwer, 1974, 1975). After eliminating those that are not really new, such as intercropping, the list is still impressive. Some are close to realization. The same moisture-conserving techniques that can be used to extend irrigation may also be used to boost yields where moisture is limiting. Twinning in cattle may be mastered and applied to reduce the part of the herd kept for breeding. A major leap is anticipated during the next few years in milk production and associated conversion efficiency.

Conventional plant breeding still promises some gains, though at some point continuing improvements must come out of genetic engineering. Plant explorers and breeders have now tapped much of the gene pool of the land races of most crops (Harlan, 1966, 1975; Jensen, 1978), though some further combinations of traits will prove advantageous. One goal is to improve upon photosynthesis (Carlson and Palacco, 1975; Zelitch, 1975), but gains thus far are slight even in the laboratory. As for genetic engineering, few have yet been transferred in higher plants, and most agricultural applications in the near future will exploit microorganisms.

New materials and engineering improvements promise to bring down the costs of greenhouses and hydroponic systems. The latter systems can be built on almost any accessible land. Extremely high yields of tomatoes and some other high-value crops are now obtained year-round in hydroponic greenhouses. No technical obstacle stands in the way of repeating this success with field crops, but capital and energy costs will not likely come down enough to make it economical unless population growth makes it necessary. In that event we must hope that cheap and abundant energy will be available.

Carbon dioxide enrichment of the atmosphere around a crop increases photosynthesis under the right conditions and may be another way to raise yields. Enrichment stimulates growth for a time in many plants, and some commercial greenhouses now find it profitable to enrich carbon dioxide to three times the atmospheric level (Cooper, 1982). The effect is greatest if other factors are not limiting, except that enrichment seems to improve the efficiency with which crops use water (Paez, Hellmers, and Strain, 1984; Wittwer, 1982), and to stimulate growth under reduced light (Wittwer, 1982). The heightened response often slows or stops as starch accumulates in the leaves, and the net effect of carbon dioxide enrichment on dry-matter accumulation varies. Yields of dry matter and of useful plant portions appear to increase the most in determinate plants (those that cease growth while fruiting) and plants with a C_3 photosynthetic pathway, including wheat, cotton, and soybean. Boosts of 40% to 50% have been obtained with carbon dioxide concentrations 3.5 to 4 times that of the normal atmosphere (Kramer, 1981).

Atmospheric carbon dioxide concentrations are projected to be twice the present concentrations by 2050. We must wonder if gains would offset or exceed losses from climatic change and rising sea levels.

ENERGY CONSERVATION. Emerging technologies promise to save energy while maintaining high yields. A paper in the USDA's 1980 *Yearbook of Agriculture* (Frye and Phillips, 1980) calls the 1970s the peak years of energy consumption in United States agriculture. Reduced tillage methods are presently having the most effect (Phillips and Phillips, 1984), but other savings are attainable. Prospects of low-input agriculture in the developed countries should improve as some new technologies become available, and less developed countries need not regard present rates of energy consumption in industrial agriculture as the unavoidable price of development.

Cultivation of perennials can save on energy used for traction and cultivation. Research on tree crops lags, in part because it takes so long to achieve test results or breed new varieties, but there is some renewed interest. Perennials have good yield potential. At least one, sugarcane, has a C_4 pathway. Temperate zone tree crops intercept sunlight efficiently over a full growing season, because they quickly extend their ground cover in the spring. Wood makes up much of the biomass of tree crops, whose future may therefore be bound to biomass energy production. Most people are now accustomed to diets based largely on annuals, and the world market for many fruits and vegetables is already glutted. New foods from tree crops and new uses are possible. Besides their use as human food, *Leucaena* and other tree legumes are being widely investigated as fodder in the tropics, and Hampshire College of Massachusetts has a research project that is growing alders for fuel and fodder.

Besides tillage, nitrogen fertilizers constitute the largest energy input into industrial agriculture. Their replacement by biological nitrogen fixation is a possible way to achieve large energy savings (chapter 10). Other research on biological nitrogen-fixation focuses on augmenting rates, maintaining fixation in the presence of high levels of combined nitrogen, and transferring the trait of symbiotic association with nitrogen-fixing bacteria to crops that now lack it. Interest in the latter approach was stimulated first by the discovery of fairly high rates of nitrogen fixation by bacteria growing in association with certain tropical grasses (Döbereiner, 1978) and then by recognition of the possibilities of genetic engineering (Hardy and Havelka, 1975). Bacteria associated with sugarcane already contribute combined nitrogen in Brazilian fields at annual rates that may be as high as 50 kg/ha, and some varieties of cane retain this property even when fertilizer nitrogen is also applied (Ruschel and Vose, 1984).

Carbon dioxide enrichment might increase biological nitrogen fixation. Several legumes responded for short periods to carbon dioxide enrichment in greenhouses, and nitrogen fixation rates increased as much as 570% (Wittwer, 1974).

Nitrogen fixation uses energy, but plants spend roughly as much to assimilate the same amount of combined nitrogen from the soil (Hardy and Havelka, 1975). On a different front but toward the same end, the energy efficiency of nitrogen fertilizer manufacture is improving.

323

Possibly, biological nitrogen fixation will meet all or most nitrogen requirements at whatever yield levels become necessary. The methods are far from proven, however. Biological nitrogen sources would be preferred to industrial synthesis in a soft energy path, and in a hard path if delivered energy is expensive. Cheap and abundant energy could favor chemical fertilizer nitrogen regardless of the effectiveness of biological nitrogen fixation.

The Near Future

Agricultural commodities presently glut world markets, with every prospect that the situation will continue. Supplies will fluctuate as always, and a run of wars, climatic anomalies, and other setbacks could conceivably produce several short years in a row, but a combination of factors combine to make overproduction more likely during the next few decades: the continuing spread of proven methods; new or forthcoming yield-raising technologies; traditional exporters who are determined to maintain their market share; a leveling-off of world population growth; the potential of the tropics; and a growing list of less developed countries that are changing from chronic food importation to net exportation.

The exporting nations are caught in a spiral of subsidies and overproduction. The United States and the EC try to hold domestic prices while bidding against one another in world markets. A review of the effect of world markets on United States farmers (Avery, 1985a, 1985b) concludes that technical improvements and slowing growth in the demand for basic commodities will keep exporters in keen competition, making it difficult to dismantle subsidy programs. The current trend is for less cropland to be used to support affluent Westerners, who are eating less meat now than they did a few years ago.

More of the less developed countries will join the ranks of exporters or at least reduce imports. We have seen India and Pakistan mount drives to end famine and overshoot the mark, becoming exporters. In China, following the economic reforms of the late 1970s, agricultural output rose 54% from 1978 to 1985, and 43% per capita (Nohre, 1985:125). Many less developed countries view import substitution in basic agricultural commodities as politically desirable, because it frees them from aid commitments, and as economically desirable, because capital is freed or jobs created. On-site research is growing in the tropics, and more yield increases can certainly be anticipated.

If any meaningful new markets are to be found for agricultural products, the buyers are likely to be the growing middle classes of the less developed countries. That group could have a large and salubrious effect on world markets and are a plausible market for the presently besieged farmers of the developed countries. The catch is that these countries need ready access to Western markets in order to prosper and increase their buying power.

Meat and dairy products are good prospects for export to the less developed countries. Even thinly populated countries may be less interested in achieving independence in meat than they are in self-sufficiency in cereals. Dairy products are not now produced as efficiently in the tropics as in cooler lands, though research could conceivably change matters.

The growing and diversifying flow of tropical fruits to the temperate, developed countries could be matched by a reverse flow of temperate zone fruits. Although Brazilian producers of orange juice concentrate are gaining a share of the United States market and would no doubt do better were it not for import restrictions, United States apple growers have tapped tropical Asian markets where import restrictions have been relaxed (Sindelar, 1985). The catch for northern growers is that breeders can more readily adapt temperate zone fruits to a lack of winter dormancy than give winter hardiness to tropicals.

Growing markets for luxury commodities will benefit a few farmers. Those who find such a market can do well indeed. Ginseng, a slow-growing medicinal herb valued in East Asia, is a boon for some in the American Midwest, but the acreage committed does little to relieve the glut of maize. Some United States growers of wine grapes did well during the wine boom of the 1970s by planting premium varieties, but too many growers jumped on the premium bandwagon, and prices accordingly came down.

Energy farming is widely touted as an outlet for excess production. To date this largely takes the form of ethanol production from surplus grain, but cropland could be put into woodland if the use of fuel wood were sufficiently expanded. So long as oil prices remain low, most such efforts will probably continue to depend on subsidies.

Substitutability and Resources for Agriculture

Optimists and pessimists dispute the substitutability of abundant resources for scarce ones. Optimists anticipate an age of substitutability in which "society would be based almost exclusively on materials that are virtually unlimited" (Goeller and Weinberg, 1976:683). Cheap and abundant energy would expedite recycling, substitution of low-grade ores for high-grade ores, and substitution of one element for another. Pessimists downplay low-grade ores (Cloud, 1968) or label vanadium, tantalum, tungsten, molybdenum, and helium as scarce "mineral vitamins" that industry must have to function properly (Ehrlich and Ehrlich, 1970:59).

My own position is one of guarded optimism. The "mineral vitamins" are dubious. Helium can be isolated from the air with presently available technology. The others go into metal alloys but hardly seem indispensable. Other alloys exist, and carbon fibers head a growing list of substitutes for metals in many applications. On the other hand, the exploitation of low-grade ores and atmospheric helium demands extra energy. So does recycling in many instances, particularly if the goal is to approach 100% recycling of materials that tend to be scattered in their end uses. In Goeller and Weinberg's model of the coming age, twice the present world population would use 12 times as much energy.

Agriculture's need for peculiarly nonsubstitutable elements tempers my enthusiasm. Huge expenditures of energy would be needed to exploit low-grade ores of fertilizer elements or to recycle them before agriculture disperses them to lower soil horizons and the sea. One optimist's argument unintentionally reveals this as the Achilles' heel of the age of substitutability. Wilfrid Beckerman (1974:188) blames his grandfather for not discovering "beckermonium," the element that is absolutely essential for society as we know it. His message is that industry might have grown dependent on beckermonium but instead does very well without it and will manage perfectly well without other elements if and when it becomes necessary. But plants and animals accept few substitutes. A critical scarcity of an essential element would necessitate redesigning them or bypassing them through industrial synthesis of food. To reply to Beckerman, if all living things have a minimum daily requirement of "vasium," we really are in trouble.

Phosphorus is by far the scarcest macronutrient in relation to fertilizer demand. The other macronutrients are not only abundant in high-grade deposits but are also good candidates for separation from crustal rocks or the sea.

Micronutrients, by definition needed in small quantities, are obviously no problem if, like iron, zinc, and chlorine, they are also abundant. Molybdenum might be the micronutrient most likely to come up short, because of its relative scarcity, widespread use in fertilizers, and competing uses in industry.

Goeller and Weinberg (1976) recognize the difference between industrial and agricultural requirements and give special attention to phosphorus and some micronutrients. They do not place reliance on very low-grade phosphorus ores—the earth's crustal rocks average only 0.12% phosphorus (Cathcart, 1980:1)—and I would add that seawater is not a viable source, because phosphorus often limits primary production in the oceans. They estimate that known or projected phosphorus resources would last at least 1,300 years at present rates of consumption, and that speculative resources are "very large." Other estimates project exhaustion in anywhere from 90 years (Institute of Ecology, 1971) to about 5,000 (Emigh, 1972).

Goeller and Weinberg (1976:684) would ultimately solve the problem through recycling: "Phosphorus can hardly be regarded as inexhaustible. This led Wells et al. many years ago to imply that ultimately we shall have to recycle bones for fertilizer, and we are in no position to refute this view. . . . In the long run, we shall undoubtedly have to return agricultural and animal wastes to the soil, particularly for the trace elements with limited resources, such as copper, zinc and cobalt."

In reality, no such reserve of now squandered wastes exists. Ninety percent of animal manures in the United States is already returned to the soil (USDA Study Team, 1980:36–37). Most other agricultural wastes are returned. Bones are a slight resource, and those from central meat-processing plants are already ground up into meal and sold for fertilizer. Efficient recycling of phosphorus is in any event singularly difficult to achieve, because so much phosphorus is immobilized in the soil, and so little removed in the crop.

When high-grade phosphorus ores are depleted, or those of another essential elements if that happens first, we will have these options:

1. Rely on low-grade ores at a high cost in energy.
2. Achieve a closed cycle of food production and utilization—say, by coupling waste disposal to hydroponics—and make up small deficits from low-grade ores.
3. Synthesize food or genetically redesign plants and perhaps livestock to do without, in either case supplying the element directly to humans from eked-out resources.
4. Settle for the best sustained yields that might be obtained in field

agriculture through waste recycling and releases of the element from soil parent material.

The choice among these options is governed by population and energy futures and to some degree by technical innovations that are yet to be made. The options are not mutually exclusive, except that option 1 is most likely if the others fail to meet needs. Deployment of options 1 and 2 rests on abundant energy supply; deployment of option 3, on radical technical breakthroughs.

The fourth option deserves special consideration as the line of least resistance. We should be able to do without fertilizer phosphorus and still obtain yields above preindustrial standards, how much above we cannot now say. Applicable research is scarce, for example, on crops that grow in association with mycorrhizae that make more soil phosphorus available; sweet potato comes to mind. Possibly, genetic engineers will transfer the trait to more crops.

The Sustainability of Future Agriculture

An agricultural system is sustainable if satisfactory yields can be indefinitely obtained without irreparably damaging its environment. A system is not sustainable if its continuation causes destruction, abandonment as yields fall to uneconomical levels, or a forced shift to a different system. Damage to the soil or other essential part of the ecosystem may be reversible or not. Reversible damage is a signal that something must be done differently; irreversible damage, that it is already too late.

That a particular system is not sustainable does not always mean that no system is sustainable in the same environment at the same or higher level of production. We have seen that low starting population pressure in less developed countries thus far makes worse the strains of feeding a rapidly growing population. The environmental threat created by the elimination of fallows could yet be met by intensification into systems that are both productive and sustainable. Those more intensive systems that readily absorb industrial inputs—tropical Asian wet rice farming in particular—may in a few decades be faced with the harder task. In one projection, only 0.08 ha of cultivated land will remain per person in Southeast Asia, half that at present (Revelle, 1986:165).

At least three approaches may be taken to grow more food by

sustainable means. One is to introduce yield-raising innovations into existing, sustainable systems. Introduction of high-yielding perennials into a permaculture system is a good example. A second approach, illustrated by the adoption of reduced tillage methods in the corn belt, is to correct specific practices that cause environmental deterioration. The third approach, what must be done on so much land below the Sahara, is to take on a wholly different system that is sustainable and meets needs.

Existing know-how, whether centuries old or learned but recently, is preserved and relied upon in the first approach and modified in the second. In the third approach, existing knowledge may be either a resource or an obstacle to the introduction of new technology.

Industrial agriculture is especially prone to falling into nonsustainable forms, but that outcome is avoidable. Soil erosion is the greatest threat. Soils can also suffer declining organic matter and deterioration of their structure or other physical properties. The reversibility of these effects varies and is not well known in many situations. Appropriate management can raise organic matter if water is not too limiting. Some physical changes, those caused by soil compaction in particular, take land out of production, but neither their reversibility nor their long-term cumulative effects are well known.

Rates of soil erosion from farmland in the United States, when averaged over all cultivated land, point to irreplaceable losses (Brown, 1981a, 1981b), but especially erodible land loses a disproportionate share, whereas vast areas are not seriously affected. Nor has the loss been uniform over time. Timmons (quoted in Batie and Healy, 1983) calculates that the average acre of Iowa cropland lost 21.1 short tons (47.4 t/ha) of soil 1949, 14.1 in 1957, and 17.2 in 1974, the last year one in which high commodity prices encouraged cultivation of marginal land. Reduced tillage methods can cut erosion 50% to 90% (Timmons, in Batie and Healey, 1983), and terracing, tie-ridging, and other methods are effective. Authorities have long urged other uses of the more erosion-prone lands, but either high market prices or subsidization encourages their cultivation. Fuel wood farming or permaculture could offer profitable alternatives in some futures.

Loss of soil built up over thousands of years is on its face a serious matter, and continued soil loss at rates greater than soil formation must ultimately destroy any soil's productivity, but the immediate consequences are far greater in some places than others. Some deep loess soils in western Iowa have lost up to 2.1 m with little effect on yields, and many badly eroded midwestern fields continue to give full yields if sufficient water and nutrients are available. Experience in the Southeast is that fertilizers cannot wholly make up for the loss of topsoil (Poincelot,

1986:138). In deep but eroding soils, plowing reaches previously untilled layers, mixing in essentially the same soil but with a lower organic matter content, requiring at the very least extra fertilizer. In other places, subsoils have low water-holding or cation exchange capacities, contain toxic amounts of aluminum ions, or are bare rock, and damage is serious and irreversible. Worldwide, deep soil profiles that can long withstand loss are exceptional.

The United States Department of Agriculture compares a value, T, "the maximum rate of erosion that can occur on a soil without reducing the soil's capacity to support sustained economic production" (USDA, 1987:4–5), with observed erosion rates, in order to estimate how much land is being used in a sustainable fashion. Sustainability is judged under projected "long-term" use, but not from the rate of soil formation, which is usually unknown, and critics estimate that many soils with rates of loss below T will begin to lose productivity in less than a hundred years (USDA, 1987:4–6). That T is greater on deep soils than on shallow ones suggests that the value exceeds the equilibrium rate at which soil formation would balance loss. Values on cropland range from 1 to 5 short tons per acre, or 2.5 to 12 t/ha (USDA, 1987:4–5).

Erosion exceeds T on 40% of cropland in the United States and is twice T or higher on 23% (USDA, 1987:2–3), but much is avoidable. Of the 175 million ha now under cultivation, about 20% cannot be economically cultivated without exceeding T. Rates on another 64% can be kept under T with known, economic conservation measures; nearly half the land at risk is not currently being managed up to that standard, accounting for most of the land on which T is being exceeded. The USDA's outlook is upbeat, in part because of continuing adoption of conservation measures, mainly from their projection that commodity gluts will force marginal land out of cultivation; higher demand or lesser yield increases on prime land would keep marginal land under the plow. Some highly erodible soils, notably many under wheat in the Palouse, give an excellent return and are not marginal in that sense.

Not only future agriculture but also its supporting systems must be sustainable. To my mind, the latter would pose the greater challenge in a high-population, high-energy future. For example, exploitation of vast granite deposits to supply uranium to breeder reactors would create spoil heaps of prodigious dimensions.

Two Estimates of
World Carrying Capacity

Numerous estimates exist of the maximum population that the world can feed (Blaxter, 1986:89–91). Two (Buringh, Van Heemst, and Staring, 1978; Klimov, Listopad, and Ustenko, 1971, cited in Kovda, 1980) are especially worth citing, because they allow for variation in climate, land capability, and resource inputs. Different working assumptions lead to quite different estimates, but both studies point toward a capacity to feed many times the present population.

Klimov et el. estimate that land under cultivation in 1970 could feed 14 billion people if all available technology were applied. To reach this level would require a massive transfer of technology, in particular to the less developed countries. However, we have in 1992 some means of achieving substantial yield increases without spending quite as much energy as seemed necessary in 1975.

Buringh et al. estimate that the "world's absolute maximum food production" could feed more than 160 billion people. Assumptions include the continued prevalence of field agriculture, yields that are very high but within the photosynthetic capacity of present crop plants, something of a *Small Planet* strategy, and environmental modification on a vast scale to provide abundant water to crops and allow extension of the cultivated area. A card-carrying optimist might arrive at an even higher "absolute maximum" limit, by assuming some future technology such as culture of cells genetically engineered for high photosynthetic efficiency or food synthesis using fusion energy.

Though these projections illustrate very well that options remain to grow more food, their optimism must be reined in if we look far into the future. Neither study really addresses sustainability; both estimate the world's technical carrying capacity, not its environmental carrying capacity. Feeding 14 billion people indefinitely would require much more effective conservation measures than are now used, and feeding 160 billion would, according to Kovda (1980:5), take "enormous quantities of irrigation water, large investments in soil reclamation, etc.," not to mention huge amounts of fertilizers. Aquifer depletion, competing demands for water, and the costs of preventing salinization are already slowing further development of irrigation; little net expansion is anticipated in the United States during the rest of this century.

The higher estimate is obviously linked to an assumption of abundant energy. Even the lower figure, if met by presently available means, would entail a large increase in the amount of energy allotted to agriculture, but energy-saving technology now under development or on the drawing boards could partially alleviate that requirement.

Ehrlich and Ehrlich (1970; also Ehrlich, 1982) argue with some passion that we are already well above the world's carrying capacity, on the grounds that species extinction is an inevitable consequence of human population growth and exploitation of land. Nature reserves on their present scale are inadequate to prevent its happening, and those extinctions will lead to the destruction of indispensable "ecosystem services." A tremendous acceleration of extinction is taking place, a loss of the world that we have known, but the judgment that we threaten our own survival in this way appears to me, like the mineral vitamins, another instance of confusing value with indispensability.

Regrettably, we can probably get away with greater extinctions than we have already wrought, favoring those species that survive in limited ranges and in habitats altered by human intervention, by drawing services from the survivors. The regret is that our acts will constitute interference without precedent. We shall miss our victims, but their extinction will not lead us to our own mass grave. Our path is an extreme extension of the process begun in the early Holocene, when we came to rely on species already favored by our intervention, the weeds of habitation, for example. Now we come close to managing, as much without intent as with, the global environment.

The possibility always remains of some colossal error. We have warnings: the creation of holes in the ozone layer and the releases of substances whose toxicity we underestimated.

Samples and Glimpses of the More Distant Future

We make the future but can barely guess the consequences of our actions. Informed opinion establishes a range of likely outcomes of population and energy, but mainly for the not too distant future. Most projections of a stable world population in the next century fall well inside the 14 billion of Klimov et al., and many are well under 10 billion. More yield-raising innovations are on the way, but the requirements of feeding that many people and the kind of society that will meet those requirements are things we should ponder. The more distant future is unclear. Stabilization is really relative, only the end of runaway growth, and by A.D. 3000 we might number 40 billion or 2 billion. We do not know what kind of energy futures lie ahead. Given these uncertainties and the various possible solutions to the phosphorus problem, any number of food production futures could be projected. Pleading artistic license more than prescience, I offer a few. Unforeseen technology is not taken into account, an inescapable omission that makes my projections probably more applicable to the next couple of centuries than to A.D. 10,000, but possibly not; if we achieve a truly stable population and an economy based on renewable or virtually inexhaustible resources, we might take our food production technology for granted and dwell on other creative outlets.

LOW POPULATION, LOW ENERGY. The challenge, if population and energy consumption are both scant, is to substitute technology and management for energy and, if the economy is not to regress to a preindustrial state, for labor. Prescriptions include the soft energy path and painstaking design of agricultural ecosystems.

Tree cropping saves labor and energy spent in tillage, planting, and weed control, more than offsetting the extra demands of the harvest, which would probably be more mechanized than it is now. Tree products might be processed to substitute for other familiar foods, and tree crop feeding systems could supplement pastures. Nuts are a versatile and storable food. Many promising legumes supply seeds and edible pods, and the foliage of many is satisfactory fodder and may to a degree be browsed or cut without substantially reducing seed and pod yields. Some possible combinations might be carob and oak in mediterranean climates, honey locust with native nuts in eastern North America or East Asia, and *Leucaena* spp. and ramon (*Brosimum alicastrum*) in the tropics. In semiarid hot lands, *Prosopis* spp. might grow with a grass understory.

Annual crops, including cereals, roots, and tubers, would be grown mainly for human consumption, because energy costs would drive up their price. Biological fixation would supply virtually all the nitrogen taken up by crops.

If demand for animal products warranted intensive pasture management, nitrogen-fixing legumes might be interplanted or undersown or fodder grasses engineered for high yields and symbiosis with nitrogen-fixing microorganisms. Cropping might be carefully controlled, and tree crops used to supplement pasture in the lean season. Or management might be more casual if per capita demand for these products does not grow much.

If available phosphorus resources become scarce or too low-grade to allow extraction without expending prohibitive amounts of energy, the remaining phosphorus fertilizers would presumably be allocated to those uses that would most directly benefit humans. These would be mainly crops for human consumption, along with aquaculture, which is generally an efficient user of fertilizer phosphorus. Pasture and feed and fodder crop systems would receive a lower priority; managed woodlands, the least of all. The last restriction would constrain biomass energy production.

HIGH POPULATION, LOW ENERGY. By high population is here meant a level higher than projected stabilization levels, perhaps close to Klimov's 14 billion.

A *Small Planet* strategy must be assumed if sustainability is to be achieved. Crops for human consumption would occupy all conceivably cultivable land. Despite mechanization, some labor would be absorbed in managing soil erosion on marginal land. Biological nitrogen fixation would have to support high yields, unless industrial nitrogen fixation were both energy efficient and run by renewable energy. Livestock would be limited to those that could be fed from crop residues, the by-products of food processing, and pastures of reduced extent, and their total contribution to the diet would be small.

Fruit and nut production might cluster on uncultivable soils, sacrificing some productivity, unless yields on cultivable land were comparable to those of the field crops. Grapevines are attractive. The highest reported dry-matter yields from the fruit alone are close to 10 t/ha/yr. Smaller but acceptable yields are obtained on many stony or thin hillside soils. Frequent fare might be a loaf of fortified nut bread and a jug of wine.

Substitution of labor for energy is probable, but management and technology should prevent our having to revert to the drudgery so often evident in involuted forms of preindustrial agriculture. The making of herbicides does not now consume much energy, and more-selective compounds might well be used in extremely small quantities. Integrated pest management could reach a state in which timely, well-chosen control measures replace nearly all chemical controls with only small expenditures of labor. Traction might be cut to a bare minimum.

If Lovins et al. (1981) are correct about how much energy we can save and still have our affluence, a society could arise that eats lean yet enjoys diverse consumer goods and advanced media and information systems: "Have the robot check the meat ration and maybe throw a few grams into the beans and rice."

HIGH ENERGY. High-energy strategies would be a necessity if population reaches very high levels. They might also be an option for a smaller population if energy is cheap as well as abundant.

At moderate population levels a fusion or breeder economy could lead to a sharp division of the landscape into areas of concentrated production and those of minimum environmental impact, but ways would have to be found to confine the environmental effects of the reactors, including waste heat and radioactive by-products. A corridor of industry and power generation could extend from Portland, Maine, to Richmond, Virginia, with food production in a narrow adjacent belt and open forests beyond, from upstate New York and Maine to West Virginia and the Blue Ridge. At very low population densities, those produced by a decline after ZPG, perhaps New York City's Staten Island would again be agricultural and most of New Jersey a wildlife refuge.

The same population levels that would produce high population pressure in a low-energy scenario would generate moderate pressure if energy supplies were abundant. Crops and field patterns might still be familiar, but large quantities of energy would be devoted to industrial nitrogen fixation and eventually to the extraction of phosphorus and molybdenum from low-grade ores. Production systems might also be mechanized on a scale well beyond today's.

Higher population pressures would force the development and adoption of extravagantly energy-intensive food production systems. Irrigation with desalted seawater, protected cultivation on a massive scale, hydroponics, and drastic alteration of lands now classed uncultivable are among the possibilities that would have to be plugged into abundant energy sources.

Choice and Chance

One cannot write a conclusion to the future, but a contrast is in order between the ability of past peoples to shape history and the abilities of ourselves and our descendants. As was stressed so often regarding past "revolutions," historical paths turn most dramatically when the actors are only carrying on business as usual. Planning is a fact of today's world, the current popularity of laissez-faire rhetoric notwithstanding. Population programs do more than just wait for the demographic transition to run its course. We do not have a free energy market. Research is a form of long-range planning, and present strategies are at this moment establishing the future options for agriculture and industry. Present policies are shaping future environments, whether by subsidizing soil erosion or setting the pace of energy consumption and the greenhouse effect.

Our planning thus far is not long-range, however. Neither we nor our descendants are likely to gain such control over the future as to avoid the long-term dominance of unintended consequences over intended ones, but business as usual is increasingly a luxury that the world cannot afford. Our ability to destroy is just too great. We are determining population levels for some time to come and creating energy paths that will in future not be easy to alter. Barring the bomb, we will certainly survive and probably prosper for a long time yet to come. We have a number of options, so we can probably change what we must, though transitions may be painful.

Notes

1. Ideally information replaces energy in the processing of low-grade ores, but real prospects are not good. In fortunate instances the ore is a physical mixture whose components are readily separated, as in sands containing gold particles, and all that is needed is a pan or sluice. Energy demands rise as gold content falls, but at the right price, sands with an amazingly low gold content are profitably processed. But the physical mixtures in crustal rocks are less amenable to such simple solutions, and most useful elements are found in endothermic compounds; that is, energy must be expended to isolate them.

2. These figures are calculated from USDA, Economic Research Service (1981), assuming 3,000 kcal and 100 g of protein in each kilogram of cereals, 1,000 kcal and 30 g protein in each kilogram of roots and tubers, 4,000 kcal and 50 g protein in each kilogram of protein meal, and 10,000 kcal in each kilogram of edible oils.

3. Revelle (1986:163) estimates 6,000 kcal/person/day, working in reverse, beginning with known consumption of 2,600 kcal/person/day and allowing for seed, waste, and loss in livestock production. He takes into account pasture and forage crops, and I do not. Which estimate is preferable depends on its use. My aim is to show the adequacy of present food production without including pastureland that might not be readily put into crops, a conservative illustration because some pasture and virtually all land in forage crops could be in crops for human consumption.

References

Avery, D. (1985a). Agriculture in the next 20 years. In *U.S. Agriculture in a Global Economy: 1985 Yearbook of Agriculture,* U.S. Department of Agriculture, Washington, D.C., pp. 388–402.

———. (1985b). U.S. farm dilemma: The global bad news is wrong. *Science,* 230:408–412.

Batie, S.S., and R.G. Healy (1983). The future of American agriculture. *Scientific American,* 248(2):45–53.

Beckerman, W. (1974). *Two Cheers for the Affluent Society.* St. Martin's, New York.

Bhagat, N., H. Davitian, and R. Paredes (1979). *The Potential of Crop Residues as a Fuel for Power Generation.* Brookhaven National Laboratory Report no. 50982. Brookhaven, N.Y.

Blaxter, K. (1986). *People, Food, and Resources.* Cambridge University Press, Cambridge.

Boserup, E. (1981). *Population and Technological Change: A Study of Long-term Trends.* University of Chicago Press, Chicago.

Brown, L.R. (1980). *Food or Fuel: New Competition for the World's Cropland.* Worldwatch Institute, Washington, D.C.

———. (1981a). *Building a Sustainable Society.* Norton, New York.

———. (1981b). World population growth, soil erosion, and food security. *Science,* 214:995–1000.

Bupp, I.C. (1979). The nuclear stalemate. In *Energy Futures: Report of the Harvard Business School* (R. Stobaugh and D. Yergin, eds.), Random House, New York, pp. 136–182.

Buringh, P., H.D. Van Heemst, and G.I. Staring (1978). *Computation of the Absolute Maximum Food Production of the World.* Wageningen Agricultural University, Wageningen, Suriname.

Bussard, R.W. (1981). [Interview, by K.C. Cole]. *Omni,* 3(4):56–58, 90–92.

Caldwell, J.J. (1977). The economic rationality of high fertility: An investigation illustrated with Nigerian survey data. *Population Studies,* 31:5–27.

———. (1981). The mechanism of demographic change in historical perspective. *Population Studies,* 35:5–27.

Carlson, P.S., and J.C. Palacco (1975). Plant cell cultures: Genetic aspects of crop improvement. *Science,* 188:622–625.

Cathcart, J.B. (1980). World phosphate reserves and resources. In *The Role of Phosphorus in Agriculture,* American Society of Agronomy, Madison, Wis., pp. 1–18.

Clark, C. (1973). *The Myth of Overpopulation.* Advocate Press, Melbourne.

Cloud, P.E., Jr. (1968). Realities of mineral distribution. *Texas Quarterly,* 11:103–126.

Cooper, C.F. (1982). Food and fiber in a world of increasing carbon dioxide. In *Carbon Dioxide Review 1982* (W.C. Clark, ed.), Oxford University Press, New York, pp. 299–320.

Darwin, C.G. (1952). *The Next Million Years.* R. Hart-Davis, London.

Döbereiner, J. (1978). Potential for nitrogen fixation in tropical legumes and grasses. In *Limitations and Potential for Biological Nitrogen Fixation in the Tropics,* Plenum, New York, pp. 13–24.

Edmonds, J., and J. Reilly (1983). Global energy production and use to the year 2050. *Energy,* 8:419–432.

Ehrlich, P.R. (1982). Human carrying capacity, extinctions, and nature reserves. *Bioscience,* 32:331–333.

Ehrlich, P.R., and A.H. Ehrlich (1970). *Population, Resources, Environment.* W.H. Freeman, San Francisco.

Emigh, G.D. (1972). World phosphate reserves — are there really enough? *Engineering and Mining Journal,* 173:90–95.

Energy Information Administration (1986). *Monthly Energy Review, December 1985.* Energy Information Administration (U.S.), Washington, D.C.

Fege, A. (1981). Energy from biomass. In *Solar Energy Handbook* (J.F. Kreider and F. Kreith, eds.), chap. 25, McGraw-Hill, New York.

Flaim, S., and D. Hertzmark (1981). Agricultural policies and biomass fuels. *Annual Review of Energy,* 6:89–122.

Foin, T.C. (1976). *Ecological Systems and the Environment.* Houghton Mifflin, Boston.

Ford Foundation Study Group (1979). *Energy: The Next Twenty Years.* Ballinger, Cambridge, Mass.

Frey, K.J. (1984). Future crop technology. In *Future Agricultural Technology and Resource Conservation* (B.C. English, J.A. Maetzold, B. R. Holding, and E.O. Heady, eds.), Iowa State University Press, Ames, pp. 310–338.

Frye, W.W., and S.H. Phillips (1980). How to grow crops with less energy. In *Cutting Energy Costs: The 1980 Yearbook of Agriculture,* U.S. Department of Agriculture, Washington, D.C., pp. 16–24.

Garret, L.D. (1980). Forests and woodlands — stored energy for our use. In *Cutting Energy Costs: The 1980 Yearbook of Agriculture,* U.S. Department of Agriculture, Washington, D.C., pp. 101–108.

Goeller, H.E., and A.M. Weinberg (1976). The age of substitutability. *Science,* 191:683–689.

Hardy, R.W.F., and U.D. Havelka (1975). Nitrogen fixation research: A key to world food? *Science,* 188:633–644.

Harlan, J.R. (1966). Plant introduction and biosystematics. In *Plant Breeding: A Symposium Held at Iowa State University* (K.J. Frey, ed.), Iowa State University Press, Ames, pp. 55–68.

———. (1975). Our vanishing genetic resources. *Science,* 188:618–621.

Hewett, C.E., C.J. High, N. Marshall, and R. Wildermuth (1981). Wood energy in the United States. *Annual Review of Energy,* 6:134–170.

Hodges, C.N. (1980). New options for climate-defensive food production. In *Climate's Impact on Food Supplies: Strategies and Technologies for Climate Defensive Food Production* (L.E. Slater and S.K. Levin, eds.), American Association for the Advancement of Science, Selected Symposium no. 62, Westview, Boulder, Colo., pp. 181–205.

Hubbert, M.K. (1975). Tidal power. In *Perspectives in Energy* (L.C. Ruedisilli and M.W. Firebaugh, eds.), Oxford University Press, New York, pp. 359–363.

Institute of Ecology (1971). *Man in the Living Environment.* Institute of Ecology, Chicago.

Jensen, N.F. (1978). Limits to growth in world food production. *Science,* 201:317–320.

Kahn, H., and A.J. Wiener (1967). *The Year 2000.* Macmillan, New York.

Kahn, H., W. Brown, and L. Martel (1976). *The Next 200 Years.* Morrow, New York.

Klimov, A.A., G.E. Listopad, and G.P. Ustenko (1971). [*Programming of the Yield*]. Volgograd Agricultural Institute, Volgograd, USSR.

Knodel, J., A. Chamratrithirong, and N. Debavalya (1987). *Thailand's Reproductive Revolution: Rapid Fertility Decline in a Third World Setting.* University of Wisconsin Press, Madison.

Kovda, V.A. (1980). *Land Aridization and Drought Control.* Westview, Boulder, Colo.

Kramer, P.J. (1981). Carbon dioxide concentration, photosynthesis, and dry matter production. *Bioscience,* 31:29–33.

Lappe, F. M. (1975). *Diet for a Small Planet.* Ballantine, New York.

Lidsky, L. (1983). The trouble with fusion. *Technology Review,* 86 (October): 32–44.

Lovins, A.B. (1976). Energy strategy: The road not taken? *Foreign Affairs,* 55:65–96.

_____. (1977). Soft energy paths. *Annual Review of Energy,* 3:477–577.

Lovins, A.B., L. Lovins, F. Krause, and W. Bach (1981). *Least-Cost Energy.* Brick House, Andover, Mass.

Mahadevan, K., and M. Sumangala (1987). *Social Development, Cultural Change, and Fertility Decline: A Study of Fertility Change in India.* Sage, Newbury Park, Calif.

McColm, R.B. (1981). The business of fusion. *Omni,* 3(4):46–51.

Meadows, D.H., D.L. Meadows, J. Randers, and W.W. Behrens III (1972). *The Limits to Growth: A Report from the Club of Rome's Project, or The Predicament of Mankind.* New American Library, New York.

Meekhoff, R.L., W.E. Tyner, and F.D. Holland (1980). U.S. agricultural policy and gasohol: A policy simulation. *American Journal of Agricultural Economics,* 62:408–415.

Merriam, M.F. (1978). Wind, waves, and tides. *Annual Review of Energy,* 1:131–158.

Mueller, E. (1976). The economic value of children in peasant agriculture. In *Population and Development* (R.G. Ridker, ed.), Johns Hopkins University Press, Baltimore, pp. 98–153.

Muffler, L.J.P., and D.E. White (1975). Geothermal energy. In *Perspectives on Energy* (L.C. Ruedesilli and M.W. Firebaugh, eds.), Oxford University Press, New York, pp. 352–358.

Nash, H. (1979). *The Energy Controversy: Soft Path Questions and Answers.* Friends of the Earth, San Francisco.

National Academy of Sciences, Board on Agricultural and Renewable Resources (1975). *Agricultural Production Efficiency.* National Academy Press, Washington, D.C.

Nohre, C.O. (1985). Agriculture in Asia and the Pacific. In *U.S. Agriculture in a Global Economy: The 1985 Yearbook of Agriculture,* U.S. Department of Agriculture, Washington, D.C., pp. 119–144.

Notestein, F.W. (1945). Population: The long view. In *Food for the World* (T.W.

Schultz, ed.), University of Chicago Press, Chicago, pp. 36–57.

_____. (1953). Economic problems of population change. In *Eighth International Congress of Agricultural Economists, 1953,* Oxford University Press, London, pp. 15–18.

Office of Technology Assessment (1977). *Organizing and Financing Basic Research to Increase Food Production.* Office of Technology Assessment, Washington, D.C.

_____. (1986). *Technology, Public Policy, and the Changing Structure of American Agriculture.* Office of Technology Assessment, Washington, D.C.

Paarlberg, D. (1985). Factors affecting U.S. production in A.D. 2000. In *U.S. Agriculture in a Global Economy: The 1985 Yearbook of Agriculture,* U.S. Department of Agriculture, Washington, D.C., pp. 30–39.

Paddocke, W., and P. Paddocke (1967). *Famine—1975.* Little, Brown, Boston.

Paez, A., H. Hellmers, and B.R. Strain (1984). Carbon dioxide enrichment and water stress interaction on growth of two tomato (*Lycopersicum esculentum*) cultivars. *Journal of Agricultural Science,* 102:687–694.

Phillips, R.E., and S.H. Phillips, eds. (1984). *No-Tillage Agriculture: Principles and Practices.* Nostrand, New York.

Pimentel, D., G. Berardi, and S. Fast (1983). Energy efficiency and conventional agriculture. *Agriculture, Ecosystems, and Environment,* 9:359–372.

Pimentel, D., S. Fast, W.L. Chao, E. Stuart, J. Dintzis, G. Einbender, W. Schlappi, D. Andow, and K. Broderick (1982). Water resources in food and energy production. *Bioscience,* 32:861–867.

Poincelot, R.P. (1986). *Toward a More Sustainable Agriculture.* Avi, Westport, Conn.

President's Science Advisory Committee, Panel on World Food Supply (1967). *The World Food Problem.* Vol. 2. The White House, Washington, D.C.

Revelle, R. (1976). The resources available for agriculture. *Scientific American,* 235(3):164–179.

_____. (1986). Soil dynamics and sustainable carrying capacity of Earth. In *Earth and the Human Future* (K.R. Smith, F. Fesharaki, and J.P. Holdren, eds.), Westview, Boulder, Colo., pp. 161–172.

Ruschel, A.P., and P.B. Vose (1984). Biological nitrogen fixation in sugar cane. In *Current Developments in Biological Nitrogen Fixation* (N.S. Subba Rao, ed.), Rekha, New Delhi, pp. 219–236.

Simmons, G.B. (1986). Family planning programs. In *World Population and U.S. Policy: The Choices Ahead* (J. Menken, ed.), W.W. Norton, New York, pp. 175–206.

Sindelar, G.F. (1985). Fruits and vegetables around the world. In *U.S. Agriculture in a Global Economy: The 1985 Yearbook of Agriculture,* U.S. Department of Agriculture, Washington, D.C., pp. 214–224.

Singer, S.F. (1971). *Is There an Optimum Level of Population?* McGraw-Hill, New York.

Spengler, J.J. (1971). *Declining Population Growth Revisited.* Carolina Population Center, Chapel Hill, N.C.

_____. (1978). *Facing Zero Population Growth: Reactions and Interpretations,*

340

Past and Present. Duke University Press, Durham, N.C.

Teitelbaum, M.S., and J.M. Winter (1985). *The Fear of Population Decline.* Academic Press, New York.

Telegraph Herald (1986). Italians may disappear within 100 years. Dubuque, Iowa, December 7.

Tillman, D.A. (1978). *Wood as an Energy Resource.* Academic Press, New York.

Touchberry, R.W. (1984). Emerging technology for the production of food from animals through land and aquaculture systems. In *Future Agricultural Technology and Resource Conservation* (B.C. English, J.A. Maetzold, B.R. Holding, and E.O. Heady, eds.), Iowa State University Press, Ames, pp. 489–510.

USDA (1987). *The Second RCA Appraisal: Soil, Water, and Related Resources on Nonfederal Land in the United States.* Review draft. U.S. Department of Agriculture, Washington, D.C.

USDA, Economic Research Service (1981). *World Agricultural Situation.* U.S. Department of Agriculture, Washington, D.C.

USDA Study Team on Organic Farming (1980). *Report and Recommendations on Organic Farming.* U.S. Department of Agriculture, Washington, D.C.

U.S. Department of Commerce, Bureau of the Census (1983). *World Population 1983: Recent Demographic Estimates of the Countries and Regions of the World.* U.S. Department of Commerce, Washington, D.C.

Wattenberg, B. (1987). *The Birth Dearth: What Happens When People in Free Countries Don't Have Enough Babies?* Pharos, New York.

Weber, J. (1977). *Grow or Die.* Arlington House, New Rochelle, N.Y.

Weinberg, A. (1986). Burning the rocks forty years later. In *Earth and the Human Future* (K.R. Smith, F. Fesharaki, and J.P. Holdren, eds.), Westview, Boulder, Colo., pp. 110–123.

Weinberg, A.M., and R. Hammond (1970). Limits to the use of energy. *American Scientist,* 58(4):412–418.

Willrich, M., and T.B. Taylor (1970). *Nuclear Theft: Risks and Safeguards.* Ballinger, Cambridge, Mass.

Wittwer, S.H. (1974). Maximum production capacity of food crops. *Bioscience,* 24:216–223.

_____. (1975). Food production: Technology and the resource base. *Science,* 188:579–584.

_____. (1980). Carbon dioxide and climatic change: An agricultural perspective. *Journal of Soil and Water Conservation,* 35:116–120.

_____. (1982). Commentary. In *Carbon Dioxide Review 1982* (W.C. Clark, ed.), Oxford University Press, New York, pp. 320–324.

World Bank (1984). *World Development Report 1984.* Oxford University Press, New York.

Yergin, D. (1979). Conservation: The key energy source. In *Energy Future: Report of the Energy Project at the Harvard Business School* (R. Stobaugh and D. Yergin, eds.), Random House, New York, pp. 136–182.

Zelitch, I. (1975). Improving the efficiency of photosynthesis. *Science,* 188:626–633.

Glossary

aeolian soils. Soils formed from windblown materials.

agriculture. The production of food from domesticated plants and animals.

Alfisol. In the USDA Seventh Approximation, a soil order with a clayey subsoil with a moderate to high proportion of cations.

alluvium. Soil, sand, or gravel deposited by flowing water.

amaranth. The plant and grain of certain *Amaranthus* spp., not a cereal. Interest in this ancient Mexican crop plant is reviving. Some other species of *Amaranthus* are grown for pot greens in several parts of the world.

anion. A negatively charged ion.

annual cropping. The practice of taking one crop each year from permanently cultivated land.

aquifer. An underground store of water.

basin system. An Egyptian system of ancient origin, in which the annual floods of the Nile are diverted through a series of basins, which are subsequently drained and planted in quick-maturing crops.

biomass. The mass of living things in an environment.

breadfruit. The tree and fruit of *Artocarpus altilis*. Breadfruit is tropical and particularly important on some Pacific islands. The fruit is starchy.

C_3 pathway. The form of photorespiration found in most plants.

C_4 pathway. A form of photorespiration found in certain plants native to dry climates, including maize, sorghum, sugarcane, and amaranth. In comparison with plants with the C_3 pathway, plants with the C_4 pathway use water more efficiently and appear to have a greater potential yield.

carrying capacity. In general, the maximum population of humans or members of another species that an environment can support. In biological ecology, sometimes the level approached by an asymptotic growth curve, an application of questionable value for human populations. See *environmental carrying capacity* and *technical carrying capacity*.

casuarina. Valuable timber trees of the genus *Casuarina* of Australia and New Guinea. They are noteworthy for their association with nitrogen-fixing bacteria, though they are not legumes.

cation. A positively charged ion.

341

cation exchange capacity. The capacity of a soil to hold cations on its particle surfaces.

chinampa. A local name for raised fields in central Mexico, where they are ancient.

chitemene. A system of cultivation of the Zambia-Zaire borderlands. The cultivators stack and burn the slash of cleared woodland over a smaller area than that cleared. The burnt-over area is subsequently cultivated longer than the unburnt area.

Chukchi. A people of northeastern Siberia.

coevolution. The evolution of two or more species in ways such that change in each one's form or behavior alters the conditions for the other's evolution.

conversion efficiency. The efficiency with which feed or fodder is converted into meat, milk, eggs, or any other animal product for human consumption. In the text, conversion efficiency is expressed as the percentage of food energy or protein in the original feed or fodder that ends up in the edible portion.

critical fat hypothesis. The hypothesis that low body fat levels commonly and significantly limit female fecundity in underfed populations.

cultivar. Any plant under substantial human care and management, whether or not it displays any signs of change from wild forms.

decrue cultivation. Cultivation along a receding body of water.

demographic transition. As ordinarily applied in demography, a transition during modernization of a population from (1) a stage of comparatively high birth and death rates to (2) a growth stage during which death rates fall faster than birth rates, and finally to (3) a period of relative stabilization in which birth rates fall to near or below death rates.

denitrification. The loss of combined nitrogen back to the atmosphere in elemental form, N_2.

denshiring. The practice of cutting, drying, stacking, and burning sod, followed by spreading the resulting mixture of soil and ashes over the area to be cultivated.

density-dependent regulation. A property of a population whereby population growth slows or becomes negative as population density increases.

diffusion. The flow of traits from one culture to another.

domestication. Conscious or unconscious control of plant or animal breeding that results in recognizable change.

drip irrigation. A.k.a. trickle irrigation. The watering of crops with a slow, steady supply of water carefully matched to plant requirements.

dry farming. Cultivation without benefit of irrigation or floodwater in dry lands or during dry seasons. The methods that must necessarily be used to ensure success are also sometimes called dry farming but are here distinguished as *dry farming methods.*

einkorn. A form of wheat (*Triticum monococcum*) that lacks gluten. It is among the earliest cultivated forms of wheat and is still cultivated on a modest scale in central Europe and around the Mediterranean.

elastic. Said of an agricultural system if the technology is available to intensify and thereby raise production, and no significant obstacles stand in the way of implementing that technology.

emmer. A form of wheat (*Triticum dicoccum*) that lacks gluten. Emmer, a probable parent of bread wheat, is tetraploid and may have arisen through hybridization early in the domestication process.

endogeny. Change from within, due to causes within the system.

environmental carrying capacity. The maximum population an environment can support without its being degraded to a less productive state. This level is sensitive to technology, because the more productive agricultural system is not always the more destructive.

ethnographic analogy. Making sense of archaeological or historical data by drawing analogies from contemporary cultures.

ethnography. A description of a society or some part of it, based on extended intensive observation.

exogeny. Change brought about by external causes.

extensive. See *intensive*.

fallow. A period during which land has a break from cultivation, though it may be useful for grazing or for harvests or leftover crops, wild plants, timber, and so on. Fallows are often described by the vegetation that develops by the end of the fallow period, just prior to cultivation: *forest, bush, woody,* and *grass. Bare fallows* are kept more or less free of vegetation by tillage.

fecundity. Biological propensity for live births.

fertility. The propensity for live births in a population or, more precisely, in its women of reproductive age. Fertility is subject to both biological and social factors.

floodwater farming. Any one of several farming systems that more or less depend on water from floods.

foggara. Originally an Arabic word for *ganat*.

halophyte. Any plant that tolerates unusual concentrations of salt in the soil.

Holocene. The era from the end of the last ice age, about 10,000 B.C., to the present.

homeostasis. A property of a system in which deviation is slight from central values of one or more quantities. Human body temperature is a well-known example.

Imperata cylindrica. A.k.a. spear grass. A pantropical grass, especially of moderately wet soils, that tends to be a troublesome weed under continuing cultivation.

infield. Most commonly an area of permanently cultivated or nearly permanently cultivated land within an area of outfields in which cultivation and fallow periods alternate. Manure, human excrement, ashes, and food scraps, often containing nutrients originating from the outfields, usually help sustain infield yields. A similar transfer often takes place from outlying pastures to permanently cultivated land, to which the term *infield* may also be applied.

integrated pest management (IPM). Control of crop pests through carefully selected biological and chemical means, taking into account complexities of the ecosystem associated with each crop. The object is to use chemical controls sparingly.

intensive. Said of an agricultural system if its managers obtain high yields by investing a great deal of inputs (labor, energy, or capital). No commonly accepted standard determines that a system is intensive; rather, a system is intensive in comparison with some more extensive alternative in which the managers stint on inputs.

island bed. A low-lying cultivation bed, surrounded by water for all or part of the year and made by moving soil to form a system of ditches and beds. Island beds are principally used in wetlands for cultivating crops that tolerate waterlogged soils, especially taro in the Pacific islands.

land race. A.k.a. local race. A variety of a crop that displays substantial variation even in a given location, because cultivators mass-select seed, that is, more or less indiscriminately save and combine seed of many plants of that variety.

ley. A type of grass fallow that became a common feature of the northwestern European and central European landscapes from the early modern period on. Traditionally, the alternating period of cultivation is skillfully managed so that grass of good feeding quality is rapidly established at its end. Leys more recently have been seeded.

limiting factor. The one factor (e.g., heat, water, or some nutrient) that is in shortest supply relative to plant needs and therefore limits growth and development.

llano. Originally a Spanish word for *plain*. The llanos of South America are broad, low-lying plains that flood in the wet season and become quite arid in the dry season.

macronutrients. Plant nutrients needed in appreciable quantities. Macronutrients that land plants get from the soil are nitrogen, potassium, phosphorus, calcium, magnesium, and sulfur.

manioc. A.k.a. cassava, tapioca. A starchy root crop of the tropics.

mass selection. See *land race*.

micronutrients. Plant nutrients needed in trace quantities. Micronutrients of land plants are iron, copper, zinc, boron, molybdenum, cobalt, and chlorine.

multicropping. The practice of taking two or more crops each year from permanently cultivated land.

negative feedback. The action of mechanisms within a system that reduce deviation produced by internal variation or outside disturbance.

niche. In biology, the "occupation" of an organism — its place within its habitat.

nitrification. The oxidation in soils or water of ammonium ions to nitrate ions.

nitrogen fixation. The formation from atmospheric nitrogen of nitrogen compounds that are available to plants. Microorganisms are responsible for most nitrogen fixation, along with some contribution from lightning and, recently, from industrial processes.

orthogenesis. Evolution that is predetermined by an early state of the system.

outfield. See *infield.*

Oxisol. In the USDA Seventh Approximation, a soil of the tropics and subtropics with a subsurface horizon high in iron and aluminum oxides. Oxisols are often deficient in nutrients, but many are important for traditional agriculture.

paddy. A rice field, here one flooded as the crop develops.

Pandanus. A.k.a. screw pine. A genus of low trees with edible seeds. Native from Southeast Asia to New Guinea, they have been naturalized throughout much of the tropics.

pastoralism. Primary reliance on domesticated animals for subsistence.

permaculture. A food production system in which a mix of perennial crops provides food for human consumption, and often fodder.

phosphorus fixation. The process by which phosphorus in available forms is combined into unavailable forms within the soil.

phytomass. The mass of live higher plants in an environment.

pitpit. A Neo-Melanesian word for *Saccharum edule,* a grass of New Guinea and some nearby islands grown for its edible part, the aborted inflorescences.

Pleistocene. The era of the four ice ages and the three warmer periods between them. The Pleistocene ended about 10,000 B.C.

population trajectory. The ups and downs of a population over time.

positive feedback. The action of mechanisms within a system that amplify deviation produced by internal variation or outside disturbance.

primary producers. See *trophic level.*

qanat. A Persian word for a well dug horizontally from a hillside into water-bearing strata.

quinoa (*Chenopodium quinoa*). A grain crop little cultivated outside its native Andes, where it is valued for its tolerance of cool growing weather and light frosts. Not a cereal but a member of the goosefoot family.

raised field. A.k.a. drained field. A volume of well-drained soil sufficient for upland crops is built up in wetlands by moving soil, drainage, or both, forming a pattern of ditches and raised fields.

Rhizobium. A genus of nitrogen-fixing bacteria associated with legumes.

runoff farming. Farming that gets much of its water from rainfall runoff, more or less diverted before reaching a stream or an aquifer.

sago. A palm (*Metroxylon sagu*) of tropical wetlands from Southeast Asia to New Guinea. At the age of about eight years it may be cut down to extract the starch stored in its pith.

Same (Lapps). A people of the northernmost parts of Norway, Sweden, and Finland.

San. A term preferred to *Bushmen.* A people of the deserts of Namibia and Botswana, southwestern Africa, who until recently lived mainly by food collecting, in small seminomadic bands.

savanna. A tropical grassland in which trees grow at wide intervals.

seepage area. A place where groundwater seeps upward through surface soil.

self-regulating system. A system in which one or more variables tend more or less strongly toward central values because of regulating mechanisms operating within the system itself, not imposed from without.

swidden. A field cleared from forest by slashing and burning, then put in temporary cultivation.

taro (*Colocasia esculenta*). A.k.a. dalo, cocoyam. An aroid crop of the tropics and subtropics grown for its starchy underground corm.

technical carrying capacity. The maximum population an area can support using technology that is already in place.

technical economies of scale. Savings on the cost of technology by large farms.

threshold temperature. The temperature above which a plant grows and develops. Threshold temperatures vary from one species to the next.

Tilapia. A genus of fish, mostly of African origin. Several species of *Tilapia* are valuable in aquaculture because they feed principally on plants.

transhumance. As applied to pastoralism, a strategy in which herders migrate with their herds while the rest of the community stays put.

trophic level. The level of energy consumption by organisms or communities of organisms. The first trophic level is filled by the primary producers, plants that gain energy by means of photosynthesis; the second trophic level, by organisms that feed on those of the first level; and so forth.

Ultisol. In the USDA Seventh Approximation, a soil with a clayey subsoil low in cations. Surface soils are moderately leached and may be acidic.

Vertisol. In the USDA Seventh Approximation, a soil whose surface horizons contain a large amount of clays that swell markedly when wet and shrink when dry, causing it to develop deep, wide cracks in a dry season.

wadi. Originally an Arabic word for a deeply etched gully characteristic of desert landscapes.

wildrice (*Zizania aquatica*). A cereal of the eastern North America, mostly wild but now propagated with some difficulty and cultivated in the northern United States and Canada. Not rice at all, but confused with rice for its habit of growing in shallow water.

Xanthosoma. A.k.a. tannia, cocoyam, taro kongkong. An aroid native to the American tropics, now widely grown for its starchy underground corms or cormels (branches off main corm).

yam. A root crop of the tropics and subtropics (*Dioscorea* spp.) that develops under a rambling vine. It is unrelated to the so-called yams sold in supermarkets in the United States, which are actually sweet potatoes.

Index